Foundations
in Music Bibliography

Foundations in Music Bibliography

Richard D. Green
Editor

The Haworth Press, Inc.
New York • London • Norwood (Australia)

025.348

Foundations in Music Bibliography has also been published as *Music Reference Services Quarterly*, Volume 2, Numbers 1/2 3/4 1993.

© 1993 by The Haworth Press, Inc. All rights reserved. No part of this work may be reproduced or utilized in any form or by any means, electronic or mechanical, including photocopying, microfilm and recording, or by any information storage and retrieval system, without permission in writing from the publisher. Printed in the United States of America.

The development, preparation, and publication of this work has been undertaken with great care. However, the publisher, employees, editors, and agents of The Haworth Press and all imprints of The Haworth Press, Inc., including The Haworth Medical Press and Pharmaceutical Products Press, are not responsible for any errors contained herein or for consequences that may ensue from use of materials or information contained in this work. Opinions expressed by the author(s) are not necessarily those of The Haworth Press, Inc.

The Haworth Press, Inc., 10 Alice Street, Binghamton, NY 13904-1580 USA

Library of Congress Cataloging-in-Publication Data

Conference on Music Bibliography (1986 : Northwestern University)
Foundations in music bibliography / Richard D. Green, editor.
   p. cm.
   "Has also been published as Music references services quarterly, volume 2, numbers 1/2/3/4 1993"–T.p. verso
   Includes bibliographical references and index.
   ISBN 1-56024-512-3 (acid-free paper)
   1. Music–Bibliography–Congresses. I. Green, Richard D., 1944- II. Title.
ML112.8.C66 1986
025.3′48–dc20   93-34074
                                                                                   CIP
                                                                                   MN

INDEXING & ABSTRACTING

Contributions to this publication are selectively indexed or abstracted in print, electronic, online, or CD-ROM version(s) of the reference tools and information services listed below. This list is current as of the copyright date of this publication. See the end of this section for additional notes.

- *Foreign Library and Information Service,* China Sci-Tech Book Review, Library of Academia Sinica, 8 Kexueyuan Nanlu, Zhongguancun, Beijing 100080, People's Republic of China

- *Information Science Abstracts,* Plenum Publishing Company, 233 Spring Street, New York, NY 10013-1578

- *Library & Information Science Abstracts (LISA),* Bowker-Saur Limited, c/o Reed Information Service, Ltd., Windsor Court, East Grinstead, East Sussex RH19 1XA

- *MUSIC ARTICLE GUIDE,* Information Services, Inc., Box 27066, Philadelphia, PA 19118

- *RILM Abstracts of Music Literature,* City University of New York, 33 West 42nd Street, New York, NY 10036

- *The Informed Librarian,* Infosources Publishing, 140 Norma Road, Teaneck, NJ 07666

- *The Music Index,* Harmonie Park Press, 23630 Pinewood, Warren, MI 48091

(continued)

SPECIAL BIBLIOGRAPHIC NOTES

related to indexing, abstracting, and library access services

☐ indexing/abstracting services in this list will also cover material in the "separate" that is co-published simultaneously with Haworth's special thematic journal issue or DocuSerial. Indexing/abstracting usually covers material at the article/chapter level.

☐ monographic co-editions are intended for either non-subscribers or libraries which intend to purchase a second copy for their circulating collections.

☐ monographic co-editions are reported to all jobbers/wholesalers/approval plans. The source journal is listed as the "series" to assist the prevention of duplicate purchasing in the same manner utilized for books-in-series.

☐ to facilitate user/access services all indexing/abstracting services are encouraged to utilize the co-indexing entry note indicated at the bottom of the first page of each article/chapter/contribution.

☐ this is intended to assist a library user of any reference tool (whether print, electronic, online, or CD-ROM) to locate the monographic version if the library has purchased this version but not a subscription to the source journal.

☐ individual articles/chapters in any Haworth publication are also available through the Haworth Document Delivery Services (HDDS).

Foundations in Music Bibliography

CONTENTS

Preface   xi
  Richard D. Green

The Varieties and Uses of Music Bibliography   1
  Donald W. Krummel

The Thematic Catalogue in Music: Further Reflections on Its Past, Present, and Future   27
  Barry S. Brook
  Richard J. Viano

Scholarly Editions: Their Character and Bibliographic Description   47
  Keith E. Mixter

"Perfuming the Air with Music": The Need for Film Music Bibliography   59
  Gillian B. Anderson

Supplement to Steven D. Wescott's *A Comprehensive Bibliography of Music for Film and Television*   105
  Gillian B. Anderson

General Principles of Bibliographic Instruction   145
  Evan Farber

Music Library Association Projects on Bibliographic Instruction   153
  Beth Christensen

Music Bibliographic Instruction on Microcomputers: Part I   157
  Robert Michael Fling

Music Bibliographic Instruction on Microcomputers:
   Part II   165
        Kathryn Talalay

Integrating Library User Education with the Undergraduate
   Music History Sequence   183
        Linda M. Fidler
        Richard S. James

Teaching Bibliography to Performers in a University School
   of Music   195
        Ruth Watanabe

A Core Literature for Music Bibliography   203
        David Fenske

The Problem of Definitive Identification in the Indexing
   of Hymn Tunes   227
        Nicholas Temperley

The Cataloging of Chant Manuscripts as an Aid to Critical
   Editions and Chant History   241
        Theodore Karp

The Rossini Thematic Catalog: When Does Bibliographical
   Access Become Bibliographical Excess?   271
        Philip Gossett

Italian Music and Lyric Poetry of the Renaissance   281
        Michael A. Keller

Discography: Discipline and Musical Ally   319
        Michael Gray

Varieties of Analysis: Through the Analytical Sieve
   and Beyond   327
        Arthur Wenk

Musical Ephemera: Some Thoughts About Types, Controls,
   Access   349
        James B. Coover

Reference Lacunae: Results of an Informal Survey
  of What Librarians Want   365
    Ann Basart

The Bio-Bibliography Series   385
    Don Hixon

Three Bibliographic Lacunae   391
    Susan T. Sommer

Index   397

∞ ALL HAWORTH BOOKS & JOURNALS
   ARE PRINTED ON CERTIFIED
   ACID-FREE PAPER

ABOUT THE EDITOR

Richard D. Green, PhD, is Associate Professor of Music History in the School of Music and Chairman of the Department of Academic Studies and Composition at Northwestern University in Evanston, Illinois. In addition to his publications on 19th-century German music, he has compiled an "Index to Composer Bibliographies" (Detroit Studies in Music Bibliography, No. 53 1985), a bibliography of published bibliographies on composers.

Preface

SUMMARY. Because the effect of the information explosion is now felt strongly on music bibliography, it is important for scholars and bibliographers to provide the appropriate tools in order for us to retain control of the many titles that are published annually in music. The article discusses the emergence of enumerative and analytical bibliography, bibliographic instruction, and the contributions of both scholars and librarians in these areas. The following papers were presented at a conference on music bibliography convened at Northwestern University in October, 1986.

Samuel Johnson once observed that knowledge is of two kinds, that which we know and that which we know how to find. During the 18th century, that which could be grasped by a single mind, especially what might have been known by such a brilliant one as Johnson's own, was quite large when compared to what was unknown. Today, however, that which can be known by even the greatest of minds is fractional when judged by all the knowledge that mankind has gathered and recorded. Ours has been called the age of information explosion, and with obvious justification, as virtually every relevant statistic confirms the alarming degree to which this statement is true. In 1976, for example, there were 26,983 hard and paper books produced in the U.S.; within one decade, by 1986, the number had risen to 52,637, nearly twice the number of titles.[1] In short, during each working day of 1986 over 200 new books were added to our shelves. Within the decade

---

Richard Green is affiliated with the School of Music at Northwestern University.

[Haworth co-indexing entry note]: "Preface." Green, Richard D. Co-published simultaneously in *Music Reference Services Quarterly,* (The Haworth Press, Inc.) Vol. 2, No. 1/2, 1993, pp. xiii-xxiii; and: *Foundations in Music Bibliography* (ed: Richard D. Green) The Haworth Press, Inc., 1993, pp. xi-xxi. Multiple copies of this article/chapter may be purchased from The Haworth Document Delivery Center [1-800-3-HAWORTH; 9:00 a.m. - 5:00 p.m. (EST)].

© 1993 by The Haworth Press, Inc. All rights reserved.

1977-87, the number of serial publications cited in Ulrich's International Periodicals Directory rose nearly 20%, from 60,000 to 70,800.[2] During that same decade, the total number of items acquired annually by the U.S. Library of Congress increased by over 12 million, while the number of copyrights granted each year rose by nearly 30%.[3] In 1861 three Ph.D. dissertations were completed in the U.S. Since that time, over 800,000 dissertations have been entered into the *Comprehensive Dissertation Index*, and more than 35,000 titles are added each year.[4] The conclusion is unavoidable, that we now produce information in nearly unmanageable amounts on a larger number of subjects, and in a greater variety of forms than ever before.

It may not seem too ironical to suggest, therefore, that as mankind publishes his discoveries in ever larger volumes, he increasingly places himself in danger of growing farther and farther removed from the knowledge he produces. This condition arises partly from the volume of information generated, and the degree of specialization that this knowledge assumes, so that each detail–as in a cosmological big-bang–grows more distant from the other. Concomitantly, however, the danger is a result of the increasing inaccessibility of this information, as each fact that is uncovered is buried by the next. It often appears that each new field of investigation, like celestial objects radiating from the big-bang, follows its own trajectory, acts according to its own internal laws, often without influence from allied subjects. Concern is now uttered from many academic circles over the extreme degree of specialization among certain disciplines, the resultant isolation of one field from another, and over the desultory nature of our conclusions drawn on isolated observations.

Because of this increasingly fragmented condition, the bibliographer has assumed two responsibilities essential to the health of most disciplines. By organizing information as it is produced, the bibliographer suggests patterns through which one item might be related to another, and so allows us to evaluate detailed achievements within their broader environment. Like individual dots on a Seurat canvas, isolated facts grow in significance as they are related to one another in larger perspective. It is now the bibliographer, as often as the scholar himself, who provides us with insight into the interrelatedness of all our observations by gathering systematic subject bibliographies that endow grander meaning to scholarly observations. Yet without access to the scholarship itself, the efforts of a few remain undiscovered to those who might benefit from their work. Justifiably assuming a position as a discipline of the humanities, music bibliography has emerged from both music librarianship and modern musicology, and can now boast its own philosophical canon, methodologies and history, however nascent these may yet be.

A second function that the bibliographer has assumed, or better has continued to assume, is to provide us with the reference tools to discover the information created by others. Our publications are, of course, a valuable means of disseminating information, but they are useful only insofar as they are available to us. By providing access to the information we create, bibliography is a useful means to an end, an object that becomes obsolete the moment it is created. Yet without adequate bibliographical control over the massive amounts of sources that are currently being produced, it will become increasingly difficult for one generation to benefit from the insights of the previous. It is, therefore, ironical, even heretical, to claim that the discipline of bibliography now contributes to the problems of bibliographical access and control, as well as to their solutions.

In earlier centuries, bibliography was largely restricted to lists of related items, gathered, as they continue to be today, for the purpose of creating order out of chaos. For that reason, modern bibliography began to emerge following the invention of printing, when information could be produced more rapidly and in greater quantities. From its beginning, music bibliography was concerned with written sources, treatises and eventually secondary studies, as much as it was with manuscripts and editions of music. Today, the bibliographic distinctions between "literature on music" and "musical literature" have become even more specialized. It was believed during earlier centuries that most of what was important to know about music could be cited within the covers of one volume. In 1703, for example, Sébastien de Brossard attempted to bring all secondary sources on music together into one volume by citing in his *Dictionaire de musique* nearly 900 writers on music from ancient times to his day. In 1792 Johann Forkel, in what has been recognized as the first comprehensive bibliography on music literature, the *Allgemeine Literatur der Musik,* listed nearly 3,000 titles of publications treating musical subjects from the Greeks to modern European music. Yet this book, at least judged from its full title, was considered by its compiler to have been only an "introduction" to secondary sources, an "Anleitung zur Kenntniss musikalischer Bücher." To the next generation, Forkel's work was already inadequate, and was supplemented by Pietro Lichtenthal in his *Dizionario e Bibliografia della musica* of 1826. Following the appearance of Carl Becker's *Systematisch-chronologische Darstellkung der musikalischen Literatur* in 1836, and its supplement three years later, few scholars of distinction have attempted to compile comprehensive bibliographies of all sources on music. The two supplements to Becker's work were quite limited in scope; Adolf Bückting's *Bibliotheca musica* (1867-72) cited German publications exclusively, while Robert Eitner's *Bücherverzeichnis der Musikliteratur* (1885) covered the years 1839 to 1846 only. Most succeeding bibliographies of this type were either selective or restricted by chronological range, national bias, or by subject. Today we must consult such varied bibliographies of secondary sources as Dayton C. Miller's *Catalogue of Books and Literary Material Relating to the Flute and other Instruments* (1935) and Siegfried Kross's *Brahms-Bibliographie* (1983). One part of the present anthology is devoted to essays on the bibliographical control of secondary sources.

Many early bibliographies of music served the same purpose that union lists and library catalogues do today. Once a large enough number of items had been collected, either on a scholarly subject or publications in a musical genre, bibliophiles felt compelled to make sense of the morass, like ordering a disheveled closet. For this reason the major bibliographical tools were created first for those composers for whom unmanageable amounts of scholarship and musical publications had been produced. With the establishment of large music publishing houses during the 18th century, bibliography came to serve a commercial as well as a scholarly purpose, by acting as advertisements for works available or as verification of copyright. Trade bibliographies, such as those compiled by Whistling and Hofmeister as the *Handbuch der musikalischen Litteratur,* served as models for modern lists of music in print, such as those published now as *Music in Print* by Musicdata. Similarly specialized enumerative bibliographies now also serve as useful lists of repertoire for specific instruments, as in Bernhard Brüchle's *Horn-Bibliographie* (1970-75). In the first part of this book, there are four contributions addressing issues of bibliographical control of primary sources.

The traditional two-part division of bibliography into enumerative bibliography of primary and secondary sources conveniently accounted for much of what was published before World War II, but is today inadequate in view of the expansion of the discipline. One must now add to these two the newer field of analytical bibliography in which, by using techniques borrowed from other disciplines, bibliography is used as a tool in the verification of sources, in establishing their authenticity, and in the description of their chronology. Exemplary studies of this sort have been conducted by Daniel Heartz (*Pierre Attaingnant: Royal Printer of Music,* 1969) and by Donald Krummel (*Guide for Dating Early Published Music,* 1974). There is a sense now that, in subject and methodology, the fields of musicology and analytical bibliography have begun to move closer together, as traditional boundaries separating the two disciplines have been challenged. There are now numerous publications that draw upon enumerative bibliographical compilations while addressing issues of chronology and provenance. For example, the study by Johnson, Tyson and Winter of The *Beethoven Sketchbooks* (1985) builds upon the union catalogue of the sketches by Hans Schmidt, the "Verzeichnis der Skizzen Beethovens," *Beethoven Jahrbuch* (1965-68), but confronts such problems of book production as ink, watermarks, and rastrology, and stitching. One section of our book, "Current Trends in Analytical and Descriptive Bibliography," is devoted to essays of this sort.

Lately both musicologists and librarians have become more insistent on the importance of bibliographic instruction, to the extent that this concern has now emerged as a separate facet of the discipline. A variety of programs have been developed involving both course-related and course-integrated instruction in music bibliography. Librarians have lead the way in refining services for library instruction, including that afforded by modern computers, and in developing plans for user assistance. Musicologists acquaint students with modern reference resources in academic courses on music bibliography and research. Most of the public discussion of these topics, it must be admitted, has been conducted in meetings of the Music Library Association, rather than in the American Musicological Society or even the College Music Society. Nevertheless, under the conventional method of bibliographic instruction, still followed in many institutions, sources are evaluated in courses as they are used as tools in research. The study of bibliography is approached exclusively as a means to an end. By this method, one discovers Vogel's *Bibliografia della musica italiana vocale profane,* for example, in the process of investigating the printed sources of Palestrina's secular music. Other institutions now treat the study of music bibliography within a separate course, in which research sources are studied as objects that can answer a variety of questions. By this method students would examine Vogel's book for its potential as a research tool, and discover that it is a union catalogue that cites the contents of individual printed volumes of Palestrina's works. Bibliographic instruction being now a very current topic, one part of this anthology is devoted to related issues.

While in former days enumerative bibliographies usually followed from scholarly synthesis and critical analysis, nowadays it often precedes them. Today we assemble bibliographies not only to collect and organize the information we have produced, but also to facilitate and direct future research into potentially fertile areas. The purpose of such work is not only retrospective and descriptive, to show us what has been done, but it is also prescriptive, to expose what remains to be done. Publications such as those under the Bio-Bibliography Series edited by Donald Nixon, including Hixon's own *Thea Musgrave,* collate the current state of scholarship on certain figures while furnishing a convenient basis for more advanced analytical and biographical research.

Sensing that the separation of the disciplines of musicology and scholarly music librarianship was threatening to retard progress in music bibliography, we decided to make a modest attempt to bring these two activities together. On October 10-11, 1986, a conference on music bibliography was convened on the campus of Northwestern University, in Evanston, Illinois. The first such conference ever held devoted exclusively to the problems of bibliographical research in music, the meeting was sponsored by a generous grant from the National Endowment for the Humanities and by several private donations, and was held in conjunction with regional meetings of the American Musicological Society and the Music Library Association. Twenty-seven scholars and music librarians of international reputation were invited to contribute papers of original research for the meeting. The topics, ranging in subject from chant studies to film music, undergraduate bibliographic instruction to discography, were organized into five sessions according to methodological focus: enumerative bibliography of primary sources; enumerative bibliography of secondary sources; bibliographic instruction; analytical bibliography; and bibliographical lacunae. In addition, there was a keynote address on the varieties of music bibliography, and a closing paper on the contributions by Robert Eitner to the field.

The purpose of the meeting, which was attended by approximately 300 people from throughout the United States and Canada, was to bring together historical musicologists and scholarly music librarians in order to promote the exchange of ideas and information on the subject and methods of music bibliography. While, to be sure, not all aspects of such a diverse field as music bibliography could ever be represented by a single conference, the topics addressed in this volume are sufficiently broad to suggest the limits of this new domain. We hope, therefore, that one result of the conference will be the broader recognition throughout the scholarly community of music bibliography as a unique, multi-disciplinary field of research, one that in its methodology and pedagogy crosses the boundaries of both music librarianship and musicology.

In the long period between the conference and this publication, some of the information contained in these papers has of course changed. I regret that three papers have been withdrawn for various reasons from the original collection. However, much remains current. The papers from the conference that are published in the present volume have been edited only slightly to correct obvious inconsistencies and errors. As these essays were originally intended to be read before an audience, it was occasionally necessary to modify certain passages presented verbally to ones more appropriate for publication. The bibliographies attending the papers, it will be observed, follow varying formats according to the styles of individual authors. An attempt has been made to unify common bibliographical terms and abbreviations through this volume. The fact that some of the information from the conference has been provided to the publisher in camera-ready form may account for certain irregularities.

The organizers of the conference would like to express sincere appreciation to the National Endowment for the Humanities for its support, to the Music School and Music Library of Northwestern University for their sponsorship, and to the following organizations for their generous donations: AR-Editions; The Audio Buff Co.; The Forest Fund; Garland Publishing Inc.; Information Coordinators, Inc.; The *Instrumentalist* Magazine; Music Library Association, Midwest Chapter; Scarecrow Press, Inc.; The Selmer Company. I am grateful to Jennifer Doctor and Lynn Gullickson for their assistance in the preparation of this text for publication.

Richard D. Green

NOTES

1. *The Bowker Annual of library and Book Trade Information* (New York: R. R. Bowker) 23rd ed., edited and compiled by Nada Beth Glick and Filomena Simora, 1987, p. 308; 33rd ed., compiled and edited by Filomena Simora, 1988, p. 403.

2. *Ulrichs International Periodicals Directory* (New York: R. R. Bowker), 17th ed., 1977; 26th ed., 1987.

3. *Annual Report of the Librarian of Congress* (Washington: Library of Congress), 1977, p. 117, A-3; 1987, p. 122, A-7.

4. *A Catalog of Selected Doctoral Dissertation Research* (Ann Arbor: University Microfilms International), 1984, ii-iii.

APPENDIX

ABBREVIATIONS

AACR-2	Anglo-American Cataloging Rules, 2nd edition
A&HCI, AHCI	Arts and Humanities Citation Index
ABC	American Broadcasting Companies, Inc.
ADD	*American Doctoral Dissertations*
AMS	American Musicological Society
ASCAP	American Society of Composers, Authors and Publishers
ASCII	American Standard Code for Information Interchange
ASIS	American Society for Information Science
Baker's	*Baker's Biographical Dictionary of Musicians.* Revised by Nicholas Slonimsky. 7th ed. New York: Macmillan Publishing Co. G. Schirmer, 1984.
BdM	*Bibliographie des Musikschrifttums*
BGSU	Bowling Green State University
BITNET	Because It's Time (inter-university communications network)
BMI	Broadcast Music, Inc.
Brook	Brook Barry S. *Thematic Catalogues in Music . . .* Hillsdale, N.Y.: Pendragon Press, 1972.
BRS	Bibliographic Retrieval Services, Inc.
CDI	*Comprehensive Dissertation Index*
CD-ROM	Compact Disc-Read-Only-Memory
Charles	Charles, Sidney. *A Handbook of Music and Music Literature in Sets and Series.* New York: Free Press, 1972.
CMS	College Music Society
DA	*Dissertation Abstracts*
DARMS	Digital Alternate Representation of Musical Symbols
DDT	*Denkmäler Deutscher Tonkunst*
DIALOG	Dialog Information Services
DTÖ	*Denkmäler der Tonkunst in Oesterreich*

ERIC	Educational Resources Information Center
Gerboth	Gerboth, Walter. *An Index to Musical Festschriften and Similar Publications.* New York: W.W. Norton, 1969.
Gribenski	Gribenski, Jean, comp. *French Language Dissertations in Music: An Annotated Bibliography.* New York: Pendragon Press, 1979.
Grove	see New Grove
Harvard	*New Harvard Dictionary of Music.* Edited by Don Randel. Cambridge, Mass.: Belknap Press, 1986.
Heyer	Heyer, Anna. *Historical Sets, Collected Editions and Monuments of Music: A Guide to Their Contents.* 3rd ed. Chicago: American Library Association, 1980.
IAML	International Association of Music Libraries, Archives and Documentation Centers
IIDM	*International Index of Dissertations and Musicological Works in Progress*
IMS	International Musicological Society
JAMS	*Journal of the American Musicological Society*
Larousse	*Larousse de la musique.* 2 vols. Paris: Larousse, 1957.
LC	Library of Congress
MAG	*Music Article Guide*
MARC	Machine-Readable Cataloging
MGG	*Die Musik in Geschichte und Gegenwart.* Edited by Friedrich Blume. 14 vols. Kassel: Bärenreiter, 1949-68. 6 supplements in 2 vols.
MI	*Music Index*
MIDI	Musical Instrument Digital Interface
MIR	Music Information Retrieval
MLA	Music Library Association
MUMS	Multiple-Use MARC System
NGD/Grove/ New Grove	*The New Grove Dictionary of Music and Musicians.* Edited by Stanley Sadie. 20 vols. Washington D.C.: Macmillan, 1980.

NM	*National Music Council. Bulletin*
Notes/NOTES	*Music Library Association Notes*
NyPL	New York Public Library
OCLC	Online Computer Library Center
PBS	Public Broadcasting Service
RAMH	*Resources of American Music History* . . . Edited by D.W. Krummel et al. Urbana: University of Illinois Press, 1981.
RCA	Radio Corporation of America
RILM	*Répertoire International de Littérature Musicale*
RIPM	*Répertoire International de la Presse Musicale*
RISM	*Répertoire International des Sources Musicales*
RLG	Research Library Group
RLIN	Research Libraries Information Network
Schaal	Schaal, Richard. *Verzeichnis deutschsprachiger musikwissenschaftlicher Dissertationen 1861-1960.* Kassel: Bärenreiter, 1963. *Supplement, 1961-1970.* Kassel: Bärenreiter, 1974.
SCIPIO	Sales Catalog Index Project Input On-line
SIGLE	System for Information on Grey Literature in Europe
SPIRES	Stanford Public Information Retrieval System
Tyrrell	Tyrrell, John, and Wise, Rosemary. *A Guide to International Congress Reports in Musicology, 1900-1975* New York: Garland, 1979.
USMARC	United States Machine-Readable Cataloging
UTLAS	UTLAS International Canada
Wettstein	Wettstein, Hermann. *Bibliographie musikalischer thematischer Verzeichnisse.* Laaber: Laaber Verlag, 1978.
WLN	Western Library Network
WPA	Works Progress Administration

The Varieties and Uses of Music Bibliography

Donald W. Krummel

SUMMARY. This overview of the morphology of music bibliography argues for an appreciation of the necessary inter-relationships between its major components. The article summarizes the current status of music bibliography and the practical issues facing bibliographers today: bibliographic standards and selectivity, problems of classification, and the concerns of the new school of physical bibliography and reference bibliography. It is useful to view the components of music bibliography in the overall framework of general bibliography. The context further needs to be viewed critically as well as descriptively: the very success of recent scholarship justifies our beginning to consider what might be called the "ecology of music bibliography."

A conference devoted entirely to music bibliography has no precedents, at least on the scale of the present one. The Vienna Beethoven centenary of 1927 included several landmark bibliography sessions but only as one part of a general music history congress.[1] Furthermore, its papers, however provocative and occasionally even productive, were essentially musicological. This is clearly appropriate, considering not only the auspices and context of this particular conference, but also the necessarily strong relationship between musicology and bibliography. The theoretical dividing line between

---

Donald W. Krummel is affiliated with the University of Illinois.

[Haworth co-indexing entry note]: "The Varieties and Uses of Music Bibliography." Krummel, Donald W. Co-published simultaneously in *Music Reference Services Quarterly*, (The Haworth Press, Inc.) Vol. 2, No. 1/2, 1993, pp. 1-25; and: *Foundations in Music Bibliography* (ed: Richard D. Green) The Haworth Press, Inc., 1993, pp. 1-25. Multiple copies of this article/chapter may be purchased from The Haworth Document Delivery Center [1-800-3-HAWORTH; 9:00 a.m. - 5:00 p.m. (EST)].

© 1993 by The Haworth Press, Inc. All rights reserved.

the two is not as easily drawn as many librarians think it ought to be; nor is the practical difference as significant as many musicologists often wish it could be. Most of America's music libraries today, for instance, were founded because musicologists or other historically-minded musicians needed collections and services which were being badly provided in a general library, and for which music institutions were even more poorly equipped. Even today the flourishing state of many a music library is due to the heavy use and strong support from its musicological community. It is not only for purposes of paying respects that a music bibliography congress like this one should be held jointly with a musicology convention. Indeed, one good way to define the relationship between scholarship and bibliography is to view each as the other one's *Doppelgänger*, and rather than try to figure out some wonderful insight somewhere in that fuzzy idea, it is better to propose that the present conference is essentially a commentary on what it means.

The Vienna conference is instructive to review, insofar as many of the issues its papers addressed are the very subject of sessions at this conference. Much has happened over the sixty years. General libraries have awakened–at least they say they have–to the needs of "special users" of all kinds. Meanwhile, thanks to the likes of that sometime general librarian and music professor Otto Kinkeldey, music bibliography is today installed as the foundation course in most graduate music programs. The successful mounting of a conference like this one is clear evidence of a flourishing activity. The program for another conference on the subject even twenty years from now is as forbidding a prospect as this one would have been in 1927.

It is useful at the outset then to view the components of music bibliography in the overall framework of general bibliography. The context further needs to be viewed critically as well as descriptively: the very success of recent scholarship justifies our beginning to consider what might be called the "ecology of music bibliography." Several classic homilies are usefully introduced at the outset. First: the desirability of a yin-yang relationship between centralized planning from above, which ultimately seeks to set standards and priorities, and grass-roots activities from down below, tailored to serve particular musical communities, and along the way to frustrate the central planning from on high. Second: the counterproductive confusion that results, on the one hand when librarians preach user-friendliness but are afraid of any serious dialogue with their users, and on the other hand when scholars demand high-quality bibliographical services but fail to recognize in them any inherent intellectual dignity. Third: the essential synergism of bibliography. The platitude is too easily forgotten–learning is cumulative, in such a way as to render today's monument obsolete tomorrow–and the role of bibliography in the process comes to be overlooked, as much by its practitioners as by its users.

Bibliography creates at once both tools and objects; it may thus be useful, or fine–or both, or neither. Emphasis on the useful tools, together with the labor-intensive activity it entails, can all too easily leave bibliography vulnerable to being taken for granted. Close attention to the objects, on the other hand, too easily allows us to overlook their essential function in the growth of knowledge. Whether in 1927 Vienna or 1986 Evanston, the great problem, I shall be arguing, is one of credibility.

Music bibliography clearly means different things to different people–be they librarians working with the public or behind the scenes, in general or specialized music libraries; scholars at work in their own areas or looking afield to other specialties; or readers in search of the scores, recordings, or writings they seek as performers, listeners, or students. One otherwise respectable musicologist once proposed–albeit with due pain and lame excuses–that music today is a "many-clangored thing." The counterpart dictum would hold that bibliography is a "many-splintered" thing–fragmented both by a concern for individual statements and objects, and by the diversity of its goals and methods. In a sense the objective of this essay is both to describe the varieties of the kindling wood, and to suggest the uses to which it may ultimately be put–whether to build great scholarly Walhallas and necessitate some brand new ones, or, best of all, both of these at once.

Such posturing aside: it is reassuring to be reminded that today's generally accepted paradigm of an overview probably finds its best rationalization in an essay by a musicologist. Lloyd Hibberd, to my knowledge, did no other major bibliographic work apart from music bibliography, although he was, appropriately, an avid music collector. While his 1957 article[2] has been subjected to qualifications and reservations,[3] it still represents the best explanation of how things are viewed today. Just as it had a variety of divergent predecessors, no doubt it will some day be succeeded by a new conception. For now, however, Hibberd's model more or less prevails, so as to allow us first to talk about "reference bibliography," which is the study, compilation, and use of lists of titles, and "physical bibliography," which is the study of the physical objects of communication.

* * *

The bulging reference shelves in our music libraries clearly confirm that reference bibliography is flourishing. Vincent Duckles was blessed not only for being a fine gentleman and scholar, but also for living in an arcadian age when–to quote an ancient commonplace–it was possible for one person to comprehend the totality of his world. Future compilers will scarcely be so fortunate, thanks to the proliferation of tools, systems, programs, visions and ideals–many of them described specifically at this conference. Several worries still need to be heard.

What are the component activities requisite for bibliographical listing? Intelligence, to begin with–a matter that begs many questions. Next, medium of presentation, of which we today have essentially four: cards, books, fiche, or on-line data bases. Third, we must at least mention the ubiquitous computers here, although their function is as yet–and no doubt always will be–ambiguous. Are they mostly an adjunct to brains, for instance? Downloading clearly allows us to grind out copy at a much faster pace, to undertake revision with a new and benign respect for perfectionist ideals. For this computers are greatly to be praised. Their brains may eventually supersede ours, insofar as artificially intelligent machinery may yet seek its own enrichment in a new art form tantamount to the music of the spheres. For now in the mundane world, however, computers as such are usefully separated from each of the four mediums, although they obviously enhance each of them. Libraries, for instance, have used them for some years now to produce catalogue cards, publishers to set type for books. Most fiche today is computer generated, and one associates data bases with computers. In fact any of the four mediums can be created without computers–

even data bases. As reference librarians laboriously wend their way through the thirty annual bound volumes and eighty-five unbound monthly issues of the *Music Index,* for instance, they console themselves in observing that they are here dealing with a data base that soon, God willing, may be merged.

Let us go back to the four mediums of bibliography. Each has its particular advantages and disadvantages. Card files, first of all, seem to be a thing of the past. The demise of the library card catalogue is perhaps not that great a loss in the music library, since the fast fingers required to work it effectively were those not of a good instrumentalist so much as of a good card-shark. More regrettable is the feather-bedding innovation of the computer era known as the "cataloguing work sheet"–clear evidence that the field of librarianship has learned to program automation in order to achieve efficiency and economy at all costs. As for the scholar's venerable shoebox, many of us who learned music bibliography by the so-called "Kinkelclone method," are still left to ask what pedagogical substitute could teach anyone so thoroughly. The scholar's working file, of course, is clearly moving into the computer, with effects on practices of scholarly documentation that are yet to be even predicted. (Whither the footnotes in an age when everything is at our fingertips? The extremes of even more shameless over-documentation, and even more irresponsible under-documentation, somehow fail to stimulate any clear picture of any new happy medium.) The scholar's working files, meanwhile, seem also to be moving back into, of all things, the commonplace book, a diary in which the scholar records facts and ideas, much as Beethoven used his sketchbooks. The event sounds curious until one observes how laboratory researchers today are speaking of "paper trails": in a curious role-reversal, scientists re-discover the principle as humanists re-discover the means.

The published book bibliography, meanwhile, might appear to be headed down the drain along with the card catalogue. At least conventional wisdom might appear to hold that everything will soon be on-line, so as to obviate the need for committing lists to print. Indeed it is hard to deny that separate bibliographies are indeed expensive to buy and keep, awkward to use, limited in availability, and above all, out of date well before they appear. In point of fact, for better or worse, just now such lists are flourishing–and in all areas of bibliography. Musicological stenographers[4] are enjoying a veritable hey-day, if not in fact an orgy. The reference shelf may be groaning in the music section a bit more than elsewhere, but to be sure the groans come from all over the library. One of the more painful complaints comes from those who accuse librarians of looking out for themselves first, and other readers second: why buy the bibliographies–especially in some of the arcane specialty areas that one sees them in today–when the library does not bother with the materials being described? Why get the new lists when the library has so little of the music itself and shows no intention or expertise in getting it? Today's conceptions of library resource-sharing (along with sheer common sense) prescribe that two libraries in the same area collecting Patagonian piccolo methods ought to get together. But reaching even this point is some years off even now; in the meantime, is it really necessary for all libraries to collect the superb new bibliography of Patagonian piccolo methods?

Whatever the sense it makes, bibliographies are proliferating, thanks to two phenomena: the increasingly academic character of music in general, and the technology of camera-copy publication. Given an Underwood portable with a new ribbon, vast amounts of time and enthusiasm, and a decent (but not necessarily flawless) eye for locating citation sources and spotting errors, there is sure to be a publisher somewhere who will pick up your bibliography of Patagonian piccolo methods–provided it is not encumbered by too meaty an introduction, or too many of the indexes that make a reference book truly useful but so as to consume pages and push up the price. These are the very books, furthermore, that librarians feel duty-bound to buy, and without the benefit of critical evaluation: even *Notes* comes too late to help. This is not to say that all of the lists are either good or bad. Rigorous critical review and careful copy-editing–such as have always been the sign of a good publisher–if they take place at all, are rarely publicized: indeed the concept of camera-copy works against them; and thus, under the circumstances, the imprint counts for naught. The effect in the larger world of scholarship is hardly to the advantage of bibliography. The bio-bibliography of–you enter the name of your favorite *Kleinmeister*–

will be publishable, while the music itself, along with the critical analyses that exposes him as the pathetic *Kleinmeister* that he really is, prove to be unavailable. Under such conditions bibliography does have credibility problems.

There are exceptions: deserving bibliographical studies still go untouched by publishers. (I have a particular title in mind here, in fact, the worthy successor to a work that would be recognized by most readers.) The library market is too problematic, the personal market having disappeared; laudatory reviews will come too late to help recover a capital investment, libraries in the meantime having acquired other titles, without the benefit of critical consideration. Indeed, the cycles are out of whack: librarians talk about the austerity and resource sharing of the 1980's but continue to buy bibliographies as in the 1960's: the only thing that has really changed, alas, is that the antiquarian program has gotten lost in the shuffle. Reference librarians continue to prepare their invaluable "pathfinders" for particular patrons, but rarely see either their work or their insights become part of the larger "bibliographical infra-structure" of the profession: the only thing that has really changed is that some of the librarians, and many of the professors, get promoted and tenured by fitting their efforts to the constraints of publishers rather than of readers.

This is not to suggest that all bibliographies today are to be frowned on. For all their frequently ugly appearances, and absence of indexes and clarifying devices, in user-friendliness they are almost always an improvement on *Die Musik in Geschichte und Gegenwart*. Several recent lists in particular that deserve special respect, for instance, are the Henle sequel to Kinsky-Halm, which at once advances several variant approaches to Beethoven bibliography without actually undertaking the problematical task of preparing a new edition; on a more modest scale, Paul Bierley's 1984 John Philip Sousa list, which in its extensive annotations establishes the context of the music in day and afterward; and the brand new Pendragon study of Virgil Thomson's portraits, which so clearly appreciates the delightful personal element that becomes a composer biography as few other books could.[5] So amply evident in all three of these books is a recognition of the synergism that can result from an awareness of both of the ways in which bibliographies are used. Bibliographies are intended to be consulted, and to be read. They become at once both respectable tools and respectable objects, as intellectual content and as physical books.

Despite all the cumbersomeness of their form, printed bibliographies are still the best device for serving readers in search, first of serendipity, second of context. Un-annotated lists, when well laid out, can be scanned with latent ease. Chronological lists suggest the very history of the scholarship its entries reflect, while classified lists suggest the character of the whole of the literature on a particular topic, also the inter-relationships between the topics themselves as well as between the adjacent entries. Much as scholarly perversity prescribes that the best scholars should read the footnotes of a new article before the text, so it admits that the most important readers of a bibliography will not be those after a particular citation or two, but those who read through whole sections of a list in search of some bibliographical insight. It is almost inevitable, then, that bibliographies should provide a specially important contact with the global villages of music–the mayors and aldermen, leaders and gatekeepers, gossips and reporters in those special circles of modern *Kenner und Liebhaber* who bring the art form to life and keep it changing. Music bibliographies at the so-called "microscopic level," in sum, should continue to flourish insofar as they help libraries to reach into particular communities that are most likely to be ill-served by the massive, expensive, and ostensibly comprehensive "macroscopic" programs, to which we next turn.[6]

The goal of universal bibliographic control is glorious to contemplate; a complete record of the output of the world's press, in which music enjoys a special nook–and only the churlish would complain about its being in the appendix.[7] Compatibility of cataloguing practice is presumed, namely that of the AACR-2 rules, as facilitated by MARC computer formats, and rigorously enforced through high standards, for instance of authority control and subject access. An emerging field in its own right has thus emerged, variously called bibliographical planning, or bibliographical policy studies, or information access research. A new kind of theorist has the committee meetings devoted to bibliographical planning. Indeed the strong respect earned by a number of present and former music librarians in this arena suggests that music theory has its serendipitous uses.

The agendas discussed probably have counterparts that musicians know all too well: Zarlino, Goetschius, Piston, Schenker, Boulez, and Lowell Mason all deliberating over policy. A high level of adrenaline is clearly needed–all the more so as one remembers that the cataloguing practices of continental Europe are still largely incompatible with (or, to use the favored euphemism, "upgradable to") those in America. Meanwhile, literally dozens of absolutely indispensable bibliographies–in music and elsewhere–go their own way, perhaps justifiably, as a reflection of a kind of original sin. Indeed, we seem today inspired by a biblio-theocratic ideal worthy of John Calvin: "Turn Back, O Man," sung to Psalm 124, but ending with: "bibliography will be complete, and all her entries compatible." Indeed it is probably no coincidence that the best national bibliographies today should come from behind the Iron Curtain.

The implications are indeed very worrisome. One of the gurus of modern librarianship, for instance, proposes that "there will be no *samizdat* in a totally electronic system."[8] The danger comes with a concern for standards, which are laudable, even necessary to facilitate communication, but dangerously suppressive as they may tend to inhibit communication–in other words as they fail to take into account the open-ended nature of scholarship. The classic recourse invokes the placating spirit of economic priorities: we can afford this if you are willing to give up that. Unfortunately the system itself is built into the weighing process. Its deliberate stance of being "value neutral" is too readily re-read as "market driven"–not at all the same thing. Adorno has argued cogently that the greatness of Arnold Schoenberg lies in his refusal to compromise his audience.[9] On such grounds, the two of them both could be among the very first passengers on the great cultural lifeboat of Western Civilization that will be launched by the computer key marked "Delete."

Standards may be a buzz-word in hi-tech bibliography, but they are inevitable standards of form, not of content. Herein lies one of the over-riding challenges of bibliography–namely, selectivity. The idea of value judgements is an oppressive one, both to our liberal sensibilities and to our all too frequent experience. We proudly acknowledge the legitimacy of all viewpoints: our libraries are "free as the town pump," open to society at large. And our lists should be so as well. Furthermore, historical experience shows us that we too often throw away the wrong things. Oscar Sonneck at the Library of Congress was happy to relegate most copyright deposits to what was labelled the "rejects," which his successor, Carl Engel, labelled the "bunk and junk." Yet we discover that this decision has deprived us of some early scores by Scott Joplin, and much of the music by early women composers. The issue is further beclouded by two varieties of hubris, one technological and the other commercial. The technological version contends that computers hold such vast capacities for storage of information that we need only work out systems of access. It is mostly in addressing questions of subject access that we are learning that there is a price to any total lack of qualitative control, in operational complexity if not always in political credibility. If not for humanity's sake, at least for sanity's sake there is a crying need to address the proliferating output of the press. The rise of modern bibliography has rather unwittingly called attention to the problem.

As for the commercial hubris, we may be proud of a society that is "market driven," but yet fail to recognize any particular responsibility attached to it. We are caught up in a spending cycle, perhaps best described in Howard Bowen's classic laws of the economics of higher education:[10] excellence costs money; we want excellence, therefore we spend all we can lay our hands on. Without wishing to engage in a Marxist sermon on the evils of capitalism, I still need to mention that there are always entrepreneurs at hand to find ways to spend our money: the reprinters of the immediate post-Sputnik era, the bibliography publishers and data-base vendors of today, and no doubt someone else tomorrow. Fighting back costs money, takes time, and demands above all an informed empathy. If it is to maintain credibility, bibliography needs both data standards, and qualitative standards.

Subject access, meanwhile, is a topic that music bibliographers have by no means been the only ones to neglect. The rhetoric, whether of bibliography, librarianship, or information science, reflects a pervasive earnestness: what are our materials "all about"; and how can one find, with some precision, those writings truly relevant to a given subject? Several components of this problem need to be addressed briefly.

Music classification is obviously in a decrepit state: the Dewey scheme is now a century old, and it has never appreciated so basic a point as the value of separating scores and books. The LC classification is approaching ninety, and for all his vaunted Germanic thoroughness, Sonneck was never able to handle even trio sonatas, let alone able to anticipate Stockhausen and Cage. Libraries are reduced to a cynical attitude known as "mark it and park it," while other aspiring systems–from Dickinson to the *British Catalogue of Music*–wither from neglect.[11] As for alphabetical subject headings, it is well-known that the low respect deserving of the Library of Congress scheme is reflected in the fact that the Library itself does not use it. But where is there any concerted effort to improve on it? The *RISM* thesaurus has both heroism and intelligence to recommend it; but how are its 1960's mainframe concepts relevant to the PC circumstances of the 1980's? There are of course additional obstacles posed by the very nature of music itself. Aestheticians argue over the questions of musical meaning; how relevant are these to the arguments of librarians and bibliographers over whether the "Eroica" is about Napoleon, or whether *Porgy and Bess* is about black society or about a New Yorker's conception about black society? Indeed, the information scientist's concept of relevance promises to introduce a whole new range of arguments.

While librarians and bibliographers tinker with call numbers and subject headings, the theories of general classification and thesaurus construction have been flourishing. Numerous musicological studies have traced the history and explored the rationales and contexts of the vocabulary. The sequel to this present conference, I should like to propose, ought to be devoted to music nomenclature, its theory, history, sociology, and lexicography. Terms such as motet, band, improvisation, mode, amateur, masterwork, royalties, clavier, and countless others, have meant different things at different times, in different countries, and to different musical communities. The study of terminology in context obviously deserves a rich future.

Working against the cause (and at this point the question of user-friendliness enters the discussion) is the unfortunate evolution of library cataloguing practices. Down in the trenches, classification assignments are not necessarily made by cataloguers with specialized knowledge of the context of the material in question, but often by those who by circumstance are employed by the library that owns the particular item being described. The cataloguer with a master's thesis on medieval chant ends up classifying acid rock, while the person excited by Gottschalk (or often with no special musical competence at all) ends up deciding whether to assign "Vespers" or "Litanies" to the odd *unicum* Renaissance partbook that has wandered into the collection. The absence of dialogue is pernicious in the area of subject access as it is nowhere else. The possible exception is in the area of authority control where, however, the stakes are lower insofar as the user is more likely to be merely bemused by the curiosities of present library practice. Admittedly the Renaissance scholar may object strongly at finding Josquin mis-parked as he is today; and while the search for Bach's "Italian concerto" in any sizeable catalogue usually involves several false starts, there is usually a patient reference librarian at hand to bail out the system. If not, the problems will likely be soluble when George Hill's forthcoming "super-Heyer" is converted to an on-line system with permuted access.[12]

In sum, the temptation of all reference bibliography is to lose contact with reality. By concentrating on form at the expense of content, it may fail to realize the critical dimensions that must eventually be addressed. Rather than addressing the over-riding objective involving the reader's assimilation of facts in order to gain understanding, reference bibliography too easily savors its operational assignment, thereby coming to store information and worship data in themselves. What is lacking is the governing awareness of an informed empathy–an awareness of why the founders of the Music Library Association came to direct the primary focus of the profession toward the journal, *Notes*. The provision of bigger, more detailed, and more expensive bibliographical systems may be a healthy sign of growth; but it also has led one of the more pragmatic music librarians to entitle his polemic, "Dinosaurs to Crush Flies: Computer Catalogues, Classification, and Other Barriers to Library Use."[13] Reference bibliography has clearly been spectacularly successful–and so quite naturally it has developed its own problems.

* * *

The danger of losing touch with reality reaches in two directions, one toward the reader, the other toward the material itself. The latter is the subject of what Hibberd considers to be the other side of the field, so-called physical bibliography. Some argue that this whole domain of study is a thing of the past. Everything will be on-line soon, and so much the better: texts will be more widely accessible, and thus libraries will no longer need to store so much paper. One copy of a text is as valid as the next, if indeed texts matter at all. Furthermore, to the considerable extent that it requires careful inspection, physical bibliography is bound to be highly labor intensive. Descriptive cataloguing, with rules worked out in rigorous detail, can be much more "accountable." To be sure, physical bibliographers do have a justifiable retort. If descriptive cataloguing is already unaffordable, usable subject analysis threatens to ruin our budgets completely–not to mention our credibility, when readers discover their choral octavos done up in a manner reminiscent of Stokowski doing up poor Bach. From the very beginnings of modern bibliographical practice at the turn of the century, the concept of "degressive bibliography"–of tailoring the detail of the citation to the material, or to the likely kind of use–has been assumed.[14] Physical bibliography is above all a process, not for production-line inputting, but for scholars willing to commit their time when particularly promising questions emerge that deserve to be addressed. As a scholarly process, to be sure, it cannot answer all the questions it raises. Nor should it ever cease to raise even more unanswerable questions. It is something that no responsible librarian can totally ignore, nor is it a device for shaming music cataloguers into bigger backlogs. It is no Victorian mansion, scheduled to be razed for the next bibliographical skyscraper; in other words, it is of the very essence of a bibliographer's, a scholar's, and a librarian's sense of responsibility.

The defenses of physical bibliography further run a gamut from the flippant to the intricate: from slogans about "the medium is the message" to impressive displays of scholarly evidence and inference–and it is to the latter of these that we now turn. Indeed, media and messages can perfectly well be separated: the only thing to suffer is understanding. Lucien Febvre once proposed that the true historian is rather like the French ogre, aroused only by the scent of human flesh.[15] By the same token, the bibliographer becomes credible only by addressing the human circumstances that may be manifest in physical objects and primary evidence. Indeed it is interesting to note that in a time when librarians often become contemptuous of physical artifacts, and scholars bemused and confused by them, it is the serious performers who express the most passionate commitment to the graphic object. Milton saw books as being "not absolutely dead things," but rather as containing "a potency of life in them so as to be as active as that soul was whose progeny they are." This is something that scrupulous and serious performing musicians understand, insofar as their basic assignment is one of showing us just how active that potency can be. As a result, performers look to the notes themselves–Beethoven *wie er eigentlich gewesen ist*–with a naïve faith that ought to make editors at once proud and humble.

Physical bibliography, unlike reference bibliography, originated largely as an English discipline, finding its scientific beginnings just over a century ago in the work of the Cambridge University librarian Henry Bradshaw, and his "natural history method"–the grouping of similar objects together in search of commonalities, interrelationships, and causalities. It was perhaps understandable that continental scholarship should find little that was either new or exciting in such a wondrously simple process. What is more regrettable is that there should be so little activity on the continent–in paleography, yes, but in bibliography, no. Musicology has been largely dominated by German masters around and after the turn of the century, and music is often quite different from the study of books that typifies general bibliography. The paucity of signature formulas in even our best music bibliographies is a case in point: but how does one collate a Renaissance partbook; or a chamber-music set, for that matter; or the unsigned gatherings in a Romantic opera vocal score, which may be imposed differently in another copy?

In general, physical bibliography today seems to be moving in two highly productive directions: what I shall call a "classical school" and a "new school." The two are not necessarily in conflict, although–as I hope to make clear in fairness to both–they are quite different in their means and ends. The prospect that the second is seen by some as supplanting the former does not make for good feelings; nor is the difference any the clearer insofar as so many major bibliographical works of the past few decades partake in various proportions of both. Over the course of the years, what we may be witnessing is the demise of the Hibberd paradigm–perhaps even the demise, or more likely the realignment, of bibliography itself as a discipline. For present purposes, we will be talking not so much about scholars and studies as we will about objectives, methods, and affinities.

The classical school continues the venerable lineage of Bradshaw, Proctor, Pollard, McKerrow, Greg, and Bowers. In modern academic jargon, it is "hard" in its emphasis on rigorous scientific method. It reflects a rather incongruous mixture of textual criticism and high technology–the former responsible for the agenda, the latter for the method. The agenda is one well-known to musicology: authorial intent, identification of variants and development of separative rationales, the search for evidence within narrow constraints and the interpretation of factual statement. The only true difference is that, instead of seeking the authentic texts of Shakespeare or Melville, musicologists look for that of Josquin or Verdi. Indeed, since there is still much to be done in musicological Denkmälerwesen, musicologists no doubt have useful methods and technologies to learn from classical bibliography in general.

The recent landmarks of the classical school are clearly the great series of articles by G. Thomas Tanselle in *Studies in Bibliography*,[16] remarkable not only for their annual appearance over nearly twenty years now, but also for the range of their coverage, from binding variants to terminology, from classical stemmatics to American copyright records. No bibliographer can be considered well equipped without knowing these writings. If Tanselle's studies provide our protein and vitamins, the *pièce de resistance* of the meal is (happily) not *flambé,* even if it is cooked on, of all things, a cyclotron. This particular machine at the Cal-Davis Crocker Lab will, when given ink samples (and, very important, in a "non-destructive" way) significantly contribute to our knowledge of the date, place, and auspices of rather specific printing activities.[17] Well publicized have been the Davis studies on Gutenberg documents involving Paul Needham of the Morgan Library, and those on J.S. Bach's Bible. It seems only a matter of time, and availability of equipment, before the machinery could address classic perplexing questions of music bibliography, for instance the printing of Bach's *Clavierübung* or the chronology of Mozart's manuscript copying activity. The horrified humanist may lament that scholarship is moving out of the library and into the laboratory. Really it is not quite so: rather the laboratory seems to be moving into the library. There may, however, be a historical dialectic at work here, insofar as the amateur scholars of past generations saw themselves superseded by the professional scholars–who now may see themselves giving way to the technological specialists trained in analytical chemistry, microscopy, and other forensic skills. Personally, for my own studies of early music typography, I very much look forward to the work of someone in creating a hologram in microscopic detail, so as to confirm, for example, the chronology of two copies printed from the type that was minutely worn down by successive impressions. Technology clearly stands to enrich physical as much as reference bibliography.

The agenda that remains to be addressed concerns the understanding of content, whether literary or musical. In a sense, the agenda is philological, one of moving backwards from the manifest text, toward the fullest comprehension of the way in which the printed copy presents the text, and perchance distorts it–always with the text as the key concept and fundamental goal. Even when the authorial element is not primary, as for instance in Paul Needham's Gutenberg studies, a kind of *Begriffletzter Hand* is involved, whether addressing the question of the printer's intent or the locus of ideal copy. Examples from music bibliography come quickly to mind, Alan Tyson's scholarship on Beethoven being the obvious landmark.[18] Furthermore, with very little effort the very same technology can address an agenda of *Kulturgeschichte*, concerned with the study of the changing impact of particular works, composers, or genres on future musical tastes. Alec Hyatt King's *Mozart in Retrospect*[19] seems an increasingly remote model for the burgeoning field of musical reception history. With such studies, in a sense, the "great chain of bibliographical being" stretches not backward, from the extant artifact into the mind of the composer, but forward, from the artifact into the mind of the historical listener. The relevance of classic bibliography in addressing the plenum is well defended, for instance, in another powerfully persuasive essay by Tanselle, which argues the case for book collectors seeking out not only first editions, but also subsequent editions of a chosen text.[20]

The contrasting "new school" of physical bibliography has come to emerge within the past decades, and is still far from solidified. In fact, grouped together in the following discussion are the works of an assortment of scholars from various disciplines, who themselves may not admit others to the group that I have included here. It is impossible, however, to deny that there is a strong contrary spirit at work, asking provocative questions ranging from the productive to the outrageous. Classical bibliography itself stands clearly in the line of fire: one can understand why it feels threatened.

Ideologically, the "new school" has positioned itself at the opposite end of several sensitive spectrums. Its intellectual roots, for instance, are largely French rather than English. Indeed, the landmark text is that by Febvre and Martin of 1958, *L'Apparition du livre*,[21] while the most widely acclaimed scholarly study in the tradition, at least for English-speaking audiences, is Robert Darnton's study of the publication of the French *Encyclopédie*.[22] One also hears due respect for the *annales* school, also more diffusely and perhaps mostly as window-dressing, evocations of Barthes and Foucault. Musicians, in fact, may recognize kindred sentiments in the recent book by another Frenchman, Jacques Attali.[23] How French the "new bibliography" is can be much argued, all the more so, for instance, in light of the fact that some of the most provocative sessions devoted to the topic have taken place at, of all places, Wolfenbüttel and Worcester, Massachusetts.[24] Even so, in place of the accepted terms "historical bibliography" or "history of books," one now hears the French equivalent, *histoire du livre*.[25]

Equally strategic is the way in which the "new bibliography" has in general moved out of the traditional academic home of bibliography–which is the English department with its Shakespearean critics and scholarly editing programs–and across the hall to the history department. How happily the historians welcome the study may be another question. *Histoire du livre,* of course, rarely brings its own funding, and historians have so often been heard to despair of late about the "burden of history," that their cups were already runneth-ing over. Welcome or not, the "new bibliography" seems bent on asking questions more attractive to historians than to literary schol-ars. Elizabeth Eisenstein's *The Printing Press as an Agent of Change*,[26] a classic example, asks how was the world different because of Gutenberg: how exactly has the impact of printing on Renaissance and later civilization been recognized by later com-mentators? Precious little of the answer is directly relevant to textu-al studies; nor does the agenda call for thorough knowledge of books as physical objects–clearly a historian's viewpoint. The "im-pact business," of course, is flourishing–never mind that we have yet to understand what exactly we mean by historical causality–and the questions are indeed exciting ones.

Still another cast of characters–perhaps better to say several of them–are seen in its footnotes to be drawn into the world of the new bibliography. The students of communications theory range from William S. Ivins and Harold Innis through Marshall McLuhan to Walter J. Ong.[27] Among the Frankfurt Marxists, Walter Benjamin is a favorite figure, in part because of the tragic story of his personal library.[28] Adorno will perhaps in time emerge as the more provoca-tive figure, along the way drawing bibliography and musicology even more closely together. Finally, due mention should be made of the assorted schools of structuralism, semiotics, deconstruction, and post-deconstruction, for it is through these that the "new bibliogra-phy" finds its ways to apply the *coup de grace* to "classical bibliog-raphy," as it questions the very concept of "text"[29]–a term beloved of philologists and other literary scholars, which is replaced by the term beloved of historians, "context."

Clearly the questions are important for musical studies of all kinds: the bibliographer's agenda becomes the agenda of scholar-ship in general, and not only for historians but also for music mer-chants, educators, and sociologists. For instance, any responsible study of early partbooks must recognize two questions: who paid for the printing, and who used the copies? Patronage and literacy, in other words: and we must at least acknowledge them, along with their ultimate unanswerability. In working with music since roughly 1700, one must recognize the continuing maxim, "pay the piper, call the tune." How otherwise can one address the charge of Marxist scholars, i.e., that capitalist institutions–like music publishers–ultimately undermine democracy, as their activities erode the political institutions and culture that are essential to an informed citizenry? How many contemporary performers could actually read a Renaissance partbook? What would have become of great composers without their publishers? What would Gershwin have been without Tin Pan Alley, or later English music in general without Playford? Such questions are neither irrelevant, nor boring–merely unanswerable.[30]

The "new bibliography," now rather amorphous in the absence of any heavy intellectual baggage, is thus all the more mobile. Obviously the questions are more important than the answers; and the method (or more often, the preferred obfuscation, the "methodology") favors trendy new guises, quite literally from chi-squares to massacred cats. Classical bibliographers complain: "Do you even know how to collate a book?" to which the response is, "Do we really need to?" The dialogue will become more productive when the questions become, "Have you worked with primary bibliographical evidence," and–more threateningly to both sides–"Show us the weaknesses in our arguments that would have been addressed by primary bibliographical evidence."[31] The trappings of method play an interestingly contrasted role for each side. In classical bibliography, statistics are likely to be played down in the prose, but they are crucial to the basic objective. They are very important and mostly inferential, so as to enable us, for instance, to say when things first happened, or what the probabilities are that something happened at all. In the new bibliography, in contrast, the statistics are likely to be quite overwhelming in their prosopographic objectives–conspicuous charts and tables, but in truth mostly descriptive, if not indeed mostly decorative. The result is an inquiry that looks very "hard" but turns out to be very "soft." Even the detractors of the "new bibliography" are usually quick to concede that we are witnessing a very good show. In effect, both sides stand to lose credibility in the absence of the other: the need for dialogue is obviously great, although considering how specialized and busy the major proponents are, the obstacles are equally great.

It is also well to recognize that the questions which engage the new bibliography are ones that have long been around–not only to bibliography in general, but even to music bibliography as well. Students of Renaissance printing, for instance, can ignore the labors of Rudolf Hirsch, or Margaret Stillwell for that matter, only at their peril. Studies of the politics of typography continue to build on the work of Stanley Morison and Harry Carter, perhaps for the good reason that they understood politics and typography. The laborious accumulaters and organizers of paper, imposition practices, ownership markings, and authentication of evidence may find a few of their concepts altered in the light of new ways of looking at things. Bibliography like all other sciences witnesses a succession of paradigms–although the intellectual structure needs to be sustained by the bibliographer as much as the original evidence itself needs to be preserved by the librarian.

In many ways the most exciting thing about the new bibliography is its spiritual timeliness. In our emphasis on tools, we too easily fail to appreciate objects. The essence of bibliographical thought in general has always reflected a high seriousness of purpose, vulnerable to giving an impression of great dullness to the layman, of sterile positivism to the scholar. It could only lead to the well-known pleas for more and more expensive and intricate systems, most of them very useful but profoundly unconvincing. They provide instant bibliographical gratification, but little long-term significance. Can universal bibliographical control really lead to more than information overload? Will the fine-tuning that is possible through more and better bibliographies result in much of anything more than still more bibliographies, and bibliographies of the bibliographies? Does the pursuit of classic bibliography lead us into the composer's workshop and the commerce of ideas, or into a deeper sense of indeterminacy? Bibliography, as a relatively new subject, still largely interdisciplinary in its auspices, has yet to appreciate some of the shattering events that music has experienced over the past generation or two. As a student around 1950 I was profoundly impressed when one favorite professor could announce, "If music ever goes through another Romantic era, the art form will be done for–completely." Yet today we are attracted more to the exuberant minimalists and the darker spirits more comfortably than the over-intellectualized heirs to the classical ideals. If this predicament is little appreciated by the practitioners of bibliography, its appreciation by the community of users of bibliography is inevitably ambiguous. Better bibliographical work is needed not only to call attention to texts that we missed–which can at most be mildly bewildering–but also to place our very work in the overall historical and communal context of scholarship–which can be profoundly threatening, particularly in a field as dependent on aesthetic experience as music is.

* * *

This overview of the morphology of music bibliography has argued for an appreciation of the necessary inter-relationships between its major components. A healthy state of scholarship cannot result, at least in any motivating way, only from the practice of citing musical objects; nor exclusively from the examination of the physical objects, whether in hopes of understanding the composer's or the historical listener's mind; nor solely from the construction of exciting questions or hypotheses, with or ostensibly without an agenda in anyone's mind. The other way to say the same thing is to propose that bibliographers, whatever their goals, deal with citations, physical objects, and ideas, and state that ignoring one of these necessarily works to the detriment of the others. Naïve fears of–or naïve fascination with–computers; disrespect for–or preoccupation with–the practices of listing; contempt for–or doting on–the historical musical icon; ignorance of significant ideas–whether through deliberate aversion or irresponsible concoction–these are what today threaten to deprive music bibliography of its appropriate credibility. Music bibliography becomes intellectually respectable only when citations, copies, and questions are in some kind of ecological balance. The range of balance remains a wide one for individual scholars, as the papers of this conference make amply evident. But the overall balance is a matter librarians and scholars, individually and collectively, can afford to ignore only at their jeopardy. This balance is also ultimately what provides bibliographers with the satisfaction of being intellectually honest as they provide both the tools and objects for the worlds of scholarship, libraries, and music.

NOTES

1. The papers for this session appear in the *Beethoven Zentenarfeier . . . Internationaler Musikhistorischer Kongress* (Wien: Universal-Edition, 1927), pp. 263-97. They include Hermann Springer on scholarly bibliography in general; Constantin Schneider on Austrian activities; Otto Erich Deutsch on cataloguing original editions of the classic masters; Friedrich Noack on musicology seminar libraries; Fritz Zobeley on "practical problems"; Josef Schmidt- Phiseldeck on dating; Wilhelm Altmann on thematic catalogues; Robert Haas on holographs of the masters; Wilhelm Hitzig on the importance of publishers' archives; and Paul Nettl on libretti. For a recent appreciation of their significance, see Hans Lenneberg, "Dating Engraved Music: The Present State of the Art," *Library Quarterly*, 41(1971): 128ff. Also notable is the 1959 Cambridge conference of the International Association of Music Libraries and the Galpin Society, as summarized in *Music, Libraries, and Instruments* (London: Hinrichsen Edition), 1961; (Hinrichsen's Eleventh Music Book), particularly section 5, "Music Bibliography," pp. 147-55.

2. Lloyd Hibberd, "Physical and Reference Bibliography," *The Library*, 5th series, 20 (1965): 124-34.

3. Among the most perceptive of these is G. Thomas Tanselle, "Bibliography and Science," *Studies in Bibliography*, 27 (1974): 57. Other important writings that address the definition are cited in my *Bibliographies: Their Aims and Methods* (London: Mansell, 1984), p. 5.

4. The phrase itself, along with a number of other concepts in this essay, are derived from an unpublished paper by my colleague Alexander Ringer, who in turn has reflected the editorial sense of Jacque Barzun's "musical stenographers."

5. The three works mentioned are, specifically, *Beiträge zur Beethoven-Bibliographie: Studien und Materialien zum Werkverzeichnis von Kinsky-Halm*, hrsg. von Kurt Dofmüller (München: G. Henle, 1978); Paul Bierley, *The Works of John Philip Sousa* (Columbus, Ohio: integrity Press, 1984); and Anthony Tommasini, *Virgil Thomson's Musical Portraits* (New York: Pendragon, 1986).

6. The "micro/macro" distinction, which is basic to the theory of bibliography, is reflected in the landmark writings of Jesse H. Shera and Margaret E. Egan, notably their *Bibliographic Organization: Papers Presented before the Fifteenth Annual Congress of the Graduate Library School, July 24-29, 1950* (Chicago: University of Chicago Press, 1951). See also Shera's "Bibliographic Management," *American Documentation*, 2 (1951): 47-54; and their "Foundations of a Theory of Bibliography," *Library Quarterly*, 22 (1952): 125-37.

7. The major statement is Dorothy Anderson, *Universal Bibliographic Control: A Long Term Policy, A Plan for Action* (München-Pullach: Verlag Dokumentation, 1974). See also Henriette Avram, "Whatever Happened to the National Data Base," *Library Quarterly*, 53 (1983): 269-78. Other writings are cited in my *Bibliographies*, p. 6. See note 3.

8. Maurice B. Line, "Some Questions concerning the Unprinted Word," in Philip Hills, ed., *The Future of the Printed Word: The Impact and Implications of the New Communications Technology* (1980), p. 30.

9. Theodore W. Adorno, *Philosophy of Modern Music,* trans. Anne G. Mitchell and Wesley V. Blomster (New York: Seabury Press, 1973), pp. 29-133 *passim.*

10. Howard Bowen, *The Costs of Higher Education* (San Francisco: Jossey-Bass, 1980).

11. The major writings relevant to the theory of music classification are mentioned in my historical overview of "The origins of Modern Music Classification," *Festschrift Albi Rosentahl,* Rudolf Elvers, ed (Tutzing: Schneider, 1984), pp. 181-98. The model developed by the IAML committee, as laid forth in *Fontes artis musicae,* 22 (1975): 48-49, does indeed seem to be sound. Further effort is now greatly needed.

12. The best summary to date of this project is in *Notes,* 43 (1986): 36-37.

13. Brain Redfern's text appears in *Brio,* 21/1 (Spring/Summer 1984): 4-8.

14. The principle itself, simply put, allows for "varying a description according to the difference of the period treated or of the importance of the work described." Falconer Madan's "Memorandum" of 1906 and other later writings that address the question are cited in my *Bibliographies,* p. 63 (see note 3). Indeed, the concept of the "difference of the period treated" is amply in evidence in standard music bibliographies, beginning with the great catalogues of Squire and Sonneck at the turn of the century, and continuing through *RISM* (at least so far as British and American libraries are concerned–but this is another matter). For a recent discussion suggesting the implications on modern cataloguing activities, see Lawrence J. McCrank, "The Bibliographic Control of Rare Books: Phased Cataloging, Descriptive Standards, and Costs," *Cataloging and Classification Quarterly,* 5/1 (Fall 1984).

15. Quoted in Eugene Weber, "The Pleasures of Diversity," *TLS,* August 22, 1986, p. 906.

16. The most important of these are collected in his *Selected Studies in Bibliography* (Charlottesville: University Press of Virginia, 1979). See also his essay "The State of Bibliography Today," *Papers of the Bibliographical Society of America,* 73 (1979): 289-304.

17. The text most accessible to general readers, if not the latest writing on the subject, is probably Richard N. Schwab, "The History of the Book and the Proton Milliprobe: An Application of the PIXl Technique of Analysis," *Library Trends,* 36 (1987): 53-107. Also pertinent are the earlier essays here by Jeffrey Abt ("Objectifying the Book: The Impact of Science on Books and Manuscripts," pp. 23-38) and Paul S. Koda ("Scientific Equipment for the Examination of Rare Books, Manuscripts and Documents," pp. 39-51). See also Richard N. Schwab, "The Cyclotron and Descriptive Bibliography: A Progress Report on the Crocker Historical and Archaeological Project at U C Davis," in the Book Club of California's *Quarterly News-Letter,* 47(1981): 3-12.

18. *The Authentic English Editions of Beethoven* (London: Faber and Faber, 1963).

19. A. Hyatt King, *Mozart in Retrospect* (London: Oxford University Press, 1955).

20. G. Thomas Tanselle, "Non-Firsts," in *Collectible Books: Some New Paths,* ed. Jean Peters (New York: Bowker, 1979), pp. 1-31.

21. Lucien Febvre and Henri-Jean Martin, *L'Apparition du Livre* (Paris: Albin Michel, 1958), translated (however unimpressively) by David Gerard as *The Coming of the Book: The Impact of Printing,* 1450-1800 (London: NLB; Atlantic Highlands, N.J.: Humanities Press, 1976).

22. *The Business of Enlightenment: A Publishing History of the Encyclopédie* 1775-1800 (Cambridge, Mass.: Belknap Press, 1979).

23. Jacques Attali, *Bruits: Essai sur l'économie politique de la musique* (Paris: Presses Universitaires de France, 1977), translated by Brian Massumi as *Noise: The Political Economy of Music* (Minneapolis: University of Minnesota Press, 1985). See in particular the review by George Steiner, "The Politics of Music," *TLS,* 6 May 1977, p. 577.

24 Among the major events of the American Antiquarian Society is a conference of 1980 that resulted in the book, *Printing and Society in Early America,* ed. William L. Joyce, David D. Hall, Richard D. Brown, and John B. Hench (Worcester, 1983). The program of the Herzog-August Bibliothek in Wolfenbüttel has included an impressive series of colloquia on topics of library history and bibliography.

25. Major essays include Darnton's "What is the History of Books?" *Daedalus,* vol. 3, no. 3 (Summer 1982): 65-83; Paul Raabe, "Library History and the History of Books: Two Fields of Research for Librarians," in *Essays in Honor of James Edward Walsh* (Cambridge: Goethe Institute of Boston, Houghton Library, 1983), pp. 7-22, also in *Journal of Library History,* 19 (1984): 282-97.

26. *The Printing Press as an Agent of Change: Communications and Cultural Transformations in Early-Modern Europe* (2 vols. Cambridge: Cambridge University Press, 1979); abridged revision as *The Printing Revolution on Early Modern Europe* (Cambridge: Cambridge University Press, 1983).

27. Among these are Harold Innis, *The Bias of Communication* (Toronto: University of Toronto Press, 1951); William M. Ivins, *Prints and Visual Communication* (Cambridge, Mass.: Harvard University Press, 1953); Marshall McLuhan, *The Gutenberg Galaxy: The Making of Typographic Man* (Toronto: University of Toronto Press, 1961); and Walter J. Ong, *The Presence of the Word: Some Prolegomena for Cultural and Religious History* (Minneapolis: University of Minnesota Press, 1967), as well as his *Orality and Literacy: The Technologizing of the Word* (London: Methuen, 1982). See also James W. Carey, "Harold Adams Inns and Marshall McLuhan," *Antioch Review,* 27 (1967): 5-39.

28. Of special importance are two essays in his *Illuminations* (New York: Harcourt, Brace, World, 1968): "Unpacking my Library: A Talk About Book Collecting," (pp. 59-67) and "The Work of Art in the Age of Mechanical Reproduction" (pp. 219-53).

29. Perhaps the most important recent example is D. F. McKenzie's inaugural Panizzi lectures, published as *Bibliography and the Sociology of Texts* (London: The British Library, 1986).

30. One musicological classic that comes to mind, which addresses an agenda oriented more to the interests of historians than of literary critics, is the "Historical Study" sections of Daniel Heartz's *Pierre Attaingnant, Royal Printer of Music* (Berkeley, Los Angeles: University of California Press, 1969). These sections summarize the particulars in such a way as to enable one confidently to predict that future studies will consist mostly of glosses on this presentation.

31. My remarks suggest cavalier attitudes in need of sensitive consideration. For more sober-minded reflection on the subtleties of the question see G. Thomas Tanselle, *The History of Books as a Field of Study* (Chapel Hill: University of North Carolina, Rare Book Collection, 1981), also printed in *Times Literary Supplement,* June 5, 1981.

The Thematic Catalogue in Music: Further Reflections on Its Past, Present, and Future

Barry S. Brook
Richard J. Viano

SUMMARY. A survey of the history of thematic catalogs from Köchel to the present, marking the years 1955, 1965, and 1972 as significant turning points. A brief account is given of the problems involved in the production of *RISM A/II* and to predictions for thematic catalogs of the future. It includes bibliographies of thematic catalogs used in the Library of Congress Uniform Titles (as of 1972), and thematic catalogs in series (1969-1987), plus a selected bibliography of secondary literature.

The fundamental significance of both the eighteenth-century incipit index and the more recent scientifically prepared thematic catalogue as primary research implements is completely accepted today. Yet this was not always the case.[1] The early inventories were created mainly by publishers, by court and church librarians, for sales and record-keeping purposes. The value of the incipit "... to differentiate one [work] from another as one differentiates books by their titles ...," was recognized (and implemented) by Johann Gottlob Immanuel Breitkopf [167][2] as early as 1762[3] and con-

---

Barry S. Brook and Richard J. Viano are affiliated with City University of New York.

[Haworth co-indexing entry note]: "The Thematic Catalogue in Music: Further Reflections on Its Past, Present, and Future." Brook, Barry S., and Richard J. Viano. Co-published simultaneously in *Music Reference Services Quarterly*, (The Haworth Press, Inc.) Vol. 2, No. 1/2, 1993, pp. 27-46; and: *Foundations in Music Bibliography* (ed: Richard D. Green) The Haworth Press, Inc., 1993, pp. 27-46. Multiple copies of this article/chapter may be purchased from The Haworth Document Delivery Center [1-800-3-HAWORTH; 9:00 a.m. - 5:00 p.m. (EST)].

© 1993 by The Haworth Press, Inc. All rights reserved.

firmed by Charles Burney in 1775.[4] However, its potential for dating, authenticating, and dissemination studies was not fully appreciated until almost two centuries later.

Similarly, although the first scholarly model of a composer thematic catalogue appeared in 1862 with Ludwig von Köchel's *Chronologischthematisches Verzeichniss* [871], and the first comparable library thematic catalogue was published in 1893 with Otto Kade's *Die Musikalien-Sammlung des Grossherzoglich Mecklenburg-Schweriner Fürstenhauses* [1192], it took several decades before scholars began–all too slowly–to grasp their practical and historical potential and to debate their structure and content. Perhaps the first to do so was Leo R. Lewis in an article from 1912* entitled "The Possibilities of thematic indexing," (see "Assorted Literature I, General" below, referred to here by an asterisked date). Lewis describes the advantage of a melodic index in library and publishers' card files. In 1927,* William Altmann pointed out the value of collective, e.g., genre and period, thematic catalogues to historical research and made recommendations as to their organization. With Alfred Einstein's third edition of Köchel in 1937 (871d), the art of thematic cataloguing took a giant step forward. The catalogue itself represented a revised scientific model that was to stand unchallenged for years, while its introduction provided the rationale for its expanded size and scope.

Except for Otto Erich Deutsch's rather general article on bibliography of 1943* and Kathi Meyer's 1944* essay on the Breitkopf catalogues, the 1940's were devoid of published discussion of thematic indexing. In the early 1950's however, four outstanding scholars were heard from on the subject: Nanie Bridgman in 1950* and 1954* lamented the lack of interest in compiling thematic indexes, and recommended "l'établissement d'un catalogue par incipit musicaux," which was a clarion call for international union cataloguing. Otto Erich Deutsch, in two essays published in 1951*, dealt with the history of the genre and the definition of the term "theme"; Bruno Stäblein (1951*) examined the problems of cataloguing medieval monophonic music; and Alexander Hyatt King (1954*) contributed a classic article dealing with the "past, present, and future" of composer thematic catalogues and presented a plan for their effective organization.

In the very same year, 1954, the fifth edition of *Grove's Dictionary* appeared with a comprehensive nine-page entry on "Dictionaries and Encyclopedias" by none other than Alec King. Grove's, however, had not seen fit to ask Mr. King (or anyone else) to write an entry on thematic catalogues, a topic that was apparently not yet considered worthy of lexicographic coverage. This, despite the fact that the Music Library Association checklist of thematic catalogues, compiled by Helen Joy Sleeper [1221]–the first bibliography in this field–had appeared the year before. It was not until the following decade, 1955-1965, that the thematic catalogue as an entity–old or new, manuscript or printed, be it of a composer's compositions, a library's holdings, or a publisher's wares–began to be fully recognized in scholarly writings as a bibliographic tool of prime musical, practical, historical, and social significance. If before the year 1955, only about half a dozen scholarly writings on the subject had been published, in the following ten years there were three times as many. In the appended list of "Selected Literature I, General," one can find for those years such authors as: H.C. Robbins Landon (1955), Paul Mies (1955, 1959), François Lesure, (1958), Jan LaRue, (1959,1960), Jan Racek (1962), Claude Palisca (1963), Wolfgang Schmieder (1963), Lenore Coral (1965), Franklin B. Zimmerman (1965), and Alphons Ott (1965).

The last mentioned, Alphons Ott, refers to his *MGG* article from 1965 on thematic catalogues, the first solid lexicographical treatment of the subject.[5] Since then, the term has become a standard entry in music dictionaries and encyclopedias in the western world. The 1955-1965 decade also represents a similar "golden age" in the production of thematic catalogues per se. Table 1, "Thematic Catalogues Used in Library of Congress Uniform Titles as of 1972," lists thirteen designated catalogues from the half-century 1900-1953 and twelve from the decade in question.

The year 1965 marks another significant turning point in this recital, for it was around 1965 that automation entered the picture, and musicologists by the score fell in love with computers. As is not uncommon in amorous liaisons, the initial excitement ran high. A brave new world was described in passionate declarations both published and proclaimed (see below "Assorted Literature II, Computers and Catalogues"). Intimate new languages were created to

TABLE 1

Thematic Catalogues Used in Library of Congress
Uniform Titles (as of 1972), Arranged by Publication Date

Date	Composer	Compiler	TCinM number
1900	Dittersdorf	Krebs	304
1905	C.P.E. Bach	Wotquenne	40
1907	Michael Haydn	Perger	569
1912	Charpentier	Ecorcheville	233
1913	W.F. Bach	Falck	64
1939	Pugnani	Zschinsky-Troxler	1009
1941	C.S. Binder	Fleischer	122
1945	Albinoni	Giazotto	12
1949	Torelli	Giegling	1311
1950	J.S. Bach	Schmieder	62
1951	Schubert	Deutsch	1181
1952	Loeillet	Priestman	752
1953	D. Scarlatti	Kirkpatrick	1157
1955	Beethoven	Kinsky/Halm	93
1955	Roman	Bengtsson	1105
1955-68	R. Strauss	Müller von Asow	1269
1956	Vanhal	Bryan	1327
1956	Viotti	Giazotto	1344
1957	J. Haydn	Hoboken	569
1960	Schütz	Bittinger	1189
1960	Dvorak	Burkhauser	332
1962	Georgi	Feininger	449
1964	Mozart 6	Köchel *et al.*	871i
1964	Koželuch	Poštolka	682
1964	Pasquini	Haynes	957

facilitate communication–input and output–between cataloguer and machine; they all bore such exotic names as Numericode, Plaine and Easie, MIR, Ford/Columbia/DARMS, etc. Expectations for living happily ever after–in or out of wedlock–were never doubted. In those euphoric days, as some readers may remember, IBM had arranged for one of its executives and chief matchmaker, Edmund Bowles (a moonlighting musicologist) to organize conferences in a dozen universities throughout the country under such headings as "Computers in the Arts and Humanities." After all, the mating process had worked so well in the sciences, why would it not also work in the arts?

Alas, the optimism was short-lived. Within a few years the number of broken engagements and failed marriages far exceeded the lasting liaisons. Those few relationships that survived into the 1970's had to overcome tribulations galore: inadequate funding, underdeveloped software, illegible printers, inelegant notation, and exaggerated expectations engendered by overzealous computer salesmen. This murky picture has brightened considerably in the 1980's, as we shall see.

Another significant trend of the late sixties was the growth of large union catalogues, first without, and later usually with, computer assistance. Examples include the following: Nanie Bridgman's incipit index of secular renaissance works; Jan LaRue's union catalogue of 18th century symphonies [712]; my own catalogue of *symphonies concertantes* [186]; Harry Lincoln's indexes of the frottola repertory [733]; Raymond Meylan's catalogue of concertos for the flute and oboe, [823, 833]; Hubert Unverricht's catalogue of 18th century string trios [1319]; and many others. Some of these include many thousands of entries–which brings us to the year 1972 and to the most ambitious union thematic catalogue possibly of all time, past, present, or future: *RISM A/II, Music Manuscripts 1600-1800*. The series A/II may ultimately comprise as many as two million individual entries.

The year 1972 was crucial to the matter at hand, not merely because a modest offering entitled *Thematic Catalogues in Music* was first published then, but because it was in that year that *RISM A/II* narrowly avoided a disaster. I beg the reader's indulgence while I tell a story, a bibliographic cliffhanger. As the reader may know, there is a meeting of *RISM* at each annual IAML conference. When IAML met in Jerusalem in 1972, in addition to the regular open *RISM* meeting there were two special sessions of *RISM's* newly formed Advisory Research Commission (ARC), its decision-making body for scholarly matters. I had to miss the first ARC meeting, during which *RISM A/II* problems were discussed, and was informed as I arrived for the second session that my urgent suggestion, made in advance, to revise the existing A/II guidelines to include incipits had been rejected. The Commission had quickly decided, for seemingly strong and valid reasons, that it would not be feasible to incorporate incipits in *RISM A/II*. First of all, it would be too expensive. Furthermore, it was too late to do so, for A/II had been underway for several years and some of the work had already been done, a few countries had even completed their task and could not be required to recatalogue everything. (The United Kingdom's card files–without incipits–had just been brought to Kassel by motorcar in 90 shoe boxes!)

I objected to this decision with such vehemence that Kurt Dorfmüller, chair of ARC, was later to claim that the explosion was heard in both Tel Aviv and Cairo. "Whatever the cost," I argued, "we must have incipits. Without incipits, we might as well just forget the whole thing. *RISM A/II* would be little better than useless. Without incipits there would be no precise means of identification for each entry and hence no way of putting order into the hundreds of file cards sent in from all over the globe, all reading, say, *Trio in D Major* by Telemann. Without incipits the work would have to be completely redone in a future generation." A heated debate ensued; it was touch-and-go for over an hour; as exhaustion was about to set in, the decision was reversed; the pro-incipit faction was victorious. Eventually a new set of guidelines for *RISM A/II–with incipits–*was drawn up. (And the United Kingdom's 90 shoe boxes were returned to London for recataloguing!)

The problems of *RISM A/II* manuscript cataloguing were just beginning. The problems included: funding the project both nationally and internationally; creating the sophisticated computer programs that could deal with the oceanic quantity of manuscripts involved; developing effective means of disseminating the collected information; and, most formidable and frustrating of all, obtaining the world-wide cooperation necessary to complete the gathering and initial cataloguing of the data. I have discussed some of these problems in a *JAMS* review (1979*) and in the Alec Hyatt King Festschrift (1980*). Suffice it to say here that:

1. Given the difficulties to be overcome, the job now being done in many national *RISM* centers throughout the world, and by Joachim Schlichte and his colleagues in the central office in Kassel is superb.
2. In the national *RISM* centers of many countries, *A/II* thematic cataloguing has proceeded on an impressive scale (e.g., West Germany which included incipits from the outset; Denmark where the manuscript cataloguing was largely completed a decade ago and published separately in microfiche form; Sweden and Czechoslovakia which have included post-1800

materials). In Italy, France, and the United States major efforts have been made to begin cataloguing with incipits. As of late 1986, index cards for over 250,000 manuscripts have been received from 26 countries. Impressive as these figures appear to be, they represent (very approximately) little more than 12 percent of the total number of manuscripts in existence for the period covered. Furthermore, several countries have not yet begun to add incipits to previously catalogued items. Others have indicated that they do not intend to do so. Nonetheless, in those countries where the work is proceeding, invaluable and sometimes surprising information is being gathered.
3. The current method of disseminating *RISM A/II* catalogue data is by microfiche.[6] Two editions have been published thus far containing 20,000 and 40,000 items respectively, listed alphabetically by composer in summary form and (to my chagrin) without incipits. The data base from which the microfiches were automatically printed does of course contain the complete record for each item including its incipits. Fortunately the third edition, scheduled to appear in 1990 and expected to contain ca. 100,000 items, will–at last–include incipits. Meanwhile the entire data base (i.e., what has been input thus far) may be consulted by correspondence.
4. A detailed, up-to-date, country by country report of *RISM A/II* activities world-wide will appear in the second edition of my *Thematic Catalogues in Music*.

We return now to the recent past and to the historiographic overview left hanging, for story-telling purposes, in the year 1972. There have been several notable developments since then. A glance at the post-1972 publications on the attached list, "Selected Literature I: General," (computer-related matters will be discussed later), reveals a slowdown in the production of articles, and at the same time, a new interest in library thematic cataloguing (Brook 1979*, 1980*), in standardising the format of composer catalogues (Basart 1980*), and in exploring the history and theory of the thematic catalogue genre (Brook 1972*, 1973*, Michalowski 1980*). Kornel Michalowski's contribution, a volume unto itself, is the most thorough and thoughtful discussion of the subject to date. The most complete lexicographic coverage is found in *The New Grove* entry.

By contrast, the production of thematic catalogues per se has shown a dramatic, geometric increase in quantity, as well as a marked, if only arithmetic improvement in quality since 1972. Many long-awaited catalogues for major composers were published: Berlioz (Holoman), Bruckner (Grasberger), Brahms (McCorkle), Charpentier (Hitchcock), Chopin (Kobylanska), Lully (Schneider), Handel (Baselt), Pergolesi (Paymer), Teleman (Menke, Ruhnke), Wagner (Deathridge et al.), and Vivaldi (Ryom). Hundreds of new catalogues for lesser composers—some very little known—have been produced not only in individual volumes, but also in dissertations, periodical articles, card files, and computer data banks. The same is true of catalogues for specific genres and obscure codexes.

Of special interest is the rise in the number of thematic catalogues produced in Eastern Europe, mainly Poland, Hungary, Czechoslovakia, and Yugoslavia, both in series and in individual volumes. Disheartening news from Czechoslovakia should be reported, however: that country possesses probably more music manuscripts than all the rest of Europe combined. Estimates run to over one million. A dozen years ago, a well-trained team of more than thirty specialists were regularly occupied in the detailed cataloguing of the country's vast court, church, and library holdings. Some 100,000 entries, abbreviated to comply with *RISM* guidelines, were sent to Kassel. At the present time, unfortunately, the team is down to three members, which may mean that decades will be required before the work can be completed.

The most remarkable expansion of all has occurred in library thematic cataloguing. Much of the impetus for this increased activity has been provided by *RISM A/II* and, as will be seen in Table 2, the results are being published by national or regional organizations in several series. Although all of the appropriate information from these catalogues is being incorporated in the *RISM A/II* data bank, several have exceeded the *A/II* temporal limitations, 1600-1800, by encompassing a wider time span, e.g., 1500-1900, or even, more

TABLE 2

Thematic Catalogues in Series (1969-1987)

N.B. Both the capitalized word and the bracketed number in each listing indicate how the annotated entry for that listing may be located in the second edition of *Thematic Catalogues in Music.*

I. **Austria**
  A. *Tabulae musicae Austriacae* (Wien: Verlag der Österreichischen Akademie der Wissenschaften, 1973--) Catalogues for the following library collections:
  1. TULLN, St. Stephan [1314.1]
  2. WIEN, St. Karl Borromäus [1407.1]
  3. WIEN, Österreichische Nationalbibliothek [1416.1]
  4. WILHERING, Zisterzienserstift, [1420.5]
  5. MELK, Benediktinerstift [812]

II. **Czechoslovakia**
  A. *Catalogus artis musicae in Bohemia et Moravia cultae. Artis musicae antiquioris catalogorum Series* (Praha: Supraphon, 1972--) A major thematic cataloguing project undertaken by the Czech State Archives. Six catalogues published, three in preparation.
  1. PRAHA, Loreta archiv [1000]
  2. BEROUN, Okresný archiv [118.1]
  3. BREZNICE [172.5]
  4. PRAHA, St. Vitus Cathedral Collection [1001.4]
  5. BAKOV nad Jizerou, in prep [66.2]
  6. KLAŠTEREC nad OHŘÍ, in prep [662.2]
  7. KROMĚŘÍZ, Zámecký hudební archiv, in prep [699.1]
  8. KRUMLOV, Česky, in prep [701.2]
  9. KUKS, in prep [704.1]
  B. *Súpis hudobnín z bývalého premonštrátskeho kláštora v Jasove* (Martin: Matica slovenská,1967--) Bozena Ornusivá- Záhumenská, editor.
  1. JASOV, Zbierka z bývalého Jezuitského kostola sv. Trojice v Kosiciach [624.1]
  2. JASOV, Zbierka z Bývaléj Dominikánskej knižnice v Košiciach [624.2]
  3. JASOV, Zbierka z Bývaného Hornouhorského Rákocziho múzea v Košiciach [624.3]
  4. JASOV, Zbierka hudobnín z chóru kostola sv. Jána Krstitela v Jasove, in prep [624.4]
  C. *Súpis hudobnín z rím.-kat. kostola v Banskej Stiavnici* (Martin: Matica slovenská, 1969--), Emanuel Muntág, editor.
  1. BANSKA ŠTIAVNICE, Súpis zbierky rukopisných hudobnín Jána Jozefa Richtera [66.5]
  2. BANSKA ŠTIAVNICE, Súpis zbierky hudobných autografov Frantiska Hrdin [66.5]
  3. BANSKA ŠTIAVNICE, Súpis zbierky hudobnín z rokov 1753-1840 [66.6]
  4. BANSKA ŠTIAVNICE, Súpis zbierky kniznice grófov Zayovcov z Uhrovca [66.7]
  5. BANSKA ŠTIAVNICE, Súpis zbierky noteveho archivu Eduarda Schoszthala, in prep [66.8]

TABLE 2 (continued)

III. Germany (BRD)
   A. *Kataloge bayerischer Musiksammlungen* (München: G. Henle, 1971) Robert Münster, general editor. (Produced in collaboration with *RISM*). Eleven catalogues published; nine in preparation.
   1. WEYARN, Tegernsee, Benediktbeuern [1403.5]
   2. FRAUENWÖRTH AUF FRAUENCHIEMSEE, Benediktinerinnenabtei, Pfarrkirchen Indersdorf, Wasserburg am Inn, Bad Tölz [398]
   3. HARBURG, Fürstlich Oettingen-Wallerstein'sche Bibliothek [498.1]
   4. MÜNCHEN, Bayerische Staatsbibliothek: Tabulaturen und Stimmbücher bis zur Mitte des 17. Jahrhunderts [885.3]
   5. MÜNCHEN, Theatinerkirche St. Kajetan [887.2]
   6. MÜNCHEN, Bayerische Staatsbibliothek: Collectio musicalis Maximilianea [885.4]
   7. REGENSBURG, Fürst Thurn und Taxis Hofbibliothek [1032.1]
   8. MÜNCHEN, Bayerische Staatsbibliothek: Maria Anna, Kurfürstin von Bayern [884.1]
   9. MÜNCHEN, St. Michaelskirche [887.3]
   10. OTTOBEUREN, Beneditiner-abtei [934.1]
   11. MÜNCHEN, Dom zu Unserer Lieben Frau (Frauenkirche) [886]
   12. EICHSTZÄTT, Benediktinerinnenabtei St. Walburg; Doms, in prep [348.1]
   13. EICHSTÄTT, Sammlung Schlecht; Seminarbibliothek St. Willibald, in prep [349.1]
   14. FRANKEN, Diözese Würzburg, in prep [395.1]
   15. LAUFEN, Kollegiatstift, in prep [722.1]
   16. MÜNCHEN, Bayerische Staatsbibliothek: Chorbücher und Handschriften in Chorbuchartiger Notierung, in prep [885.5]
   17. POLLING, Pfarrkirche, in prep [980.1]
   18. REGENSBURG, Bischöfliche Zentralbibliothek: Proske Musikbibliothek, in prep [1034.2]
   19. TEGERNSEE, Sammlung Herzog Wilhelm in Bayern, in prep [1292.1]
   20. URSBERG, St. Josefs-Kongregation, in prep [1324.1]
   B. *Kataloge der Stadt-und Universitätsbibliothek Frankfurt am Main* (Frankfurt am Main: Vittorio Klostermann, 1979--)
   1. FRANKFURT, Kirchlichen Musikhandschriften des 17. und 18. Jahrhunderts [396.1]
   2. FRANKFURT, Opernsammlung, in prep [396.2]
   C. *Musikwissenschaftliche Schriften* (München-Salzburg: Emil Katzbichler, 1976--)
   1. Joseph EYBLER [365.1]
   2. Georg Anton KREUSSER [690]
   3. Sigismund NEUMANN [907.3]
   D. *Studien zur Landes- und Sozialgeschichte der Musik* (München-Salzburg: Emil Katzbichler, 1979--)
   1. GÖTTWEIG, Austria, Benediktinerstift [471.1]
   2. *Die Vertonung liturgischer Sonntaqsoffertorien am Wiener Hof.* Gabriela KROMBACH, compiler [698.1]
   3. Franz Joseph AUMANN [33.1]
   E. Tutzing: Hans Schneider
   1. *Der mehrstimmige Introitus in Quellen des 15.Jahrhunderts*, Würzburger musikhistorische Beiträge, 3. Frohmut DANGEL-HOFMANN, compiler [277.1]
   2. Anton BRUCKNER, Publikation des Inst. für Österreichische Musikdokumentation VII [196.2]
   3. Jacob BUUS, Wiener Veröffentlichungen zur Musikwissenschaft 6 [211.1]
   4. WIESENTHEID,Veröffentlichungen der Gesellschaft der Musikgeschichte [1420a]

IV. Italy
   A. *Cataloghi di fondi musicali italiani,* a cura della Società Italiana di Musicologia (Produced in collaboration with *RISM*) (Torino: E.D.T./ Musica, 1984--)
      1. PADOVA, Conservatorio "Cesare Pollini" [941.1]
      2. BRESCIA, Archivio Capitolare del Duomo [172.2]
      3. VENEZIA, Fondazione "Querini-Stampalia" [1330.1]
V. Poland
   A. *Musicalia vetera. Katalog tematyczny rekopiśmiennych zabytków dawnej muzyki w Polsce* [Ancient music. Thematic catalogues of early music manuscripts in Poland] (Kraków: Polskie Wydawnictwo Muzyczne, 1969--) Zygmunt M. Szweykowski, general editor. Eight catalogues of collections in Poznań, Kraków, and Wawel have been published, plus one genre catalogue not part of the series.
      1. WAWEL: Opracowała, I/I [1390]
      2. KRAKÓW, Jagellónian Library [684.1]
      3. WAWEL, I/2 [1390.1]
      4. POZNAŃ, Adam Mickiewicz U. Library [983.1]
      5. WAWEL, I/3 [1390.3]
      6. WAWEL, I/4 [1390.2]
      7. WAWEL, I/5 [1390.4]
      8. WAWEL, I/6 [1390.5]
      9. *Polonez* (4 v.). Stephen BURHARDT, compiler [206]
VI. United States
   A. *Thematic Catalogue Series* (Stuyvesant, NY: Pendragon Press, 1972--) Twelve composer catalogues, plus one in facsimile; two early publisher's catalogues in facsimile; the Danish *RISM* catalogue in microfiche.
      1. Giovanni Battista PERGOLESI [965.2]
      2. Ignace PLEYEL [976]
      3. John COPRARIO [256.1]
      4. *Three HAYDN Catalogues,* Facsimile reissue [550a]
      5. Franz SCHNEIDER [1169.1]
      6. *The Danish RISM Catalogue: Music manuscripts before 1800 in the Libraries of Denmark,* 20 microfiches [1163.3]
      7. Jean-François LESUEUR [729]
      8. *Melodic Index to HAYDN'S Instrumental Music* [555f]
      9. Johann PEZEL [968.1]
      10. Franz BENDA [97.1]
      11. Alfonso FERRABOSCO the Elder [373.1]
      12. Giovanni Battista VIOTTI [1345.2]
      13. *Virgil THOMSON's Musical Portraits* [1304.2]
      14. *The Breitkopf Thematic Catalogue, The Six Parts and Sixteen Supplements, 1762-1787,* Facsimile reissue [167d]
      15. *Christian Ulrich RINGMACHER Thematic Catalogue (1773)* Facsimile [1065.2]
   B. *The Symphony, 1720-1840* (New York: Garland Publishing, 1979-1986) Barry S. BROOK, editor-in-chief. This sixty-volume series, which contains 549 full scores for 244 composers, provides thematic catalogues of the complete symphonic output of some 200 composers. Volume 61, *Reference Volume: Contents of the Set and Collected Thematic Indexes* (1986) gathers in one place all the thematic indexes published in the series plus thirteen thematic indexes not originally included in the set.

TABLE 2 (continued)

- C. *Detroit Studies in Music Bibliography* (Detroit: Detroit Information Coordinators, 1970--)
  1. Jeremiah CLARKE, [248]
  2. Christoph NICHELMANN, [912a]
  3. Carlos d'ORDOÑEZ, [930.1]
  4. *Fuging Tunes in the Eighteenth Century.* Nicholas TEMPERLEY, compiler [1299.5]
- D. (Hackensack, NJ: Joseph Boonin, Inc., 1972--)
  1. Salamon ROSSI [1112]
  2. Florian Leopold GASSMANN [433.1]
  3. Benedetto PALLAVICINO [946.1]

VII. **Yugoslavia**
- A. *Musical Evenings in Osor* (Zagreb, Osor: Music Information Center) Stanislav Tuksar, general editor.
  1. Giovanni Mane GIORNOVICHI [451.1]
  2. Antun SORKOČEVIĆ [1223.4]
  3. Jelena Pucic SORKOČEVIĆ [1223.5]
  4. Luka SORKOČEVIĆ [1223.6]

ambitiously, by dealing with the complete manuscript holdings of the library in question.

The publication of thematic catalogues in series, both by government-supported organizations and commercial firms, is the single most positive new trend of the recent past, one that is continuing to this day. Table 2 lists these many series by country and publishing house, and reveals the great number and variety of catalogues they contain, e.g., composer, library, genre, facsimile, and microfiche. It affirms as well the ultimate recognition by scholars and publishers of the significance and sales potential (even for minor composers), of thematic catalogues of all kinds. While most of the series listed in the chart contain thematic catalogues *only*, there are some more general bibliographic collections, containing two or more thematic indexes that have also been included, e.g., in Germany: those of publishers Katzbichler, Klostermann, and Schneider; in the United States: those of Boonin and the Detroit Information Coordinators.

Not evident from Table 2, which lists primarily conventionally produced catalogues, is the recently renewed interest in the use of the computer for thematic cataloguing purposes. Following the overly optimistic discussions in the 1960's of the potentials of automation (see appended list of "Selected Literature II: Computers and Catalogues") and the many resultant stillborn computer projects, there was a period during much of the 1970's when computer applications to thematic cataloguing were relatively limited.

A major deterrent to success in this field was the failure to produce an efficient, elegant, and inexpensive method of computer-driven music printing. "Efficient" in this context may be defined as "easy-to-use, versatile, and highspeed." By "elegant," I mean *highest engraving quality;* to accept anything less today is inexcusable and unnecessary. By "inexpensive" I mean *really* inexpensive, not merely competitive with other music-printing processes; not limited to the simple representation of the manuscript score, but inexpensive also for such automatically-produced (and easily-programmable) by-products as orchestral parts, transposed parts and vocal scores, etc. Such a method, considered immanent in 1965,[7] indeed, "just around the corner," did not in fact begin to be realized until the 1980's. Today, with the advent of personal computers, with hard-disk storage capabilities and laser printers, with the transfer of previously developed, sophisticated, software from mainframe to microcomputers, the above mentioned criteria are slowly being met.

Indeed, we are in the midst of encouraging advances in automated music printing–and in other computerized music research processes as well. The new technologies are causing radical changes in the way musicologists and music publishers function. The background and current status of that "revolution" can best be seen in the two final documents listed under "Selected Literature II" below: the late Philip Drummond's detailed and masterfully annotated bibliography, *Computer Applications to Music; A Survey and Review of the Literature 1949-1979* (Deta Davis's *Computer Applications in Music* [Los Altos, California 1986] was not yet available at this writing); and the Walter B. Hewlett/Eleanor Selfridge-Field *Directory of Computer Assisted Research in Musicology 1986* which opens with a superb essay, "Printing Music by Computer," summarizing current developments and 24 reproductions of computer-produced pages of music. The main body of the Directory presents compact descriptions of over one hundred computer applications to music from 1980 to the present, including a dozen thematic cataloguing projects.

Other projects currently under way include catalogues for Rameau by Catherine Massip, which is in its initial stages; for Offenbach, by Antonio de Almeida, which is virtually complete but is having publication problems; for Saint-Saëns by Sabina Rabson; a new edition of the Schmieder *Bach-Werke-Verzeichnis* is in press; and the new Kinsky *Beethoven*, edited by Kurt Dortmüller is several years away. A catalogue of the works of Johann Vanhal was completed some years ago, with Paul Bryan doing his symphonies and Alexander Weinmann all the other genres. The plan to publish their work in a two-volume set, in English and German respectively, has not yet materialized.

The *Bach Compendium,* a mega-catalogue edited by Christoph Wolff and Hans-Joachim Schulze, scheduled to appear in four volumes, represents a new and extremely detailed model for future scientific thematic cataloguing of a major composer's works. Two large indexes completed by Czech scholars, one for Dittersdorf by Oldrich Pulkert and the other for the Brixi family by Vladimir Novak have not found publishers. The catalogue of the works of Mislivecek is being compiled separately by two scholars; attempts to open communication between the two compilers have thus far been unsuccessful. In the beginning stages are much-needed catalogues for two composers whose output is both large and multi-editioned: Liszt and Villa-Lobos. Also in progress but with much still to do is a composite thematic index of 75 pre-1830 multiple-composer thematic catalogues, both printed and in manuscript.

Predictions are inevitable in a paper such as this; I would like to make a few. The production of thematic catalogues will continue on its merry pace. Computers will become a *sine qua non* of the genre. Quality will improve, but standardization in the format of composer catalogues will never be achieved. There will be greater emphasis on authenticity determination as methods of style analysis improve; the Anhänge of doubtful works are thus likely to decrease in size. Union catalogues and huge data bases will become increasingly fashionable, and enormously useful in identifying anonymi and solving multiple-parent riddles. Finally, the second edition of *Thematic Cataloques in Music,* scheduled to appear in 1988, will contain almost twice as many entries as its predecessor which was published only a decade and a half earlier.

NOTES

1. I refer only to "art music" cataloguing. Folk music researchers had the good sense, as early as 1899, to offer a historic challenge with a prize (the complete works of Sweelinck!) to the author of the best method for classifying folk song materials melodically and to hold several conferences on the subject. See Daniel Scheurleer [116], Koller [676], and Krohn [698], etc. See note 2 for explanation of numbers in brackets.

2. Numbers given in square brackets refer to citations in Barry S. Brook, *Thematic Catalogues in Music: An Annotated Bibliography*, (Hillsdale, N.Y.: Pendragon Press, 1972). These numbers will remain the same in the second edition now being prepared for publication with the indispensible collaboration of Professor Richard Viano, (Stuyvesant, N.Y.: Pendragon Press, 1988). N.B. Dates given with asterisks in the text refer to citations in the appended "Selected Literature I: General."

3. The quotation is from Breitkopf's perceptive *Nacherinnerung* to Parte 1ma of his thematic *Catalogo delle Sinfonie* . . . (Leipzig, 1762 p. 29). The complete catalogue, one of the first, largest, and most important ever published, was reprinted in facsimile in 1966 by Dover Publications under the title, *The Breitkopf Thematic Catalogue; the Six Parts and Sixteen Supplements 1762-1787*; the reprint, which has been unavailable for many years, will be reissued by another publisher in 1989.

4. *The Present State of Music in Germany, the Netherlands and the United Provinces*, 2nd ed., London, 1775, Vol 2, p. 73-74. "[Breitkopf] seems . . . to have been the first who gave to his catalogues an index in notes, containing the *subjects* or two or three first bars, of the several pieces in each musical work; by which a reader is enabled to discover not only whether he is in possession of an entire book [e.g., a collection of six trios] but of any part of its contents."

5. A hasty check has shown no prior dictionary articles. An interesting tidbit may be found in Michel Brenet's *Dictionaire de la musique* (1926). This astute and indefatigable French scholar was the first to point out confusion between "incipit" and "theme." I quote her entry in its entirety: "Thématique, adj. qual. *Qui se rapport à un theme. On emploie à tort ce vocable en nominant *table thématique* la table des *incipit* de morceaux de musique contenu dans un recueil."

6. A pilot catalogue of the holdings of a single collection, that of the Fürstlich Hohenlohe-Langenburgsche Schloßbibliothek, was published by the RISM staff in *Fontes artis musicae*, 25/4 (1978): 295-411. Incipits were given in both conventional notation and plaine and easie code. The introduction describes *RISM A/II* processes, including computer usage.

7. In May of 1965, following a Symposium on "Input Languages to Represent Music," the co-director of Ford Columbia Project which was designed " . . . to enable us to print music under computer control . . . ," announced that "next month we will become fully operational." A dozen years later, that promise, and many others made in the name of both commercial and noncommercial ventures,

remained unfulfilled. See "Selected Literature II," Stephan Bauer-Mengelberg, 1970*.

SELECTED LITERATURE I: GENERAL

N.B.: Numbers in brackets at the end of each entry refer to citations in *Thematic Catalogues in Music*, see note 2.

1912 Lewis, Leo R. "The Possibilities of Thematic Indexing," *Proceedings of the Music Teachers National Association*, 7(1912): 180-88. [732]

1927 Altmann, Wilhelm. "Über thematische Kataloge," *Bericht Über den Internationalen Musikwissenschatlichen Kongress der Beethoven-Zentenarfeier* (Wien: Universal Edition, 1927), p. 283-89. [24]

1943 Deutsch, Otto Erich. "Music Bibliography and Catalogues," *The Library*, 23/4 (March 1943): 151-70. [294]

1944 Meyer, Kathi. "Early Breitkopf & Härtel Thematic Catalogues of Manuscript Music," *The Musical Quarterly*, 30 (April 1944): 163-73. [167b]

1950 Bridgman, Nanie. "L'Établissement d'un catalogue par incipit musicaux," *Musica disciplina*, 4/1 (1950): 65-68. [174]

1951 Deutsch, Otto Erich. Preface to Schubert, *Thematic Catalogue of All His Works in Chronological Order* (London: Dent; New York: Norton, 1951), p. ix-xx. [295]

1951 _____."Theme and Variations, with Bibliographical Notes on Pleyel's Haydn Editions," *The Music Review*, 12/1 (Feb. 1951): 68-71. [296]

1951 Stäblein, Bruno. "Der thematische Katalog der mittelalterlichen einstimmigen Melodien," *Zweiter Weltkongress der Musik-bibliotheken Lüneburg 1950* (Kassel, 1951?). p. 52-54. [1232]

1954 Bridgman, Nanie. "À propos d'un catalogue central d'incipits musicaux," *Fontes artis musicae*, 1 (1954): 22-23. [175]

1954 King, Alec Hyatt. "The Past, Present and Future of the Thematic Catalogue," *Monthly Musical Record*, 84/953, 954 (1954): 10-13; 39-46. [659]

1955 Landon, H.C. Robbins. *The Symphonies of Joseph Haydn* (London: Universal Edition, 1955) 862 p. Thematic catalogue, p. 605-823. [554]

1955 Mies, Paul. "Komponisten-Werkverzeichnisse. Ein Hilfsmittel für Musiker, Musikliebhaber und Musikalienhändler," *Musikhandel*, 6/4-5 (1955): 102-03; 6/6-7 (1955): 156-57. [829]

1958 Deutsch, Otto Erich. "Thematische Kataloge," *Fontes artis musicae*, 5/2 (1958): 73-79. [297]

1958 Lesure, François. "Musique et musicologie dans les bibliothèques Parisiennes," *Bulletin des bibliothèques de France*, 3 (1958): 265. [730]

1959 Bridgman, Nanie. "Le classement par incipit musicaux, histoire d'un catalogue," *Bulletin des Bibliothèques de France*, 4/6 (1959): 303-08. [176]

1959 LaRue, Jan. "A Union Thematic Catalogue of 18th Century Symphonies," *Fontes artis musicae*, 6/1 (1959): 18-20. [712a]

1959 Mies, Paul. "Tematické seznamy hudebních skladeb [Thematic Indexes of Musical Compositions]," *Hudební rozhledy*, 12/4 (1959): 146-48. [830]
1960 LaRue, Jan. "Major and Minor Mysteries of Identification in the 18th Century Symphonies," *Journal of the American Musicological Society*, 13/1-3 (1960): 181-96. [712b]
1960 _____."Union Thematic Catalogues for 18th Century Chamber Music and Concertos," *Fontes artis musicae*, 7/2 (1960): 64-66. [713a]
1961 Bridgman, Nanie. "Nouvelle visite aux incipit musicaux," *Acta musicologica*, 33/2-4 (1961): 193-96. [177]
1962 Racek, Jan. "Hudební inventáře a jejich význam pro hudebněhistorické bádání [Music inventories and their meanings for musicological research]," *Ada musei Moraviae*, 47 (1962): 135-62. [1018]
1962 Thiel, Eberhard. "Thematisches Verzeichnis," *Sachwörterbuch der Musik. Kröners Taschenausgabe*, Bd. 10 (Stuttgart: Kröner, 1962), p. viii. 602p. [1302.1]
1963 Palisca, Claude. "American Scholarship in Western Music," *Musicology*, Frank L. T. Harrison, Mantle Hood and Claude V. Palisca, compilers (Englewood Cliffs, N.J.: Prentice Hall, 1963), p. 163-66. [946]
1963 Schmieder, Wolfgang. "Menschliches-Allzumenschliches oder einige unparteiische Gedanken über thematische Verzeichnisse," *Otto Erich Deutsch, Festschrift . . . zum 80. Geburtstag*, W. Gerstenberg, ed. (Kassel, 1963), p. 309-18. [1167]
1964 Noble, Richard D. C. "Editorial [on thematic catalogues]," *Consort*, 21 (Summer 1964): 241-47. [914]
1965 Coral, Lenore. *An Historical Survey of Thematic Catalogues with Special Reference to the Instrumental Works of Antonio Vivaldi* (M.A. thesis: U. of Chicago Graduate Library School, 1965) (typescript). [257]
1965 Ott, Alfons. "Thematische Verzeichnisse," *Die Musik in Geschichte und Gegenwart*, vol. 13 (1965), p. 311-21. [934]
1965 Zimmerman, Franklin B. "Melodic Indexing for General and Specialized Use," *Music Library Association Notes*, 22/4 (June 1966): 1187-92. [1439]
1966 Fukač, Jiři. "Tschechische Musikinventare," trans. by Adolf Langer. *Tschechische Musikwissenschaft. Geschichtliches. Musica Antiqua Europae Orientalis* (Praha: Tschechoslovakisches Musik-Informationszentrum, 1966), p. 1-64. [413]
1966 Riedel, Friedrich Wilhelm. "Zur Geschichte der Musikalischen Quellenüberlieferung und Quellenkunde," *Acta musicologica*, 38/1 (1966): 3-27. [1054]
1967 Riemann, Hugo. *Riemann Musik Lexikon* (1967), "Thematische Kataloge," p. 952-53. [1060]
1972 Brook, Barry S. "The First Printed Thematic Catalogues," *Festskrilt Jens Peter Larsen 1902-14 VI-1972. Studier udgivet af Musikvidenskabeligt Institut ved Københavns Universitet* (København: Wilhelm Hansen Musik-Forlag, 1972), p. 103-12. [193]
1973 _____."A Tale of Thematic Catalogues [On the Definitions, History,

Functions, Historiography, and Future of the Thematic Catalogue]," *Music Library Association Notes*, 29/3 (March 1973): 407-15.

1975 Johansson, Carl. "From Pergolesi to Gallo by the Numericode system," *Svensk tidskrift för musikforskning*, 47/2 (1975): 67-68. [633.1]

1979 Brook, Barry S. Review of: Robert Münster and Robert Machold, eds. *Thematischer Katalog der Musik-Handschriften der ehemahligen Klosterkirchen Weyarn, Tegernsee amd Benediktbeuern* (Munich: Henle Verlag, 1971); Ursula Bockholdt, Robert Machold, and Lisbet Thew, eds. *Thematischer Katalog der Benediktin-erinnenabtei Frauenworth und der Pfarrkirchen Indersdorf, Wasserburg am Inn und Bad Tolz* (Munich: Henle Verlag, 1975); Gertraut Haberkamp, ed. *Thematischer Katalog der Musik-Handschriften der Fürslich Oettingen-Wallerstein-schen Bibliotek Schloss Harburg* (Munich: Henle Verlag, 1976), *Journal of the American musicological society*, 32/3 (1979): 549-55.

1980 _____. "The Past, Present and Future of the Music Library Thematic Catalogue," *Music and Bibliography: Essays in Honor of Alec Hyatt King*, O.W. Neighbour, ed. (New York: K. G. Saur, 1980) p. 215-42.

1980 _____. "Thematic Catalogue," *New Grove Dictionary of Music and Musicians*, vol. 18 (London: Macmillan, 1980), p. 732-36.

1980 Michałowski, Kornel. *Katalogi tematyczne: Historia i teoria* (Kraków: Polish Music Publishers PWM, 1980) 150p. [826.1]

1982 Basart, Ann. "Bringing Order into a Preposterous Muddle: Recent Trends in Thematic Catalogs," *Cum notis variorum*, No. 67 (Nov. 1982): 5-17. [73.1]

1984 Brook, Barry S. "Christian Ulrich Ringmacher (1743-1781): His Heritage, His Firm, and His Catalogue," *Music and Civilization: Essays in Honor of Paul Henry Lang*, Edmond Strainchamps and Maria Rika Maniates, eds. (New York: W. W. Norton, 1984), p. 243-61.

SELECTED LITERATURE II: COMPUTERS AND CATALOGUES

1964 Bernstein, Lawrence F. "Data Processing and the Thematic Index," *Fontes artis musicae*, 11/3 (1964): 159-65. [117]

1964 Brook, Barry S. and Murray Gould. *Notating Music with Ordinary Typewriter Characters (A Plaine and Easie Code System for Musicke)* (Flushing, N.Y.: Queens College, 1964). [187]

1964 Heckmann, Harald. "Neue Methoden der Verarbeitung musi-kalischer Daten," *Die Musikforschung*, 17/4 (1964): 381-83. [574]

1965 Brook, Barry S. "The Simplified Plaine and Easie Code System for Notating Music, a Proposal for International Adoption," *Fontes artis musicae*, 12/2-3 (May-Sept. 1965): 156-60. [188]

1965 _____. "Utilization of Data Processing Techniques in Musical Documentation," *Fontes artis musicae*, 12/2-3 (May-Sept. 1965): 112-22. [189]

1965 Collins, Walter S. "A New Tool for Musicology," *Music and Letters*, 46 (1965): 122-25. [255]
1965 Meylan, Raymond. "Utilisation des calculatrices électroniques pour la comparaison interne du répertoire des basses danses du quinzième siècle," *Fontes artis musicae*, 12/2-3 (May-Dec. 1965): 128-35. [824]
1966 LaRue, Jan and George W. Logemann. "E[lectronic] D[ata] P[rocessing] for Thematic Catalogues," *Music Library Association Notes*, 22/4 (June 1966): 1179-86. [719]
1967 Brook, Barry S. "Some New Paths for Music Bibliography," *Computers in Humanistic Research: Readings and Perspectives*, Edmund A. Bowles, ed. (Englewood, N.J.: Prentice-Hall, 1967), p. 204-11. [190]
1967 _____. "Music Bibliography and the Computer," *Computer Applications in Music*, Gerald Lefkoff, ed. (Morgantown, W. Va.: West Virginia University Library, 1967). [191]
1967 Heckmann, Harald. *Elektronische Datenverarbeitung in der Musikwissenschaft* (Regensburg: Gustav Bosse Verlag, [1967]). [575]
1967 Lincoln, Harry B. "Some Criteria and Techniques for Developing Thematic Indices," *Der Computer in Musikwissenschaft und Musikdokumentation*, Harald Heckmann, ed. (Regensburg: Gustav Bosse Verlag, 1967). [735]
1967 _____. "Thematic Index of 16th-Century Italian Music,"-*Computers and the Humanities*, 2/2 (Nov. 1967): 86. [736]
1967 Meylan, Raymond. "Symbolisierung einer Melodie auf Lochkarten," *Elektronische Datenberarbeitung in der Musikwissenschaft*, Harald Heckmann, ed. (Regensburg: Gustav Bosse Verlag, 1967), p. 21-24. [825]
1967 Pulkert, Oldřich. "Hudba, samočinné počítače a jiné novinky" [Music, computers, and other novelties], *Hudební věda*, 3 (1967): 479-84. [1011]
1968 LaRue, Jan. "The Thematic Index: A Computer Application to Musicology," *Computers and the Humanities*, 2/5 (May 1968): 243. [717]
1968 Lincoln, Harry B. "The Thematic Index: A Computer Application to Musicology," *Computers and the Humanities*, 2/5 (May 1968): 215-20. [738]
1969 Bernstein, Lawrence F. "Computers and the 16th-Century Chanson; A Pilot Project at the University of Chicago," *Computers and the Humanities*, 3/3 (Jan. 1969): 153-61. [118]
1970 Bauer-Mengelberg, Stefan. "The Ford-Columbia Input Language," *Musicology and the Computer*, Barry S. Brook, ed. (New York: City University of New York Press, 1970), p. 48-52. [77]
1970 Brook, Barry S. "Music Documentation of the Future," *Musicology and the Computer*, Barry S. Brook, ed. (New York: City University of New York Press, 1970), p. 28-36. [192]
1973 Ottosen, Knud. "Le classement par ordinateur des listes de repons liturgiques: le traitement des données," *Informatique musicale: journées d'étude 1973*, textes des conférences, E.R.A.T.T.O. Calcul et sciences humaines (Paris: CNRS, 1973). [934.1]
1975 Remmel, Mart. *Automatic Notation of One-Voiced Songs* (Tallin: Academy of Sciences of the Estonian SSR, 1975). 23p. [1043.3]

1984 Drummond, Philip J. *Computer Applications to Music; A Survey and Review of the Literature 1949-1979.* (Master's essay: University of New South Wales, 1984) 441 p. (Copy in CUNY Ph.D. Program in Music)
1986 Hewlett, Walter B. and Eleanor Selfridge-Field. *Directory of Computer Assisted Research in Musicology 1986* (Menlo Park, CA: Center for Computer Assisted Research in the Humanities, 1986). 86 p. (Available from the above Center, 535 Middlefield Road, Suite 120, Menlo Park, CA 94025)

Scholarly Editions: Their Character and Bibliographic Description

Keith E. Mixter

SUMMARY. This paper addresses the problems of bibliographical description from a historical viewpoint. Some distinction is drawn between the "monumental edition" of music and the complete works set. The nature of the critical edition is examined, and the author offers an outline of documents which should be considered in compiling a list of sources for a musical work. Finally, a plea for a wider and more detailed use of the critical apparatus is advocated on the part of both performer and scholar.

I am pleased to have been asked to speak at this Conference on Music Bibliography. Music bibliographers are the unsung heroes of musical scholarship, and we owe a debt to Kären Nagy and Richard Green for their recognition of the vital role which this art plays in supplying a basis for that scholarship. Tribute should also be paid to the Music Library Association for the various awards which it has instituted in recent years to recognize bibliographical scholarship.

I have chosen to speak to you on the subject of scholarly and critical editions. As you will see later, I am using these terms advisedly, since older editions, generally those of the 19th century and earlier, may not be thought of as critical editions, although they are

---

Keith E. Mixter is affiliated with the School of Music, Ohio State University.

[Haworth co-indexing entry note]: "Scholarly Editions: Their Character and Bibliographic Description." Mixter, Keith E. Co-published simultaneously in *Music Reference Services Quarterly*, (The Haworth Press, Inc.) Vol. 2, No. 1/2, 1993, pp. 47-58; and: *Foundations in Music Bibliography* (ed: Richard D. Green) The Haworth Press, Inc., 1993, pp. 47-58. Multiple copies of this article/chapter may be purchased from The Haworth Document Delivery Center [1-800-3-HAWORTH; 9:00 a.m. - 5:00 p.m. (EST)].

© 1993 by The Haworth Press, Inc. All rights reserved.

frequently used by scholars. My remarks will address the following aspects: bibliography, monumental editions, complete works, and critical editions. I am hoping that my observations as bibliographer and editor will be of interest to you. Certainly the importance of scholarly editions for the fields of librarianship and musicology calls for this closer look.

BIBLIOGRAPHIC DESCRIPTION

Within the field of bibliographic description the pre-Heyer era is irregular in coverage. In 1871, the indefatigable bibliographer Robert Eitner published a listing of new editions of early music from the "earliest period" to the year 1800 as volume three of his *Monatshefte für Musikgeschichte,* with supplements issued in 1877 and 1878. Eitner intended the list as an aid to the development of the field of musicology, then in its infancy. This bibliography, which reached back at least to the year 1757, but which excluded by design complete works sets, embraced general collections, collections of German secular songs (Eitner's immediate interest), editions of older sacred music, a few collections of arrangements, and titles about which Eitner had gathered information only from catalogues. There followed then a partial index to these collections, together with a brief biographical identification of the composers. The entire listing extended to 208 pages.

In 1934, the fourth edition of Arnold Schering's *Tabellen zur Musikgeschichte,* published by Breitkopf and Härtel, contained a self-serving section devoted to *Denkmäler* and *Gesamtausgaben* published by that firm. The large number of such publications nevertheless made that listing a valuable one for those days. A well-intentioned, but short-lived, series compiled by Walter Lott was published from 1937 to 1943 under the title *Verzeichnis der Neudrucke alter Musik.* Published in Leipzig, the series covered the years 1936 to 1942, and included composers active to about the year 1800. Publications of the American firms of Ditson and G. Schirmer were represented. Following the basic bibliographic listing we find a systematic index and a title and text index. Lott's series was presumably aborted by the war, and indeed the final slim issue for 1942 was printed on markedly inferior paper.

Today we are grateful for the exemplary efforts of Anna Harriet Heyer in her *Historical Sets, Collected Editions, and Monuments of Music*, especially in the expanded third edition of Chicago, 1980. It is to be regretted, however, that so many of her volume titles appear in translation, a fact which diminishes the bibliographical value of the citations. Less well known is her *A Check-List of Publications of Music*, her University of Michigan master's thesis of 1944, which provided very helpful American locations for publications listed.

MONUMENTAL EDITIONS

For purposes of this discussion, I am excluding complete works sets from a consideration of monumental editions. In a sense, however, this distinction is a clouded one, since some editions, such as *Das Erbe deutscher Musik*, the *Monumentos de la Música Española*, and *Musica Britannica*, include complete works sub-sets, and thereby present a classification dilemma to the music cataloguer. Despite this problem, the approach taken by writers in encyclopedias such as *Die Musik in Geschichte und Gegenwart* and *The New Grove Dictionary of Music and Musicians* has also been to distinguish between monumental editions and composers' complete works sets.[1] Although the methodology of these genres has much in common, this seems a reasonable direction to take, and I shall follow it here.

Many commentators, for example Carl Dahlhaus, have observed that the monumental edition was born of the nationalistic fervor of the 19th century.[2] Indeed, titles such as "monuments," "Denkmäler," "monumentos," and the like, complemented by descriptive words such as "Bohemica," "Britannica," or "Polonia," bear out this view. Dahlhaus has also suggested (surely tongue-in-cheek) that in this fervor old clefs, mensurations, key signatures, and other attributes of earlier notation were placed under the protection of the national heritage *(Denkmalschutz)*. The political importance of Bavaria is reflected in its being accorded a separate sub-series of the *Denkmäler deutscher Tonkunst*, whereas other areas of Germany have had to be content with being subsumed within the pan-Germanic series I.

It is remarkable how politically astute the early promoters of these monumental series were. Three years prior to the inception of the

DDT, in the year 1889, Philipp Spitta published the musical works of Frederick the Great, a publication heralded by Emperor William I. In 1892, two years before the first publication of the series *Denkmäler der Tonkunst in Österreich,* Guido Adler brought out a series of musical works by the Emperors Ferdinand III, Leopold I, and Joseph I. In demonstrating the involvement of these sovereigns with music, surely the role of music as a national monument was established and state subsidy for further publication was assured.[3]

Monumental editions are often categorized as national or international. Although this is a practical approach, it leads to some ambiguities. We find, for example, the Trent Codices, containing works by such non-Austrians as John Dunstable and Guillaume Dufay, published as several volumes of the *DTÖ,* and we see that same series embracing an edition of Marcantonio Cesti's opera *Pomo d'oro.* The latter can be explained away as a spectacle first performed at the Viennese court; indeed, we were for many years grateful to have this edition available, important as it is as an example of Venetian opera of this period.

The practice of teutonic publishers of monumental sets in assigning *Jahrgang,* or yearly issue, numbers to their volumes, is lamentable as it serves no practical purpose and leads to confusion. In this practice, volumes one to three of the *DTÖ,* for example, published in 1894, 1894, and 1895, respectively, are numbered *Jahrgang I-number 1, Jahrgang I-number 2, and Jahrgang II*. Most modern scholars do not observe this in citation. Heyer's ambivalent approach in this regard is reflected in her treatment of the *DTÖ,* wherein *Jahrgang* numbers appear in parentheses behind the volume numbers, and in her description of the *DDT,* second series, where the primary numbering appears to be by *Jahrgänge.*

COMPLETE WORKS

The purpose of a collected edition of a composer's works is to present the entirety of his works, even the minor ones, and to publish them in an authoritative edition. Probably the only place in which one can follow, for example, the fascinating creative stages of Franz Liszt's tone poem *Mazeppa* is in the *Musikalische Werke,* published in Leipzig 1907 to 1936. An authoritative edition is usually construed to mean a critical edition–but I will return to this later.

Karl Vötterle, the founder of the Bärenreiter Verlag, has called the immediate post-World War II period the "hour of the complete works edition."[4] Indeed, the number of such editions has grown almost exponentially since 1945, chiefly at the hands of that firm and the American Institute of Musicology. The hand-to-mouth existence of such publications of earlier days has been replaced by sales which extend to the western hemisphere and even to the orient.[5] American librarians, recalling the scarcity of scholarly editions in domestic libraries in the 1940's and 1950's, when musicology was a burgeoning discipline, realize that they can ill afford to neglect this phase of acquisition. Support for these publications is badly needed, despite the financial help of such companies as Volkswagen, which is reported to have contributed, prior to the year 1975, 5,533,775 Marks toward the new complete works editions of Mozart, Haydn, Bach, Gluck, Schubert, and Wagner.[6]

In 1947, J.M. Coopersmith published an article entitled "The First *Gesamtausgabe:* Dr. Arnold's Edition of Handel's Works."[7] As it turns out, the edition was neither Gesamt nor was it the "first." The late fourteenth-century manuscript Paris, Bibliothèque nationale f. fr. 1584 contains all but five compositions of Guillaume de Machaut, with the note "Here is the order that G. de Machaut wishes to have in his book."[8] Efforts up to 1851 involved largely abortive attempts at complete publications such as Arnold's Handel edition of 1787 to 1797, publications of piety such as Lassus' *Magnum opus musicum* of 1604, or the publication of works in public demand such as the Haydn *Oeuvres complètes* of 1802 to 1843. As we all realize, 1851 saw the inception of the Bach-Gesellschaft edition of the Bach *Werke*, a collection comprehensive enough that we may herald it as the beginning of a new epoch in which we may reasonably assume completeness in so-called complete works sets.

But what of the changing character of such collections? Two features stand out. The first of these is an organization into series, or sub-series, which represent compositional genres. While the Bach *Werke* (1851-1926) were published in nearly random order, the Mozart *Sämtliche Werke* (1876-1905) were laid out in series, of one or more volumes each, representing compositional types. This has largely been the practice in the more comprehensive latter-day sets such as Haydn's *Kritische Gesamtausgabe,* which began publication in 1950. This organization facilitates on-shelf searching without resort to cumbersome conspectuses or thematic indexes.

A second feature is the inclusion of materials not essentially musical or not from the composer's own hand. This was begun by Friedrich Chrysander in his Handel *Werke* (1858-1902) in a most felicitous way. Here we find six supplementary volumes containing compositions by various composers from whom Handel borrowed material for his own works. In the more recent *Neue Ausgaben* of Mozart and Schubert, begun in 1956 and 1964 respectively, iconographic and biographical documents are included. Efforts have recently been made toward the recording of the complete works of a composer, of which an example is the recording of Anton Webern's music, issued by Columbia in 1957. We can hope that this modest beginning will lead to more such endeavors.

I would like to say a word regarding footnote and bibliographic entries for complete works sets. Too often, editors are given as author entries, seeming to disavow the conceptions of the composers. This is appropriate only for documentation to material such as a foreword, where the author is indeed the editor. Confusion is also sown by the literal adoption of such titles as *Guillelmi Dufay Opera Omnia,* maintaining the inflected composer's name as part of the title, a practice excusable for a Latin title page, but hardly for a bibliographic entry, where alphabetical placement may be highly important.

CRITICAL EDITIONS

If nineteenth-century nationalism inspired the publication of monumental editions and complete works sets in music, so also did the application of the nineteenth-century scientific method influence the critical aspects of the editing of these sets. Alfred Foulet and Mary Speer have observed that this scientific philological method, based on a classification of manuscripts, succeeded the earlier empirical method in which one source was utilized and improved upon in the edition.[9] Along this line, Alfred Dürr has recently introduced two new terms into musicological parlance: *Quellenedition* (source edition) and *Werkedition* (composition edition).[10] These refer, respectively, to the editing of one particular musical source, more typical of nineteenth-century musical editions, and the editing of one particular work, drawing upon its manifold sources. It is the latter procedure that is more typical of modern critical editions. These are useful terms, and should be borne in mind throughout the ensuing discussion.

Following the selection of the composition or compositions to be edited, there are five steps entailed in the creation of a critical edition: (1) the establishment of a source bibliography, (2) the collection of these sources, (3) the collation and comparison of the sources, (4) the editing of the music and, where appropriate, the verbal texts, and (5) the compilation of the critical commentary. Because of time limitations I can comment only briefly on each of these.

In source bibliography, one must determine what the sources for a particular composer's *oeuvre* might be. Although historiographers are reluctant to define the nature of a "source," understandably because this may vary from case to case, Norman F. Cantor and Richard F. Schneider state that "a primary source is a work that was written at a time that is contemporary or nearly contemporary with the period or subject being studied."[11] We might add that anything originating after the time during which it might have been reviewed in one way or another by the composer lies more appropriately in the realm of "reception history" rather than in the category of source materials. While the identification and location of sources has been much eased by bibliographies such as the *Répertoire international des sources musicales,* which began publication in 1960, we can but plead for greater precision in descriptive cataloging in the hope that such improvements will aid the scholar in the closer identification of sources. I offer the following outline of documents which should be considered in compiling a list of sources for a musical work:

I. Antecedent Works
   A. Foreign to the Composer
   B. The Composer's Own

II. Manuscripts
   A. Autograph
      1. Sketch
      2. Composing Score
      3. Revision Copy
      4. Fair Copy
   B. Amanuensis (Engraving?) Copy

III. Prints
   A. Proofs
   B. First Edition (Impression)
   C. Further Issues of the First Edition
   D. Second and Subsequent Editions (Throughout the Life of the Composer)

Obviously not all of these "states" will be present for each and every composer or composition.[12] One must always be alert to corrections by the composer which may be expressed within one or several of the above states or through performance parts, letters, or lists of corrections.

The task of the collection of sources is self explanatory and needs little comment. It should be undertaken at the earliest moment since it can be time consuming and may otherwise lead to undue delay in the editorial process. The collation and comparison of sources is a difficult undertaking, often entailing decisions concerning authenticity, which become especially problematic in the case of youthful works. Georg von Dadelsen has observed that whereas style criticism was earlier frequently applied in such judgement, this procedure has largely been superseded by source criticism.[13] He pleads for an appropriate balance of methods in such matters. In any case, a hierarchy of sources should be attempted, if at all possible.

There are two recent books on the process of editing: *Editionsrichtlinien musikalischer Denkmäler und Gesamtausgaben* (Kassel, 1967), edited by Georg von Dadelsen, and John Caldwell's *Editing Early Music* (Oxford, 1985), both of which provide useful guidelines. Additionally, *Musikalische Edition im Wandel des historischen Bewusstseins* (Kassel, 1971), edited by Thrasybulos Georgiades, renders an account of earlier editing methods within the confines of various genres or periods. The method of editing may be eclectic, that is, utilizing two or more sources, or the editing may follow an *editio princeps,* in which one source is followed without exception. In the former case, one may, for example, choose one source for the editing of the musical text and another for the editing of the verbal text of a vocal composition. Or, for a comprehensive work such as an opera, various parts may be edited according to various sources, a procedure found necessary in the editing of Mozart's *La finta giardiniera* for the *Neue Ausgabe* volume of 1978 because the autograph had disappeared during World War II, only to show up later in the Biblioteka Jagiellonska in Cracow.[14] Computer application to the process of collating has been described by Arthur Mendel. The program involves the encoding of the sources, part by part, and the automated preparation of the score, following which the sources are compared and the variants listed.[15]

Once the sources of a composition have been collated and evaluated and the edited text established, the final step is the compilation of the critical report (*Revisionsbericht*). This document falls into two parts: the description of the sources and an account of the places where these sources depart in their readings from those of the edited text. At times, source description may be as detailed as descriptive cataloguing. The more common sources, however, such as the Trent Codices, for which a certain amount of bibliographic description is already present in musicological literature, do not require as much elaboration as do those for which an adequate bibliography does not exist; for the former, reference to existing bibliography will suffice. On the other hand, we welcome such abundance of detail as that provided by Higinio Anglès in certain volumes of the *Monumentos de la Música Española* or by Albert Smijers in his edition of the Josquin *Werke,* for often this is our only resort in approaching less well-known sources.

Fredson Bowers makes two points in remarking on textual criticism: (1) it is necessary for the literary critic to base his remarks on a textually pure edition, and (2) we will understand a work better if we are able to follow the several stages of its creation.[16] It follows that there are two goals of musical textual criticism, i.e., the investigation of the creative process and the establishment of a textually pure text. While to some extent the methods employed are the same,

I submit that some elements are more basic to the one than to the other. For example, the matter of chronology, it seems to me, is more important for the investigation of the creative process than for the establishment of the pure text, while the opposite may be true of style criticism.

The most wearisome process is the listing of variants–wearisome to arrive at and wearisome to read and understand. Because of typographical problems, publishers are generally not sympathetic to the drawing up of such lists, and even some musicologists, Georg Feder, for example, do not favor the process.[17] Arthur Mendel, on the other hand, speaks eloquently in favor of a full listing of variants, even suggesting that without a critical report no edition can be trusted.[18] I am in full agreement with Mendel; a full listing of variants is vital. The matter of whether or not to provide such a listing is a little like the question of the selective or comprehensive bibliography–I would rather make the selection myself than to have it imposed upon me, for neither the editor nor the bibliographer can fully anticipate the purpose to which these tools may be put. However, there may be matters which can and should be left out of variant lists, such as differences in orthography which do not lead to differences in meaning.

Critical commentaries are certainly among the most unused types of musicological literature and should be an object of bibliographic instruction. The mature performer (by "mature," I mean the graduate student through the concert artist) might benefit from the study of variant readings by becoming acquainted with ornaments, accidentals, or tempo indications which the performing editions do not reflect and which might greatly enhance a thoughtful performance. For the historian, other lessons might be learned. Here I am reminded of changes in fifteenth-century dissonance practice which may be seen in variants in manuscripts dating twenty years apart.

* * *

I hope that this brief excursion into the nature of monumental and complete works series has been informative, for these editions offer something for everyone, the composer, the performer, the theorist, and the historian. Such editions are likely to increase in number in the future, and they are certain to play an even larger role in our musical life. A grasp of their complexities is certain to reward us with a greater understanding of our art.

NOTES

1. See Wolfgang Schmieder, "Denkmäler der Tonkunst," Die Musik in Geschichte und Gegenwart, ed. Friedrich Blume, vol. 3 (Kassel: Bärenreiter, 1949-), cols. 166-92, and Sydney Robinson Charles, "Editions, Historical," *The New Grove Dictionary of Music and Musicians,* ed. Stanley Sadie, vol. 5 (London: Macmillan, 1980), p. 848-69.
2. Carl Dahlhaus, "Zur Ideengeschichte musikalischer Editionsprinzipien," *Fontes ariis musicae,* 25 (1978): 20.
3. For further information, see Hans Joachim Moser, *Das musikalische Denkmälerwesen in Deutschland* (Kassel: Bärenreiter, 1952), p. 20-21.
4. Ludwig Finscher, "Musikalische Denkmäler und Gesamtausgaben," *Musikalisches Erbe und Gegenwart* (Kassel: Bärenreiter, 1975), p. 10
5. See, for example, the lament of Hans Joachim Moser regarding the sale of the Weber complete works in his *Das musikalische Denkmälerwesen in Deutschland* p. 15.
6. Hanspeter Bennwitz, "Die Förderung von Musiker-Gesamtausgaben durch die Stittung Volkswagenwerk," *Musikalisches Erbe und Gegenwart* (Kassel: Bärenreiter, 1975). p. 101.
7. J.M. Coopersmith, "The First *Gesamtausgabe:* Dr. Arnold's Edition of Handel's Works," *Music Library Association Notes,* 4 (1946-47): 277-91; 439-49.
8. Richard H. Hoppin, *Medieval Music* (New York: Norton, 1978), p. 399.
9. Alfred Foulet and Mary Blakeley Speer, *On Editing Old French Texts* (Lawrence: Regents Press of Kansas, 1979), p. 3-8.
10. Wolfgang Rehm, "Quellenforschung und Dokumentation im Verhältnis zur Editionstechnik, aufgezeigt an einem Beispiel aus der *Neuen Mozart-Ausgabe,*" *Quellenforschung in der Musikwissenschaft* ed. Georg Feder (Wolfenbüttel: Herzog August Bibliothek, 1982), p. 95.
11. Norman F. Cantor and Richard F. Schneider, *How to Study History* (New York: Crowell, 1967). p. 22-23.
12. See the list of states in Hubert Unverricht, *Die Eigenschriften und die Originalausgaben von Werken Beethovens in ihrer Bedeutung für die modernen Textkritik* (Kassel: Bärenreiter, 1960). p. 25, and the complex filiation of the Piano Sonata op. 111 on p. 44.
13. Georg von Dadelsen, "Methodische Bemerkungen zur Echtheitskritik," *Musicae Scientiae Collectanea, Festschrift Karl Gustav Fellerer zum siebzigsten Geburtstag,* ed. Heinrich Hüschen (Köln: Arno Volk, 1973). p. 78.

14. Rehm, *Quellenforschung in der Musikwissenschaft* 97-101. For a fascinating account of this and other Berlin manuscripts, see Nigel Lewis, *Paperchase* (London: Hamish Hamilton, 1981).

15. Arthur Mendel, "The Purposes and Desirable Characteristics of Text-Critical Editions," *Modern Musical Scholarship*, ed. Edward Olleson (Stocksfields: Oriel Press, 1978), p. 23-24.

16. Fredson Bowers, *Textual and Literary Criticism* (Cambridge: University Press, 1959), 1-34.

17. Georg Feder, "Gedanken über den kritischen Apparat aus der Sicht der Haydn-Gesamtausgabe," *Colloquium amicorum; Joseph Schmidt-Görg zum 70. Geburtstag*, ed. Siegfried Kross and Hans Schmidt (Bonn: Beethovenhaus, 1967), p. 73-75.

18. Mendel, *Modern Musical Scholarship*, p. 22.

"Perfuming the Air with Music":[1]
The Need for Film Music Bibliography

Gillian B. Anderson

SUMMARY. To demonstrate the need for a film music bibliography, the author recounts the struggle to identify the composers of four popular film tunes, to locate the scores and to compile a list of related secondary literature. An evaluation of the bibliographical problems encountered in the search, and of a few of the sources consulted.

[Ms. Anderson played brief recorded examples at the outset of her paper. Ed.] I have begun this presentation by playing four selections which most of you will recognize:[2] Leigh Harline's "When You Wish Upon a Star" from *Pinocchio;*[3] Victor Young's "Around the World" from *Around the World in 80 Days;*[4] Paul Simon's "Mrs. Robinson" from *The Graduate;*[5] and John William's *Star Wars* theme.[6] To demonstrate the need for film music bibliography, I would like to pretend that I knew nothing about the music for these four films, *Pinocchio, Around the World in 80 Days, The Graduate,* and *Star Wars.* I would like to show you what happened when I tried to identify the composers, to locate the scores, and to compile a list of secondary literature.

I started with James Limbacher's *Film Music: From Violins to*

Gillian B. Anderson is affiliated with the Music Division at the Library of Congress.

[Haworth co-indexing entry note]: " 'Perfuming the Air with Music': The Need for Film Music Bibliography." Anderson, Gillian B. Co-published simultaneously in *Music Reference Services Quarterly,* (The Haworth Press, Inc.) Vol. 2, No. 1/2, 1993, pp. 59-103; and: *Foundations in Music Bibliography* (ed: Richard D. Green) The Haworth Press, Inc., 1993, pp. 59-103. Multiple copies of this article/chapter may be purchased from The Haworth Document Delivery Center [1-800-3-HAWORTH; 9:00 a.m. - 5:00 p.m. (EST)].

© 1993 by The Haworth Press, Inc. All rights reserved.

Video[7] and Limbacher's *Keeping Score. Film Music 1972-1979.*[8] In the later, more recent volume, Limbacher cites John Williams as the composer for Twentieth Century Fox's 1977 production of *Star Wars.* In the first volume Limbacher lists Victor Young as the composer for United Artists' 1956 film *Around the World in 80 Days* and Dave Grusin for Avco-Embassy's 1967 film *The Graduate.* Unfortunately, not only is Walt Disney's *Pinocchio* absent from both of Limbacher's books, but there are also other errors of commission or omission. Paul Simon is not credited with the songs for *The Graduate,* and Avco-Embassy was incorrectly cited as the releasing company, rather than Embassy.[9] At least Limbacher got the dates of the three films correct (which he frequently does not).[10]

I next checked Clifford McCarty's *Film Composers in America. A Checklist of Their Work.*[11] It listed only Disney-RKO's 1940 production of *Pinocchio,* because McCarty's excellent work was published in 1953, before the other three films had been released. McCarty listed Leigh Harline and Paul Smith as the composers, and gave Edward Plumb, Charles Wolcott, and Frederick Stark as the orchestrators for *Pinocchio.* I had now identified the composers for three of the films. However, Limbacher listed Dave Grusin as the composer of *The Graduate,* not also Paul Simon, and I needed to reconcile this discrepancy.

I found all the credits for *The Graduate* in *The American Film Institute Catalog of Motion Pictures Produced in the United States,* Volume 2, *Feature Films, 1961-1970.*[12] It listed all the musical credits for the film, and indicated that Simon had written the songs, while Grusin had done the underscoring. To summarize my attempt to identify the composers: no single reference work contained all the information on the composers of film scores, and some of the works consulted were unreliable. None of them contained information about the location of scores.

My next step was to locate the scores. I first looked in the Library of Congress (henceforth LC) Music Division card catalog under the titles of the four films, then under all the composers' names. The LC Music Division has microfilmed its extensive holdings of film scores, and I might have expected to locate several of the four scores in its collection. The negative results of my search, however, are listed in Tables 1 through 4. From Table 1 one can see that there are many settings under the title *Pinocchio* listed in the LC catalog. Only the third entry tentatively refers to a film. In Table 1, under the name Leigh Harline (the last two entries) there are only two arrangements of the same song, but no score. In Table 2 for the title *Around the World in 80 Days* it is much the same story. In Table 3 under the title *The Graduate,* or under the name Paul Simon, there is only one entry, but no score. Under the title *Star Wars* in Table 4 there are unexpectedly fewer entries than under the name John Williams, but this is probably because the individual sections from the film score are not cross-referenced to the film title in the music title catalog.[13]

Not one of the four film scores is found in the LC Music Division card catalog. All the entries in Tables 1 through 4 are arrangements or excerpts. As a general rule the Music Division receives published copyright deposits. The LC Copyright Office retains unpublished copyright deposits at its Landover, Maryland, storage facility, and the majority of the LC's film scores are unpublished copyright deposits.[14] Several years ago, for example, two unpublished copyright deposits–Bernard Herrmann's scores for *Vertigo* and *The Egyptian*–were transferred from the Copyright Office to the Music Division.

After not finding the scores in the Music Division, I checked the Copyright Office Catalog to see whether the scores were listed as unpublished copyright deposits either under the film titles or under the composers' names. The results are listed in Tables 5 through 8. When one consults the first entry of Table 5, "As I Was Say'n to the Duchess," one immediately sees why using the copyright cards can be difficult. The entry does not contain a reference to the film title. Although "As I Was Say'n to the Duchess" is from *Pinocchio,* there is no reference to the film on the card filed under Harline's name in the Copyright Office catalog. Nor does the title of the film appear on the main entry card for "As I Was Say'n to the Duchess" under "Disney, Walt Productions" in the catalog of the Copyright Office.[15] How, then, is one to know that "As I Was Say'n to the Duchess" was from *Pinocchio*? Fortunately, the song is listed under *Pinocchio* in Stanley Green's *Encyclopedia of the Musical Film.*[16] However, one is not always so lucky. A close perusal of the copyright entries under Harline shows that musical deposits for *Pinocchio* were registered from July 1, 1938, to September 28, 1939, that is, well before the film was released in 1940. However, the whole score was never deposited for copyright.

In Table 6, the letters "EU" indicate an unpublished copyright deposit, "EP" a published deposit. Under Victor Young there are a number of unpublished copyright deposits, especially if one gets past the famous "Around the World" theme. Through the 1950's the movie studios customarily copyrighted every cue of a score separately, so one has to compare all the cues with the film before one can be sure the whole score is present. Altogether these unpublished deposits for *Around the World in 80 Days* may constitute the entire score, but we cannot be certain.

From Table 7 one learns that no music for *The Graduate* by Dave Grusin was copyrighted. All the songs by Paul Simon were copyrighted, but they appear to be lead sheets that were written down after the performance. In Table 8, the double asterisks refer to deposits of music in hard copy. All are arrangements. Towards the end of the Table, one will encounter the entry for the suite from the score for *Star Wars* marked with a triple asterisk. However, the film score itself was not deposited. Instead, the music was copyrighted by making a PA (Performing Arts) registration on every band of the two record soundtrack. (See all the single asterisks.[17]) The soundtrack does not represent the whole score and may not even be in the right order. To summarize the LC search, the score for *Around the World in 80 Days* may be in the Copyright Office, but the scores for three of the most popular films produced since 1940 are not in the Library of Congress collections. My next step, therefore, was to try and find them elsewhere.

I checked *Resources of American Music History: A Directory of Source Materials from Colonial Times to World War II.*[18] There was a Leigh Harline Collection at the College-Conservatory of Music at the University of Cincinnati, and a Victor Young Collection at the Boston Public Library. I telephoned and found that piano short scores for *Pinocchio* and for *Around the World in 80 Days* are in each place. The Harline Collection contains autograph material, but the Victor Young Collections at the Boston Public Library and at

TABLE 1[41]

Sample Entries Under *Pinocchio* in the M Title Catalog of the Music Division, Library of Congress

PN6120 .A5F554	Frank, Yasha... *Pinocchio* (a musical legend) by Yasha Frank, from the story by A. [i.e., C.] Collodi [pseud.] text and lyrics by Yasha Frank, prepared for publication by Bernice Zaconick; music by Eddison Von Ottenfeld and Armando Loredo...New York, N.Y., Edward B. Marks Music Corp., © 1939.
M1995 .G265P4	*Pinocchio*. (An operetta in three acts from the Italian story by C. Collodi) Gaul, Harvey Bartlett. Vocal score, pfte. acc., with dialogue and stage directions.
M1508	Harline, Leigh. "Pinocchio," lyrics by Ned Washington, music by L. Harline...n.p., 1938. Film? LC has excerpts.
M1350.H	Harline, Leigh...(*Pinocchio*) When You Wish Upon a Star; by Leigh Harline, arr. for orchestra by Merle Isaac...Appl. states prev. reg. 1/50/40, EP82126. © on arrangement; Bourne, Inc., New York; 4 Mar 53; EP69646.
M1350.H	Helger, Ludig...*Pinocchio;* Bourleske [by] Lutz Helger ...© Edition Melodia Hans Gerig, Koeln, Ger.; 9 Apr. 54; EF0-27608.
M1356.R	*Pinocchio;* cha-cha-cha, musique de Robert Rapetti. Orchestre parties separees. Paris, New York, Editions P. Beuscher...(Series tropicale) (With Fiesta a Brazilia) © Editions Musicales Paul Beuscher; 31 Mar 64; EF0-100735.
M24 .P897P5	Pozzoli, Ettore...*Pinocchio;* piccola suite per pianoforte ...© G. Ricordi & C., Milano; 30 Dec 55; EF22254.
M1731.2.S	*Pinocchio*. Piano & chant. Paroles de Bernard Michel, musique de Henri Salvador. France...© Editions Musicales Henri Salvador & Walt Disney Productions (France); 25 Nov 75; EF0-180872.
M1995 .S3A55	Schaefer, George Alfred Grant...arr. *Adventures of Pinocchio;* an operetta in three acts based on C. Collodi's Italian story, Pinocchio. Dramatized and adapted by Theodosia Paynter, adapted and arranged from Italian folk melodies by G.A. Grant-Schaefer. Chicago, The Raymond A. Hoffman Co., 1935.
M1731.2.V	*Pinocchio;* (d'apres le conte de Collodi), texte de Romi, pseud. of Robert Miquel, & Franck Terran, musique de Michel Villard...Neuilly sur Seine [France] Vogue International. © Editions Vogue International; 20 Nov 72; EF0-161867.
M1245.Y	Yoder, Paul...*The Adventures of Pinocchio;* [by] Paul Yoder...[Band and parts] © Neil A. Kjos Music Co., Chicago; 8 Mar 54; EP79170.

Entries For *Pinocchio* Under Liegh Harline in the M Composer Catalog of the Music Division, Library of Congress

M1350.H	(*Pinocchio*) When You Wish Upon a Star;... arr. for orchestra by Merle Isaac. [Piano-conductor score and parts]...Appl. states prev. reg. 1/50/40, EP82126. © on arrangement; Bourne, inc., New York; 4 Mar 53; EP69646.

TABLE 1 (continued)

M1420 .H27P5   [*Pinocchio*. When You Wish Upon a Star; arr.] When You Wish Upon a Star; from *Pinocchio*, lyrics by Ned Washington, arr. by C. Paul Herfurth. Score (7p.) and parts. [For band; without words]...NM; arrangement. © Bourne, Inc., New York; 16 Apr 56; EP98789.

---

[41] In the following tables, we have attempted to reproduce the LC entries exactly as they appear in the catalogue, including all peculiarities in orthography and abbreviations. [Ed.]

TABLE 2

Sample Entries Under *Around the World in Eighty Days* in the M Title Catalog of the Music Division, Library of Congress

M1356.2.F   Porter, Cole. [*Around the World in Eighty Days*. Suez dance]. Suez dance: from productions Around the World.--s.l.: s.n., 1977. Lead sheets.

M1572.Y   Around the World; from the film *Around the World in 80 Days*, 2-part chorus, arr. William Stickles, lyrics by Harold Adamson, m Victor Young. Chappell. Score. NM: arr. © Victor Young Publications Inc.; 25 Sep 57; EP112594.

M1553.Y   Around the World;...3-part mixed voices, SAB, arr. William Stickles... Chappell...© Victor Young Publications Inc.; 25 Sep 57; EP112595.

M1564.Y   Around the World;...4-part male voices, TTBB, arr. William Stickles... Chappell...© Victor Young Publications Inc.; 25 Sep 57; EP112596.

M1630.2.Y   Young, Victor. Around the World; lyrics by Harold Adamson. $.50. Appl. states prev. reg. as EU444506. © Victor Young Publications, Inc., Beverly Hills, Calif.; 18 Oct 56; EP102869.

M14.85Y   Around the World...arr. Ashley Miller, for Hammond preset & spinet organs. Chappell...© Victor Young Publications Inc.; 20 Sep 57; EP112443.

M1356.Y   Around the World...dance & vocal background arr. Johnny Warrington. 3 piano-conductor scores & parts. (A Masterscore arrangement) [Versions for orchestra alone or with male vocal or female vocal]...© Victor Young Publications, Inc.; 8 Jul 57; EP121107.

M1258.Y   Around the World...arr. for band by Alfred Reed. Chappell...[The Chappell group band library]...© Victor Young Publications, Inc.; 30 Aug 57; EP112441.

M1268.Y   Around the World; half time show, compilation & arr. Al Davis (Albert 0. Davis) & Al Polhamus. Condensed score & parts...© Hal Leonard Music, Inc.; 24 Jun 57; EP112019.

M1258.Y   Around the World;...arr. for band by Alfred Reed... Chappell. Condensed score & parts. (The Chappell group band library)...© Victor Young Publications, Inc.; 30 Aug. 57; EP111873.

M175.A4Y   Around the World;...accordion solo, arr. Pietro Deiro, Jr. Liza Music Corp...© Victor Young Publications, Inc.; 1 Oct 57; EP121109.

M1552.Y   Around the World...Duet: soprano and baritone...arr. by William Stickles. New York, Chappell [c1957]

M1508   Around the World; w Harold Adamson, m Victor Young, arr. Albert Sirmay. Rev. ed. Chappell. NM: "editorial revision." © Victor Young Publications, Inc.; 15 Aug 57; EP121252. [NOTE: Full title of film does not appear on this card]

M1258.Y   Around the World...arr. by W.J. Duthoit for brass and reed band. London, Chappell, 1957.

M1508   *Around the World in Eighty Days.* [Musical drama] Various publishers, © 1879-80. Various composers. LC has excerpts.

M1503   Leibinger, Gilbert. *Around the World in Eighty Days;* a musical comedy.
.L5415A7   Book and lyrics by Peter Gurney, based upon the book by Jules Verne.
1962   [Chicago] Dramatic Pub. Co. [1962].

M1508   *Around the World in 80 Days.* Fain, Sammy, 1902- Selections for voice and piano not separately cataloged.

ML96   Porter, Cole. [*Around the World in Eighty Days.* Selections] Around the
.B4673   World. [194-?] Orchestrator's Ms.in ink. Scored by Robert Russell
No.14Case   Bennett.

Sample Entries for *Around the World in Eighty Days* Under Victor Young in the M Composer Catalog of the Music Division, Library of Congress

M1356.Y   [*Around the World in 80 Days*] Around the World, arr. for orch by Jimmy Lally. Lyrics by Harold Adamson. London, Chappell, 1957.

M1552.Y   ...Around the World from Michael Todd.s award-winning show *Around the World in Eighty Days.* Duet: Sop & baritone. Words by Harold Adamson, arr. William Stickles. N.Y., Chappell, 1957.

M1362.Y   Around the World...Arr. Pietro Deiro, Jr. Accordion band. N.Y., Chappell, © 1958.

M1527.2.Y   *Around the World in Eighty Days.* Selections... Arr. by Felton Rapley. London, Chappell; Beverly Hills, Calif. V. Young Publications, [c. 1957]

M1200.A.   *Around the World in Eighty Days;* Selections...Arr. for military band by
No. 806   Denis Wright. London, Chappel, c. 1956. [The Army Journal for full military band no. 806.] Includes Derby day by Robert Farnon arr. for military band by W.J. Duthoit.

M1258.Y   Around the World... Arr. by W.J. Duthoit for brass & reed band. London, Chappell, c. 1957.

M1508   Away Out West...Lyrics by Harold Adamson. Beverly Hills, Calif. V. Young Publications, © 1956.

M1527.2.Y   India Countryside...Arr. for piano solo by Felton Rapley. London, Chappell; Beverly Hills, Calif. V. Young Publications, © 1957.

TABLE 3

**Entries Under Paul Simon and *The Graduate* in the
M Composer and Title Catalog of the Music Division, Library of Congress**

M1508   *The Graduate*. Simon, Paul Frederic, 1941- Selections for voice and piano not separately cataloged.

TABLE 4

**Entries Under *Star Wars* in the M Title Catalog of the
Music Division, Library of Congress**

M1630.18   [Songs based on the movie *Star Wars*.] -- [s.l.]: Bonwit House
.S64554   of Music, 1977. [19] p. in various pagings. Melodies with chord symbols.

M1527.2.W   Williams, Johnny...[*Star Wars*. Selections; arr.] *Star Wars;* deluxe souvenir folio of music selections, photos, and stories from the Twentieth Century-Fox motion picture. -- Hialeah, Fla.: Columbia Pictures Publications, 1977. ["Piano solo" or "sketch score"]

**Entries from *Star Wars* Under John Williams in the
M Composer Catalog of the Music Division, Library of Congress**

M13.W   Cantina Band. From 20th Century-Fox Motion Picture *Star Wars*. m John Williams. arr. LeRoy Davidson. ©Fox Fanfare Music, Inc.; 4 Nov 77; EP377425.   Prev. reg. 25 May 77; LP47760; prev. pub. 29 Jul 77. EP371988.

M1527.2.W   Cantina Band...arr. Jerry Mascaro...Fox Fanfare Music, Inc. 21 Sep 77. EP374984.

M129.W   Main title; classical guitar solo...arr. Michael Scott... prev. pub. 6 Jul 77, EP371274.

M13.W   Main title. from... *Star Wars*...arr. Champ Champagne ...prev. pub. 1977. Fox Fanfare Music Inc., 16 Jul 77. EP371986.

M35.W   Main title...arr. Dan Coates...prev. pub. 1977. © Fox Fanfare Music, Inc.; 16 Jul 77; EP371985.

M1380.W   Main title...arr. Dan Coates...prev. 6 Jul 77. EP371274 ...Fox Fanfare Music, Inc. 8 Sep 77. EP374978.

M1527.2.W   Main title...arr. Jerry Mascaro...6 Jul 77. EP371274 ...Fox Fanfare Music Inc.; 1 Oct 77. EP375489.

M13.W   Princess Leia's Theme...arr. Champ Champagne. prev...6 Jul 77. EP371273...Fox Fanfare Music, Inc. 28 Jul 77. EP373820.

M1380.W   Princess Leia's Theme...arr. Dan Coates...6 July 77. EP371273...Fox Fanfare Music, Inc.; 7 Sep 77. EP374979.

TABLE 5

Sample Entries Under Harline, Leigh in the Copyright Catalog

NOTE: Entries that were obviously not from *Pinocchio* were not included [*Pluto's Dream Show* or *Follow the Boys* for example]. Entries dated before 1938 and after 1941 were not included unless specifically from *Pinocchio*. The copyright dates in brackets were supplied from the cards under Disney, Walt, productions as were the "(From *Pinocchio*)" phrases which did not appear on the cross reference cards under Leigh Harline.

EU178257   As I Was Say'n to the Duchess. Disney, Walt, productions, ltd. [1 Oct 38]

EU202202   Figaro and Cleo. Berlin, Irving, inc.

EP86408   July 5, 1940. Give a Little Whistle. (Fox-trot) (In *Pinocchio*) (New matter: orchestra arrangement) Harline, Leigh, music; Mason, Jack, new matter, employee for hire; Washington, Ned, words. Berlin, Irving, inc.

EP82012   Jan. 5, 1940. Give a Little Whistle. (In *Pinocchio*) (Symbols for guitar, chords for ukulele and banjo). Berlin, Irving, inc.

EU170931   Got No Strings. (From *Pinocchio*). Disney, Walt, productions, ltd.; [1 July 38]

EP85283   May 13, 1940. Hi-diddle-dee-dee. (New matter: band arrangement) Harline, Leigh and Washington, Ned, composers; Leidzen, Erik W.G., employee for hire, arranger. Berlin, Irving, inc.

EU190818   Hi-diddle-dee-dee, an actor's life for me (From *Pinocchio*). Disney, Walt, productions; 17 May 39.

EU197240   Honest John (From *Pinocchio*). Disney, Walt, productions; [7 June 39]

EP81672   Dec. 20, 1939. Honest John. (New matter: Arrangement for orchestra) (Kresa). Berlin, Irving, inc.

EU193843   How Lovely You Are. ABC music corp.

EP86409   July 5, 1940. I've Got No Strings. (Fox-trot) (In *Pinocchio*) (New matter: orchestra arrangement). Harline, Leigh, music; Washington, Ned, words; Camarata, Toots, new matter, employee for hire. Berlin, Irving, inc.

EP79463   Jiminy Cricket. Berlin, Irving, inc.

EP81674   Dec. 20, 1939. Jiminy Cricket. (New matter: Arrangement for orchestra) (Kresa). Berlin, Irving, inc.

EU170932   Little Wooden Head. (Gepetto's song in *Pinocchio*) (In folk song style). Disney, Walt, productions, ltd.; [1 July 38H

EP113234   Apr. 20, 1943. Little Wooden Head. (New matter: simplified piano arr.) Harline, Leigh, music; James, Milton, arranger, employee for hire. Berlin, Irving inc.

EU202205   Monstro the Whale. Berlin, Irving, inc.

EP81673   Dec. 20, 1939. Monstro the Whale. (New matter: Arrangement for orchestra) (Kresa). Berlin, Irving, inc.

TABLE 5 (continued)

EU192454   n.d. Music Box. (From *Pinocchio*). Disney, Walt, productions; [31 Mar 39]

EU199641   *Pinocchio*. (To be used in connection with our production of the same name.) Disney, Walt, productions; [23 July 39]

EU199642   *Pinocchio*. (The Guessing Song) Disney, Walt, productions; [23 July 39]

Efor62895   May 9, 1940. *Pinocchio*. (Selection) (New matter: orchestra arrangement) Harline, Leigh, music; Zalva, George L., arranger.

EU201466   *Pinocchio*. (Sequence 2) (Pastoral opening) (Piano-conductor). Disney, Walt, productions; 11 Aug 39.

EU198380   Three Cheers for Anything. (from *Pinocchio*) (2003) Disney, Walt, productions; [16 June 39]

EP82379   Jan. 18, 1940. Three Cheers for Anything. Harline, Leigh, music; Washington, Ned, words. Berlin, Irving, inc.

EP112314   Mar. 13, 1943. Turn on the Old Music Box. (New matter: simplified piano arr.) Harline, Leigh, music; James, Milton, arranger, employee for hire. Berlin, Irving, inc.

EU176054   When You Wish Upon a Star (from *Pinocchio*). Disney, Walt, productions, ltd.; [23 Aug 38]

EP86411   July 5, 1940. When You Wish Upon a Star. (Fox-trot) (In *Pinocchio*) (New matter: orchestra arrangement). Harline, Leigh, music; Kresa, Helmy, new matter, employee for hire; Washington, Ned, words. Berlin, Irving, inc.

EP84969   June 6, 1940. When You Wish Upon a Star. (New matter: band arrangement) Harline, Leigh, and Washington, Ned, composers; Leidzen, Erik W.G., arranger. Berlin, Irving, Inc.

TABLE 6

Entries for *Around the World in Eighty Days* Listed Under Victor Young in the Copyright Catalog

EU492895   Aouda's Rescue; from *Around the World in 80 Days*, m Victor Young, arr. Leo Shuken. © Victor Young Publications, Inc.; 6 September 57.

EP121107   Around the World; from *Around the World in 80 Days*, waltz, lyrics by Harold Adamson, m Victor Young, dance & vocal background arr. Johnny Warrington. 3 piano-conductor scores & parts. (A Masterscore arrangement) [Versions for orchestra alone or with male vocal or female vocal] NM: arr. © Victor Young Publications, Inc.; 8 July 1957.

EP117173   Around the World; from Michael Todd.s award-winning show *Around the World in 80 Days*, lyrics by Harold Adamson, m Victor Young, accordion band, arr. Pietro Deiro, Jr. Chappell. Parts. NM: arr. © Victor Young Publications, Inc.; 7 Mar 58.

EF23575   Around the World; selection, from the production *Around the World in 80 Days,* arr. for military band by Denis Wright, m Victor Young. London, Chappell, Band Music Dept. Condensed score & parts. (In The Army Journal for Full Military Band, no. 806)   NM: arr.   ©Victor Young Publications, Inc.; 9 Oct 57.

EF23319   Around the World; from the production *Around the World in 80 Days,* arr. for orchestra by Jimmy Lally, lyrics by Harold Adamson, m Victor Young. London, Chappell. Piano-conductor score & parts. NM: arrangement. © Victor Young Publications, Inc.; 17 May 57.

EP112595   Around the World; from [the] show *Around the World in 80 Days,* 3-part mixed voices, SAB, arr. William Stickles, lyrics by Harold Adamson, m Victor Young. Chappell. Score. NM: arr. © Victor Young Publications, Inc.; 25 Sep 57.

EP113543   Around the World; from [the] show *Around the World in 80 Days,* duet, soprano & baritone, w. Harold Adamson, m Victor Young, arr. William Stickles. Chappell. Score. NM: arr. ©Victor Young Publications, Inc.; 1 Nov 57.

EP112443   Around the world; from [the] show *Around the World in 80 Days,* lyrics by Harold Adamson, m Victor Young, arr. Ashley Miller, for Hammond preset & spinet organs.   Chappell [Without words] NM: arr. © Victor Young Publications Inc.; 20 Sep 57.

EF23484   Around the World in 80 Days; piano selection, m Victor Young, arr. Felton Rapley. London, Chappell. © Victor Young Publications, Inc.; 3 Sep 57.

EP106705   Away Out West; from *Around the World in 80 Days,* lyrics by Harold Adamson, m Victor Young. Appl. states prev. reg. as EU459040. © Victor Young Publications, Inc.; 11 Mar 57.

EU494947   Entrance of the Bull March; from *Around the World in 80 Days,* m Victor Young. © Victor Young Publications, Inc.; 30 Aug 57.

EU494941   Epilogue; from *Around the World in 80 Days,* m Victor Young. © Victor Young Publications, Inc.; 30 Aug 57.

EU494951   India Countryside; from *Around the world in 80 days,* m Victor Young. © Victor Young Publications, Inc.; 30 Aug 57.

EU494942   Invitation to a Bullfight; from *Around the World in 80 Days,* m Victor Young. © Victor Young Publications, Inc; 30 Aug. 57.

EU494949   Land Ho!; from *Around the World in 80 Days,* m Victor Young. © Victor Young Publications, Inc.; 30 Aug 57.

EU558887   Long Live the English Scene; w. Harold Adamson, m Victor Young, arr. Liza Music Corp. NM: w & new arr. ©Liza Music Corp.; 21 Jan 59[?].

EU494946   The Pagoda of Pillaji; from *Around the World in 80 Days,* m Victor Young. ©Victor Young Publications, Inc.; 30 Aug 57.

70   FOUNDATIONS IN MUSIC BIBLIOGRAPHY

TABLE 6 (continued)

EU494950 Paris Arrival; from *Around the World in 80 Days*, m Victor Young. © Victor Young Publications, Inc.; 30 Aug 57.

EU494945 The Prairie Sailcar; from *Around the World in 80 Days*, m Victor Young. © Victor Young Publications, Inc.; 30 Aug 57.

EU494944 Sky Symphony; from *Around the World in 80 Days*, m Victor Young. © Victor Young Publications, Inc.; 30 Aug 57.

EU494948 The Temple of Dawn; from *Around the World in 80 Days*, m Victor Young. © Victor Young Publications, Inc.; 30 Aug 57.

TABLE 7

Entries Under Paul Simon in the Copyright Office Catalog 1956-70: Songs from *The Graduate*

EU961603 The Big, Bright Green Pleasure Machine. w & m Paul Simon. 2 p. © Paul Simon; 4 Oct 66.

EU890832 April Come She Will. w & m Paul Simon. © Eclectic Music Co.; 1 Jul 65.

EP274171 Mrs. Robinson. w & m Paul Simon, arr. Johnny Warrington (John Warrington). Stage band arr. Charing Cross Music. Condensed Score. 4 p. & parts. Without words. Appl. author: Paul Simon, employer for hire. Appl. states prev. reg. 11 Apr 68, EU53372; prev. pub. 24 May 68, EP246273. NM: arr. ©Paul Simon; 20 Jan 70.

EP246273 Mrs. Robinson. (from the motion picture *The Graduate*) w & m Paul Simon. New York, Charing Cross Music. 6 p. App. states prev. reg. 11 Apr 68, EU53372. © Paul Simon; 24 May 68.

EU53372   Mrs. Robinson, from *The Graduate*. w & m Paul Simon. 3 p. © Paul Simon; 11 Apr 68.

EU961608 Scarborough Fair-Canticle. w & m Paul Simon & Art Garfunkel. 3 p. © Paul Simon; 4 Oct 66.

EP210635 Sound of Silence. w & m Paul Simon (In *The Paul Simon Song Book*. London, Lorna Music Co., p. 18) Appl states prev. reg. 1 Jun 64, EU827993. © Eclectic Music Co.; 24 Sep 65.

EU827993 Sound of Silence. w & m Paul Simon. © Eclectic Music Co.; 1 June 64.

TABLE 8

Sample Entries Under *Star Wars* in the Copyright Catalog 1971-77

NOTE: * indicates that the copyright is for a sound recording.
      ** indicates that the copyright is for sheet music.

** EP377425 Cantina Band. From the Twentieth Century-Fox motion picture *Star Wars*. m John Williams, arr. LeRoy Davidson. 8 p. Appl. au: Fox Fanfare Music, Inc., employer for hire of LeRoy Davidson. Prev. pub. 25 May 1977, LP47760; 29 Jul 77, EP371988. NM: all organ solo arr. © Fox Fanfare Music, Inc.; 4 Nov 77.

* PA62-946 The Desert and the Robot Auction. music composed and conducted by John Williams. From the 20th Century-Fox film *Star Wars*. -- Performed by the London Symphony Orchestra...2T-541...side 1, band 4. © Fox Fanfare Music, Inc. Appl. au.: Fox Fanfare Music, Inc., as employer for hire of...

* PA62-944 Imperial Attack. music composed and conducted by John Williams... London Symphony...20th Century Records 2T-541...side 1, band 2. © Fox Fanfare Music, Inc...

* PA62-957 Inner city. music composed and conducted by John Williams...London Symphony...20th Century Records 2T-541...side 2, band 4. © Fox Fanfare Music, Inc...

SR1-460 Juan Torres. [Juan Torres, organista; acompanamiento Orquesta de Jean Poll]. Musart EDM-1722, p1977. 1 sound disc: 12 in. 33 1/3 rpm, stereo. Title on container: *Discotheque*. © Disco Musart, S.A. Appl. au.: sound recording: Discos Musart, S.A., employer for hire. DCR 1977; PUB 28 Nov 77; REG 31 May 78.

* PA62-949 The Land of the Sandpeople. music composed and conducted by John Williams...London Symphony... 20th Century Records 2T-541...side 3, band l...© Fox Fanfare Music, Inc.

* PA62-947 The Last battle. music composed and conducted by John Williams... London Symphony...20th Century Records 2T-541...side 4, band 1. © Fox Fanfare Music, Inc.

** EP374978 Main title. From the Twentieth Century-Fox motion picture *Star wars*. m John Williams, arr. Dan Coates. 5 p. (Big Note Color Me Series) Appl. au: Fox Fanfare Music, Inc., employer for hire of Dan Coates. Prev. pub. 25 May 77, LP47760; 6 Jul 77, EP371274. © on piano arr.; Fox Fanfare Music, Inc.; 8 Sep 77.

** EP373819 Main title. From the 20th Century-Fox motion picture *Star Wars*. m John Williams, arr. Bob Lowden. 8 p. & parts in folder. Appl. au: Fox Fanfare Music, Inc., employer for hire of Bob Lowden. Prev. pub. 6 Jul 77, EP371274. NM: marching band arr. © Fox Fanfare Music, Inc.; 29 Jul 77.

TX176-899 The Marvel Comics Illustrated Version of *Star Wars*. adapted by Roy Thomas and Howard Chaykin from the screenplay by Geroge Lucas; special introd. by Stan Lee. -- lst ed. -- New York: Ballantine Books, 1977. 124 p. ISBN 0-345-27492-X. © 20th Century-Fox Corporation. Appl. au.: 20th Century-Fox Corporation, employer for hire. NM: introd., pref., compilation. DCR 1977; PUB 28 Oct 77; REG 16 Jan 79.

N47477 More Movie Themes and Other Original Themes Played by the Magnificent 101 Strings Orchestra. Alshire S-5344. Phonodisc (2 s. 12 in. 33 1/3 rpm. stereo) Appl. au: Alshire International. P Alshire International; 1 Oct 77; Contents: Main theme from *Star Wars*.

TABLE 8 (continued)

N46772 Not of This Earth. Peformed by Neil Norman. GNP Crescendo CNPS 2111. Phonodisc (2 s. 12 in. 33 1/3 rpm) Appl. au: GNP-Crescendo Record Company, Inc. Appl. states all new except side 1, band 2 & side 2, band 5. P GNP-Crescendo Record Company, Inc.; 1 Sep 77. Contents: *Star Wars*...

N44840 Patrick Gleeson's *Star Wars;* selections from the film performed on the world's most advanced synthesizer. m composed by John Williams from the 20th Century Fox film *Star Wars,* performed by Patrick Gleeson. Mercury SRM-1-1178. Phonodisc (2 s. 12 in. 33 1/3 rpm. stereo) Appl. au: Phonogram, Inc. P Phonogram, Inc.; 15 Aug 77.

** EP371273 Princess Leia's theme. from the 20th Century-Fox motion picture *Star Wars*. m John Williams, arr. Bert Dovo. 3 p. Appl. au: Fox Fanfare Music, Inc., employer for hire of Bert Dovo. NM: piano solo arr. ©Fox Fanfare Music, Inc.; 6 Jul 77.

* PA62-956 Rescue of the Princess. music composed and conducted by John Williams...London Symphony...20th Century Records 2T-541...side 2, band 3. © Fox Fanfare Music, Inc.

* PA62-951 The Return Home. music composed and conducted by John Williams...London Symphony...20th Century Records 2T-541...side 3, band 3. © Fox Fanfare Music, Inc.

SR3-815 The Sky's the Limit. [performed by] Glenn Derringer. Win Mil Records WINMIL-203, p1977. 1 sound disc: 33 1/3 rpm, stereo; 12 in. Contents: Main title theme from *Star Wars*. 2...© Hal Leonard Publishing Corporation. Appl. au.: sound recording: Hal Leonard Publishing Corporation, employer for hire of Glenn Derringer. DCR 1977; PUB 12 Dec 77; REG 28 Feb 78.

***EU858030 *Star wars;* suite from the motion picture score. m John Williams. 185 p. Prev. reg. 25 May 77. NM: new & adapted music. © Fox Fanfare Music, Inc.; 5 Dec 77.

K128455 *Star Wars*. No. 1133. X-wing fighters & TIE fighter. T-shirt, serigraph on fabric. © 20th Century-Fox Film Corporation; 6 Sep 77.

K126836 *Star Wars*. Man & woman holding pistols. By Tom Jung, author of the print; 20th Century-Fox Film Corporation. Col. reproduction of painting; poster. ©20th Century-Fox a.a.d.o. 20th Century-Fox Film Corporation; 15 Jun 77.

** EP371988 *Star Wars*. m John Williams, arr. Bob Lowden. 63 p. Appl. au: Fox Fanfare Music, Inc., employer for hire of Bob Lowden. NM: arr. & sketch scores. © Fox Fanfare Music, Inc.; 29 Jul 77.

K125725 *Star Wars*. Man with glowing sword & woman holding gun-like weapon, robots behind them, space surrealism background. By Hildebrandt, author of the print: 20th Century-Fox Film Corporation. Col. print; poster. © 20th Century-Fox Film Corporation; 22 May 77.

LP47760	*Star Wars.* Lucasfilm, Ltd. Released by 20th Century-Fox Film Corporation. 121 min., s.d., color, 35 mm, Panavision. © 20th Century-Fox Film Corporation; 25 May 77.
N43555	*Star Wars;* main title theme. Princess Leia; theme. By John Williams, performed by Jon Ellis & The Survival. Atlantic 3409. Phonodisc (2 s. 7 in. 45 rpm. stereo) App. au: Atlantic Recording Corporation. P Atlantic, generally known a.d.o. Atlantic Recording Corporation; 20 Jun 77.
** EP374986	*Star Wars* Medley. From the 20th Century-Fox motion picture *Star Wars.* m John Williams, arr. Bob Lowden. 5 p. 6 parts in folder. Appl. au: Fox Fanfare Music, Inc., employer for hire of Bob Lowden. prev. pub. 25 May 77, LP47760; 6 Jul 77, EP371273 & EP371274. NM: pop stage band arr. © Fox Fanfare Music, Inc.; 23 Aug 77.
VA4-518	Technical readout, master computer banks, death star: droid recognition, file 137529/ drawn by Geoffrey Mandel. Mechanical drawing; 2 p. Plans for robot & squat tripedal automaton. -- Based on the motion picture, *Star Wars.* (In *The Newspaper of Science Fiction and Fantasy,* Special Collector's ed., v. 1, no. 1, p. 18-19) © Geoffrey Manel. NM: artistic interpretation, explanatory notes, technical details and text. DCR 1977; PUB 15 Jun 77; REG 4 May 78.
N44540	Themes from *Star Wars*... Performed by Birchwood Pops Orchestra. Pickwick SPC -3582. Phonodisc (2 s. 12 in. 33 1/3 rpm. stereo) App. au: Pickwick International, Inc. P Pickwick International, Inc. (in notice: Pickwick International, Inc. Pickwick Records Division); 8 Jul 77.

Brandeis University appear to contain only short scores prepared by copyists.[19] Now, what about *The Graduate* and *Star Wars?*

A call to John Williams' assistant at the Boston Symphony Orchestra[20] led me to call the music librarian at Twentieth Century Fox.[21] Surprisingly, both John Williams and Twentieth Century Fox have copies of the score for *Star Wars.* Often, composers do not retain copies of their own scores, and theoretically the producing company for *Star Wars,* Lucas Films, should have had the score. However, for complicated legal reasons a copy had been sent to the releasing company for the film, Twentieth Century Fox.

Next, I telephoned Dave Grusin who said, however, that he no longer had any material pertaining to *The Graduate* and suggested that I contact Larry Shayne in New York.[22] As the agent for Diplomat Music, Shayne had controlled the rights for the underscoring for *The Graduate.* Larry Shayne was not in the Manhattan phone directory. The telephone number in Los Angeles cited in the *Music Industry Guide* was for a real estate firm. Finally, John Shepherd of the New York Public Library found the number for Larry Shayne

Music in Santa Monica, California. They had a list of all the cues and all the business records regarding the financial arrangements and use of each cue, but they did not have the score. Although Larry Shayne controlled the rights to the music, he had left the score with Embassy, which had subsequently changed hands a number of times. Whether all of Embassy's records survived all the transfers is still an open question. Larry Shayne is still trying to locate the score.

To summarize the search for the scores: only three were traceable. One of these, *Around the World in 80 Days,* may be in the Library of Congress in the Copyright Office. However, in order to examine it, one must pay a search fee of $10 an hour to the Copyright Office and must examine it on the premises under constant scrutiny. These are not ideal circumstances if one wants to determine whether the score really is complete. Two of the three, *Pinocchio* and *Around the World in 80 Days,* are in libraries where they can be consulted, although the scores are only piano short scores. *Star Wars* can be examined at the Twentieth Century Fox music library, but only if permission from John Williams has first been obtained. The full score for *Pinocchio* may be consulted in the music library at the Disney Studios.

I am disappointed that I was able to find so many of the scores, because it is often more difficult or impossible. Few of us would know, for example, that the Franklin J. Schaffner Collection at Franklin and Marshall College in Pennsylvania has Jerry Goldsmith's scores to *Patton, Planet of the Apes* and several other films.[23] More astonishingly, MGM has buried all of its scores and parts in a landfill. Alex North's scores for *Death of a Salesman* (1951) and *Member of the Wedding* (1953), both Stanley Kramer/Columbia productions, have been destroyed.[24] At present, film music specialists must often rely on personal information acquired by serendipity in order to locate scores—a most unsatisfactory state of affairs.

Having found the scores, I next wanted to find out about the secondary literature on these works and on their composers. First, I checked in Rita Mead's *Doctoral Dissertations in American Music,*[25] then, in the Adkins/Dickinson *Doctoral Dissertations in Musicology*[26] and James R. Heintze's *American Music Studies: A Clas-*

sified Bibliography of Master's Theses.[27] There were no listings under the names of any of the composers for the four films under discussion here. However, in the time since Heintze's book was compiled, Sharon S. Prado at the University of Cincinnati has written a very fine and extremely useful master's thesis entitled "Leigh Harline's *Pinocchio.*"[28]

I also looked in Steven D. Wescott's *A Comprehensive Bibliography of Music for Film and Television.*[29] Steven Wescott's book is fabulous. If your library does not yet have it, get it. For those of us who have been fumbling along without it, it is a miracle. Film music articles are scattered in a myriad of diverse newspapers and journals. Because Wescott went to all those places and compiled a listing, no one else will have to repeat his work. Wescott lists three articles on Dave Grusin, five articles on Leigh Harline, none for Paul Simon, five for Paul Smith, fifty for John Williams, and thirteen for Victor Young. Although he does not list them, there are several books on Paul Simon and on Simon and Garfunkel[30] which contain information about *The Graduate*. However, there are no books on any of the other composers and, except for the Prado thesis on Harline, no theses either.

Table 9 cites additions to Wescott's book, in which references to Leigh Harline, John Williams and Victor Young appear. I searched through more bibliographies than Wescott did, including, for example, *The Arts and HumanitiesCitation Index,*[31] the *Chicorel Index to Film Literature,*[32] the *International Index to Film Periodicals,*[33] *The Readers Guide to Periodical Literature,*[34] and the W.P.A. *The Film Index: A Bibliography.*[35] I also searched through the LC Music Division's Periodical Index, and with the help of my colleague, Robert Palian, I conducted a computer search on the Dialogue System.[36] My favorite article on the Dialogue System was for *Pinocchio:* "Pinocchio becomes a father; first proboscis monkey born in captivity; with photographs."[37] In spite of having consulted the extra bibliographies I discovered only a few additional citations for our composers, most of which were obituaries and reviews of videotapes and soundtracks. Obviously, I found many articles about other subjects and composers that Wescott missed, actually about twice as many as are given in Table 9. Time did not permit me to

TABLE 9

ADDITIONS TO STEVEN D. WESCOTT A COMPREHENSIVE BIBLIOGRAPHY OF MUSIC FOR FILM AND TELEVISION (Detroit, Information Coordinators, 1985).
Gillian B. Anderson
Library of Congress, 9/15/86.

NOTE: The citations below were found in a number of sources, both original and secondary. [Unverified] means that I tried but was unable to locate the journal in the Library of Congress Collections. The short summaries that follow some citations were taken primarily from Richard Dyer MacCann and Edward S. Perry, The New Film Index. A Bibliography of Magazine Articles in English, 1930-1970 (N.Y., E.P. Dutton & Co., Inc., 1975). Some article titles are listed in brackets in English. These citations came from The Arts and Humanities Citation Index which does not give citations in the original language. I was unable to locate the the original article and thus the original title.

I. HISTORY
SURVEYS

5a. Atkins, Irene Kahn. Interview with Eric M. Berndt. The Development of Optical Sound Reproduction. American Film Institute/Louis B. Mayer Oral History Collection, Part I, No. 1. [New York Times Oral History Program] Glenn Rock, N.J., Microfilming Corp. of America, 1977.
5b. Atkins, Irene Kahn. Interviews with Early Sound Editors. Ibid., Part I, No. 6.
5c. Atkins, Irene Kahn. Interview with James G. Stewart. Developments in Sound Technique. Ibid., Part I, no. 22.
13a. Caps, John. "TV Music: Music Makes All the Difference," IN Luc van de Ven, ed. Motion Picture Music. Mechelen, Belgium, Soundtrack, 1980, p. 64ff.
136. van de Ven, Luc. Motion Picture Music. Mechelen, Belgium: Soundtrack, 1980.
    Twenty Four articles which originally appeared in Soundtrack (SCN). Includes discography and filmography. Articles about Les Baxter, Richard Rodney Bennett, Goldsmith, Herrmann, Kaper, Mancini, Rusticelli, Sarde, Shire and John Williams; The Ghost and Mrs. Muir, Nicholas and Alexandra, Jaws, and Towering Inferno.
    Reviewed in Kosmorama 27, No. 155 (1981), 196-7.
145a. Belluso, Paolo and Flavio Merkel. Rock-Film. Milan, Gammalibri, 1984. [ML128.R684 1984]
155a. Friedman, Norman. "Theory Number Two: Studying Film Impact on American Conduct and Culture," Journal of Popular Film 3 (Spring 1974), 173-81.
173a. Leyda, Jay,ed. The Voices of Film Experience. N.Y., Macmillan, 1977. Interviews with Bernard Herrmann and Miklos Rozsa.
177a. McBride, Joseph, ed. Filmmakers and Filmmaking. (The American Film Institute). Los Angeles, J. P. Tarcher, 1983. Interview with Leonard Rosenman, p. 114-9.
190a. Steen, Mike. Hollywood Speaks! An Oral History N.Y., G.P. Putnam's Sons, 1974. Interviews with Busby Berkeley (p. 296), Bernard Freericks (p. 314), John Green (p. 326).
197a. American Film Institute/ Louis B. Mayer Oral History Collection, Part I and American Film Institute Seminars and Dialogues on Film [New York Times Oral History Program]. Glenn Rock, N.J., Microfilming Corp.

of America, 1977. [Guide: AI3.07 Nos. 1-3] Part I contains transcripts of interviews with Eric M. Berndt, Early Sound and Music Editors, Hugo Friedhofer, Joseph Gershenson, George R. Groves, Bronislaw Kaper, James G. Stewart, and Harry Warren. [Microfilm 49528 micRR] Seminars and Dialogues contains transcripts of interviews with Elmer Bernstein, Jerry Goldsmith, Henry Mancini and Dory Previn. [Microfilm 5185 micRR] NOTE: Each interview is listed separately under Irene Kahn Atkins, the interviewer, or under the name of the composer according to Wescott's format.

211a. Care, Ross. "Mickey Mouse Music," Funnyworld 22 (1981), 47-9.

231a. Denbo, Doris. "He's the Big Noise Behind the Talkies," American Magazine 3 (June 1931), p. 82+. See also Literary Digest 105 (28 Jan 1930), 37. Profile of Count Cutelli, sound effects artist for Disney and others.

234a. English, M. "How Mickey Mouse Inspired Song Hits," Down Beat 20 (Nov. 4, 1953), 5.

235a. Farren, Jonathan. Cine-Rock. Paris, A. Michel, 1979. [PN1995.9.M86F37]

237a. Finch, Christopher. The Art of Walt Disney from Mickey Mouse to the Magic Kingdoms. N.Y., Harry Abrams, Inc., [1973]. Contains numerous references to the composers for Disney's films.

237b. Ford, Charles. L'univers des images animés. Paris: Editions Albin Michel, 1973. The Sherman Brothers on p. 52, 103-5, 175-6, 236.

242a. George, Lee. "Aspects of Industrial Film Music," M.A. Thesis, Wayne State University, 1964. 90 p. illus.

248a. The Illustrated Disney Song Book. New York, Hal Leonard Pub. Corp., 1979. Contains information about Disney composers.

253a. Jones, Isabel Morse. "Film Music. The Composer Emerges. A Man of Importance in New Hollywood Releases," Musical America 67 (Feb. 1947), 19, 362.

253b. Jones, Isabel Morse. "Golden Anniversary. Music a Willing Handmaiden in 50 Years of Film-Making," Musical America 64 (May 1944), 4-5,10.

257a. Krasnoborski, W. F. "T.V. Music: Roots and Offshoots," in van de Ven, Luc. Motion Picture Music. Mechelen, Belgium, Soundtrack, 1980, p. 60ff. [See 136]

262a. McConnell, Frank D. The Spoken Seen: Film and Romantic Imagination. Baltimore, John Hopkins University Press, 1975, p. 19, 21, 104.

262b. Madsen, Roy Paul. The Impact of Film: How Ideas Are Communicated Through Cinema and Television. New York, MacMillan, 1975, p. 571.

263a. Maltin, Leonard. The Disney Films. New York, Crown Publishers, 1973.

263b. Maltin, Leonard. "Unearthing Jazz Heritage You Can See and Hear," Jazz Magazine (Northport, N.Y.) (Fall 1976), 36-41. Filmography.

265a. Mary Poppins. New York, National Publishers, 1964.

287a. Sands, Pierre Norman. "A Historical Study of the Academy of Motion Picture Arts and Science (1927-47). Ph.D., University of Southern California 1966. 267p. UM67-8027. DA XXVIII/1 p180-A. Discusses musicians.

301a. Taylor, John Russell. Hitch: The Life and Times of Alfred Hitchcock. New York, Pantheon, 1978. Covers composers who worked for Hitchcock.

TABLE 9 (continued)

312a. Weis, Elisabeth and John Belton. Film Sound. Theory and Practice. New York, Columbia University Press, 1985.
312b. Weis, Elisabeth. The Silent Scream. Alfred Hitchcock's Sound Track. East Brunswick, N.J., Associated University Presses, Inc., 1982. This book is about all sounds on the soundtracks except the music. It is extremely well done.

SILENT AND EARLY SOUND ERA

315a. "Accuracy in Talkie Equipment," Scientific American 143 (Aug. 1930), 102-3.
322a. Ahern, Maurice L. "Diggin' in the Graveyard," Commonweal 14 (12 Aug. 1931), 358-60. Since 1928 over 130 silents remade into talkies.
322b. Ahern, Maurice L. "Hollywood Horizons," Commonweal 12 (21 May 1930), 71-3. Suggests talkies have revolutionized audience viewing and impact.
322c. Ahern, Maurice L. "An Overseas Headache," Commonweal 13 (11 Mar 1931), 519-21. Surveys European beginnings in competing with American talkies.
322d. Alaleona, Domenico. "A proposito del 'Cavaliere della Rosa'. Melodramma cinematografico e melodramma parlato." Musica J.5, no. 37 (1911), 1.
322e. "All-Talking Pictures Are Lost on Japanese Audiences," Trans-Pacific 18 (3 July 1930), 12.
327a. Anderson, Gillian B. "The Thief of Bagdad and its Music," Institute For Studies In American Music Newsletter, XIV, No. 1 (Nov. 1984), 8-10.
339a. Audisio, Gabriel. "Le language des films," La revue musicale 11, No. 106 (July 1930), 23-32.
342a. Austin, Cecil. "Art and the Peep Show," Chesterian 6, No. 41 (Oct.1, 1924), 1-4.
343a. Austin, Cecil. "The Cinema Organ," The Organ 4, No. 13 (July 1924), 45-51.
348a. Balestreri, Giuliano. "Euterpe o Cenerentola? Musica e cinematografo," Musica d'oggi 16, No. 5 (May 1934), 171-4.
459a. Blum, Carl Robert. "Tonkunst und Tonfilm," Der Auftakt 9, No. 7/8 (1929), 170-2.
460a. Boblitz, K. Sherwood. "Moving Picture Music and How It Impresses the Child," Musical Observer 24 (1916), 319, 353; Metronome 32, No. 8 (1916), 42.
460b. Boehme, C. "Die Begleitmusik im kinematographen Theater," Zeitschriften fuer Instrumentenbau, J. 30 (1910), 491-2.
462a. Bonardi, Pierre. "L'Infirme, la Muse e le Titan," [La film sonore], La revue musicale 15, No. 151 (Dec. 1934), 348-9.
462b. Boone, Andrew R. "Canning Nature's Noises for the Talkies," Popular Science 119 (Nov. 1931), 54-55ff.
462c. Boone, ANdrew R. "Prehistoric Monsters Roar and Hiss for Sound Film," Popular Science 122 (Apr. 1933), 20-21+.
462d. Boone, Andrew R. "Shooting Sound from Arctic to Equator," Travel 64 (Feb. 1935), 32-4.
462e. Boone, Andrew R. "Talkie Troubles," Scientific American 147 (Dec. 1932), 326-9. About conditions under which Trader Horn, Igloo, and Eskimo were filmed by W. S. Van Dyke.
471a. "Britain's Talkies Come To," Living Age 340 (Apr 1931), 207-8. John Maxwell, British producer, sees new prosperity in sound film.

471b. Bronstein, N. "Tonfilm," Anbruch 13, No. 8/10 (Nov./Dec. 1931), 186-9.
479a. C., K.S. "Practical Way to Uplift 'Movie' Music," Musical America 22, No. 18 (1915), 4.
479b. Cadman, Charles Wakefield. "The Musical Enigma of the Soundies," Music World 1, No. 4 (Sept. 1930), 9,20; 1, No. 5 (Oct. 1930), 6,21.
481a. Carls, Carl Dietrich. "Der Opernfilm," Der Auftakt 10, No. 11 (1930), 235-8.
481b. Carter, Gaylord. Interview on music for silents in You Must Remember This, ed. by Walter Wagner. N.Y., G. P. Putnam, 1975, p. 68-70.
490a. Chelsey, John. "Cinema Music," Musical Standard 9 (1917), 151-2.
490b. Chevaillier, Lucien. "L'augure et l'etoile," Le Monde Musicale 42, No. 11 (Nov. 1931), 325-7.
492a. Collins, F. L. "First Year Was the Loudest," Woman's Home Companion 58 (May 1931), 11.
501a. Cousins, E. G. "Talkies Wield a Duster," Bookman 80 (Apr. 1931), 52-3. The coming of sound will revive many forgotten classics.
501b. Crain, Hal. "Leaders of Joint Interests United Under the Motto 'Finer Film-Music'," Musical America 33, No. 14 (Jan. 29, 1921), 1,3-4.
501c. "Credit Should Go to Barrymore for First Sound Motion Picture," Scholastic 49 (23 Sep 46), 16T. John Barrymore's 1926 Don Juan.
505a. Davison, A. E. "Picture Music," Musical News No. 1423 (Dec. 7, 1918), 163.
505b. Delehanty, Thornton. "The Film Cycle from Music to Guns to Music," Literary Digest 116 (8 July 1933), 27. Patterns of talkies.
511a. D'Esterre, Neville. "Music and Talk in the Picture Theatre," British Musician 6, No. 2 (Feb. 1930), 38-41.
512a. Dittmer, Eugen. "'Kino und Oper.' Eine Epistel," Allgemeine Musik Zeitung J. 40 (1913), 480-81.
512b. Donaldson, Leonard. "Bioscope Music. A Plea for the Picture-Pianist," Musical Standard 37 (1912), 148-9.
512c. Donaldson, Leonard. "Bioscope Music," Musical Standard 37 (1912), 166-7, 193-5.
513a. Draper, John. "Sound Tricks in the Talkies," Popular Mechanics Magaine 55 (Feb. 1931), 236-40.
515a. D'Udina, Jean. "La musique et le cinema," Le Ménestrel 4527.85 année, No. 5 (2 Feb. 1923), 49-51; 4528.85 année, No. 6 (9 Feb. 1923), 61-2; 4529.85 année, No. 7 (16 Feb. 1923), 73-4.
518a. Eaton, Quaintance. "Reading Music from Shadows. The 'Sound Track' on a Movie Film is Not Yet an Open Book to Technicians," Musical Digest 14, No. 9 (1929), 15-16.
521a. Davy, Charles. "Is There a Future for Talkies?" Bookman 86 (Aug. 1934), 248. Realistic sound and abstract black and white images do not mix well.
524a. Epstein, Margot. "Gezeichnete Musik. Oskar Fischingers Toenende Ornamente," Allgemeine Musikzeitung 59, No. 47 (Nov. 25, 1932), 591.
540a. "Ethelbert Nevin's A Day in Venice (Un Giorno in Venezia); a New Tone Film Presentation Which Is Commanding National Attention," The Etude 52, No. 6 (June 1934), 337.
545a. Febvre-Longeray, Albert. "En merge du film sonore; de l'adaption musicale," Le courrier musical 31, No. 21 (Dec. 15, 1929), 685-8.

TABLE 9 (continued)

559a. Florian, Felix. "Picture Theater Music," *Musical Standard* 12, No. 283 (July 20, 1918), 28.
562a. Fox, Joseph. "Playing the Picture," *Melody* VI, No. 1 (Jan. 1922), 24-5.
562b. Fox, Julian. "Casualties of Sound. Part One: King Mike," *Films and Filming* 19, No. 1 (Oct. 1972), 34-40; Part Two: 19, No. 2 (Nov. 1972), 33-40. Actors and actresses who had difficulty making the transition to sound films.
564a. Freeland, Matthew. "I Remember," *Sight and Sound* 14, No. 56, (Winter 1945-46), 126-7. Memories of early uses of sound in films.
569b. "Galsworthy on the Talkies," *Living Age* 338 (15 May 1930), 349-50. Playwright gives views on coexistence of silents and talkies.
572a. Gaumont, Leon. "L'industrie du film parlant," *Le courrier musical* 31, No. 21 (Dec. 15, 1929), 691-4.
573a. Gerwig, H. C. "The Photo-Play Organist," *Musician* 21 (1916), 54-5.
573b. Gilbert, Henry F. "My Summer in the Movies," *Musical Courier* 86, No. 3 (Jan. 18, 1923), 6, 46.
573c. Gillett, John. "Laughter," *Sight and Sound* 40, No. 1 (Winter 1970-71), 45. Observations on the change to sound films; *Spite Marriage* (Keaton, 1929) and *Laughter* (D'Abbadie D'Arrast, 1930).
575a. Glinski, Mateusz. "... O filmie dzwiekowym i dzwieku filmowym," *Muzyka* 8, No. 11/12 (Dec. 1931), 484-5.
575b. Goldbeck, Frederik. "La Joie de Vivre," *La revue musicale* 15, No. 151 (Dec. 1934), 419-20. Reference to Tibor Harsanyi and Film Music.
575c. Goldsmith, Alfred N. "The Jack in the Box," *Musical Digest* 15, No. 2 (Feb. 1930), 24, 47. About the phonograph and moving pictures.
576a. "Good Word for the Talkies," *Literary Digest* 108 (21 Mar 1931), 17. Suggests *City Lights* cannot bring back silents.
581a. Grant, J. P. "Popular Opera via 'the Movies,'" *Musical America* 24, No. 9 (1916), 36-7.
582a. Graves, Charles. "Significant Speech," *Cinema Quarterly* 1, No. 2 (Winter 1932), 89-92. Struggles with sound film compared with crude days of theater before Shakespeare.
584a. Greenland, Blanche. "'Faking' in 'Movie' Music Corrupting Public's Taste," *Musical America* 22, No. 22 (1915), 12.
587c. Grierson, John. "The G.P.O. Gets Sound," *Cinema Quarterly* 2, No. 4 (Summer 1934), 215-21. Documentary uses; examples.
598a. Hadley, Henry. "Henry Hadley Talks on Writing Music for the Movies," *Musical Courier* 93 (Dec. 9, 1926).
602a. Halliwell, Leslie. "Merely Stupendous," *Films and Filming* 13, No. 5 (Feb. 1967), 4-12; No. 6 (Mar. 1967), 48-56; No. 7 (Apr. 1967), 33-38; 14, No. 4 (Jan. 1968), 10-15; No. 5 (Feb. 1968), 38-44; No. 6 (Mar. 1968), 42-47; No. 7 (Apr. 1968), 49-53. Seven articles on the decade when films first learned to talk; the last two are on British cinemas of 1930s.
602b. Hallowes, Malcolm. "Organs in Cinema," *The Organ* 1, No. 1 (July 1921), 26-30.
604a. "The Hand of Death on the Screen," *Literary Digest* 105 (5 Apr. 1930), 19-20. French author Bernard Fay says sound is killing art of the film.
604b. Hansford, M. M. "Mortimer Wilson," *American Organist* 15, No. 5 (May 1932), 307-8. Obituary.
604c. Hansford, M. M. "Motion Picture Playing - An Outlook," *The Musician* 24, No. 11 (1919), 8, 10.

609a. Harding, Henry J. "Music and the Pictures," Cadenza 21, No. 8 (1915), 2-4.
610a. Harsanyi, Tibor. "Sur la musique de Dessin animé," La revue musicale 15, No. 151 (Dec. 1934), 412-8.
613a. Henry, Leigh. "The Filming of Music," Musical News and Herald 62, No. 1563 (Mar. 11, 1922), 314, 316.
615a. Herring, Robert. "Twenty-three Talkies," Close Up 6, No. 2 (1930), 134-40. On the Use of Sound.
616b. Hinrichs, Gustav. "A Plea for the Musician Who Creates the Musical Score for Feature Pictures," Musical Courier 86, No. 25 (June 21, 1923), 7.
621a. Howard, Clifford. "The Menace Around the Corner," Close Up 6, No. 1 (1930), 59-66. The effect on Hollywood of sound and other technologies.
626a. Huxley, Aldous and Robert E. Sherwood. "Do You Like the Talkies," Golden Book 11 (April 1930), 51-4. Pro and con, with Huxley for silents.
626b. Huxley, Aldous. "Film Folio 3: Silence Is Golden," Sight and Sound 23 (July-Sep 53), 47-48. A reprint from an article written in 1929 in which Huxley lamented the coming of sound with a scathing review of The Jazz Singer.
632a. "Il film nella didattica pianista," Musica sacra 60, No. 9 (Sept. 25, 1934), 140-43.
632b. Isaacson, Charles. "Specialized Knowledge Is Need of Moving Picture Musicians," Musical America 33, No. 18 (Feb 26, 1921), 37.
647a. Keeley, Joseph C. "Talking Movies and Opera," New Music Review 28, No. 332 (July 1929), 286.
648a. Kegl, Zoltan J. "Crackup of Mighty Glazier Caught for First Time by Sound Camera," Popular Science 123 (Dec. 1933), 24-6.
650a. Kent, George. "New Crisis in the Motion Picture Industry," Current History 33 (Mar 1931), 887-91. Coming of sound destroyed internationalism of movies.
656a. Kirsanoff, Dmitri. "De la synthèse cinématographique," La revue musicale 15, No. 151 (Dec. 1934), 350-51.
656b. Klaren, Georg. "Die Frage der Filmmusik," Der Auftakt J. 3, No. 8 (1923), 194-6.
668a. Koechlin, Charles. "Le problème de la musique de cinéma," Le monde musical 45, No. 10 (Oct. 31, 1934), 269-71.
677a. L., R. "Le film sonore au service de l'émission vocale," La revue musicale 15, NO. 151 (Dec. 1934), 425-6.
677b. Lachenbruch, Jerome. "Jazz and the Motion Picture," Metronome 38, No. 4 (Apr. 1922), 94.
677c. La Forge, Frank. "Will the Radio and Talking Pictures Compel a Revolution in Methods of Teaching Singing," The Etude 48, No. 5 (May 1930), 313-4.
679a. Lanauer, Jean. "In Praise of Simplicity," Close Up 6, No. 2 (1930), 134-40. For sound film.
679b. Landry, Lionel. "Musique et cinema," La revue musicale 8, No. 4 (Feb. 1, 1927), 136-41.
682a. Lange, Francisco Curt. "La mecanización de la música y la supersaturación musical," Boletin de la Universidad Nacional de la Plata 17, No. 3 (1933), 114-29.
685a. Lawler, H. "Opera on the Screen," The Etude 54 (May 1936), 349-50.
696a. Lingisch, Herbert. "Musikalische Probleme des Tonfilms," Allgemeine Musikzeitung 61, No. 41 (Oct. 12, 1934), 560-61.

TABLE 9 (continued)

704a. Lorentz, Alfred. "Der gefilmte Kapellmeister," Neue Zeitschrift fuer Musik J. 8 (1914), 377-8.
704b. Lovewell, S. Harrison. "A New Field of Activity for Organists," Musician 20 (1915), 346-7.
708a. Luciani, S. A. "La musica y el cinematografo," La revista de musica 1, No. 1 (July 1929), 12-18.
708b. Luciani, S. A. "Le visioni della musica e il cinematografo," Harmonia 2, No. 6 (1914), 1-5.
715a. Maitland, Rollo F. "Some Difference between Church and Motion Picture Organ Playing," Musician 22 (1917), 226.
720a. Marshall, Norman. "Music in the Talkies," Bookman 84 (July 1933), 191-2. Cinematic reality is now threatened by the unnatural effects of musical accompaniment.
721a. Martin, Linton. "Operating on the Operas. Will History Repeat Itself When the Lyric Drama Goes Talkie?" Musical America 49, No. 15 (June 25, 1929), 16-17.
736a. Meuer, Adolf. "Staatsoper und Tonfilm; die Gefahren der Filmoper," Signale 88, No. 21 (May 21, 1930), 633-35.
736b. Michaud, Jean. "The Film Drama of the Future," Sackbut 3, No. 6 (Jan. 1923), 183-5.
737a. Mila, Massimo. "Canzoni e musiche de cinematografo," La rassegna musicale 4, No. 4 (July 1931), 205-15.
740a. Miller, Don. "Movie History on TV," Films In Review 11, No. 2 (Feb. 1960), 65-9. Review and discussion of single program in TV's 20th Century series, dealing with coming of sound to movies.
740b. Miller, George. "The Organ in the Theatre," Musician 20 (1915), 414-5.
741a. Milne, A. Forbes. "Good Music and the Kinema," The Music Teacher 14 (1922), 297, 302.
746a. "Mortimer Wilson," Fischer Edition News VIII, No. 1 (Jan.-Feb. 1932), 15. Obituary.
746b. "Mortimer Wilson...[and] Franz Xavier Arens," Musical Courier 104, No. 6 (Feb. 6, 1932), 14. Obituary.
746c. "Mortimer Wilson Dies," Pacific Coast Musician 21, No. 5 (Jan. 30, 1932), 11.
748a. "'Movie' Organs," Musician 21 (1916), 246.
749a. "Multilingual Talkies," Literary Digest 106 (12 July 1930), 15. Marie Dressler doubts foreign talkie appeal.
749b. Murphy, Robert. "The Coming of Sound to the Cinema in Britain," Historical Journal of Film, Radio and Television 4, No. 2 (1984), 143-160.
749c. "Music and the Films," Musical News and Herald 62, No. 1554 (Jan. 7, 1922), 19.
749d. "Music at Cinemas," Musical News 48 (1915), 271-2.
749e. "Musica e cinematografo," Musica d'oggi Anno III, No. 12 (Dec. 1921), 340.
764a. "New Arbiter of Women's Movie Styles," Literary Digest 105 (10 May 1930), 23. Predicts tomorrow's cinema styles will be influenced by demands of microphone.
764b. "New Magic Movies," Popular Mechanics Magazine 55 (Apr. 1931), 539-41.
766a. Newman, Ernest. "A Talk on the Talkies," Musical America 49, No. 16 (July 10, 1929), 5-6.
766b. Newman, Ernest. "These Cinema Organs and Organists," Musical Times 72, No. 1055 (Jan. 1931), 45-6.

766c. Nichols, Robert. "Cinema-To-Be," Spectator 146 (24 Jan 1931), 103-4. Effects on film form with coming of sound; predictions on use of color, stereoscopic projection, and animation.
771a. Obey, Andre. "Musique et cinema," Le monde musical 36, No. 11-12 (June 1925), 213-5.
773a. "Opera via Talkies," Musician 40 (June 1935), 4. Surveys recent interest in movie operas.
773b. "The Organ, the Organist, and the Motion Picture," The Music Trade Review 67, No. 13 (Sep. 28, 1918), 15.
773c. "Organ Music and Movies," Cadenza 21, No. 8 (1915), 8-10.
775a. O'Sullivan, Joseph. "Adaptation of Music to Motion Pictures," Metronome 33, No. 7 (1917), 58.
778a. Ottich, Maria. "Tonfilm und Rundfunk als Objekte der Musikwissenschaft," Die Musik 27, No. 1 (Oct. 1934), 41-3.
783a. "Paramount's Paris Studio," Living Age 339 (Oct. 1930), 206-7. U.S. firm producing talkies in eleven languages.
786a. Pasche, Hans. "Runkfunk und Tonfilm im Musikunterricht," Signale 88, No. 10 (March 5, 1930), 261-2.
799a. Potamkin, Harry Alan. "In the Land Where the Images Mutter," Close Up 6, No. 1 (1930), 11-19. Critical comments on recent sound films.
799b. Potamkin, Harry Alan. "Movie: New York Notes," Close Up 7, No. 4 (Oct. 1930), 235-52. Comments on recent films and film writing.
807a. Preussner, Eberhard. "Situation des Tonfilms." Melos 8, No. 12 (Dec. 1929), 540-3.
808a. Prunières, Henry. "Le cinema au service de la technique pianistique," La revue musicale 15, No. 151 (Dec. 1934), 424-5.
808b. Pudovkin, Vsevolod. "The Global Film," Hollywood Quarterly 2, No. 4 (July 1947), 327-32. Wonders if film can still be international after the advent of sound.
808c. Quarry, Edmund. "Midwife to the Talkies," Sight and Sound 18 (Summer 1949), 94. About a sound film made in England as early as 1924-25.
808d. R., B. "Film sonoro e cataloghi musicali," Bolletino bibliografico musicale 5, No. 5 (May 1930), 21-31.
810a. Romain, Paul. "Capacité auditive du spectateur au cinéma," Le courrier musical 31, No. 21 (Dec. 15, 1929), 684-5.
814a. Rathaus, Karol. "Problemy Muzczne w Filmie Dziekowym," Muzyka 8, No. 10 (Oct. 1931), 408-10.
825a. Romberg, Sigmund. "Screen Operetta," Pacific Coast Musician 19, No. 18 (May 3, 1930), 16.
828a. Rowe, E. B. "A Letter,"[Article on Talking Movies] Musical Courier 101, No. 10 (Sep. 6, 1930), 22.
833a. Sacerdote, Eduardo. "Music and the Films," Pacific Coast Musician 25, No. 11 (June 6, 1936), 3-4.
835a. Schaff, Edward. "Jazz and the Picture House," Musical Advance 16, No. 10 (May 1929), 3.
837a. Scherber, Ferdinand. "Tonfilm und Theater," Signale 88, No. 41 (Oct. 8, 1930), 1133-1136.
837b. Scherber, Ferdinand. "Der Tonfilmschlager," Signale 92, No. 45 (Nov. 7, 1934), 636-7.
838c. Schertzinger, Victor. "The Composer of 'Marcheta' Talks About the Talking Pictures," Music Trade News 8, No. 4 (Sept. 1929), 15-16.
869a. Schmidt, Leopold. "Lichtbild und Laut - Lautapparat im

TABLE 9 (continued)

Musiklehrsaal," *Signale* J. 72 (1814), 298-300.
871a. "A Scholar Examines Sound Films," *Musical Leader* 57, No. 4 (May 25, 1929), 5.
872. Schuenemann, Georg.
872a. Schuenemann, Georg. "Tonfilm und Rundfunk im Musikunterricht," *Rheinische-Musik-und Theater-Zeitung* 30, No. 39/40 (Nov. 16, 1929), 421-23.
873a. Scott, Cyril. "The Cinema and Programme Music," *Monthly Musical Record*, 63, No. 752 (Dec. 1933), 225.
883a. Sherwood, R. E. "Renaissance in Hollywood," *World Today* 56 (Nov. 1930), 564-70.
885a. Simons, Rainer. "Theater, Tonfilm und Radio," *Signale* 89, No. 13 (March 25, 1931), 327-9.
885b. Singer, Kurt. "Opernfilm," *Anbruch* 12, No. 6 (June 1930), 212-14.
991a. Skinner, Richard Dana. "A Letter to Walter Damrosch," *North American Review* 240, (Sept. 1935), 278-83. Bring Wagner operas to screen.
994a. Spies, A. "Der Tonfilm," *Deutsche Musikzeitung* 32, No. 10 (May 23, 1931), 145.
994b. Spinola, Helen. "That Terrible Talkie Test," *Delineator* 118 (May 1931), 17 +. Humorous article on Hollywood activities.
1008a. Strobel, Heinrich. "Tonfilm und Lehrstueck," *Melos* 8, No. 7 (July 1929), 315-7. Review of the Deutsches Kammermusikfest, Baden-Baden, 1929.
1015a. "The Talkies' Future," *Nation* 130 (15 Jan 1930), 61-2. Suggests movies could go beyond technique.
1015b. "Talkies Preferred," *Living Age* 340 (Aug. 1931), 606-7. Columbia students and Spanish correspondent prefer talkies to theatre and opera.
1015c. "Talking Motion Pictures," *Science* 71 (17 Jan 30) Supp. 10+.
1016a. Tavano, C. F. "Cinema sonore - cinéma parlant," *Le courrier musical* 31, No. 21 (Dec. 15, 1929), 694-5.
1019a. Tessner, Hans. "Kinomusik," *Neue Musik Zeitung* J. 37 (1915/16), 56-7.
1027a. Tibbett, L. "Opera can be saved by the Movies," *Pictorial Review* 34 (Feb. 1933), 8-9+.
1027b. Tibbett, Lawrence. "A Talk on the Talkies," *The Etude* 49, No. 8 (Aug. 1931), 539-40. As told to R. H. Wollstein.
1027c. "Der Tonfilm und die Musiker," *Oesterreichische Musiker-Zeitung* 37, No. 12 (June 16, 1929), 65-6.
1030a. Tootell, George. "Cinema Music and its Future," *The Chesterian* New Series, 38 (April 1924), 179-85.
1030b. Torchet, Julian. "Spectacles fictifs et musiques re'elles," *Le guide musical* 54 (1908), 769-70.
1031a. Troy, William. "Retrospect: 1933," *Nation* 138 (3 Jan 1934), 27-28. Talkie reflects evasion, abandonment, and confusion of period.
1031b. Trumbo, Dalton. "Frankenstein in Hollywood," *Forum* 87 (Mar 1932), 142-6. Struggle between those who believe in talkies and those who wait for return of silents.
1036a. "Union Musicians Fight Sound Pictures in Advertising Campaign," *Music Trade News* 8, No. 6 (Nov. 1929), 13-14.
1037a. "Urban and Kinemacolor," *Cadenza* 21, No. 7 (1915), 14,15,33.
1037b. Ursel, Comte d'. "A Propos D'Images Sonores," *La Revue Musicale* 15, NO. 151 (Dec. 1934), 361-4.

1039a. "Using Moving Pictures as Aid to Concert Business," Musical America 22, No. 14 (1915), 11.
1044a. Vidor, King. "The End of an Era," Films and Filming 1, No. 6 (Mar. 1955), 8-9. The friendship between William Randolph Hearst and Marion Davies; the coming of sound. Reprinted from A Tree Is A Tree (Harcourt, 1953).
1045a. Vildrac, Charles. "En guise d'introduction," La revue musicale 15, No. 151 (Dec. 1934), 321-3.
1048a. Vuillermoz, Émile. "La musique et la cinégraphie," Le ménestrel Anne 82, No. 3 (Jan. 16, 1920), 17-18.
1048b. Wachten, Edmund. "Auf Krise der Europaischen Musikkultur," Allgemeine Musikzeitung 61, No. 14 (April 6, 1934), 185-8. [See 771a]
1048c. Wagner, Rob. "Lend Me Your Ears," Collier's 85 (11 Jan 1930) 10-11+; 86 (13 Dec 1930), 16-18. Review of progress made in talkies.
1049a. Wallfisch, J. H. "Parsifal im Kino," Neue Zeitschrift fuer Musik J. 79 (1912), 734.
1056a. Waters, Thorold. "Music's winning chance in the 'Talkies.' Cine-opera the most natural development," Australian Musical News 18, No. 11 (June 1, 1929), 3-4.
1059a. Weiss, E. H. "Le phonograph au cinéma," Le courrier musical 31, No. 21 (Dec. 15, 1929), 689-91.
1059b. Weiss, Trude. "The First Opera-Film," Close Up 9, No. 4 (Dec. 1932), 242-5.On The Bartered Bride, by Max Ophuls from Smetena.
1062a. Welsh, W. H. "Orchestras in Cinemas," Musical News 51 (1916), 313-4.
1063a. Whipple, Leon. "Gone Talkie," Survey 64 (1 July 1930), 321-22. Assesses power of sound film emotionally and intellectually.
1063b. White, Alvin C. "After Two Years of the Talkies in America," The Strad 40, No. 471 (July 1929), 129-31.
1063c. White, E. B. "Mood Men: Playing for Silent Pictures," Readers Digest 33 (July 1938), .

SEE ALSO:
312a (Weis), 2512b (Osborne).

SOUND TECHNIQUES AND TECHNOLOGY

1143a. Collins, Chester. "First Movie Soundtracks: The Edison Kinetophone Cylinders (Mark 56 Records: No. 856)," The Antique Phonograph Monthly 7, No. 10 (19??), 10.
1146a. Fabrizio, T. C. "Before the Jazz Singer," Antique Phonograph Monthly 5, No. 5 (19??), 3-6.
1162a. Lightman, Herb A. "The Film Finds Its Voice," American Cinematographer 50, No. 1 (Jan., 1969), 84-7.
1162b. "Making of a Sound Fable," Popular Mechanics Magazine 54 (Summer, 1930), 353-55. How animated films are made.
1171a. Yates, Raymond Francis. "A Technician Talks About the Talkies," Scientific American 143 (Nov. 1930), 384-5. Points out some failings of talkies and ways to overcome these.

1935-1949

1185a. Arvey, Verna. "Music of Worth to the Movies," The Etude 57, No. 7 (July 39), 434.

TABLE 9 (continued)

1191a. "Behind the Golden Curtain," *Harper's* 196 (Jan. 48), 96. The Metropolitan opera goes to the multitudes via cinema.
1210a. Breger, Renee. "Opera at the Cinema," *Musical Mercury* 6 (Oct. 1938), 23-30.
1210b. "Bringing the Symphony Orchestra to Moving Picture Patrons," *The Etude* 55, No. 11 (Nov. 1937), 710.
1243a. Clifford, Hubert. "British Film Music Comes of Age," *Musical America* 66 (Jan. 10, 1946), 29, 34.
1247a. Crichton, Kyle, (ed.), "Gamble with Music," *Collier's* 117 (23 Mar 1946), 22-23. Problems in filming a music versus stage musical production.
1248a. Currie, John B. "Of Human Bondage, The Killers, Notorious," *Film Music Notes* 6, No. 1 (Sep.-Oct. 1946), 16-20. Reviews of scores by Korngold, Rozsa and Roy Webb.
1251a. Davenport, M. "Machine-Made Prima Donnas," *Readers Digest* 28 (May 1936), 91. Only best operas and performances recorded. Excerpt from *Stage*.
1288a. Gronostay, Walter. "Beethoven im Film," *Deutsche Musikkulture* 2, No. 2 (June/July 1937), 119-21.
1304a. "Hen Tracks on Sound Tracks," *Popular Mechanics Magazine* 91 (Apr. 1949), 168-9.
1315b. Huntley, John. "Film Music," *Penguin Film Review* 2 (Jan. 1947), 21-25. Methods of studying film music.
1322a. Huntley, John. "The Magic Bow", *Film Music Notes* 6, No. 1 (Sep.-Oct. 1946), 16. Review.
1344a. Janssen, Werner. "Score Conceived before Filming of Picture," *Music and Musicians* 22, No. 8 (Sep. 1936), 6.
1352a. Keefer, Lubov. "Soviet Film Music Plays Leading Role," *Musical America* 63 (Sept. 1943), 6-8,34.
1354a. Keller, Hans. "Film Music - Some Objections," *Sight and Sound* 15, No. 60 (Winter 1946-7), 136. SEE 1766.
1359a. Keller, Hans. "Revolution or Retrogression?" *Sight and Sound* 16, No. 62 (Summer 1947), 63-4. Critical reactions to the film version of the opera, *The Barber of Seville*.
1374a. Laine, Juliette. "Operetta and the Sound Film," *The Etude* 56 (June 1938), 359-60. Advice to aspiring movie singer actresses by Jeannette MacDonald.
1400a. Martin, Donald "Fine Scores for New Musical Pictures," *The Etude* 58, No. 2 (Feb. 1940), 85, 88.
1400b. Martini, Nino. "And Now the Movies," *The Etude* 54 (June 1936), 349-50. Opera films.
1443a. "Movie mirrors Music-Mindedness," *Musician* 43 (Apr. 1938), 75.
1464a. Paul, E. "Musical and Low," *Atlantic* 176 (July 1945), 109+. Humorous attack on movie musicals.
1481a. Robins, S. "Disney Again Tries Trailblazing: *Fantasia*," *New York Times Magazine* (3 Nov. 1940), 6-7+.
1495a. Saunders, Richard Drake. "Fitting the Music to the Film," *Musical Courier* 121 (Jan. 1, 1940), 5,25.
1496a. Saunders, Richard Drake. "'Rhythm Sheet' Aids in Hollywood Film," *Musical Courier* 121 (March, 1940), 7.
1505a. Smith, Paul J. "The Music of the Walt Disney Cartoons," *The Etude* 58 (July 1940), 438, 494.
1511a. Sternfeld, Frederick W. "Music and the Feature Films," *Musical Quarterly* 33 (Oct. 1947), 517-32.
1523a. Tindall, Glenn M. "Music and the Movies," *School and Society* 48 (3 Dec. 1938), 721-4. Tribute to the musical film.
1526a. Trautwein, Friedrich. "Der Schallfilm, das Schallaufzeichnungs

Geraet der Zukunft," <u>Deutsche Musikkultur</u> 2, No. 3 (Aug./Sept. 1937), 170-4.
1530a. "The Use of Standard Musical Compositions in Motion Pictures," <u>Music Educators Journal</u> 25, No. 2 (Oct. 1938), 56.

<u>SEE ALSO</u>:
253 a & b (Jones)

SOUND TECHNIQUES AND TECHNOLOGY 1935-1949

1561a. Coldby, J. "Electronic Techniques of Making Talking Pictures," <u>Radio News</u> 25 (Jan. 1941), 8-10+
1573a. "Manufacturing Quiet for the Movies," <u>Popular Science</u> 139 (Dec. 1941), 98.
1579a. "Sounder Sounds: RCA Demonstrates Ultraviolet Ray Recording for Movies," <u>Business Week</u> (29 Feb. 1936), 27.
1579b. "Sound Tricks of the Movies," <u>Popular Mechanics Magazine</u> (Sep. 1944), 56-61.
1580a. "Voomp, Clank, Bonk: Name Your Noise and the Movies' Sound Makers Will Give It to You," <u>Popular Science</u> 138 (Mar. 1941), 106-9.

1950's

1596a. Bauer, Leda. "Twice-Told Tales," <u>Theater Arts</u> 35 (June 1951), 39-41+ Opera into film - limitations and failures; emphasis on <u>Tales of Hoffman</u>.
1687a. Graham, Ronnie. "Stale, Flat and Profitable," <u>Films in Review</u> 2 (Feb. 1951), 25-27+. Informal Survey of Hollywood Musicals.
1722. ADD: Vol. 19 (Dec. 1950), 336; 19 (Feb. 1951), 416.
1786. ADD:
Stallings showed films made by the Calvin Co.; Phelps described his work for an Ohio State promotional film; Gould played some of his title music and commented on practical problems of working with musicians.
1813a. "MGM Musicals," <u>Life</u> (14 Apr. 1952), 116-8. Fred Astaire, Gene Kelly and the Champions.
1817. ADD:
<u>Broken Arrow</u>, <u>Carrie</u>.

SOUND TECHNIQUES AND TECHNOLOGY 1950's

1939a. Ryder, Loren L. "A New Method of Handling Sound for Foreign Releases," <u>American Cinematographer</u> 33, No. 4 (April 1952), 158+.

1960's

1980a. Assayas, Olivier. "[SPFX News or Science Fiction Films as Reference Points]," <u>Cahiers du cinéma</u> (1980), 34-40. Sound effects and music.
2057a. Garel, Alain. "La musique de film," <u>La revue de cinema</u> (Nov. 1982), 133-6.
2057b. Garel, Alain. "La musique de 'Country and Western Music,'" <u>La revue du cinema</u> 368 (Jan. 1982), 131-3; 369 (Feb. 1982), 135-8.
2062a. Gross, M. "Anyway They Spell It, Shermans Make Music Universal

TABLE 9 (continued)

Language," Billboard 79 (Nov. 11, 1967), 22.
2071b. Hicks, Jimmie. "Fantasia's Silver Anniversary," Films in Review 16, No. 9 (Nov. 1968), 529-35.

SOUND TECHNIQUES AND TECHNOLOGY 1960's

2204a. Ebel, Fred E. "That Old Regenerative Set of Mine," Popular Electronics 28 (Jan. 1968), 50-51. About film sound effects.
2204b. Kingery, R. A. "The Man Who Taught the Movies How to Speak," Saturday Review 51 (6 Apr. 1968) 56-8. About Joseph Tykocinski-Tykociner, researcher in sound engineering.

1970's

2261a. Britt, Stan. "EMI Sound Tracks," Cassettes and Cartridges (July 1975), 138-40. Discography. [Unverified]
2273a. Byrd, Katherine and Allan Byrd. "The Quest for Organic Sound," Stereo (Summer, 1974), 54-7. [Unverified]
2273b. Calum, P. "Musikken," Kosmorama 23, No. 136 (1977), 253. Music in New York, New York.
2274a. Care, Ross. "Lisztomam," Film Quarterly 31, No. 3 (1978), 55-61. [Unverified]
2276a. Champlin, Charles. "Don't Shoot the Piano Player," The Ragtimer (Mar/Apr, 1974), 15-16.
2328a. Cook, Page. "The Sound Track," Films in Review 28 (Jan. 1977), 44-6+.
2346a. Criscione, G. "[Estate-Romana-1979. A Roman Festival of Films, Plays, Dances and Music]," Studi Romani 27, No. 4 (1979), 570-72.
2351a. Daney, Serge. "[Deemphasis of Sound in Film (5 Films at Nantes)]," Cahiers du cinéma 275 (1977), 63-4.
2367a. Ehrlich, Cindy. "Nagel on 'Exorcist': Doin' the Devil's Sound Effects," Rolling Stone (Feb. 28, 1974), 16
2428a. Hiemenz, Jack. "Play It Again Sam. And Again, And Again...," Zoo World (Mar. 28, 1974), 18-19. [Unverified]
2435a. Jacobson, Robert and Irving Kolodin. "Weber and Wagner at the Lincoln Center Opera Festival," Saturday Review 53 (Aug. 1970), 35. Hamburg Opera's contribution to "Opera on Film" festival.
2440a. Jones, Robert T. "Movie Time at the Opera," Time 96 (27 July 70), 56. Report on festival of operatic films.
2486a. Marcus, Leonard. "Videotape and 'Dueling Banjos,'" High Fidelity and Musical America 23, No. 6 (June 1973), 4.
2493a. Mérigeau, J. L. C. and Pascal Merigeau. "Tabous, violence et mort: le grand rendez-vous," Revue de cinema 371 (1982), 96-106. Taboos, violence and death main themes in rock films.
2504. ADD:
Arnold Schoenberg's Musical Accompaniment to Imaginary Film.
2512a. "Opera on Film," Opera News 35 (5 Sep 70), 21. Weber's Der Freischuetz.
2512b. Osborne, Conrad L. "Song O' My Heart," High Fidelity and Musical America 23, No. 2 (Feb. 1973), 67-8.
2517a. Patterson, Richard. "Motion Picture Sound: A Long Way from the 'Ice Box,'" American Cinematographer 52, No. 4 (April 1971), 320-3.
2537a. "Rolf Lieberman," New Yorker 46 (29 Aug 1970), 21-22. Interview. His work on operatic films.
2541a. Schepele, Peter. "Ingmar Bergman og Musikken," Kosmorama 24,

No. 137 (1978), 44-6. Music in Bergman's films.
2546a. "The Score: the Writers in Profile," BMI, the Many Worlds of Music 1 (1974), 31-2.
2557a. Smith, Chris. "Bluesing the Screen," Blues-Link 4 Incorporating 'Blues World' (1974), 13-14. Film acknowledgements. [Unverified]
2557b. Smith, Richard Langham. "Debussy and the Art of the Cinema," Music and Letters 54 (Jan. 1973), 61-70.
2601a. Watts, Michael. "Dylan: The Film's a Loser," Melody Maker (June 2, 1973), 32-3.
2601b. Watts, Michael. "The Man Called 'Alias'," Melody Maker (Feb. 3, 1973, 28-30.
2601c. Watts, Michael. "Michael Oldfield and Allan Jones. The Young Ones," Melody Maker (Aug. 31, 1974), 27-31.
2604a. Wick, Ted. "Creating the Movie-Music Album," High Fidelity and Musical America 26, No. 4 (Apr. 1976), 68-71.

SOUND TECHNIQUES AND TECHNOLOGY
1970's

2629a. Bigbee, Lynn. "Basic Elements of Sound Recording," Filmmakers Newsletter 3, No. 12 (Oct. 1970), 36-42. Reprinted from "MPL Table Talk' No. 3, a publication of Motion Picture Laboratories, Inc.
2633a. Fodor, J. "[Film Dubbing, Phonetic, Semiotic, Esthetic and Psychological Effects]," Filmkritik 21, No. 3 (1977), 170.
2646a. Oldfield, Michael. "Fun! Fun! Fun!" Melody Maker (April 20, 1974), 28.
2649a. Purchese, John. "Recording Sound for 'Song of Norway'," American Cinematographer 52, No. 4 (April 1971), 324-7+.

1980's

2707a. Abdrashitov, A. "Music and Cinema," Soviet Film 1 (1983), 15. Konstantin Lopushansky.
2715a. Anderson, Lindsay. "This Sporting Life." Tempo: A Quarterly Review of Modern Music 139 (Dec. 1981), 33-4. Analysis of Roberto Gerhard's composition of musical score for film.
2746a. Chion, Michel, "Entretien avec Jean Neny. Le regard du mixeur," Cahiers du cinema 340 (Oct. 1982), X-XI. The view of the films sound mixer.
2746b. Chion, Michel. "Entretien avec Marie-Josèphe Yoyotte. Le sens de l'ellipse," Cahiers du cinéma 341 (Nov. 1982), X, XII. Sound mixing in films direct or not direct.
2746c. Chion, Michel. "Filmer la musique. Où ça se passe?" Cahiers du cinéma 332 (Feb. 1982), XI. Filming a musical performance (Glenn Gould).
2746d. Chion, Michel. "Lumière avec son," Cahiers du cinéma 338 (July-Aug. 1982), XI. Film sound editing.
2746e. Chion, Michel. "Les Maillons les Plus Faibles," Cahiers du cinema 333 (Mar. 1982), XII. Film soundtracks (The technicians).
2746f. Chion, Michel. "[Silence as a metaphor in sound films]," Cahiers du cinéma 330 (1981), 5-15.
2746g. Chion, Michel. "[The current status of sound-mixing technology - neglect and fetishism]," Cahiers du cinema 330 (1981), IX-X.
2783a. Davies, H. "Electronic Music (Gerhard, Roberto Adaptation of Music

TABLE 9 (continued)

Techniques for Theater, Radio and Film)," Tempo 139 (Dec. 1981), 35-8.

2899a. Garel, Alain. "Musique de films," La revue de cinema 378 (1982), 123-5. Film scores and original soundtracks.

2820a. Ivanava, S. "Music Silhouettes in the Cinema," Obzor - A Bulgarian Quarterly Review of Literature and Arts 58 (1982), 90-3.

2826a. Kennedy, Evelyn. "Film Music Editor," Music Educators Journal 69, No. 2 (Oct. 1982), 54. Career opportunities.

2840a. Levine, Steven A. "Structures of Sound Image in The Rules of the Game (Renoir)," Quarterly Review of Film Studies 7, No. 3 (1982), 210.

2845a. McCarthy, Todd. "Schmidt's Score Doesn't Score in L. A. Reconstruct of Dreyer's 'Arc'," Variety (June 1, 1983), 4, 76.

2847a. "The Men Who Made Music," Variety 303 (July 1, 1981), 54.

2864a. Perle, George. "Das Film-Zwischenspiel in Bergs Lulu," Oesterreichische Musik Zeitschrift 36, No. 12 (Dec. 1981), 631-8.

2895a. "La Traviata de Franco Zeffirelli," Cahiers du cinéma 346 (May 1982), 66.

2896. ADD: On the music of John Williams for E.T. and of Jerry Goldsmith for Poltergeist and other films.

2899a. Verniere, James D. "Franco Zeffirelli Discusses 'La Traviata' and Opera on Film," Ovation (July, 1983), 8-11.

2901a. "Voix in-ouies?" Cahiers du cinema 343 (Jan. 1983), XIII. Unheard voices. Computerized voices in films.

II. COMPOSERS

George Antheil

2983a. Sternfeld, Frederick W. "Specter of the Rose, An Analysis with Musical Excerpts," Film Music Notes 6, No. 1 (Sep.-Oct. 1946), 7-14.

John Barry

3021a. "Aboard the Bandwagon," Time 87 (14 Jan 66), 62+.

Elmer Bernstein

3052a. Bernstein, Elmer. "The DeMille Legend," Chapter IV in Gabe Essoe and Raymond Lee. DeMille: The Man and His Pictures. N.Y., A.S. Barnes, 1970, p. 277-82. Reprinted from The Los Angeles Times, 1966.

3052b. Bernstein, Elmer. Elmer Bernstein: An American Film Institute Seminar on his Work. Glen Rock, N.J.: Microfilming Corp. of America, 1977. [No. 16 in the series entitled The American Film Institute Serminars and Dialogues.] [SEE 197a (Seminars 16)]

3060b. Brown, Royal. "'To Kill a Mockingbird': Original Film Score," High Fidelity and Musical America 27 (Apr 1977), 119.

3075a. Salmi, Markku. "Elmer Bernstein," Film Dope 3 (Aug. 1973), 37-8.

SEE ALSO:
2328a (Cook)

Joseph Carl Breil

3100a. Allen, Clyde. Notes for recording, The Birth of a Nation Label X, LXDR-701-2, 1986.
3102a. "Joseph Carl Breil Passes Away," Musical America 43, No. 15 (Jan. 30, 1926), 39.

SEE ALSO:
720 (Marks)

Charlie Chaplin

3127f. "Charlie Chaplin and Talkies," Review of Reviews 86 (Aug. 1932), 49-50. Reprint of La revue mondiale article by Rene Fonjallaz suggesting superiority of silents over talkies.
3127g. "Charlie Chaplin and Talking Pictures," Theater Arts 14 (Nov. 1930), 908. Speculates on whether City Lights will use sound.
3134a. Mass, Robert F. Charlie Chaplin. N.Y., Pyramid, 1975.
3138b. Schepelern, P. "Chaplin 4: Som Komponist," Kosmorama 19 (Aug. 1973), 261-2.

SEE ALSO: 576a(Good word)

Aaron Copland

3144a. "[Aaron Copland concerning his score for North Star]," Film Music Notes 3, No. 3 (Dec. 1943), 10-11.
3144b. Badder, D. J. "Aaron Copland," Film Dope 8 (Oct. 1975), 7-9.
3146a. Cochran, Alfred W. "Style, Structure and Tonal Organization in the Early Film Music of Aaron Copland," Ph.D., Catholic University of America, 1986.
3156a. London, Kurt. "Film Music of the Quarter," Films 1, No. 1 (Nov. 1939), 76-80.
3157a. Morton, Lawrence. "The Red Pony," Hollywood Quarterly 3, No. 4 (1948-49), 395-402.
3161a. Rolandadams, G. "Copland Appalachian Spring (original version), Music for Movies ARGO 2RG-935," Strad 93 (1982), 43.
3163. CORRECT: Musical Quarterly 37, No. 2 [Not 7, No. 2].

SEE ALSO:
3743a (Raksin), 4035a(Thomson)

Adolph Deutsch

3188a. Deutsch, Adolph. "The Composer: Forgotten Man of the Movies," Musical America 66 (June, 1946), 5, 38.

Brian Easdale

3203. ADD: Another Edition. The Red Shoes Ballet; The Tales of Hoffmann. N.Y., Garland Pub., 1977.

Hugo Friedhofer

3269. Atkins, Irene Kahn. ADD: Microfilm version 197a (Part I, #7)
3270a. "Biography of Hugo Friedhofer, Excerpts from The Bandit of Sherwood," Film Music Notes 5, No. 9 (May 1946), 36-40.
3279. "Hugo Friedhofer." ADD: New York Times 130, p. 21 (N), A26(LC)

TABLE 9 (continued)

May 20, 1981; Skoop 17 (July 1981), p. 5; Obituaries.
3279a. Koldys, Mark. "Friedhofer: The Young Lions," American Record Guide 46 (May 1983), 76.
3286a. "Theater and Film: 'Best Years of Our Lives': Original Film Score By Hugo Friedhofer," High Fidelity and Musical America 29 (Nov. 1979), 29.

SEE ALSO: 82(Huntley/Manvell), 104(Prendergast), 197a (Part I, #7).

Jerry Goldsmith

3298a. Alien (Soundtrack reviews) American Record Guide 42 (Sept. 1979), 54; Audio 63 (Nov. 1979), 134; Christian Science Monitor 71 (June 18, 1979), 18; Consumer Reports 45 (Feb. 1980), 131; High Fidelity 29 (Oct. 1979), 124; Pro Musica Sana 8, No. 1 (Winter 1979-80), 9; Stereo Review 43 (Aug. 1979), 106.
3298b. Anobile, Richard. Alien. N.Y., Avon, 1979.
3300a. Bryce, Allan. "Jerry Goldsmith on 'Star Sound'," SCN Soundtrack Collector's Newsletter 4, No. 18 (July 1979), 23.
3300b. Caps, John. "The Ascent of Jerry Goldsmith," SCN Soundtrack Collectors Newsletter 5, No. 19 (Oct. 1979), 3-8; No. 20 (Jan. 1980), 3-8.
3306a. Cook, Page. "The Sound Track," Films in Review 27 (Oct. 1976), 495-9.
3312a. Feather, Leonard. "From Pen to Screen - Jerry Goldsmith," International Musician 69, No. 6 (Dec. 1970), 4.
3316-18. ADD: SEE 197a (Seminars #66).
3320a. Harrington, Richard. "Goldsmith Goes for It," Washington Post 106 (Apr. 12, 1983), D7.
3323a. Quigley, Michael. "Alien," SCN Soundtrack Collector's Newsletter 5, No. 19 (Oct. 1979), 20-21.
3324a. Scanlon, Paul and Michael Gross. The Book of Alien. N.Y., Simon and Schuster, 1979.
3324b. Serrin, William. "The Hired Man, a Vanishing American," New York Times 128 (Aug. 4, 1979), 6.
3328a. Williams, J. "Business File: Jerry Goldsmith Calls the Tune," Films Illustrated 5 (Feb. 1976), 218.
3328b. Wright, John. "Jerry Goldsmith Lecture," SCN Soundtrack Collector's Newsletter 4, No. 7 (Apr. 1979), 3-7.

SEE ALSO: 136(Van de Ven), 197a(Seminars #66), 2896(Vallerand).

John Green

SEE ALSO: 190a(Steen).

Leigh Harline

3349a. Prado, Sharon S. "Leigh Harline's Pinocchio: A Consideration of Music for Films," (Master's Thesis, Division of Graduate Studies College-Conservatory of Music, University of Cincinnati, 1984). This is a fine work which contains an inventory of the Harline Collection at U. of Cincinnati.

SEE ALSO: 1400a (Martin).

Bernard Herrmann

3359a. "Bernard Herrmann." New York Times 125 (26 Dec. 1975), 34. Obituary.
3359b. The Bernard Herrmann Society Journal Aug. 1981+. San Diego (Kevin Fahey, 5523 Denny Ave., N. Hollywood, Calif. 61601).
3363a. Brown, Royal. "A Film-Music Milestone from Bernard Herrmann," High Fidelity and Musical America 24 (Oct. 1974), 122.
3366a. Brown, Royal. "The Mysterious Film World of Bernard Herrmann," High Fidelity and Musical America 25 (Dec. 1975), 120-21.
3368a. "'Citizen Kane' Classic Film Scores of Bernard Herrmann," High Fidelity and Musical America 25 (Jan. 1975), 104.
3384. ADD: No. 228/9 and 234 (Mar/Jun 1976) and (Nov. 1976), 18-19 and 26-7.
3388a. Harris, Steve. "An Afternoon with Bernard Herrmann," The Bernard Herrmann Society Journal 5-6 (Fall 1982), 16ff.
3397a. Kinkaid, F. "Herrmann Wuthering Heights," Opera News 47 (1983), 43. Music performance review.
3398a. Krasnoborski, W. F. "Mrs. Muir and Mr. Bernstein," SCN Soundtrack Collector's Newsletter 2, No. 7 (July 1976), 10-11.
3398b. Krasnoborski, W. F. "Mrs. Muir and Mr. Herrmann," SCN Soundtrack Collector's Newsletter 5, Reprinted in 136(Van de Ven), p. 7-11.
3403a. Murphy, A. D. "Bernard Herrmann, 64, dies," Variety 281 (Dec. 31, 1975), 6.
3419a. Vallerand, F. "Musique de films," Sequences 104 (Apr. 1981), 61-2.
3421a. Zador, Leslie. "Movie Music's Man of the Moment," Coast FM and Fine Arts (July 1971), 30.
   SEE ALSO: 90 (O'Toole), 104(Prendergast), 136(Van de Ven), 173a (Leyda, p. 198-9), 301a(Taylor), 312a(Weis), 2252(Bernstein), 2329 (Cook), 4953(Watts).

Maurice Jarre

3454a. "Three Screen Composers: Maurice Jarre, Dimitri Tiomkin and Henry Mancini," Cinema (Los Angeles) 3, No. 3 (July 1966), 8-10+. Interview.

Bronislau Kaper

3478. Atkins, Irene Kahn. SEE 197a (Part I, #13).
   SEE ALSO: 136(Van de Ven).

Erich Wolfgang Korngold

3497a. Arvey, Verney. "Composing for the Pictures. An Interview with Erich Wolfgang Korngold," The Etude 55, No. 1 (Jan. 1937), 15-6.
3517a. Miller, Frank. "Evaluation of the cello in Deception," Film Music Notes 6, No. 2 (Nov. 1946), 7-9(?)
   SEE ALSO: 1248a (Currie).

Henry Mancini

3549a. Feather, Leonard. "From Pen to Screen," International

TABLE 9 (continued)

<u>Musician</u> 69, No. 4 (Oct. 1970), 7.
3557-8. See 197a (Seminars #118 and 199).
3560a. "Never Too Much Music," <u>Time</u> 79 (25 May 62), 70+. Henry Mancini and <u>Moon River</u>.
3560b. Paisley, Rom. "Henry Mancini - Doint It Right," <u>ASCAP Today</u> 9, No. 1 (Spring 1978), 6-10.
SEE ALSO: 104(Prendergast), 136(Van de Ven), 197a(Seminars 118, 199), 2847a(The man who..), 3454a(Three screen comosers).

Mario Nacimbene

SEE ALSO: 136(Van de Ven).

Alex North

3659a. <u>Cleopatra</u>. N.Y., National Publishers, Inc., 1963.
3662a. "Film Music By Alex North," <u>High Fidelity and Musical America</u> 28 (Feb. 1978), 102.
SEE ALSO: 104(Prendergast).

David Raksin

3734a. Morton, Lawrence. "David Raksin's Score for <u>Forever Amber</u>," <u>Film Music Notes</u> 7, No. 2 (Nov.-Dec. 1947).
3737a. Pechter, William. "Abraham Polonsky and <u>Force of Evil</u>," <u>Film Quarterly</u>, 15, No. 3 (1962).
3743a. Raksin, David. "A Note for Aaron Copland," <u>Perspectives in New Music</u> 19 (1981), 47.
3745a. Raksin, David. "Notes on <u>The Bad and the Beautiful</u>," <u>Film Music</u> 12, No. 4 (1953), 14.

Alan Rawsthorne

3753. ADD: A critical analysis of <u>Ivory Hunter</u>(alt. title in England: <u>Where No Vultures Fly</u>).

Hugo Riesenfeld

3757a. Buhrman, T. Scott. "Photoplays DeLuxe," <u>The American Organist</u> 3, No. 5 (1920), 157-175. Illus.
3758a. Herzog, Dorothea B. "Smiling his Way to the Goal of Ambition," <u>National Brain Power Monthly</u> (Nov. 1922), 24. Illus.
3762a. Riesenfeld, Hugo. "Music and the Movies," <u>The Violinist</u> 35, No. 6 (Dec. 1924), 211.
3762b. Riesenfeld, Hugo. "Musical Classics for Millions," in Cooke, James Francis. <u>Great Musicians on the Art of Music</u>. Philadelphia, Theo. Presser Co., 1925, p. 408-13.
3763a. van Broeckhoven, J. "Hugo Riesenfeld, Concertmaster, Composer, and Director of the Rivoli, Rialto and Criterion Theatres, New York City," <u>Musical Observer</u> 19, No. 5 (May, 1920), 18, 28.
3764. ADD: vol. 94, no. 7 (Feb. 17, 1927), 48-9.
SEE ALSO: 602(Hall).

Ann Ronell

3770a. Spaeth, Sigmund. "Ann Ronell, George Gershwin and Richard

Rodgers," <u>Film Music Notes</u> 5, No. 1 (Sept. 1945), [17].

Leonard Rosenman

SEE ALSO: 177a (McBride, p. 114-9).

Miklos Rozsa

3811a. Brown, Royal. "Spellbound: Classic Film Scores of Miklos Rozsa," <u>High Fidelity and Musical America</u> 25 (July 1975), 97-8.
3811b. Brown, Royal. "Theater and Film," <u>High Fidelity and Musical America</u> 26 (Oct. 1976), 140-1.
3835a. Evans, Colin. "Overtones of Hollywood," <u>Times Educational Supplement</u> 3071 (Apr. 4, 1975), 103.
3841a. "Happy 70th Birthday to Miklos Rozsa," <u>Film Music Notebook</u> 2, No. 4 (1976), 3-5.
3858. CHANGE: <u>Film Music</u> to <u>Film Music Notes</u>.
3865. Reviewed in <u>Music and Letters</u> 58, No. 1 (1977), 103-4.
3872a. <u>Pro Musica Sana</u> (Miklos Rozsa Society Journal).
3885a. Rozsa, Miklos. "An Outline of University Training for Musicians in Motion Picture Work," <u>Film Music Notes</u> 5, No. 2 (Oct. 1945), 25-9.
3885b. Rozsa, Miklos. "Scoring the <u>Jungle Book</u>," <u>Film Music Notes</u> 1, No. 7 (Apr. 1942), 4.
3891a. Smith, Bethia. "Review of <u>The Strange Loves of Martha Ivers</u>," <u>Film Music Notes</u> 6, No. 2 (Nov. 1946), 10-11.
3893a. <u>The Story of Ben Hur</u>. N.Y., Random House, 1959.
3893b. Vallance, Tom. "Soundtrack: Classic Waxman and Rozsa: Vintage Garland," <u>Film</u> 26 (May 1975), 10.
SEE ALSO: 104(Prendergast), 1248a(Currie), 173a (Leyda[p. 409-410), 3419(Vallance).

Philippe Sarde

SEE ALSO: 136(Van de Ven).

Max Steiner

3971a. Maffett, James D. "<u>Cassablanca</u>: The Classic Film Score for Humphrey Bogart," <u>Stereo Guide</u> (Christmas, 1974), 74-6. [Unverified]
3990a. Max Steiner, interviewed in <u>The Real Tinsel</u>, edited by Bernard Rosenberg and Harry Silverstein. N. Y., Macmillan, 1970, p. 392-3.

Virgil Thomson

4035b. Thomson, Virgil. <u>American Music Since 1910</u>. London, Weidenfeld and Nicolson, 1971.

Dimitri Tiomkin

4073a. Tiomkin, Dimitri. "A New Field for Composers," <u>Musical Observer</u> 20, No. 7 (July 1930), 5, 16.
SEE ALSO: 3454a(Three screen composers).

Franz Waxman

TABLE 9 (continued)

4130a. Cleave, Alan. "Record Review: Sunset Boulevard: the Classic Film Scores of Franz Waxman," Movie Maker 9 (Aug. 1975), 547.
4134a. Hart, Elsepth. "Peyton Place," Films in Review 9, No. 1 (Jan. 1958), 26-8.
4136a. "Interview with Franz Waxman," Film Music Notes 3, No. 6 (March, 1944), 5.
4141a. Pratley, Gerald. "Franz Waxman," Hollywood Quarterly 5, No. 2 (Winter, 1950), 132-7.
4141b. "'Sunset Boulevard': Classic Film Scores of Franz Waxman," High Fidelity and Musical America 25 (Apr. 75), 102-3.
4141c. Waxman, Franz. "The New Music of Motion Pictures," Film Music Notes 5, No. 1 (Sept. 1945), [27-29].
 SEE ALSO: 3893b(Vallance).

John Williams

4187a. Caps, John. "[John Williams]," Soundtrack! The Collector's Quarterly 3 (Sep. 1984), 22-23.
4190a. Colon, C. "El sinfonismo como lenguaje historico de la musica cinetomatografica," Casablanca 30 (June 1983), 18-21. About the importance of John Williams and his contribution to symphonic scores in contemporary film.
4193a. Doherty, J. "Out of This World," Soundtrack! The Collector's Quarterly 2 (Dec. 1983), 28.
4198a. Lehti, S. J. "In the Valley of the Sequels," Soundtrack! The Collector's Quarterly 3, No. 11 (Sep. 1984), 16-20. Discusses the scores of John Williams, James Horner and Basil Poledouris for three recent sequels.
4198b. Libbey, T. W., Jr. "Disks Attest to the Versatile Talents of John Williams," New York Times 132 (Feb. 27, 1983, sec. 2), 21-2.
4202a. Pugliese, Roberto. "John Williams, L'Extraterrestre," Segnocinema 8 (May, 1983), 30-32.
4204a. Raynes, D. "Star Tracks," Soundtrack! The Collector's Quarterly 3 (Dec. 1984), 21.
 SEE ALSO: 136(van de Ven), 2896(Vallerand).

Roy Webb

 SEE ALSO: 1248a(Currie).

Victor Young

4213a. Ayotte, Jeannine M. "The Victor Young Collection in the Music Department of the Boston Public Library." Typescript. Boston Public Library, 1982. Card Index for Collection.
4215a. "Doedsbud," Orkester Journalen 24 (Dec. 1956), p. 21.
4217a. "Music Figures Fall Before Grim Reaper," Billboard 68 (Nov. 24, 1956), 15+.
4217b. Obituary. Musical America 76 (Dec. 1, 1956), 33; Newsweek 48 (Nov. 19, 1956), 89; Time 68 (Nov. 19, 1956), 94; Variety 204 (Nov. 14, 1956), 79.
4218a. "Victor Young Dead at 56," Down Beat 33 (Dec. 12, 1956), 10.
4218b. "Victor Young Dies," Melody Maker 31 (Nov. 17, 1956), 4.
4221a. Victor Young Collection at Brandeis University (movie short

scores, Oscar for Around the World in 80 Days, recordings). Typescript Finding Aid. The Victor Young Collection was originally donated to Brandeis. Then a part of it was transferred to the Boston Public Library. Although only printed sheet music was supposed to be transferred, in fact, recordings and movie scores also were transferred. Thus, the score for Around the World in 80 Days is not at Brandeis but at the Boston Public Library.
SEE ALSO: 1795 (Lewin. Around the World in 80 Days).

Additional Composer Profiles

4222a. Atkins, Irene Kahn. Interview with Harry Warren. Hollywood Song Writer. The American Film Institute/Louis B. Mayer Oral History Collection, Part I, #4. [N.Y. Times Oral History Program] Glenn Rock, N.J., Microfilming Corp. of American, 1977.
4223. Atkins, Irene Kahn. ADD: See 197a(Part I, #9).
4273a. Tynan, John. "The Sherman Brothers," BMI, The Many Worlds of Music 5 (1972), 28-9.

III. AESTHETICS
Silent and Early Sound Era

4329a. Fuerst, Leonhard. "Grundfragen des Films," Melos 13, No. 4 (April, 1934), 132-5.
4331a. Fuerst, Leonhard. "Ueber die Grundlichen der Filmwissenschaft," Die Musik 26, No. 4 (Jan. 1934), 254-8.
4337a. Gutman, Hanns. "Aussichten des Tonfilm," Die Musik 21, No. 2 (Nov. 1928), 123-5.

SOUND ERA. Form and Function:Aural/Visual Relationships in Film Art

4823. Previn, Dory. ADD: See 197a(Seminars, #137).

Sociology and Culture: The Impact of Industry and Art

5074. ADD: UM69-1108. DA XXIX/8 p.2809-10-A (Sociology).
5104. ADD: UM71-2227;DA XXXI/11 p6210-A (Theater).
5239. ADD: Another edition The Red Shoes; The Tales of Hoffman. N.Y., Garland Pub., 1977.

IV. SPECIAL TOPICS

Musical Performance on Film
1950's

5262. Kracauer, Siegfried. ADD: Some analysis of Gance's Louise(1939), Menotti's The Medium(1951), Powell and Pressburger's Tales of Hoffmann(1951).
5285a. "Opera Season To Taste," Harper's 210 (Jan. 1955), 87. Differences in Italian and American treatments of opera on film.
1960's
5331a. Fry, Annette. "Opera on Main Street," Opera News 26 (31 Mar 1962), 8-13. A "Grand Opera Film Festival" series for local theaters.
5757. ADD: Another edition. Flint, Mich., National Opera Association, 1973.

98   FOUNDATIONS IN MUSIC BIBLIOGRAPHY

TABLE 9 (continued)

Musical Performance on Television
1980's

5844a. Bauer, Gerd. "Unterhaltungsmusik im Fernsehen," Musica 34, No. 1 (Jan.-Feb. 1980), 21-4.

Film Musicals

5892a. Applebaum, Stanley. The Hollywood Musical. N. Y., Dover Publications, 1974.

Bach, Steven, SEE 1981.

5892b. Baker, Peter. "Tough Guys Set a New Pattern," Films and Filming 2, No. 4 (Jan. 1956), 15. Serious dramatic material has changed the movie musical.

5899a. "Big Season for Musicals: Jumbo, Gypsy, and Bye Bye Birdie," Look 26 (14 Aug 1962), 38-9+.

5926a. Chion, Michel. "La comedie musical. Un amour pudique," Cahiers du cinéma 331 (Jan. 1982), X. Review Alain Masson: La Comédie Musicale, Editions Stock.

Crichton, Kyle. SEE 1247a.

5946a. Cutts, John. "On the Bright Side," Films and Filming 16, No. 11 (Aug. 1970), 17-18. Illus. Interview with Charles Walters. Musicals generally. Walters dance director.

5953a. Dietz, Howard. "The Musical Band Wagon Keeps on Rollin' Along," Look 17, No. 16 (11 Aug 1953), 93-5. History of the Hollywood musical, esp. The Band Wagon.

5958a. "Elephant's Eye," New Yorker 31 (10 Sep 1955), 33-5. Interchange of discussion about set designing for Oklahoma! and publicity for Guys and Dolls.

Graham, Ronnie. See 1687a.

6003. ADD: Reviewed by T. Manns in Filmrutan 24, No. 4 (1981), 40.

6040a. Lee, Edward. Jeanette MacDonald. N.Y., Jove Publications, 1977.

6010. ADD: 14 (Nov.-Dec. 1957), 16-19; and No. 15 (Jan.-Feb. 1958), 17-18.

6010a. Hudson, Peggy and Roy Hemming. "The Lively Arts," Senior Scholastic 91 (28 Sep 1967), 42-3. On the Kraft Music Hall special The Hollywood Musical.

6027a. Kimball, Robert. "Those Glorious MGM Musicals," Stereo Review 33, No. 9 (Sept. 1974), 98-9.

6052a. Mahieu, Jose Agustin. "El cine musical," Cuadernos Hispano-Americanos 379 (Jan. 1982), 119-30. The musicals (representations in the cinema).

MGM Musicals. See 1813a.

Paul, E. See 1464a.

6085a. Peck, Seymour. "Again the Movies Sing and Dance," New York Times Magazine (1 July 1961), 16-17. Production stills from recent musicals.

6094a. Rickey, Carrie. "Let Yourself Go," Film Comment 18, No. 2 (1982), 43-7. The musical as experimental film genre & 3 musicals sing one from the libido.

6094b. Ringgold, Gene. Chevalier. Secaucus, N.J., Citadel, 1973.

6095a. Ronan, Margaret. "The Lively Arts," Senior Scholastic 94 (7 Feb. 1969), 16+. A quick history of film musicals.

6109a. Silke, James. "Mary Poppins," Cinema 2, No. 4 (Dec.-Jan. 1964-5), 48.

6117a. "Song and Dance," Sight and Sound 24 (Oct.-Dec. 1954), 95-100. Photo section on American and British musicals.
6126a. Sutton, Martin. The Hollywood Musical Film. M. A. Thesis. Exeter University, 1976.
6133a. Thompson, Thomas. "Tuning U.S. Musicals to Overseas Box Office," Life 58 (12 Mar 1965), 55+.
     Tindall, Glenn. See 1523a.
6143a. Vallence, Tom. "Soundtrack," Film 49 (Autumn 1967), 35-7. Return of the film musical.
6145. ADD: Singin' in the Rain, An American in Paris, Guys and Dolls, etc. represent decline from On the Town.
6148a. Warner, Alan. "Busby Berkeley: Dream Maker," Cassettes and Cartridges (Mar. 1974), 556, 558. [Unverified]
     SEE ALSO: 190a(Steen), 1247a(Crichton), 3770a(Spaeth).

Guides to Primary Sources

6198a. Anderson, Gillian B. Silent Film Music (1894-1929): A Guide. D.C., Library of Congress, 1987.

Filmographies

6265. ADD: Reviewed FIN 11 (1) (1978), 87-8.
6269. ADD: Reviewed in American Music 3, No. 3 (Fall, 1985), 354-5.
6273a. "Walt Disney Presents," Film Dope 12 (June 1977), 2-29.

Discographies

6273a. Affelder, P. "Sound-Track Favorites on Discs," Cosmopolitan 141 (Oct. 1956), 6. A list of popular, semiclassical, classical musicals; special emphasis on Pinocchio, Moby Dick and Trapeze.
6281a. "Magical Music of Walt Disney: Fifty Years of Original Motion Picture Soundtracks. High Fidelity and Musical America 29 (Mar. 1979), 130.
6340. Woll, Allen L. ADD: Reviewed in Filmkritik 21, No. 3 (1977), 169.

include them all here. Like some of the other tools in this field, Wescott is a superb source, but remains incomplete.

The literature on film music covers a wide spectrum in quality. Although most of it is about two pages long and is of marginal value, some works by the following scholars are excellent: Lawrence Morton, Clifford McCarty, Elisabeth Weis, Philip Tagg, Martin Marks, Fred Steiner, Win Sharples. My conclusion after searching for literature about Leigh Harline, Paul Smith, Paul Simon, Dave Grusin, John Williams, and Victor Young is that much remains to be written. The book by Wescott and the thesis by Prado are examples of good recent work, and more is being done.[38] I do not have the space to discuss what is involved in finding copies of the four films, except to say that there is no bibliography which tells us where copies of 35mm prints are located. The videotape reference guides did not list *Pinocchio*;[39] however, since I personally own a copy of it I know that it exits.

I have used my four examples to demonstrate what has been and what still needs to be done in the field of film music bibliography. We do not yet have a reliable, comprehensive bibliography of film scores or a *RISM* for film scores. The Library of Congress has published a guide to silent film scores and cue sheets in four of the major silent film music collections in the United States.[40] The Society for the Preservation of Film Music is working toward the establishment of a National Union Catalog of Film Scores, but this effort is in its infancy. We do have a comprehensive bibliography of the literature on film music, and there is a small but growing core of excellent secondary literature. We do not have comprehensive bibliographies on films yet either, but I would like to conclude on a more complicated note. [At this point Ms. Anderson played a brief recorded example of the real *Star Wars* theme, followed immediately by the fourth recorded example she had played at the outset of her paper, which was from the opening theme of Korngold's score for *King's Row*. Ed.] The imposter was from Erich Wolfgang Korngold's score for *King's Row*. As you can hear, the two excerpts are strikingly similar for several measures, and both themes share certain characteristics with some of Wagner's heroic trumpet themes.

I have concluded this deception among my musical examples, because I want to emphasize that the language of film music works by association. Some are grounded in actual physiological responses. Low sounds cause anxiety in most humans, so many scary scenes are accompanied by low bass notes. Some associations are grounded in the Hollywood composers' traditions, in stereotypes, cliches, and innovations that they have worked out. Some associations may be grounded in the vaudeville, pantomine, opera, and ballet traditions. Some associations may derive purely by chance. Others may be a function of politics or the times. Ultimately, the goal in film music studies will be to explore the relationship between music and image, to describe why and how the music works for both the audience and the composers, and to trace the development of film music's language from Wagner to *King's Row* to *Star*

Wars, for example, and beyond. Ultimately, there will need to be a bibliography of musical associations.

The movies and their music are part of our culture, part of who we are. They affect the ways in which we express ourselves, and they bear some relationship to the development of our values. "When You Wish Upon a Star, Your Dreams Come True" is not only a great song, it is part of my value system, figuratively anyway. Many of us have been similarly touched. Although movie music can be cloying as well as exalting, its study ultimately holds the promise of national, cultural and self revelation. Such a dynamic end must be preceded by down-to-earth bibliographies of film music; I hope I have made my case for them.

NOTES

1. Gaylord Carter, interviewed on the playing of organ accompaniments for silent films in *You Must Remember This,* Walter Wagner, ed. (New York: G.P. Putnam, 1975), p. 68-70.

2. If you had not known them, you could have identified the titles of the two songs from the words, but someone would have had to tell you what the titles of the instrumental numbers were. Then you could have found them in Shapiro's *Popular Music 1920-1979. A Revised Cumulation.* Nat Shapiro and Bruce Pollock, eds. (Detroit: Gale Research Company, 1985).

3. Disney-RKO. 1940.

4. Todd-United Artists, 1956.

5. Embassy. 1967.

6. Lucas Films-Twentieth Century Fox, 1977.

7. Metuchen, N.J.: The Scarecrow Press, Inc., 1974.

8. Metuchen, N.J.: The Scarecrow Press, Inc., 1981

9. Furthermore, Limbacher omits the names of the orchestrators and of the producers, Mike Todd, for *Around the World in 80 Days,* and Lucas Films for *Star Wars.* Such information can become critical In the attempt to locate original scores.

10. See my review in *American Music,* 3/3 (Fall, 1985): 354-5.

11. New York: Da Capo, 1972 (originally 1953).

12. Richard P. Krafsur, ed. (New York: R.R. Bowker Co., 1976), p. 422. The song "Sound of Silence" is erroneously listed as "Sounds of Silence." Currently, this great reference work is of value only for films of the 1960's and 1920's. Fortunately, other volumes are currently underway. [The catalog for the period 1911-1920 was published in 1988. Ed.]

13. Normally, with popular music there are more entries in the title catalog than in the composer name catalog. From the 1950's throughout the 1970's, copyright cards were filed by title in the M title catalog but not in the composer catalog.

14. In 1977-76, the Copyright Office and the Music Division reproduced the copyright cards for the music deposits by thirty of the major movie studios between 1898 and 1956. These files were then cross-referenced by the films' titles and composers and remain the Music Division. Most of the deposits were unpublished EU's and remain in the Copyright office.

15. Main entry cards, found under the copyright claimant's name, frequently contain more information than can be found on cross reference cards. The cards under "Disney, Walt Productions" supplied the film's title and registration dates for a number of the other incomplete entries found under Harline.

16. New York: Oxford University Press, 1981, p. 224.

17. This kind of registration (with recordings instead of hard copy) has been made with increasing frequency since just before 1978 when the new copyright law took effect.

18. D.W. Krummel, Jean Geil, Doris J. Dyen, Deane L. Root, compilers. (Urbana: University of Illinois Press, 1981).

19. The Victor Young Collection was given to Brandeis. Later, the sheet music was transferred to the Boston Public Library. Although Brandeis intended to retain all the film scores and recordings, the score for *Around the World in 80 Days* was inadvertently transferred to Boston Public. However, the film scores appear to be copyists' scores, and there appear to be no full scores or autograph sketches. I am grateful to Robert Evanson, fine arts librarian, at Brandeis for this information.

20. Nancy Knutsen in September, 1986.

21. Jo Ann Kane Music Service, 10201 West Pico Blvd., Los Angeles, CA 90035.

22. c/o Group 555, West 57th St., No. 122, N.Y., N.Y. 10019

23. Christian Chun. *Inventory of the Franklin J. Schaffner Collection 1949-1982*. Archives and Special Collections, Shadek-Fackenthal Library, Franklin and Marshall college, Lancaster, Pa., 17603, p. 6,9,13, & 15. I am indebted to Kathleen Moretto for calling this source to my attention.

24. "Alex North Receives S.P.F.M. Career Achievement Award," *The Cue Sheet*, 3/3 (September 1986): 32f.

25. *A Classified Bibliography*. (New York: Institute for Studies in American Music, Brooklyn College of the City University of New York, 1974)

26. Cecil Adkins and Alis Dickinson, ed. Seventh Edition/Second Edition. (Philadelphia: The American Musicological Society, 1984.)

27. Detroit: Information Coordinators, 1984.

28. "Leigh Harline's *Pinocchio:* A Consideration of Music for Films," (Master's Thesis, Division of Graduate Studies College-Conservatory of Music, University of Cincinnati, 1984).

29. Detroit: Information Coordinators, 1985.

30. Mitchell S. Cohen. *Simon & Garfunkel: A Biography in Words & Pictures,* Greg Shaw, ed. (s.l.: Sire Books; New York: distributed by Chappell Music Co., 1977.)

Spencer Leigh. *Paul Simon-Now and Then.* (Liverpool: Raven Books, 1973.)

Agustin Sanchez Vidal. *Simon & Garfunkel.* (Madrid: Ediciones Jucar, 1975.)

31. Philadelphia: Institute for Scientific Information, 1976-.
32. Marietta Chicorel, ed. (New York: Chicorel tibrary Pub. Corp., [1975]).
33. New York: R.R. Bowker Co., 1972-.
34. New York: H.W. Wilson Co., 1901-.
35. New York: The Museum of Modern Art, 1941-1985.

36. We searched the *National Newspaper Index,* the *Magazine Index* and the *Biography Master Index.*

37. *Science Digest,* 61 (February 1967): 61. We had equal trouble searching for common names such as Paul Smith, Paul Simon and John Williams.

38. For excellent summaries on the state of film music research, see Martin Marks, "Film Music: The Material, Literature, and Present State of Research," *Music Library Association Notes,* 36 (December 1979): 314-25. Martin Marks, "Film Music: The Material, Literature, and Present State of Research," *Journal of the University Film and Video Association,* 34/1 (Winter, 1982): 3-40. Also see a review of Stephen Wescott's book by Clifford McCarty, "Publications," *The Cue Sheet,* 3/3 (September 1986): 41.

39. *The Video Source Book,* 7th ed Professional Volume. (Syosset, New York: The National Video Clearinghouse, Inc. 1985). James L. Limbacher, *Feature Films, A Directory of Feature Films on 16mm and Videotape Available for Rental, Sale, and Lease.* (New York and London: R.R. Bowker Co., 1985).

40. Gillian B. Anderson, compiler. *Silent Film Music (1894-1929) A Guide.* (Washington, D.C., 1988).

Supplement to Steven D. Wescott's *A Comprehensive Bibliography of Music for Film and Television*[1]

Gillian B. Anderson

SUMMARY. The following citations, drawn from a variety of sources, supplement Steven D. Wescott's *A Comprehensive Bibliography of Music for Film and Television*. Short summaries that follow some citations were taken primarily from Richard Dyer MacCann and Edward S. Perry, *The New Film Index: A Bibliography of Magazine Articles in English, 1930-1970*.

The citations below were found in a number of sources, both original and secondary. The designation "[Unverified]" indicates that I was unable to locate the journal in the Library of Congress collections. The short summaries that follow some citations were taken primarily from Richard Dyer MacCann and Edward S. Perry, *The New Film Index: A Bibliography of Magazine Articles in English, 1930-1970* (New York: E.P. Dutton & Co., Inc., 1975). Titles listed in brackets in English have been drawn from *The Arts and Humanities Citation Index*, which does not give citations in the original language; I was unable to locate the original article.

Gillian B. Anderson is affiliated with the Music Division at the Library of Congress.

1. Detroit: Information Coordinators, 1985.

[Haworth co-indexing entry note]: "Supplement to Steven D. Wescott's *A Comprehensive Bibliography of Music for Film and Television*." Anderson, Gillian B. Co-published simultaneously in *Music Reference Services Quarterly*, (The Haworth Press, Inc.) Vol. 2, No. 1/2, 1993, pp. 105-144; and: *Foundations in Music Bibliography* (ed: Richard D. Green) The Haworth Press, Inc., 1993, pp. 105-144. Multiple copies of this article/chapter may be purchased from The Haworth Document Delivery Center [1-800-3-HAWORTH; 9:00 a.m. - 5:00 p.m. (EST)].

© 1993 by The Haworth Press, Inc. All rights reserved.

I. HISTORICAL SURVEYS

5a. Atkins, Irene Kahn. Interview with Eric M. Berndt. The Development of Optical Sound Reproduction. *American Film Institute/Louis B. Mayer Oral History Collection,* Part 1, No. 1. New York Times Oral History Program. Glenn Rock, New Jersey: Microfilming Corp. of America, 1977.

5a. _____. Interviews with Early Sound Editors. *American Film Institute/Louis B. Mayer Oral History Collection,* Part I, No. 6.

5b. _____. Interview with James G. Stewart. Development in Sound Technique. *American Film Institute/Louis B. Mayer Oral History Collection,* Part I, no. 22.

13a. Caps, John. "TV Music: Music Makes All the Difference," in Luc van de Ven, ed., *Motion Picture Music.* Mechelen, Belgium: Soundtrack, 1980, p.64 passim.

136. van de Ven, Luc. *Motion Picture Music.* Mechelen, Belgium: Soundtrack, 1980. Twenty-four articles which originally appeared in *Soundtrack (SCN).* Includes discography and filmography. Articles about Les Baxter, Richard Rodney Bennett, Goldsmith, Herrmann, Kaper, Mancini, Rusticelli, Sarde, Shire and John Williams; *The Ghost and Mrs. Muir, Nicholas and Alexandra, Jaws,* and *Towering Inferno.* Reviewed in *Kosmorama,* 27, No. 155 (1981): 196-97.

145a. Belluso, Paolo and Flavio Merkel. *Rock-Film.* Milan: Gammalibri, 1984. [ML 128.R684 1984]

155a. Friedman, Norman. "Theory Number Two: Studying Film Impact on American Conduct and Culture, *Journal of Popular Film,* 3 (Spring 1974), 173-81.

173a. Leyda, Jay, ed. *The Voices of Film Experience.* New York: Macmillan, 1977. Interviews with Bernard Herrmann and Miklos Rozsa.

177a. McBride, Joseph, ed. *Filmmakers and Filmmaking.* The American Film Institute. Los Angeles: J. P. Tarcher, 1983. Interview with Leonard Rosenman, p. 114-19.

190a. Steen, Mike. *Hollywood Speaks! An Oral History.* New York: G . P. Putnam's Sons, 1974. Interviews with Busby

Berkeley (p. 296), Bernard Freericks (p. 314), John Green (p. 326).

197a. *American Film Institute/Louis B. Mayer Oral History Collection, Part I* and *American Film Institute Seminars and Dialogues on Film.* New York Times Oral History Program. Glenn Rock, New Jersey: Microfilming Corp. of America, 1977. [Guide: AI3.07 Nos. 1-3]
Part I contains transcripts of interviews with Eric M. Berndt, Early Sound and Music Editors, Hugo Friedhofer, Joseph Gershenson, George R. Groves, Bronislaw Kaper, James G. Stewart, and Harry Warren. [Microfilm 49528 micRR]
Seminars and Dialogues contains transcripts of interviews with Elmer Bernstein, Jerry Goldsmith, Henry Mancini and Dory Previn. [Microfilm 5185 micRR]
Each interview is listed separately under Irene Kahn Atkins, the interviewer, or under the name of the composer according to Wescott's format.

211a. Care, Ross. "Mickey Mouse Music," *Funnyworld,* 22 (1981), 47-49.

231a. Denbo, Doris. "He's the Big Noise Behind the Talkies," *American Magazine,* 3 (June 1931), 82f. See also *Literary Digest,* 105 (28 January 1930), 37. Profile of Count Cutelli, sound effects artist for Disney and others.

234a. English, M. "How Mickey Mouse Inspired Song Hits," *Down Beat,* 20 (4 November 1953), 5.

235a. Farren, Jonathan. *Cine-Rock.* Paris: A. Michel, 1979. [PN1995.9 .M86F37]

237a. Finch, Christopher. *The Art of Walt Disney from Mickey Mouse to the Magic Kingdoms.* New York: Harry Abrams, Inc., [1973] Contains numerous references to the composers for Disney's films.

237b. Ford, Charles. *L'univers des images animés.* Paris: Editions Albin Michel, 1973. The Sherman Brothers on pp. 52, 103-105, 175-76, 236.

242a. George, Lee. "Aspects of Industrial Film Music," M.A. Thesis, Wayne State University, 1964. 90 p. Illus.

248a. *The Illustrated Disney Song Book.* New York: Hal Leonard Pub. Corp., 1979. Contains information about Disney composers.

253a. Jones, Isabel Morse. "Film Music. The Composer Emerges. A Man of Importance in New Hollywood Releases," *Musical America,* 67 (February 1947), 19, 362.

253b. Jones, Isabel Morse. "Golden Anniversary. Music a Willing Handmaiden in 50 Years of Film-Making," *Musical America,* 64 (May 1944), 4-5, 10.

257a. Krasnoborski, W.F. "T.V. Music: Roots and Offshoots," in van de Ven, Luc. *Motion Picture Music.* Mechelen, Belgium: Soundtrack, 1980, p. 60 passim. [See 136]

262a. McConnell, Frank D. *The Spoken Seen: Film and Romantic Imagination.* Baltimore: Johns Hopkins University Press, 1975, p. 19, 21, 104.

262b. Madsen, Roy Paul. *The Impact of Film: How Ideas Are Communicated through Cinema and Television.* New York, Macmillan. 1975, p. 571.

263a. Maltin, Leonard. *The Disney Films.* New York: Crown Publishers, 1973.

263b. Maltin, Leonard. "Unearthing Jazz Heritage You Can See and Hear," *Jazz Magazine,* Northport: New York (Fall 1976), 36-41. Filmography.

265a. *Mary Poppins.* New York: National Publishers, 1964.

287a. Sands, Pierre Norman. "A Historical Study of the Academy of Motion Picture Arts and Science (1927-47)." Ph.D., University of Southern California. 1966. 267p. UM67-8027. DA XXVIII/I p 180-A. Discusses musicians.

301a. Taylor, John Russell. *Hitch: The Life and Times of Alfred Hitchcock.* New York: Pantheon, 1978. Covers composers who worked for Hitchcock.

312a. Weis, Elisabeth and John Belton. *Film Sound. Theory and Practice.* New York: Columbia University Press, 1985.

312b. Weis, Elisabeth. *The Silent Scream. Alfred Hitchcock's Sound Track.* East Brunswick, New Jersey: Associated University Presses, Inc., 1982. Concerned with those sounds on the soundtracks except the music. Extremely well done.

SILENT AND EARLY SOUND ERA

315a. "Accuracy in Talkie Equipment," *Scientific American*, 143 (August 1930), 102-103.

322a. Ahern, Maurice L. "Diggin' in the Graveyard," *Commonwealth*, 14 (12 August 1931), 358-60. Since 1928 over 130 silents remade into talkies.

322b. Ahern, Maurice L. "Hollywood Horizons," *Commonwealth*, 12 (21 May 1930), 71-3. Suggests talkies have revolutionized audience viewing.

322c. Ahern, Maurice L. "An Overseas Headache," *Commonwealth*, 13 (11 March 1931), 519-21. Surveys European beginnings in competing with American talkies.

322d. Alaleona, Domenico. "A proposito del 'Cavaliere della Rosa'. Melodramma cinematografico e melodramma parlato." *Musica*, 5, no. 37 (1911), 1.

322e. "All-Talking Pictures Are Lost on Japanese Audiences," *Trans-Pacific*, 18 (3 July 1930), 12.

327a. Anderson, Gillian B. "The Thief of Bagdad and its Music," *Institute for Studies in American Music Newsletter*, 14, No. 1 (November 1984), 8-10.

339a. Audisio, Gabriel. "Le language des films," *La revue musicale*, 11, No. 106 (July 1930), 23-32.

342a. Austin, Cecil. "Art and the Peep Show," *Chesterian*, 6, No. 41(1 October 1924), 1-4.

343a. Austin, Cecil. "The Cinema Organ," *The Organ*, 4, No. 13 (July 1924), 45-51.

348a. Balestreri, Giuliano. "Euterpe o Cenerentola? Musica e cinematografo," *Musica d'oggi*, 16, No. 5 (May 1934), 171-74.

459a. Blum, Carl Robert. "Tonkunst und Tonfilm," *Der Auftakt*, 9, No. 7/8 (1929), 170-72.

460a. Boblitz, K. Sherwood. "Moving Picture Music and How It Impresses the Child," *Musical Observer*, 24 (1916), 319, 353; *Metronome*, 32, No. 8 (1916), 42.

460b. Boehme, C. "Die Begleitmusik im kinematographen Theater," *Zeitschriften für Instrumentenbau*, 30 (1910), 491-92.

462a. Bonardi, Pierre. "L'Infirme, la Muse e le Titan," [La film sonore], *La revue musicale,* 15, No. 151 (December 1934), 348-49.

462b. Boone, Andrew R. "Canning Nature's Noises for the Talkies," *Popular Science,* 119 (November 1931), 54-55 passim.

462c. Boone, Andrew R. "Prehistoric Monsters Roar and Hiss for Sound Film," *Popular Science,* 122 (April 1933), 20-21 passim.

462d. Boone, Andrew R. "Shooting Sound from Arctic to Equator," *Travel,* 64 (February 1935), 32-34.

462e. Boone, Andrew R. "Talkie Troubles," *Scientific American,* 147 (December 1932), 326-9. Describes conditions under which *Trader Horn, Igloo,* and *Eskimo* were filmed by W.S. Van Dyke.

471a. "Britain's Talkies Come To," *Living Age,* 340 (April 1931), 207-8. John Maxwell, British producer, sees new prosperity in sound film.

471b. Bronstein, N. "Tonfilm," *Anbruch,* 13, No. 8/10 (November/December 1931), 186-89.

479a. C., K.S. "Practical Way to Uplift 'Movie' Music," *Musical America,* 22, No. 18 (1915), 4.

479b. Cadman, Charles Wakefield. "The Musical Enigma of the Soundies," *Music World,* 1, No. 4 (September 1930), 9, 20; 1, No. 5 (October 1930), 6, 21.

481a. Carls, Carl Dietrich. "Der Opernfilm," *Der Auftakt,* 10, No. 11(1930), 235-38.

481b. Carter, Gaylord. Interview on music for silents in *You Must Remember This,* ed. by Walter Wagner. New York: G.P. Putnam, 1975, p. 68-70.

490a. Chelsey, John. "Cinema Music," *Musical Standard,* 9 (1917), 151-52.

490b. Chevaillier, Lucien. "L'augure et l'etoile," *Le Monde Musicale,* 42, No. 11 (November 1931), 325-27.

492a. Collins, F.L. "First Year Was the Loudest," *Woman's Home Companion,* 58 (May 1931), 11.

501a. Cousins, E. G. "Talkies Wield a Duster," *Bookman*, 80 (April 1931), 52-53. The coming of sound will revive many forgotten classics.

501b. Crain, Hal. "Leaders of Joint Interests United Under the Motto 'Finer Film-Music,'" *Musical America*, 33, No. 14 (29 January 1921), 1, 3-4.

501c. "Credit Should Go to Barrymore for First Sound Motion Picture," *Scholastic*, 49 (23 September 1946), 16 passim. John Barrymore's 1926 *Don Juan*.

505a. Davison, A. E. "Picture Music," *Musical News*, No. 1423 (December 7,1918), 163.

505b. Delehanty, Thornton. "The Film Cycle from Music to Guns to Music," *Literary Digest*, 116, (8 July 1933), 27. Patterns of talkies.

511a. D'Esterre, Neville. "Music and Talk in the Picture Theatre," *British Musician*, 6, No. 2 (February 1930), 38-41.

512a. Dittmer, Eugen. "'Kino und Oper.' Eine Epistel," *Allgemeine Musik-Zeitung*, 40 (1913), 480-81.

512b. Donaldson, Leonard. "Bioscope Music. A Plea for the Picture-Pianist," *Musical Standard*, 37 (1912), 148-49.

512c. Donaldson, Leonard. "Bioscope Music," *Musical Standard*, 37 (1912), 166-67, 193-95.

513a. Draper, John. "Sound Tricks in the Talkies," *Popular Mechanics Magazine*, 55 (February 1931), 236-40.

515a. D'Udina, Jean. "La musique et le cinema," *Le Ménestrel*, 4527.85 année, No. 5 (2 February 1923), 49-51; 4528.85 année, No. 6 (9 February 1923), 61-2; 4529.85 année, No. 7(16 February 1923), 73-74.

518a. Eaton, Quaintance. "Reading Music from Shadows. The 'Sound Track' on a Movie Film is Not Yet an Open Book to Technicians," *Musical Digest*, 14, No. 9 (1929), 15-16.

521a. Davy, Charles. "Is There a Future for Talkies?" *Bookman*, 86 (August 1934), 248. Realistic sound and abstract black and white images do not mix well.

524a. Epstein, Margot. "Gezeichnete Musik. Oskar Fischingers Toenende Ornamente," *Allgemeine Musikzeitung*, 59, No. 47 (25 November 1932), 591.

540a. "Ethelbert Nevin's *A Day in Venice (Un Giorno in Venezia)*, a New Tone Film Presentation Which Is Commanding National Attention," *The Etude,* 52, No. 6 (June 1934), 337.

545a. Febvre-Longeray, Albert. "En merge du film sonore; de l'adaption musicale," *Le courrier musical,* 31, No. 21 (December 15, 1929), 685-88.

559a. Florian, Felix. "Picture Theater Music," *Musical Standard,* 12, No. 283 (20 July 1918), 28.

562a. Fox, Joseph. "Playing the Picture," *Melody,* VI, No. 1 (January 1922), 24-25.

562b. Fox, Julian. "Casualties of Sound. Part One: King Mike," *Films and Filming,* 19, No. 1 (October 1972), 34-40; Part Two: 19, No. 2 (November 1972), 33-40. Actors and actresses who had difficulty making the transition to sound films.

564a. Freeland, Matthew. "I Remember," *Sight and Sound,* 14, No. 56, (Winter 1945-46), 126-27. Memories of early uses of sound in films.

569b. "Galsworthy on the Talkies," *Living Age,* 338 (15 May 1930), 349-50. Playwright gives views on coexistence of silents and talkies.

572a. Gaumont, Leon. "L'industrie du film parlant," *Le courrier musical,* 31, No. 21(15 December 1929), 691-94.

573a. Gerwig, H.C. "The Photo-Play Organist," *Musician,* 21 (1916), 54-55.

573b. Gilbert, Henry F. "My Summer in the Movies," *Musical Courier,* 86, No. 3 (18 January 1923), 46.

573c. Gillett, John. "Laughter," *Sight and Sound,* 40, No. 1 (Winter 1970-71), 45. Observations on the change to sound films; *Spite Marriage* (Keaton, 1929) and *Laughter* (D'Abbadie D'Arrast, 1930).

575a. Glinski, Mateusz. ". . . O filmie dzwiekowym i dzwieku filmowym," *Muzyka,* 8, No. 11/12 (December 1931), 484-85.

575b. Goldbeck, Frederik. "La Joie de Vivre," *La revue musicale,* 15, No. 151 (December 1934), 419-20. Reference to Tibor Harsanyi and Film Music.

575c. Goldsmith, Alfred N. "The Jack in the Box," *Musical Digest*, 15, No. 2 (February 1930), 24, 47. About the phonograph and moving pictures.

576a. "Good Word for the Talkies," *Literary Digest*, 108 (21 March 1931), 17. Suggests *City Lights* cannot bring back silents.

581a. Grant, J.P. "Popular Opera via 'the Movies,'" *Musical America*, 24, No. 9 (1916), 36-37.

582a. Graves, Charles. "Significant Speech," *Cinema Quarterly*, 1, No. 2 (Winter 1932), 89-92. Struggles with sound film compared with crude days of theater before Shakespeare.

584a. Greenland, Blanche. "'Faking' in 'Movie' Music Corrupting Public's Taste," *Musical America*, 22, No. 22 (1915), 12.

587c. Grierson, John. "The G.P.O. Gets Sound," *Cinema Quarterly*, 2, No. 4 (Summer 1934), 215-21. Documentary uses; examples.

598a. Hadley, Henry. "Henry Hadley Talks on Writing Music for the Movies," *Musical Courier*, 93 (December 9, 1926).

602a. Halliwell, Leslie. "Merely Stupendous," *Films and Filming*, 13, No. 5 (February 1967), 4-12; No. 6 (March 1967), 48-56; No. 7 (April 1967), 33-38; 14, No. 4 (January 1968), 10-15; No. 5 (February 1968), 38-44; No. 6 (March 1968), 42-47; No. 7 (April 1968), 49-53. Seven articles on the decade when films first learned to talk; the last two are on British cinemas of 1930s.

602b. Hallowes, Malcolm. "Organs in Cinema," *The Organ*, 1, No. 1 (July 1921), 26-30.

604a. "The Hand of Death on the Screen," *Literary Digest*, 105 (5 April 1930), 19-20. French author Bernard Fay says sound is killing the art of film.

604b. Hansford, M.M. "Mortimer Wilson," *American Organist*, 15, No. 5 (May 1932), 307-308. Obituary.

604c. Hansford, M.M. "Motion Picture Playing–An Outlook," *The Musician*, 24, No. 11 (1919), 8, 10.

609a. Harding, Henry J. "Music and the Pictures," *Cadenza*, 21, No. 8 (1915), 2-4.

610a. Harsanyi, Tibor. "Sur la musique de Dessin anime," *La revue musicale,* 15, No. 151 (December 1934), 412-18.
613a. Henry, Leigh. "The Filming of Music," *Musical News and Herald,* 62, No. 1563 (11 March 1922), 314, 316.
615a. Herring, Robert. "Twenty-three Talkies," *Close Up,* 6, No. 2 (1930), 134-40. On the Use of Sound.
616b. Hinrichs, Gustav. "A Plea for the Musician Who Creates the Musical Score for Feature Pictures," *Musical Courier,* 86, No. 25 (21 June 1923), 7.
621a. Howard, Clifford. "The Menace Around the Corner," *Close Up,* 6, No. 1 (1930), 59-66. The effect on Hollywood of sound and other technologies.
626a. Huxley, Aldous and Robert E. Sherwood. "Do You Like the Talkies," *Golden Book,* 11 (April 1930), 51-54. Pro and con; Huxley favors silent films.
626b. Huxley, Aldous. "Film Folio 3: Silence Is Golden," *Sight and Sound,* 23 (July-September 1953), 47-48. A reprint from an article written in 1929 in which Huxley lamented the coming of sound with a scathing review of *The Jazz Singer.*
632a. "Il film nella didattica pianista," *Musica sacra,* 60, No. 9 (25 September 1934), 140-43.
632b. Isaacson, Charles. "Specialized Knowledge Is Need of Moving Picture Musicians," *Musical America,* 33, No. 18 (26 February 1921), 37.
647a. Keeley, Joseph C. "Talking Movies and Opera," *New Music Review,* 28, No. 332 (July 1929), 286.
648a. Kegl, Zoltan J. "Crackup of Mighty Glazier Caught for First Time by Sound Camera," *Popular Science,* 123 (December 1933), 24-26.
650a. Kent, George. "New Crisis in the Motion Picture Industry," *Current History,* 33 (March 1931), 887-91. Coming of sound destroyed internationalism of movies.
656a. Kirsanoff, Dmitri. "De la synthese cinematographique," *La revue musicale,* 15, No. 151 (December 1934), 350-51.
656b. Klaren, Georg. "Die Frage der Filmmusik," *Der Auftakt,* 3, No. 8 (1923), 194-96.

668a. Koechlin, Charles. "Le probleme de Ia musique de cinema," *Le monde musical,* 45, No. 10 (31 October 1934), 269-71.
677a. L., R. "Le film sonore au service de l'emission vocale," *La revue musicale,* 15, No. 151 (December 1934), 425-26.
677b. Lachenbruch, Jerome. "Jazz and the Motion Picture," *Metronome,* 38, No. 4 (April 1922), 94.
677c. La Forge, Frank. "Will the Radio and Talking Pictures Compel a Revolution in Methods of Teaching Singing," *The Etude,* 48, No. 5 (May 1930), 313-14.
679a. Lanauer, Jean. "In Praise of Simplicity," *Close Up,* 6, No. 2 (1930), 134-40. For sound film.
679b. Landry, Lionel. "Musique et cinema," *La revue musicale,* 8, No. 4 (1 February 1927), 136-41.
682a. Lange, Francisco Curt. "La mecanizacion: de la musica y la supersaturacion musical," *Boletin de Ia Universidad Nacional de la Plata,* 17, No. 3 (1933), 114-29.
685a. Lawler, H. "Opera on the Screen," *The Etude,* 54 (May 1936), 349-50.
696a. Lingisch, Herbert. "Musikalische Probleme des Tonfilms," *Allgemeine Musikzeitung,* 61, No. 41 (12 October 1934), 560-61.
704a. Lorentz, Alfred. "Der gefilmte Kapellmeister," *Neue Zeitschrift für Musik,* 8 (1914), 377-78.
704b. Lovewell, S. Harrison. "A New Field of Activity for Organists," *Musician,* 20 (1915), 346-47.
708a. Luciani, S.A. "La musica y el cinematografo," *La revista de musica,* 1, No. 1 (July 1929), 12-18.
708b. Luciani, S. A. "Le visioni della musica e il cinematografo," *Harmonia,* 2, No. 6 (1914), 1-5.
715a. Maitland, Rollo F. "Some Difference between Church and Motion Picture Organ Playing," *Musician,* 22 (1917), 226.
720a. Marshall, Norman. "Music in the Talkies," *Bookman,* 84 (July 1933), 191-92. Cinematic reality is now threatened by the unnatural effects of musical accompaniment.
721a. Martin, Linton. "Operating on the Operas. Will History Repeat Itself When the Lyric Drama Goes Talkie?" *Musical America,* 49, No. 15 (25 June 1929), 16-17.

736a. Meuer, Adolf. "Staatsoper und Tonfilm; die Gefahren der Filmoper, *Signale,* 88, No. 21(21 May 1930), 633-35.
736b. Michaud, Jean. "The Film Drama of the Future," *Sackbut,* 3, No. 6 (January 1923), 183-85.
737a. Mila, Massimo. "Canzoni e musiche de cinematografo," *La rassegna musicale,* 4, No. 4 (July 1931), 205-15.
740a. Miller, Don. "Movie History on TV," *Films In Review,* 11, No. 2 (February 1960), 65-9. Review and discussion of single program in TV's *20th Century* series, dealing with coming of sound to movies.
740b. Miller, George. "The Organ in the Theatre," *Musician,* 20 (1915), 414-15.
741a. Milne, A. Forbes. "Good Music and the Kinema," *The Music Teacher,* 14 (1922), 297, 302.
746a. "Mortimer Wilson," *Fischer Edition News,* 8, No. 1 (January-February 1932), 15. Obituary.
746b. "Mortimer Wilson . . . [and] Franz Xavier Arens," *Musical Courier,* 104, No. 6 (6 February 1932), 14. Obituary.
746c. "Mortimer Wilson Dies," *Pacific Coast Musician,* 21, No. 5 (January 30, 1932), 11.
748a. "'Movie' Organs," *Musician,* 21 (1916), 246.
749a. "Multilingual Talkies," *Literary Digest,* 106 (12 July 1930), 15. Marie Dressler doubts foreign talkie appeal.
749b. Murphy, Robert. "The Coming of Sound to the Cinema in Britain," *Historical Journal of Film, Radio and Television,* 4, No. 2 (1984), 143-160.
749c. "Music and the Films," *Musical News and Herald,* 62, No. 1554 (7 January 1922), 19.
749d. "Music at Cinemas," *Musical News,* 48 (1915), 271-72.
749c. "Musica e cinematografo," *Musica d'oggi,* 3, No. 12 (December 1921), 340.
764a. "New Arbiter of Women's Movie Styles," *Literary Digest,* 105 (10 May 1930), 23. Predicts tomorrow's cinema styles will be influenced by demands of microphone.
764b. "New Magic Movies," *Popular Mechanics Magazine,* 55 (April 1931) 539-41.
766a. Newman, Ernest. "A Talk on the Talkies," *Musical America,* 49, No. 16 (10 July 1929), 5-6.

766b. Newman, Ernest. "These Cinema Organs and Organists," *Musical Times*, 72, No. 1055 (January 1931), 45-46.

766c. Nichols, Robert. "Cinema-To-Be," *Spectator*, 146 (24 January 1931), 103-4. Effects on film form with coming of sound; predictions on use of color, stereoscopic projection, and animation.

771a. Obey, Andre. "Musique et cinema," *Le monde musical*, 36, No. 11-12 (June 1925), 213-15.

773a. "Opera via Talkies," *Musician*, 40 (June 1935), 4. Surveys recent interest in movie operas.

773b. "The Organ, the Organist, and the Motion Picture," *The Music Trade Review*, 67, No. 13 (28 September 1918), 15.

773c. "Organ Music and Movies," *Cadenza*, 21, No. 8 (1915), 8-10.

775a. O'Sullivan, Joseph. "Adaptation of Music to Motion Pictures," *Metronome*, 33, No. 7 (1917), 58.

778a. Ottich, Maria. "Tonfilm und Rundfunk als Objekte der Musikwissenschaft," *Die Musik*, 27, No. 1 (October 1934), 41-43.

783a. "Paramount's Paris Studio," *Living Age*, 339 (October 1930), 206-207. U.S. firm producing talkies in eleven languages.

786a. Pasche, Hans. "Runkfunk und Tonfilm im Musikunterricht," *Signale*, 88, No. 10 (5 March 1930), 261-62.

799a. Potamkin, Harry Alan. "In the Land Where the Images Mutter," *Close Up*, 6, No. 1(1930), 11-19. Critical comments on recent sound films.

799b. Potamkin, Harry Alan. "Movie: New York Notes," *Close Up*, 7, No. 4 (October 1930) 235-52. Comments on recent films and film writing.

807a. Preussner, Eberhard. "Situation des Tonfilms." *Melos*, 8, No. 12 (December 1929), 540-43.

808a. Prunieres, Henry. "Le cinema au service de la technique pianistique," *La revue musicale*, 15, No. 151 (December 1934), 424-25.

808b. Pudovkin, Vsevolod. "The Global Film," *Hollywood Quarterly*, 2, No. 4 (July 1947), 327-32. Wonders if film can still be international after the advent of sound.

808c. Quarry, Edmund. "Midwife to the Talkies," *Sight and Sound,* 18 (Summer 1949), 94. About a sound film made in England as early as 1924-25.

808d. R., B. "Film sonoro e cataloghi musicali," *Bolletino bibliografico musicale,* 5, No. 5 (May 1930), 21-31.

810a. Romain, Paul. "Capacite auditive du spectateur au cinema," *Le courrier musical,* 31, No. 21 (December 15, 1929), 684-85.

814a. Rathaus, Karol. "Problemy Muzczne w Filmie Dziekowym," *Muzyka,* 8, No. 10 (October 1931), 408-10.

825a. Romberg, Sigmund. "Screen Operetta," *Pacific Coast Musician,* 19, No. 18 (May 3, 1930), 16.

828a. Rowe, E.B. "A Letter," [Article on Talking Movies] *Musical Courier,* 101, No. 10 (6 September 1930), 22.

833a. Sacerdote, Eduardo. "Music and the Films," *Pacific Coast Musician,* 25, No. 11 (6 June 1936), 3-4.

835a. Schaff, Edward. "Jazz and the Picture House," *Musical Advance,* 16, No. 10 (May 1929), 3.

837a. Scherber, Ferdinand. "Tonfilm und Theater," *Signale,* 88, No. 41 (8 October 1930), 1133-36.

837b. Scherber, Ferdinand. "Der Tonfilmschlager," *Signale,* 92, No. 45 (7 November 1934), 636-37.

838c. Schertzinger, Victor. "The Composer of 'Marcheta' Talks About the Talking Pictures," *Music Trade News,* 8, No. 4 (September 1929), 15-16.

869a. Schmidt, Leopold. "Lichtbild und Laut–Lautapparat im Musiklehrsaal," *Signale,* 72 (1814), 298-300.

871a. "A Scholar Examines Sound Films," *Musical Leader,* 57, No. 4 (25 May 1929), 5.

872. ADD: [Schünemann,] Georg.

872a. Schünemann, Georg. "Tonfilm und Rundfunk im Musikunterricht," *Rheinische Musik und Theater-Zeitung,* 30, No. 39/40 (16 November 1929), 421-23.

873a. Scott, Cyril. "The Cinema and Programme Music," *Monthly Musical Record,* 63, No. 752 (December 1933), 225.

883a. Sherwood, R.E. "Renaissance in Hollywood," *World Today,* 56 (November 1930), 564-70.

885a. Simons, Rainer. "Theater, Tonfilm und Radio," *Signale,* 89, No. 13 (25 March 1931), 327-9.
885b. Singer, Kurt. "Opernfilm," *Anbruch,* 12, No. 6 (June 1930), 212-14.
991a. Skinner, Richard Dana. "A Letter to Walter Damrosch," *North American Review,* 240, (September 1935), 278-83. Bring Wagner operas to screen.
994a. Spies, A. "Der Tonfilm," *Deutsche Musikzeitung,* 32, No. 10 (23 May 1931), 145.
994b. Spinola, Helen. "That Terrible Talkie Test," *Delineator,* 118 (May 1931), 17 passim. Humorous article on Hollywood activities.
1008a. Strobel, Heinrich. "Tonfilm und Lehrstueck," *Melos,* 8, No. 7 (July 1929), 315-7. Review of the Deutsches Kammermusikfest, Baden-Baden, 1929.
1015a. "The Talkies' Future," *Nation,* 130 (15 January 1930), 61-62. Suggests movies could go beyond technique.
1015b. "Talkies Preferred," *Living Age,* 340 (August 1931), 606-607. Columbia students and Spanish correspondent prefer talkies to theatre and opera.
1015c. "Talking Motion Pictures," *Science,* 71 (17 January 1930) Supp. 10 passim.
1016a. Tavano, C.F. "Cinema sonore–cinema parlant," *Le courrier musical,* 31, No. 21 (December 15, 1929), 694-95.
1019a. Tessner, Hans. "Kinomusik," *Neue Musik Zeitung,* 37 (1915/16), 56-57.
1027a. Tibbett, L. "Opera can be saved by the Movies," *Pictorial Review,* 34 (February 1933), 8-9 passim.
1027b. Tibbett, Lawrence. "A Talk on the Talkies," *The Etude,* 49, No. 8 (August 1931), 539-40. As told to R.H. Wollstein.
1027c. "Der Tonfilm und die Musiker," *Oesterreichische Musiker-Zeitung,* 37, No. 12 (16 June 1929), 65-66.
1030a. Tootell, George. "Cinema Music and its Future," *The Chesterian,* New Series, 38 (April 1924), 179-85.
1030b. Torchet, Julian. "Spectacles fictifs et musiques re'elles," *Le guide musical,* 54 (1908), 769-70.

1031a. Troy, William, "Retrospect: 1933," *Nation,* 138 (3 January 1934), 27-28. Talkie reflects evasion, abandonment, and confusion of period.

1031b. Trumbo, Dalton. "Frankenstein in Hollywood," *Forum,* 87 (March 1932), 142-46. Struggle between those who believe in talkies and those who wait for return of silents.

1036a. "Union Musicians Fight Sound Pictures in Advertising Campaign," *Music Trade News,* 8, No. 6 (November 1929), 13-14.

1037a. "Urban and Kinemacolor," *Cadenza,* 21, No. 7 (1915), 14-15, 33.

1037b. Ursel, Comte d'. "A Propos D'Images Sonores," *La Revue Musicale,* 15, No. 151 (December 1934), 361-64.

1039a. "Using Moving Pictures as Aid to Concert Business," *Musical America,* 22, No. 14 (1915), 11.

1044a. Vidor, King. "The End of an Era," *Films and Filming,* 1, No. 6 (March, 1955), 8-9. The friendship between William Randolph Hearst and Marion Davies; the coming of sound. Reprinted from *A Tree Is A Tree* (New York: Harcourt, 1953).

1045a. Vildrac, Charles. "En guise d'introduction," *La revue musicale,* 15, No. 151 (December 1934), 321-23.

1048a. Vuillermoz, Emile. "La musique et la cinegraphie," *Le menestrel,* Anne 82, No. 3 (16 January 1920), 17-18.

1048b. Wachten, Edmund. "Auf Krise der Europaischen Musikkultur," *Allgemeine Musikzeitung,* 61, No. 14 (6 April 1934), 185-88. (See 771a.)

1048c. Wagner, Rob. "Lend Me Your Ears," *Collier's,* 85 (11 January 1930) 10-11 passim; 86 (13 December 1930), 16-18. Review of progress made in talkies.

1049a. Wallfisch, J.H. "Parsifal im Kino," *Neue Zeitschrift für Musik,* 79 (1912), 734.

1056a. Waters, Thorold. "Music's winning chance in the 'Talkies.' Cine-opera the most natural development," *Australian Musical News,* 18, No. 11(1 June 1929), 3-4.

1059a. Weiss, E.H. "Le phonograph au cinema," *Le courrier musical* 31, No. 21 (December 15, 1929), 689-91.

1059b. Weiss, Trude. "The First Opera-Film," *Close Up*, 9, No. 4 (December 1932), 242-5. On *The Bartered Bride*, by Max Ophuls from Smetena.

1062a. Welsh, W.H. "Orchestras in Cinemas," *Musical News*, 51 (1916), 313-14.

1063a. Whipple, Leon. "Gone Talkie," *Survey*, 64 (1 July 1930), 321-22. Assesses power of sound film emotionally and intellectually.

1063b. White, Alvin C. "After Two Years of the Talkies in America," *The Strad*, 40, No. 471 (July 1929), 129-31.

1063c. White, E.B. "Mood Men: Playing for Silent Pictures," *Readers Digest*, 33 (July 1938).

See also: 312a (Weis), 2512b (Osborne).

SOUND TECHNIQUES AND TECHNOLOGY

1143a. Collins, Chester. "First Movie Soundtracks: The Edison Kinetophone Cylinders (Mark 56 Records: No. 856)," *The Antique Phonograph Monthly*, 7, No. 10 (19??), 10.

1146a. Fabrizio, T.C. "Before the Jazz Singer," *Antique Phonograph Monthly*, 5, No. 5 (19??), 3-6.

1162a. Lightman, Herb A. "The Film Finds Its Voice," *American Cinematographer*, 50, No. 1 (January, 1969), 84-85.

1162b. "Making of a Sound Fable," *Popular Mechanics Magazine*, 54 (Summer, 1930), 353-55. How animated films are made.

1171a. Yates, Raymond Francis. "A Technician Talks About the Talkies", *Scientific American*, 143 (November 1930), 384-85. Points out some failings of talkies and ways to overcome these.

1935-1949

History

1185a. Arvey, Verna. "Music of Worth to the Movies," *The Etude*, 57, No. 7 (July 1939), 434.

1191a. "Behind the Golden Curtain," *Harper's,* 196 (January 1948), 96. The Metropolitan opera goes to the multitudes via cinema.

1210a. Breger, Renee. "Opera at the Cinema," *Musical Mercury,* 6 (October 1938), 23-30.

1210b. "Bringing the Symphony Orchestra to Moving Picture Patrons," *The Etude,* 55, No. 11 (November 1937), 710.

1243a. Clifford, Hubert. "British Film Music Comes of Age," *Musical America,* 66 (10 January 1946), 29, 34.

1247a. Crichton, Kyle, (ed.), "Gamble with Music," *Collier's,* 117 (23 March 1946), 22-23. Problems in filming a music versus stage musical production.

1248a. Currie, John B. *"Of Human Bondage, The Killers, Notorious,"* Film Music Notes, 6, No. 1 (September-October 1946), 16-20. Reviews of scores by Korngold, Rozsa and Roy Webb.

1251a. Davenport, M. "Machine-Made Prima Donnas," *Readers Digest,* 28 (May 1936), 91. Only best operas and performances recorded. Excerpt from *Stage.*

1288a. Gronostay, Walter. "Beethoven im Film," *Deutsche Musikkulture,* 2, No. 2 (June/July 1937), 119-21.

1304a. "Hen Tracks on Sound Tracks," *Popular Mechanics Magazine,* 91 (April 1949), 168-69.

1315b. Huntley, John. "Film Music," *Penguin Film Review,* 2 (January 1947), 21-25. Methods of studying film music.

1322a. Huntley, John. *"The Magic Bow",* Film Music Notes, 6, No. 1 (September-October 1946), 16. Review.

1344a. Janssen, Werner. "Score Conceived before Filming of Picture," *Music and Musicians,* 22, No. 8 (September 1936), 6.

1352a. Keefer, Lubov. "Soviet Film Music Plays Leading Role," *Musical America,* 63 (September 1943), 6-8, 34.

1354a. Keller, Hans. "Film Music–Some Objections," *Sight and Sound,* 15, No. 60 (Winter 1946-7), 136. See 1766.

1359a. Keller, Hans. "Revolution or Retrogression?" *Sight and Sound,* 16, No. 62 (Summer 1947), 63-64. Critical reactions to the film version of the opera, *The Barber of Seville.*

1374a. Laine, Juliette. "Operetta and the Sound Film," *The Etude*, 56 (June 1938), 359-60. Advice to aspiring movie singer actresses by Jeannette MacDonald.

1400a. Martin, Donald "Fine Scores for New Musical Pictures," *The Etude*, 58, No. 2 (February 1940), 85, 88.

1400b. Martini, Nino. "And Now the Movies," *The Etude*, 54 (June 1936), 349-50. Opera films.

1443a. "Movie mirrors Music-Mindedness," *Musician*, 43 (April 1938), 75.

1464a. Paul, E. "Musical and Low," *Atlantic*, 176 (July 1945), 109 passim. Humorous attack on movie musicals.

1481a. Robins, S. "Disney Again Tries Trailblazing: *Fantasia*," *New York Times Magazine*, (3 November 1940), 6-7 passim.

1495a. Saunders, Richard Drake. "Fitting the Music to the Film," *Musical Courier*, 121 (1 January 1940), 5, 25.

1496a. Saunders, Richard Drake. "'Rhythm Sheet' Aids in Hollywood Film," Musical Courier, 121 (March 1940), 7.

1505a. Smith, Paul J. "The Music of the Walt Disney Cartoons," *The Etude*, 58 (July 1940), 438, 494.

1511a. Sternfeld, Frederick W. "Music and the Feature Films," *Musical Quarterly*, 33 (October 1947) 517-32.

1523a. Tindall, Glenn M. "Music and the Movies," *School and Society*, 48 (3 December 1938), 721-24. Tribute to the musical film.

1526a. Trautwein, Friedrich. "Der Schallfilm, das Schallaufzeichnungs–Geraet der Zukunft," *Deutsche Musikkultur*, 2, No. 3 (August/September 1937), 170-74.

1530a. "The Use of Standard Musical Compositions in Motion Pictures," *Music Educators Journal*, 25, No. 2 (October 1938), 56.

See also: 253 a & b (Jones)

Sound Techniques and Technology

1561a. Coldby, J. "Electronic Techniques of Making Talking Pictures," *Radio News*, 25 (January 1941), 8-10 passim.

1573a. "Manufacturing Quiet for the Movies," *Popular Science*, 139 (December 1941), 98.

124 *FOUNDATIONS IN MUSIC BIBLIOGRAPHY*

1579a. "Sounder Sounds: RCA Demonstrates Ultraviolet Ray Recording for Movies," *Business Week* (29 February 1936), 27.
1579b. "Sound Tricks of the Movies," *Popular Mechanics Magazine,* (September 1944), 56-61.
1580a. "Voomp, Clank, Bonk: Name Your Noise and the Movies' Sound Makers Will Give It to You," *Popular Science,* 138 (March 1941), 106-109.

1950's

History

1596a. Bauer, Leda. "Twice-Told Tales," *Theater Arts,* 35 (June 1951), 39-41 passim. Opera into film–limitations and failures; emphasis on *Tales of Hoffman.*
1687a. Graham, Ronnie. "Stale, Flat and Profitable," *Films in Review,* 2 (February 1951), 25-27 passim. Informal Survey of Hollywood Musicals.
1722. ADD: Vol. 19 (December 1950), 336; 19 (February 1951), 416.
1786. ADD: Stallings showed films made by the Calvin Co.; Phelps described his work for an Ohio State promotional film; Gould played some of his title music and commented on practical problems of working with musicians.
1813a. "MGM Musicals," *Life,* (14 April 1952), 116-18. Fred Astaire, Gene Kelly and the Champions.
1817. ADD: *Broken Arrow, Carrie.*

Sound Techniqes and Technology

1939a. Ryder, Loren L. "A New Method of Handling Sound for Foreign Releases," *American Cinematographer,* 33, No. 4 (April 1952), 158 passim.

1960's

History

1980a. Assayas, Oliver. "[SPFX News or Science Fiction Films as Reference Points]," *Cahiers du cinema,* (1980), 34-40. Sound effects and music.

2057a. Garel, Alain. "La musique de film," *La revue de cinema,* (November 1982), 133-36.

2057b. Garel, Alain. "La musique de 'Country and Western Music'," *La revue du cinema,* 368 (January 1982), 131-33; 369 (February 1982), 135-38.

2062a. Gross, M. "Anyway They Spell It, Shermans Make Music Universal Language," *Billboard,* 79 (11 November 1967), 22.

2071b. Hicks, Jimmie. *"Fantasia's Silver Anniversary,"* Films in Review, 16, No. 9 (November 1968), 529-35.

Sound Techniques and Technology

2204a. Ebel, Fred E. "That Old Regenerative Set of Mine," *Popular Electronics,* 28 (January 1968), 50-51. About film sound effects.

2204b. Kingery, R.A. "The Man Who Taught the Movies How to Speak," *Saturday Review,* 51 (6 April 1968) 56-58. About Joseph Tykocinski-Tykociner, researcher in sound engineering.

1970's

History

2261a. Britt, Stan. "EMI Sound Tracks," *Cassettes and Cartridges,* (July 1975), 138-40. Discography. [Unverified]

2273a. Byrd, Katherine and Allan Byrd. "The Quest for Organic Sound," *Stereo,* (Summer, 1974), 54-7. [Unverified]

2273b. Calum, P. "Musikken," *Kosmorama,* 23, No. 136 (1977), 253. Music in *New York, New York.*

2274a. Care, Ross. "Lisztomam," *Film Quarterly,* 31, No. 3 (1978), 55-61. [Unverified]
2276a. Champlin, Charles. "Don't Shoot the Piano Player," *The Ragtimer,* (March/April 1974), 15-16.
2328a. Cook, Page. "The Sound Track," *Films in Review,* 28 (January 1977), 44-46 passim.
2346a. Criscione, G. "[Estate-Romana-1979. A Roman Festival of Films, Plays, Dances and Music]," *Studi Romani,* 27, No. 4 (1979), 570-72.
2351a. Daney, Serge. "[Deemphasis of Sound in Film (5 Films at Nantes)]," *Cahiers du cinema,* 275 (1977), 63-64.
2367a. Ehrlich, Cindy. "Nagel on 'Exorcist': Doin' the Devil's Sound Effects," *Rolling Stone,* (28 February 1974), 16.
2428a. Hiemenz, Jack. "Play It Again Sam. And Again, And Again...," *Zoo World,* (28 March 1974), 18-19. [Unverified]
2435a. Jacobson, Robert and Irving Kolodin. "Weber and Wagner at the Lincoln Center Opera Festival," *Saturday Review,* 53 (August 1970), 35. Hamburg Opera's contribution to "Opera on Film" festival.
2440a. Jones, Robert T. "Movie Time at the Opera," *Time,* 96 (27 July 1970), 56. Report on festival of operatic films.
2486a. Marcus, Leonard. "Videotape and 'Dueling Banjos,'" *High Fidelity and Musical America,* 23, No. 6 (June 1973), 4.
2493a. Merigeau, J.L.C. and Pascal Merigeau. "Tabous, violence et mort: le grand rendez-vous," *Revue de cinema,* 371 (1982), 96-106. Taboos, violence and death main themes in rock films.
2504. ADD: Arnold Schoenberg's Musical Accompaniment to Imaginary Film.
2512a. "Opera on Film," *Opera News,* 35 (5 September 1970), 21. Weber's *Der Freischütz*
2512b. Osborne, Conrad L. "Song O' My Heart," *High Fidelity and Musical America,* 23, No. 2 (February 1973), 67-68.
2517a. Patterson, Richard. "Motion Picture Sound: A Long Way from the 'Ice Box,'" *American Cinematographer,* 52, No. 4 (April 1971), 320-23.

2537a. "Rolf Lieberman," *New Yorker,* 46 (29 August 1970), 21-22. Interview. His work on operatic films.
2541a. Schepele, Peter. "Ingmar Bergman og Musikken," *Kosmorama,* 24, No. 137 (1978), 44-6. Music in Bergman's films.
2546a. "The Score: the Writers in Profile," *BMI, the Many Worlds of Music,* 1 (1974), 31-32.
2557a. Smith, Chris. "Bluesing the Screen," *Blues-Link 4 Incorporating 'Blues World,'* (1974), 13-14. Film acknowledgements. [Unverified]
2557b. Smith, Richard Langham. "Debussy and the Art of the Cinema," *Music and Letters,* 54 (January 1973), 61-70.
2601a. Watts, Michael. "Dylan: The Film's a Loser," *Melody Maker,* (2 June 1973), 32-33.
2601b. Watts, Michael. "The Man Called 'Alias'," *Melody Maker,* (3 February 1973), 28-30.
2601c. Watts, Michael. "Michael Oldfield and Allan Jones. The Young Ones," *Melody Maker,* (31 August 1974), 27-31.
2604a. Wick, Ted. "Creating the Movie-Music Album," *High Fidelity and Musical America,* 26, No. 4 (April 1976), 68-71.

Sound Techniques and Technology

2629a. Bigbee, Lynn. "Basic Elements of Sound Recording," *Filmmakers Newsletter,* 3, No. 12 (October 1970), 36-42. Reprinted from "MPL Table Talk" No.3, a publication of Motion Picture Laboratories, Inc.
2633a. Fodor, J. "[Film Dubbing, Phonetic, Semiotic, Esthetic and Psychological Effects]," *Filmkritik,* 21, No. 3 (1977), 170.
2646a. Oldfield, Michael. "Fun! Fun! Fun!" *Melody Maker,* (20 April 1974), 28.
2649a. Purchese, John. "Recording Sound for 'Song of Norway'," *American Cinematographer,* 52, No. 4 (April 1971), 324-27 passim.

1980's

History

2707a. Abdrashitov, A. "Music and Cinema," *Soviet Film,* 1 (1983), 15. Konstantin Lopushansky.

2715a. Anderson, Lindsay. "This Sporting Life." *Tempo: A Quarterly Review of Modern Music,* 139 (December 1981), 33-34. Analysis of Roberto Gerhard's composition of musical score for film.

2746a. Chion, Michel. "Entretien avec Jean Neny. Le regard du mixeur," *Cahiers du cinema,* 340 (October 1982), x-xi. The view of the films sound mixer.

2746b. Chion, Michel. "Entretien avec Marie-Josephe Yoyotte. Le sens de l'ellipse," *Cahiers du cinema,* 341 (November 1982), x, xii. Sound mixing in films direct or not direct.

2746c. Chion, Michel. "Filmer la musique. Ou ca se passe?" *Cahiers du cinema,* 332 (February 1982), xi. Filming a musical performance (Glenn Gould).

2746d. Chion, Michel. "Lumiere avec son," *Cahiers du cinema,* 338 (July-August 1982), xi. Film sound editing.

2746e. Chion, Michel. "Les Maillons les Plus Faibles," *Cahiers du cinema,* 333 (March 1982), xii. Film soundtracks (The technicians).

2746f. Chion, Michel. "[Silence as a metaphor in sound films]," *Cahiers du cinema,* 330 (1981), 5-15.

2746g. Chion, Michel. "[The current status of sound-mixing technology–neglect and fetishism]," *Cahiers du cinema,* 330 (1981), ix-x.

2783a. Davies, H. "Electronic Music (Gerhard, Roberto Adaptation of Music Techniques for Theater, Radio and Film)," *Tempo,* 139 (December 1981), 35-38.

2899a. Garel, Alain. "Musique de films," *La revue de cinema,* 378 (1982), 123-25. Film scores and original soundtracks.

2820a. Ivanava, S. "Music Silhouettes in the Cinema," *Obzor–A Bulgarian Quarterly Review of Literature and Arts,* 58 (1982), 90-93.

2826a. Kennedy, Evelyn. "Film Music Editor," *Music Educators Journal,* 69, No. 2 (October 1982), 54. Career opportunities.

2840a. Levine, Steven A. "Structures of Sound Image in *The Rules of the Game,* (Renoir)," *Quarterly Review of Film Studies,* 7, No. 3 (1982), 210.

2845a. McCarthy, Todd. "Schmidt's Score Doesn't Score in L.A. Reconstruct of Dreyer's Arc," *Variety,* (1 June 1983), 4, 76.

2847a. "The Men Who Made Music," *Variety,* 303 (1 July 1981), 54.

2864a. Perle, George. "Das Film-Zwischenspiel in Bergs *Lulu,*" *Oesterreichische Musik Zeitschrift,* 36, No. 12 (December 1981), 631-38.

2895a. "La Traviata de Franco Zeffirelli," *Cahiers du cinema,* 346 (May 1982), 66.

2896. ADD: On the music of John Williams for *E.T.* and of Jerry Goldsmith for *Poltergeist* and other films.

2899a. Verniere, James D. "Franco Zeffirelli Discusses 'La Traviata' and Opera on Film," *Ovation,* (July 1983), 8-11.

2901a. "Voix inouies?" *Cahiers du cinema,* 343 (January 1983), xiii. Unheard voices. Computerized voices in films.

II. COMPOSERS

George Antheil

2983a. Sternfeld, Frederick W. *"Specter of the Rose,* An Analysis with Musical Excerpts," *Film Music Notes,* 6, No. 1 (September-October 1946), 7-14.

John Barry

3021a. "Aboard the Bandwagon," *Time,* 87 (14 January 66), 62 passim.

Elmer Bernstein

3052a. Bernstein, Elmer. "The DeMille Legend," Chapter IV in Gabe Essoe and Raymond Lee. *DeMille: The Man and His*

Pictures. New York: A.S. Barnes, 1970, p. 277-82. Reprinted from *The Los Angeles Times,* 1966.

3052b. Bernstein, Elmer. *Elmer Bernstein: An American Film Institute Seminar on his Work.* Glen Rock, New Jersey: Microfilming Corp. of America, 1977. [No. 16 in the series entitled The American Film Institute Seminars and Dialogues.] [See 197a (Seminars 16)].

3060b. Brown, Royal. " 'To Kill a Mockingbird': Original Film Score," *High Fidelity and Musical America,* 27 (April 1977), 119.

3075a. Salmi, Markku. "Elmer Bernstein," *Film Dope,* 3 (August 1973), 37-38.

See also: 2328a (Cook)

Joseph Carl Breil

3100a. Allen, Clyde. Notes for recording, *The Birth of a Nation* Label X, LXDR-701-2, 1986.

3102a. "Joseph Carl Breil Passes Away," *Musical America,* 43, No. 15 (January 30, 1926), 39.

See also: 720 (Marks)

Charlie Chaplin

3127f. "Charlie Chaplin and Talkies," *Review of Reviews,* 86 (August 1932), 49-50. Reprint of *La revue mondiale,* article by Rene Fonjallaz suggesting superiority of silents over talkies.

3127g. "Charlie Chaplin and Talking Pictures," *Theater Arts,* 14 (November 1930), 908. Speculates on whether *City Lights* will use sound.

3134a. Mass, Robert F. *Charlie Chaplin.* New York, Pyramid, 1975.

3138b. Schepelern, P. "Chaplin 4: Som Komponist," *Kosmorama,* 19 (August 1973), 261-2.

See also: 576a (Good word)

Aaron Copland

3144a. "[Aaron Copland concerning his score for *North Star*]," *Film Music Notes*, 3, No. 3 (December 1943), 10-11.

3144b. Badder, D.J. "Aaron Copland," *Film Dope*, 8 (October 1975), 7-9.

3146a. Cochran, Alfred W. "Style, Structure and Tonal Organization in the Early Film Music of Aaron Copland," Ph.D., Catholic University of America, 1986.

3156a. London, Kurt. "Film Music of the Quarter," *Films*, 1, No. 1 (November 1939), 76-80.

3157a. Morton, Lawrence: *"The Red Pony,"* Hollywood Quarterly, 3, No. 4 (1948-49), 395-402.

3161a. Rolandadams, G. "Copland *Appalachian Spring* (original version), *Music for Movies* ARGO 2RG-935," *Strad*, 93 (1982), 43.

3163. CORRECT: *Musical Quarterly*, 37, No. 2 [Not 7, No. 2].

See also: 3743a (Raksin), 4035a (Thomson)

Adolph Deutsch

3188a. Deutsch, Adolph. "The Composer: Forgotten Man of the Movies," *Musical America*, 66 (June 1946), 5, 38.

Brian Easdale

3203. ADD: Another Edition. *The Red Shoes Ballet; The Tales of Hoffmann*. New York, Garland Pub., 1977.

Hugo Friedhofer

3269. Atkins, Irene Kahn. ADD: Microfil's version 197a (Part 1, #7)

3270a. "Biography of Hugo Friedhofer, Excerpts from *The Bandit of Sherwood*," *Film Music Notes*, 5, No. 9 (May 1946), 36-40.

3279. ADD: *New York Times*, 130, p. 21(N), A26 (LC) (20 May 1981); *Skoop*, 17 (July 1981), p. 5; Obituaries.

3279a. Koldys, Mark. "Friedhofer: *The Young Lions*," *American Record Guide*, 46 (May 1983), 76.

3286a. "Theater and Film: 'Best Years of Our Lives': Original Film Score By Hugo Friedhofer," *High Fidelity and Musical America,* 29 (November 1979), 29.

See also: 82 (Huntley/Manvell), 104 (Prendergast), 197a (Part 1, #7).

Jerry Goldsmith

3298a. *Alien* (Soundtrack reviews) *American Record Guide,* 42 (September 1979), 54; *Audio,* 63 (November 1979), 134; *Christian Science Monitor,* 71 (18 June 1979), 18; *Consumer Reports,* 45 (February 1980), 131; *High Fidelity,* 29 (October 1979), 124; *Pro Musica Sana,* 8, No. 1 (Winter 1979-80), 9; *Stereo Review,* 43 (August 1979), 106.
3298b. Anobile, Richard. *Alien.* New York, Avon, 1979.
3300a. Bryce, Allan. "Jerry Goldsmith on 'Star Sound'" *SCN Soundtrack Collector's Newsletter,* 4, No. 18 (July 1979), 23.
3300b. Caps, John. "The Ascent of Jerry Goldsmith," *SCN Soundtrack Collectors Newsletter,* 5, No. 19 (October 1979), 3-8; No. 20 (January 1980), 3-8.
3306a. Cook, Page. "The Sound Track," *Films in Review,* 27 (October 1976), 495-99.
3312a. Feather, Leonard. "From Pen to Screen–Jerry Goldsmith," *International Musician,* 69, No. 6 (December 1970), 4.
3316-18. ADD: See 197a (Seminars #66).
3320a. Harrington, Richard. "Goldsmith Goes for It," *Washington Post,* 106 (12 April 1983), D7.
3323a. Quigley, Michael. "Alien," *SCN Soundtrack Collector's Newsletter,* 5, No. 19 (October 1979), 20-21.
3324a. Scanlon, Paul and Michael Gross. *The Book of Alien.* New York, Simon and Schuster, 1979.
3324b. Serrin, William. "The Tired Man, a Vanishing American," *New York Times,* 128 (4 August 1979), 6.
3328a. Williams, J. "Business File: Jerry Goldsmith Calls the Tune," *Films Illustrated,* 5 (February 1976), 218.
3328b. Wright, John. "Jerry Goldsmith Lecture," *SCN Soundtrack Collector's Newsletter,* 4, No. 7 (April 1979), 3-7.

See also: 136 (Van de Ven), 197a (Seminars #66), 2896 (Vallerand).

John Green

See also: 190a (Steen).

Leigh Harline

3349a. Prado, Sharon S. "Leigh Harline's *Pinocchio:* A Consideration of Music for Films," (Master's Thesis, Division of Graduate Studies College-Conservatory of Music, University of Cincinnati, 1984). This is a fine work which contains an inventory of the Harline Collection at U. of Cincinnati.

See also: 1400a (Martin).

Bernard Herrmann

3359a. "Bernard Herrmann." *New York Times,* 125 (26 December 1975), 34. Obituary.

3359b. *The Bernard Herrmann Society Journal* (August 1981) passim. San Diego (Kevin Fahey, 5523 Denny Ave., N. Hollywood, Calif. 61601).

3363a. Brown, Royal. "A Film-Music Milestone from Bernard Herrmann," *High Fidelity and Musical America,* 24 (October 1974), 122.

3366a. Brown, Royal. "The Mysterious Film World of Bernard Herrmann," *High Fidelity and Musical America* 25 (December 1975), 120-21.

3368a. "'Citizen Kane' Classic Film Scores of Bernard Herrmann," *High Fidelity and Musical America,* 25 (January 1975), 104.

3384. ADD: No. 228/9 and 234 (March/June 1976) and (November 1976), 18-19, 26-27.

3388a. Harris, Steve. "An Afternoon with Bernard Herrmann," *The Bernard Herrmann Society Journal,* 5-6 (Fall 1982), 16 passim.

3397a. Kinkaid, F. "Herrmann *Wuthering Heights,*" *Opera News,* 47 (1983), 43. Music performance review.

3398a. Krasnoborski, W.F. "Mrs. Muir and Mr. Bernstein," *SCN Soundtrack Collector's Newsletter,* 5, Reprinted in 136 (Van de Ven), p. 7-11.

3403a. Murphy, A.D. "Bernard Herrmann, 64, dies," *Variety,* 281 (31 December 1975), 6.
3419a. Vallerand, F. "Musique de films," *Sequences,* 104 (April 1981), 61-62.
3421a. Zandor, Leslie. "Movie Music's Man of the Moment," *Coast FM and Fine Arts,* (July 1971), 30.

See also: 90 (O'Toole), 104 (Prendergast), 136 (Van de Ven), 173a (Leyda, p. 198-9), 301a (Taylor), 312a (Weis), 2252 (Bernstein), 2329 (Cook), 4953 (Watts).

Maurice Jarre

3454a. "Three Screen Composers: Maurice Jarre, Dimitri Tiomkin and Henry Mancini," *Cinema,* (Los Angeles) 3, No. 3 (July 1966), 8-10 passim. Interview.

Bronislau Kaper

3478. Atkins, Irene Kahn. See 197a. (Part 1, #13). See also: 136 (Van de Ven).

Erich Wolfgang Korngold

3497a. Arvey, Verney. "Composing for the Pictures. An Interview with Erich Wolfgang Korngold," *The Etude,* 55, No. 1 (January 1937), 15-16.
3517a. Miller, Frank. "Evaluation of the cello in *Deception,*" *Film Music Notes,* 6, No. 2 (November 1946), 7-9.

See also: 1248a (Currie).

Henry Mancini

3549a. Feather, Leonard. "From Pen to Screen," *International Musician,* 69, No. 4 (October 1970), 7.
3557-8. See 197a (Seminars #118 and 199).
3560a. "Never Too Much Music," *Time,* 79 (25 May 1962), 70 passim. Henry Mancini and *Moon River.*

3560b. Paisley, Rom. "Henry Mancini–Doin' It Right," *ASCAP Today*, 9, No. 1 (Spring 1978), 6-10.

See also: 104 (Prendergast), 136 (Van de Ven), 197a (Seminars 118, 199). 2847a (The Man who . . .), 3454a (Three screen composers).

Mario Nascimbene

See also: 136 (Van de Ven).

Alex North

3659a. *Cleopatra*. New York: National Publishers, Inc., 1963.
3662a. "Film Music By Alex North," *High Fidelity and Musical America*, 28 (February 1978), 102.

See also: 104 (Prendergast).

David Raksin

3734a. Morton, Lawrence. "David Raksin's Score for *Forever Amber*," *Film Music Notes*, 7, No. 2 (November-December 1947).
3737a. Pechter, William. "Abraham Polonsky and *Force of Evil*," *Film Quarterly*, 15, No. 3 (1962).
3743a. Raskin, David. "A Note for Aaron Copland," *Perspectives in New Music*, 19 (1981), 47.
3745a. Raksin, David. "Notes on *The Bad and the Beautiful*," *Film Music*, 12, No.4 (1953), 14.

Alan Rawsthorne

3753. ADD: A critical analysis of *Ivory Hunter* (alt. title in England: *Where No Vultures Fly*).

Hugo Riesenfeld

3757a. Buhrman, T. Scott. "Photoplays DeLuxe," *The American Organist*, 3, No. 5 (1920), 157-75. Illus.

3758a. Herzog, Dorothea B. "Smiling his Way to the Goal of Ambition," *National Brain Power Monthly,* (November 1922), 24. Illus.
3762a. Riesenfeld, Hugo. "Music and the Movies," *The Violinist,* 35, No. 6 (December 1924), 211.
3762b. Riesenfeld, Hugo. "Musical Classics for Millions," in Cooke, James Francis, *Great Musicians on the Art of Music.* Philadelphia, Theo. Presser Co., 1925, p. 408-13.
3762a. van Broeckhoven, J. "Hugo Riesenfeld, Concertmaster, Composer, and Director of the Rivoli, Rialto and Criterion Theatres, New York City," *Musical Observer,* 19, No. 5 (May 1920), 18, 28.
3764. ADD: vol. 94, no. 7 (17 February 1927), 48-49.

See also: 602 (Hall)

Ann Ronell

3770a. Spaeth, Sigmund. "Ann Ronell, George Gershwin and Richard Rodgers," *Film Music Notes,* 5, No. 1 (September 1945), [17].

Leonard Rosenman

See also: 177a (McBride, p. 114-19)

Miklos Rozsa

3811a. Brown, Royal. "Spellbound: Classic Film Scores of Miklos Rozsa," *High Fidelity and Musical America,* 25 (July 1975), 97-98.
3811b. Brown, Royal. "Theater and Film," *High Fidelity and Musical America,* 26 (October 1976), 140-41.
3835a. Evans, Colin. "Overtones of Hollywood," *Times Educational Supplement,* 3071(4 April 1975), 103.
3841a. "Happy 70th Birthday to Miklos Rozsa," *Film Music Notebook,* 2, No. 4 (1976), 3-5.
3858. CHANGE: *Film Music* to *Film Music Notes.*
3865. Reviewed in *Music and Letters,* 58, No. 1 (1977), 103-104.

3872a. *Pro Musica Sana* (Miklos Rozsa Society Journal).

3885a. Rozsa, Miklos. "An Outline of University Training for Musicians in Motion Picture Work," *Film Music Notes,* 5, No. 2 (October 1945), 25-29.

3885b. Rozsa, Miklos. "Scoring the *Jungle Book*," *Film Music Notes,* 1, No. 7 (April 1942), 4.

3891a. Smith, Bethia. "Review of *The Strange Loves of Martha Ivers*," *Film Music Notes,* 6, No. 2 (November 1946), 10-11.

3893a. *The Story of Ben Hur.* New York: Random House, 1959.

3893b. Vallance, Tom. "Soundtrack: Classic Waxman and Rozsa: Vintage Garland," Film, 26 (May 1975), 10.

See also: 104 (Prendergast), 1248a (Currie), 173a (Leyda, p. 409-410), 3419 (Vallance).

Philippe Sarde

See also: 136 (Van de Ven).

Max Steiner

3971a. Maffett, James D. "*Casablanca:* The Classic Film Score for Humphrey Bogart," *Stereo Guide* (Christmas, 1974), 74-6. [Unverified]

3990a. Max Steiner, interviewed in *The Real Tinsel,* edited by Bernard Rosenberg and Harry Silverstein. New York: Macmillan, 1970, p. 392-93.

Virgil Thomson

4035b. Thomson, Virgil. *American Music Since 1910.* London, Weidenfeld and Nicolson, 1971.

Dimitri Tiomkin

4073a. Tiomkin, Dimitri. "A New Field for Composers," *Musical Observer,* 20, No. 7 (July 1930), 5, 16.

See also: 3454a (Three screen composers).

Franz Waxman

4130a. Cleave, Alan. "Record Review: *Sunset Boulevard:* the Classic Film Scores of Franz Waxman," *Movie Maker,* 9 (August 1975), 547.

4134a. Hart, Elsepth. "Peyton Place," *Films in Review,* 9, No. 1 (January 1958), 26-28.

4136a. "Interview with Franz Waxman," *Film Music Notes,* 3, No. 6 (March 1944), 5.

4141b. "'Sunset Boulevard': Classics Film Scores of Franz Waxman," *High Fidelity and Musical America,* 25 (April 1975), 102-103.

4141 c. Waxman, Franz. "The New Music of Motion Pictures," *Film Music Notes,* 5, No. 1 (September 1945), [27-29].

See also: 3893b (Vallance).

John Williams

4187a. Caps, John. "[John Williams]," *Soundtrack! The Collector's Quarterly,* 3 (September 1984), 22-23.

4190a. Colon, C. "El sinfonismo como lenguaje historico de la musica cinetomatografica," *Casablanca,* 30 (June 1983), 18-21. Discusses the importance of John Williams and his contribution to symphonic scores in contemporary film.

4193a. Doherty, J. "Out of This World," *Soundtrack! The Collector's Quarterly,* 2 (December 1983), 28.

4198a. Lehti, S.J. "In the Valley of the Sequels," *Soundtrack! The Collector's Quarterly,* 3, No. 11 (September 1984), 16-20. Discusses the scores of John Williams, James Horner and Basil Poledouris for three recent sequels.

4198b. Libbey, T.W., Jr. "Disks Attest to the Versatile Talents of John Williams," *New York Times,* 132 (27 February 1983, sec. 2), 21-22.

4202a. Pugliese, Roberto. "John Williams, L'Extraterrestre," *Segnocinema,* 8 (May 1983), 30-32.

4204a. Raynes, D. "Star Tracks," *Soundtrack! The Collector's Quarterly,* 3 (December 1984), 21.

See also: 136 (van de Ven), 2896 (Vallerand).

Roy Webb

See also: 1248a (Currie).

Victor Young

4213a. Ayotte, Jeannine M. "The Victor Young Collection in the Music Department of the Boston Public Library," Typescript. Boston Public Library, 1982. Card Index for Collection.
4215a. "Doedsbud," *Orchester Journalen,* 24 (December 1956), p. 21.
4217a. "Music Figures Fall Before Grim Reaper," *Billboard,* 68 (24 November 1956), 15 passim.
4217b. Obituary. *Musical America,* 76 (1 December 1956), 33; *Newsweek,* 48 (19 November 1956), 89; *Time,* 68 (19 November 1956), 94; *Variety,* 204 (14 November 1956), 79.
4218a. "Victor Young Dead at 56," *Down Beat,* 33 (12 December 1956), 10.
4218b. "Victor Young Dies," *Melody Maker,* 31 (17 November 1956), 4.
4221a. Victor Young Collection at Brandeis University (movie short scores, Oscar for *Around the World in 80 Days,* recordings). Typescript Finding Aid. The Victor Young Collection was originally donated to Brandeis. Then a part of it was transferred to the Boston Public Library. Although only printed sheet music was supposed to be transferred, in fact, recordings and movie scores also were transferred. Thus, the score for *Around the World in 80 Days* is not at Brandeis but at the Boston Public Library.

See also: 1795 (Lewin, *Around the World in 80 Days*).

Additional Composer Profiles

4222a. Atkins, Irene Kahn. Interview with Harry Warren. Hollywood Song Writer. *The American Film Institute/Louis B.*

Mayer Oral History Collection, Part I, #4. [New York Times Oral History Program] Glenn Rock, New Jersey: Microfilming Corp. of American, 1977.
4223. ADD: See 197a (Part I, #9).
4273a. Tynan, John. "The Sherman Brothers," *BMI, The Many Worlds of Music,* 5 (1972), 28-29.

III. AESTHETICS

SILENT AND EARLY SOUND ERA

4329a. Fuerst, Leonhard. "Grundfragen des Films," *Melos,* 13, No. 4 (April 1934), 132-35.
4331a. Fuerst, Leonhard. "Ueber die Grundlichen der Filmwissenschaft," *Die Musik,* 26, No. 4 (January 1934), 254-58.
4337a. Gutman, Hanns. "Aussichten des Tonfilm," *Die Musik,* 21, No. 2 (November 1928), 123-25.

SOUND ERA

Form and Function: Aural/Visual Relationships in Film Art

4823. ADD: See 197a (Seminars, #137).

Sociology and Culture: The Impact of Industry and Art

5074. ADD: UM69-1108. DA XXIX/8 p. 2809-10-A (Sociology).
5104. ADD: UM71-2227; DA XXXI/11 p. 6210-A (Theater)
5239. ADD: Another edition *The Red Shoes; The Tales of Hoffman.* New York: Garland Pub., 1977.

IV. SPECIAL TOPICS

MUSICAL PERFORMANCE ON FILM

1950's

5262. ADD: Some analysis of Gance's *Louise* (1939), Menotti's *The Medium* (1951), Powell and Pressburger's *Tales of Hoffman* (1951).
5285a. "Opera Season To Taste," *Harper's*, 210 (January 1955), 87. Differences between Italian and American treatments of opera on film.

1960's

5331a. Fry, Annette. "Opera on Main Street," *Opera News*, 26 (31 March 1962), 8-13. A "Grand Opera Film Festival" series for local theaters.
5757. ADD: Another edition. Flint, Michigan: National Opera Association, 1973.

MUSICAL PERFORMANCE ON TELEVISION

1980's

5844a. Bauer, Gerd. "Unterhaltungsmusik im Fernsehen," *Musica*, 34, No. 1 (January-February 1980), 21-24.

FILM MUSICALS

5892a. Applebaum, Stanley. *The Hollywood Musical.* New York: Dover Publications, 1974.
Bach, Steven. See 1981.
5892b. Baker, Peter. "Tough Guys Set a New Pattern," *Films and Filming*, 2, No. 4 (January 1956), 15. Serious dramatic material has changed the movie musical.

5899a. "Big Season for Musicals: *Jumbo, Gypsy,* and *Bye Bye Birdie,*" *Look,* 26 (14 August 1962), 38-39 passim.
5926a. Chion, Michel. "La comedie musical. Unamour pudique," *Cahiers du cinema,* 331 (January 1982), x. Review Alain Masson: La Comedie Musicale, Editions Stock.
Crichton, Kyle. See 1247a.
5946a. Cutts, John. "On the Bright Side," *Films and Filming,* 16, No. 11 (August 1970), 17-18. Illus. Interview with Charles Walters. Musicals generally. Walters dance director.
5953a. Dietz, Howard. "The Musical Band Wagon Keeps on Rollin' Along," *Look,* 17, No. 16 (11 August 1953), 93-95. History of the Hollywood musical, esp. *The Band Wagon.*
5958a. "Elephant's Eye," *New Yorker,* 31 (10 September 1955), 33-35. Interchange of discussion about set designing for *Oklahoma!* and publicity for *Guys and Dolls.*
Graham, Ronnie. See 1687a.
6003. ADD: Reviewed by T. Manns in Filmrutan, 24, No. 4 (1981), 40.
6040a. Lee, Edward. *Jeanette MacDonald.* New York: Jove Publications, 1977.
6010. ADD: 14 (November-December 1957), 16-19; 15 (January-February 1958), 17-18.
6010a. Hudson, Peggy and Roy Hemming. "The Lively Arts," *Senior Scholastic,* 91 (28 September 1967), 42-43. On the Kraft Music Hall special *The Hollywood Musical.*
6027a. Kimball, Robert. "Those Glorious MGM Musicals," *Stereo Review,* 33, No. 9 (September 1974), 98-99.
6052a. Mahieu, Jose Agustin. "El cine musical," *Cuadernos Hispano Americanos,* 379 (January 1982), 119-30. The musicals (representations in the cinema).
MGM Musicals. See 1813a.
Paul, E. See 1464a.
6085a. Peck, Seymour. "Again the Movies Sing and Dance," *New York Times Magazine,* (1 July 1961), 16-17. Production stills from recent musicals.
6094a. Rickey, Carrie. "Let Yourself Go," *Film Comment,* 18, No. 2 (1982), 43-47. The musical as experimental film genre and three musicals sing one from the libido.

6094b. Ringgold, Gene. *Chevalier.* Secaucus, New Jersey: Citadel, 1973.
6095a. Ronan, Margaret. "The Lively Arts," *Senior Scholastic,* 94 (7 February 1969), 16 passim. A quick history of film musicals.
6109a. Silke, James. "Mary Poppins," *Cinema,* 2, No. 4 (December-January 1964-65), 48.
6117a. "Song and Dance," *Sight and Sound,* 24 (October-December 1954), 95-100. Photo section on American and British musicals.
6126a. Sutton, Martin. *The Hollywood Musical Film.* M.A. Thesis. Exeter University, 1976.
6133a. Thompson, Thomas. "Tuning U.S. Musicals to Overseas Box Office," *Life,* 58 (12 March 1965), 55 passim.
Tindall, Glenn. See 1523a.
6143a. Vallence, Tom. "Soundtrack," *Film,* 49 (Autumn 1967), 35-37. Return of the film musical.
6145. ADD: *Singin' in the Rain, An American in Paris, Guys and Dolls,* etc., represent decline from *On the Town.*
6148a. Warner, Alan. "Busby Berkeley: Dream Maker," *Cassettes and Cartridges,* (March 1974), 556, 558. [Unverified] See also: 190a (Steen), 1247a (Crichton), 3770a (Spaeth).

GUIDES TO PRIMARY SOURCES

6198a. Anderson, Gillian B. *Silent Film Music* (1894-1929): *A Guide.* D.C., Library of Congress, 1987.

FILMOGRAPHIES

6265. ADD: Reviewed *FIN,* 11 (1) (1978), 87-88.
6269. ADD: Reviewed in *American Music,* 3, No. 3 (Fall, 1985), 354-55.
6273a. "Walt Disney Presents," *Film Dope,* 12 (June 1977), 2-29.

DISCOGRAPHIES

6273a. Affelder, P. "Sound-Track Favorites on Discs," *Cosmopolitan,* 141 (October 1956), 6. A list of popular, semiclas-

sical, classical musicals; special emphasis on *Pinocchio, Moby Dick,* and *Trapeze.*
6281a. "Magical Music of Walt Disney: Fifty Years of Original Motion Picture Soundtracks," *High Fidelity and Musical America,* 29 (March 1979), 130.
6340. ADD: Reviewed in *Filmkritik,* 21, No. 3 (1977), 169.

General Principles of Bibliographic Instruction

Evan Farber

SUMMARY. Bibliographic instruction, teaching the use of the library, has only recently been given attention in library schools. There are still not many library schools that offer separate courses in bibliographic instruction. The position of bibliographic instruction within the library is new, as the discipline itself was only relatively recently recognized among professional circles. Bibliographic instruction builds confidence and efficiency in the use of the library, makes class assignments more profitable, and helps to free time for librarians while making demands on the library's resources.

Bibliographic instruction, which is not really a very happy phrase, is simply teaching the use of the library. Instruction in library use is the phrase that is used in library literature. It is nothing new, although one might infer that it is from certain bits of evidence if you look through the library literature and the history of libraries. Only recently, really, has it been given any attention in library schools. There are still not very many library schools that offer separate courses in bibliographic instruction; indeed there are a fair number of library schools that hardly pay any attention to it at all, even in courses dealing with reference sources and bibliography.

The position of a bibliographic instruction librarian is relatively

---

Evan Farber is affiliated with the Lilly Library at Erlham College.

[Haworth co-indexing entry note]: "General Principles of Biliographic Instruction." Farber, Evan. Co-published simultaneously in *Music Reference Services Quarterly*, (The Haworth Press, Inc.) Vol. 2, No. 1/2, 1993, pp. 145-151; and: *Foundations in Music Bibliography* (ed: Richard D. Green) The Haworth Press, Inc., 1993, pp. 145-151. Multiple copies of this article/chapter may be purchased from The Haworth Document Delivery Center [1-800-3-HAWORTH; 9:00 a.m. - 5:00 p.m. (EST)].

new. That is, the person on the staff–university or college library staff–whose primary responsibility is for supervising or carrying out the program of bibliographic instruction. As a matter of fact, to check my own perceptions, I went back to the *College and Research Library News* fifteen years ago, 1971, and looked through a whole year, and found only one mention of bibliographic instruction at all, among all the advertisements for reference librarians, bibliographers, and so forth. Its recognition by associations is also relatively recent. The bibliographic instruction section, which is now I think perhaps the largest section within the Association of College and Research Libraries, was established only in 1979 after some struggle. Before then there was little or no prominence given to bibliographic instruction at meetings, say at the Association of College and Research Libraries, and probably not at the other special library groups, such as the Music Library Association, Art Library Association, and so forth.

If you want a history of it and there are several, especially a new book by Larry Hardesty, John Schmitt and John Tucker called *User Instruction in Academic Libraries: A Century of Selected Readings*. It goes back into the 19th century and shows what people were doing then to teach the use of the library to undergraduates. Despite this history that goes back more than a hundred years, it was not until the 1960's that the current approach to bibliographic instruction got started, when there were many events, individuals and organizations that contributed to the movement. But it seems to me that although one must acknowledge the importance of these individuals, the events and trends–all of those that shaped the environment–they really created external circumstances, circumstances external to libraries, that produced the context which made biblio- graphic instruction possible. There was, first of all, the enormous expansion of education in the 1950's and, of course, the expansion of libraries during that time. There was the growth of collections and, at the same time the increasing complexity of libraries; and because of the growth, libraries became much more difficult, much more overwhelming.

At the same time there was a proliferation of bibliographic tools– tools that were created in the 1950's and the 1960's, none of which had existed before. There was a whole movement of educational reform–a movement toward independent study and an emphasis on research. There was a new generation of librarians, post-war librarians, educated in the post-war era who were just coming into positions as directors, heads of reference, all those kinds of activities. And then, of course, there was the movement throughout society, a movement for change that affected education as well. Finally, there was the movement in the late 1960's and the 1970's, the slowing-down of growth, the emphasis on library use rather than library buildings. This period emphasized improving services and making sure that collections were used rather than just built. In any case, bibliographic instruction grew quite rapidly, and though there are still more than just a few pockets of resistance, one certainly can say that bibliographic instruction is generally accepted in the academic librarianships. And it is still growing and developing.

Four and a half years ago, I gave a talk to the Music Library Association meeting at Santa Monica and I began by noting that bibliographic instruction was not very common in music libraries. That has changed. Not only does the literature reflect this change, but so also does the present conference, the representation on this stage, and this group of people. We are now concerned about bibliographic instruction for undergraduates, graduates, for performers, large and small institutions and a variety of approaches.

Why all this activity? Why Bibliographic instruction? Why is it needed? In libraries, where we have all kinds of things to do, why should we focus on this? Let me talk about undergraduates, for several reasons. First, they are the largest group, I think, with which most of you are concerned. Secondly, I am more familiar with that group. Thirdly, I think it is easier to make a case for undergraduates, although some of what I'm going to say about undergraduates is also appropriate for graduates, professionals, advanced students of different kinds. So, what is the case for undergraduates? Why are we so emphatic about teaching students how to use libraries? First of all, many, perhaps most, undergraduates do not especially like libraries or librarians. Now, part of that is based on stereotypes, on unfortunate high school experiences. Some of it is based on feelings of inadequacy. Some of you may have read in *College and Research Libraries* earlier this year the article on library anxiety. This was an article written by a librarian who had been a reference librarian at, I think, East Tennessee State, a fairly large state institution in which they asked freshmen to keep journals of their library experiences, their feelings and libraries. I will quote from the article:

> It was found that 75 to 80 percent of students in each class described their initial response to the library in terms of fear or anxiety. Terms like 'scary,' 'overpowering,' 'lost,' 'helpless,' 'confused,' and 'fear of the unknown' appear over and over again. A description from the journal of a freshman is typical of the feelings expressed by these students. 'Using the library's a scary prospect, especially when I think about in-depth research. I know that research can not be done without frequent visits to the library, and I know that nothing in here will hurt me, but it all seems so vast and overpowering.'

I wonder how much different that is from advanced students who have not really been trained to use the library. Music students may be different, as are most graduate students. But the point is, however, that when one feels helpless, one feels anxious–unfamiliar, not in control–and when students do not enjoy using the library they avoid it. So that is my first reason why instruction is important because students really do not use libraries, and do not like to use libraries.

The second thing is that even students who like to use libraries do not use it well. Sure, they know the *Readers' Guide* and the card catalog, but that is about all they know. And this is a case where a little knowledge is a dangerous thing, because they come into your college library and they see the card catalog or *Readers' Guide* and say, "Oh, I've got it made. That's all I need." This is what they have been taught in high school. It is worse than no knowledge. I often feel I would much rather have foreign students in my bibliographic instruction courses who know nothing about American libraries. They are much more eager, much more receptive to learn about American libraries than a good high school graduate who thinks he or she knows it all. That is probably true of graduate students, too, who they think they know a lot more about using libraries than they really do.

Thirdly, assignments do not demand effective use of the library. Most faculty members, and here again keep in mind I am talking about undergraduates, do not think about teaching students how to use the library in devising assignments. They think about the objectives of the particular discipline but not about ways of finding information in that discipline.

Fourthly, the teaching faculties and librarians do not always work together. Library assignments that are made by teaching faculty are often unrealistic or unreasonable, or both. Those are some of the negative factors that lead to the dissatisfactions. There is clearly a need for doing something about it.

Let me make a positive case for bibliographic instruction, and what I am going to be talking about is primarily course-related or course-integrated bibliographic instruction. From the student's point of view, why is it useful? Why is it helpful? What are the positive reasons? The answer is, because it permits them to be more efficient, to save time. As I tell our students: there is nothing that I show them that they could not find for themselves, sooner or later. But it might take them years to do it. They could go through every page in the library, page by page, and find the information, but there are ways of doing this a lot faster. I want them to save time and, secondly, to be more effective, to get more effective information, better information, more valid information. A good bibliographic instruction program helps students learn to evaluate sources to get to the best materials so that the students can do better work, and so that they can enjoy their research. They can discover the satisfactions of finding that elusive fact, or that gem of some obscure article that is going to be a key to whatever they're working on. This is an enormously satisfying thing. It teaches them how to act like their faculty model, to be a junior researcher, if you will.

What are the advantages for the teacher? Students become more independent, more interesting and rewarding to teach. In our program, which is a very long-term program and very well-developed, students in our senior seminar can perform on the same level as graduate students in most institutions. Most faculty members would say this simply because they have been trained to use the library independently, and to use sources well. It makes the job of the teacher a much happier one, a much more rewarding one.

From the librarian's point of view, bibliographic instruction is important. It increases use of the library and this is, from an administrator's point of view, essential. How does one justify buying all this material? I sometimes tell the story that when I first came to

Earlham as director of the libraries many years ago I made a plea in a faculty meeting for increasing the library budget to buy back-files of periodicals which were very spotty. The faculty member said, "Why do you need that? Why do you need those files of periodicals; the ones we have now aren't being used?" I was stunned because I knew that those back-files of periodicals are important. As a serials librarian, there was nothing so pleasurable as getting volume 16, number 3 and filling in that back-file. I knew they were important, this faculty member knew they were important. But why were the students not using them? Well, they were not using them because they did not know the indexes, the bibliographies, the abstracting services to get to those things.

That made me begin thinking. Why are they not using them, and how do we get them to use them? And so, essentially, it was just out of a self-cynical, pragmatic need that bibliographic instruction was used to justify funds for the library. Bibliographic instruction creates a greater demand for the library's resources, and it makes better use of librarians. Students feel more comfortable with librarians who have talked to them about ways of finding information, much more at ease in asking questions, and they ask better questions. Individual reference help is great and it is important, but it is also expensive; and why should a trained reference librarian have to answer questions like how do you use the *Music Index*. Why shouldn't the student learn that in class and then ask the reference librarian much more sophisticated questions that really make use of the librarian's training? So bibliographic instruction can take care of those basic questions in class situations, and then the reference librarians can devote themselves to the things for which they have really been trained. Bibliographic instruction does not cut down on reference work; it does not mean that you are going to need less time at the reference desk. But it means that the time is going to be spent more valuably.

That is the why of bibliographic instruction. The next question is how. There are a variety of ways. My own preference is for course-related or course-integrated instruction in which, very briefly, assignments are built into the course so that they become a part of the student's expectations in taking the course. Course-integrated means, if possible, that a symbiotic relationship is created between the librarian's objectives and those of the teacher. Those two work together in an assignment that is called a good course-integrated assignment.

My own preference is for course-related or course-integrated instruction, and it is based on as much the realities of academic politics and other practical concerns as it is on educational theory. But whatever method one chooses, make sure that it is tailored to your needs. When I talk to other institutions about our program, that is, about Earlham College's program, I try to make it clear that I am not trying to export; I am not trying to sell our program. Our program was designed for our students, our courses, our curriculum, our library, and our library staff. And so should any institution's program be uniquely designed, whether the students are freshmen, advanced undergraduates, graduate students, or possible performers. All of these factors, the courses, and the library collection should determine the nature of the bibliographic instruction program. Now, I am not saying you cannot learn from others, from what other institutions are doing, but learn from others and then adapt to your particular situations. And actually that is one reason I am so much in favor of course-related or course-integrated instruction because it is so flexible, so adaptable, so versatile. It can be adapted to the level of students, to the number of students in particular classes, to the types of assignments, to the size of the collections, and the kinds of collections. It can even adapt to the type of classroom, that is, if it is in a large classroom or a small classroom or in the reference area. But whatever you decide to do, that is your decision. But do it wisely. Whatever method you choose, keep in mind that bibliographic instruction is not an end in itself. The goal is the education of students, helping them develop into better students, better scholars, better performers, maybe just better users of information, information for their own lives, their own careers, their own working places. That is the goal, to support the development of those students. And bibliographic instruction should be used with that in mind. It may not guarantee that those students are going to develop in the ways you want, but it surely can help. I will leave that up to you to decide how to do it.

Music Library Association Projects on Bibliographic Instruction

Beth Christensen

SUMMARY. This article outlines the Music Library Association's activities in bibliographic instruction, which include both presentations and publications, at the Midwest Chapter and national levels during the years 1978-1986. Although there has been emphasis on bibliographic instruction within the general library profession since the 1960's, work with bibliographic instruction in the Music Library Association did not begin until 1978. The first committee on bibliographic instruction originated in the Midwest Chapter at that time, with a subcommittee at the national level being organized in 1983. Several publications and a variety of conference presentations have resulted from the work of these committees.

This paper is presented in my capacity as Chair of the Music Library Association Midwest Chapter's Bibliographic Instruction Committee. Another panelist on this session, Linda Fidler, is Chair of the National Committee. I will briefly summarize the work of both committees. The MLA Midwest Chapter and national Bibliographic Instruction Committees have a unique and special relationship. Although there has been a great deal of emphasis on bibliographic instruction within the library profession since the early 1960's, there was no committee devoted to bibliographic instruction within MLA until 1978. At that time, the Midwest Chapter Biblio-

---

Beth Christensen is affiliated with St. Olaf College.

[Haworth co-indexing entry note]: "Music Library Association Projects on Bibliographic Instruction." Christensen, Beth. Co-published simultaneously in *Music Reference Services Quarterly*, (The Haworth Press, Inc.) Vol. 2, No. 1/2, 1993, pp. 153-156; and: *Foundations in Music Bibliography* (ed: Richard D. Green) The Haworth Press, Inc., 1993, pp. 153-156. Multiple copies of this article/chapter may be purchased from The Haworth Document Delivery Center [1-800-3-HAWORTH; 9:00 a.m. - 5:00 p.m. (EST)].

© 1993 by The Haworth Press, Inc. All rights reserved.

graphic Instruction Committee was formed. Until the national committee was organized in 1983, the Midwest Chapter Bibliographic Instruction Committee considered itself to be, in effect, a quasi "national" committee.

The Midwest Committee began, as many of these things do, through an informal and enthusiastic conversation among MLA members interested in bibliographic instruction; Linda Fidler and Richard Jones were the founding mother and father of the Committee. As it developed its charge, it became clear to those of us on the Committee that our first task should be to assess where we stood; to know just who was doing what in bibliographic instruction within the Midwest Chapter. A survey was sent to all music departments within the Midwest Chapter in 1979, and, in 1982 this information was published as a *Directory of Bibliographic Instruction Programs in the Midwest*. Kathryn Talalay of Indiana University was largely responsible for collating and presenting this information. This process is now being repeated at the national level. A questionnaire was distributed and collected, and published information about it is forthcoming.

In 1980, two significant sessions relating to bibliographic instruction were presented at MLA meetings. The national meeting provided a session on teaching a bibliographic course, hosted by the Public Services Interest Group. Although this presentation was not concerned with bibliographic instruction on a general level (and certainly not, in most cases, at the undergraduate level), it was at least tangential to bibliographic instruction, and it stimulated some discussion about the topic at the national level. Later that year, the Midwest Chapter Committee hosted a program during which bibliographic instruction programs at specific institutions were described. Music faculty and librarians from Oberlin Conservatory, St. Olaf College and the University of Wisconsin at Milwaukee talked about their experiences in working with each other to educate music students in library use.

In 1982, a day-long pre-conference on public services and bibliographic instruction preceded the national MLA meeting. Evan Farber, Annie Thompson, and Don Krummel were featured speakers. The afternoon was devoted to small group discussions which focused on a variety of topics including course-related instruction, evaluation, graduate music bibliography courses, and textbooks for bibliographic instruction. In October of that year, the Midwest Chapter Committee sponsored a session on "Teaching Librarians to Teach" in which I provided a sample classroom lecture which was then critiqued by Sharon Rogers of Bowing Green State University. Following the demonstration and specific comments, Dr. Rogers provided more general guidance on effective classroom lecture techniques.

At the same meeting, the Midwest Chapter Committee put finishing touches on a list of standards or competencies of library skills at the undergraduate level which was published in the March 1984 issue of *Notes*. The list compiled for this article emphasized skills we believe every music student should obtain during his/her college career. Although examples of specific reference tools are provided, it does not prescribe specific titles, for obvious reasons: they vary greatly from library collection to collection, from teacher to teacher, and the specification of individual books would immediately date the list. We did not designate the methods by which students would develop these skills. These, too, would vary greatly, and in addition, the Committee did not feel it was within its scope to define "how." The Committee agreed unanimously, however, that regardless of how or where they acquired them, music students should have these skills by the time they graduate from college.

The article was designed to serve two purposes: first, to provide librarians with a document endorsed by some level of the MLA which could be used as they defend bibliographic instruction programs to library administrators; second, to stimulate dialog between music faculty and librarians. We held our collective breath as we sent it out. We thought it was controversial, but we have not had a single response. We decided that this was due to one of two reasons: (1) no one read it (it *was* in small print between two much larger articles in an issue published at a busy time of year), or (2) everyone agreed with it. Having given ourselves the option, we decided that everyone agreed. The Committee would still be pleased to receive comments or to answer questions regarding this report.

This brings us to the year 1984. Once we had surveyed "who" was doing "what," had learned about various techniques of bibliographic instruction, and had established common goals for ourselves through the competency list, we decided that it was time to complete the process and take on the controversial subject of evaluation. The Committee sponsored a panel on evaluation at its 1984 Chapter meeting. Virginia Tiefel from Ohio State University served as guest speaker, and music librarians from Oberlin, Bowling Green State University, and Goshen College participated. It became obvious that librarians' experiences with evaluation varied greatly. Although the evaluation of bibliographic instruction is unquestionably one of our most difficult and easily ignored challenges, this meeting stressed that it is also an important ingredient as we strive to create effective and responsive bibliographic instruction programs.

Having thus completed our circle, the last two years have been a time of self-reflection for the Midwest Chapter Bibliographic Instruction Committee. We have taken the time to sit back, to think "now what?" and to question our constituency. It has become clear that one of the major concerns on librarians' minds is how to better communicate with our music faculty as we work together toward our common goal of educating music students. To this end, we are planning a session on "marketing" bibliographic instruction programs for the 1987 Chapter meeting. Without any impetus of our own, however, today's meeting has already taken a giant step in this direction. It has provided us with an opportunity to come together, to share our common concerns, and to educate each other in the process of educating our students.

Music Bibliographic Instruction on Microcomputers: Part I

Robert Michael Fling

SUMMARY. The Indiana University Music Library uses microcomputer programs to instruct undergraduate students about the structures and uses of uniform titles for music, and about core music reference sources. An introductory interactive tutorial describes "form," "distinctive," and "collective" uniform titles, followed by examples from the works of J.S. Bach, Mozart, Monteverdi, and Bartók, and concluding with a graded quiz.

The music librarians at Indiana University have long pondered the question of how best to teach to undergraduate music majors some basic skills for using the music library. During recent years we have used a variety of methods, including slide presentations, printed guides, videotape presentations, walking tours, and classroom lectures. Each of these, for one reason or another, has proved to be flawed: The slide show loaded too much information into one sitting; 40 minutes of color photos of catalog cards and music dictionaries seemed to do more to promote sedation than education. Our videotape was more condensed, and it brought some liveliness and humor to the topic, but it was produced on a shoestring by

---

Robert Michael Fling is affiliated with the Music Library at Indiana University.

[Haworth co-indexing entry note]: "Music Bibliographic Instruction on Microcomputers: Part I." Fling, Robert Michael. Co-published simultaneously in *Music Reference Services Quarterly*, (The Haworth Press, Inc.) Vol. 2, No. 1/2, 1993, pp. 157-163; and: *Foundations in Music Bibliography* (ed: Richard D. Green) The Haworth Press, Inc., 1993, pp. 157-163. Multiple copies of this article/chapter may be purchased from The Haworth Document Delivery Center [1-800-3-HAWORTH; 9:00 a.m. - 5:00 p.m. (EST)].

© 1993 by The Haworth Press, Inc. All rights reserved.

reference librarians rather than by Metro-Goldwyn Mayer, and its shortcomings were obvious to all who viewed it. Walking tours have the advantage of allowing questions and answers between librarians and students, but a tour guide can impart only a limited amount and variety of information, and only a few students can comfortably be ushered around at once. The class lecture format, with follow-up written exercises requiring use of some reference books, seems in general to be an excellent one for bibliographic instruction, but it has had limited success at Indiana because of the size of the enrollment in the School of Music.

Core classes for freshmen and sophomore music majors typically have 200 or more students, and herd behavior invariably brings them in to do their library assignments in large groups, all to use the same few volumes at once. Consequently, when in 1983 the School of Music placed four Apple+ microcomputers in a newly remodeled room adjacent to the reference area of the library, the music librarians were ripe to experiment with something new in the way of bibliographic instruction. It seemed that microcomputer-assisted instruction could offer several advantages: students could be involved in an interactive learning experience, with immediate feedback about correct and incorrect responses; they could control the sequence and pacing of the lessons; and each student could reserve a computer in advance for a convenient time. There were disadvantages, too: there would be limited contact between students and librarians; students would be working at screens rather than turning the pages of real encyclopedias and indexes; and finally, there seemed to be no appropriate existing software. We would have to design and program such a system ourselves.

The plan we envisioned called for three independent lessons that would teach some very basic tools and skills that undergraduate music students would be likely to require. One lesson would teach a few essential music reference sources, and the other two would instruct about some of the more arcane aspects of how music is cataloged in a library: in particular, the essential filing and locational elements of uniform titles, and Library of Congress subject headings for music. The program would be named "Making the Most of the Music Library."

Our decision to devote two parts of the program to catalog use was based upon observations over the years about how undergraduates use the Music Library at Indiana University. Music research papers usually are not assigned until well into undergraduate studies, but the performance emphasis at our school means that freshmen need to locate scores and recordings in the library from day one of classes. One of our driving forces was the sight of new students standing before open catalog drawers, scratching their heads in bewilderment. And many inquiries to the reference librarian indicated clearly that there was a high rate of failure by students to locate even the most standard of repertoire.

Consequently, the first module of the program to be created concerns uniform titles for music. It was designed and written during Spring semester 1984 by a team of two librarians: David Fenske (Head of the Music Library) and myself; and two graduate students in music librarianship: Shirlene Ward (now a music librarian at Northwestern University), and Brenda Nelson (now a librarian at the Archives of Traditional Music, Indiana University). Programming was by John Schaffer (now a member of the music faculty at the University of Wisconsin-Madison). After several weeks of collective brainstorming, the design that resulted was quite a simple one, due partly to constraints of hardware that was less than state-of-the-art; partly to a desire to keep programming costs low; and partly because it seemed to us that a straightforward design would teach as effectively as a more complicated one.

The initial challenge was to identify and to distill out of the cataloging rules those characteristics of uniform titles that seemed most basic. (See Example 1: Sample Titles.) We decided that the tutorial portion of the program would define three categories of titles, and we characterized these as "Form Titles" (those based on the name of a form or type of composition), "Distinctive Titles," and "Collective Titles" (those for collections of several works by one composer, whether in the same form or for the same medium, or not). Next would come description of those additions to titles that help distinguish among different editions and formats of the same work: "Chorus score," "Libretto," language designations, and so forth. (See Example 2: Flowchart.)

The program itself is in three sections: Section One is a tutorial, which is itself divided into the four categories defined above. Each

Example 1
Sample Titles

Form Titles:
   Bartók, Béla.
     [Quartets, strings, no. 6]
     String Quartet Number Six ...

Distinctive Titles:
   Mozart, Wolfgang Amadeus.
     [Zauberflöte]
     The Magic Flute ...

Collective Titles:
   Bach, Johann Sebastian.
     [Organ music]
     Complete organ works ...

   Mozart, Wolfgang Amadeus.
     [Works]
     Neue Ausgabe ...

Additions to Titles:
   Kodály, Zoltán.
     [Psalmus hungaricus. Chorus score]
     Psalmus Hungaricus: für Tenorsolo ...

   Bizet, Georges.
     [Carmen. Libretto. English & French]
     Carmen: an Opera ...

of these four sections includes illustrations drawn from our catalogs, and concludes with a short quiz. The text was written with the idea that the four sections would be taken in the order shown on the flowchart, but the student also has the option of skipping or repeating sections.

In Section Two, slightly more complicated examples are used than in the tutorial. The student selects one of four composers to work with: Bach, Mozart, Bartók, or Monteverdi. The four were chosen for the program for the collective variety of forms, genres, and languages in which they wrote music. After choosing a composer, the student is shown two or three screens of "hints" about the forms and languages commonly used by that composer, and about any appropriate and unique numbering schemes for his compositions. Then follow about fifteen multiple-choice questions about titles of some works by that composer. (See Example 3: Sample Question 1.)

Example 2
Flowchart
Making the Most of the Music Library: Using Uniform Titles

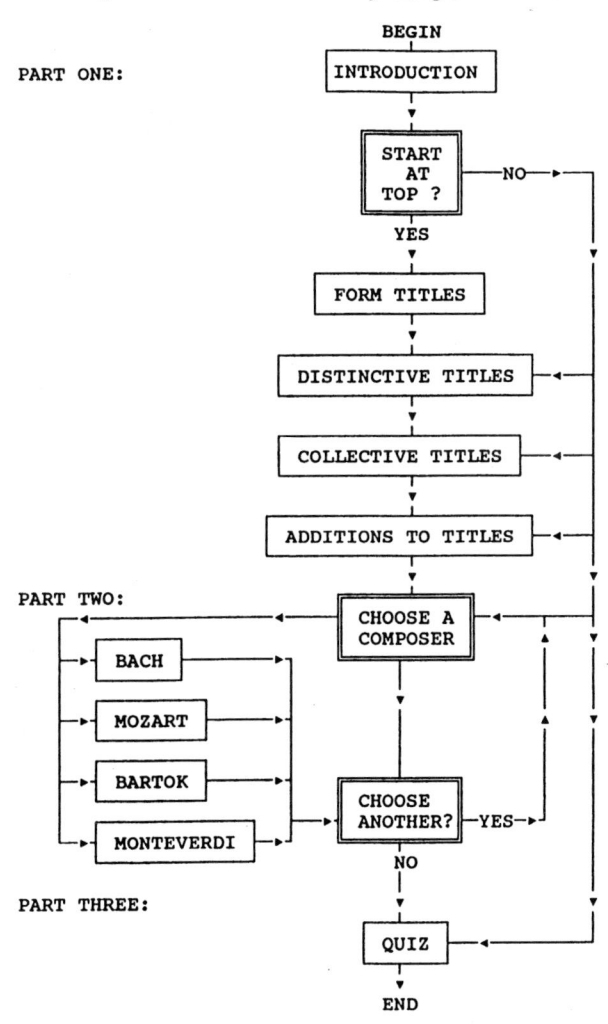

PART ONE:

BEGIN
↓
INTRODUCTION
↓
START AT TOP? —NO→
↓ YES
FORM TITLES
↓
DISTINCTIVE TITLES ←
↓
COLLECTIVE TITLES ←
↓
ADDITIONS TO TITLES ←

PART TWO:

CHOOSE A COMPOSER
→ BACH →
→ MOZART →
→ BARTOK →
→ MONTEVERDI →
↓
CHOOSE ANOTHER? —YES→
↓ NO

PART THREE:

QUIZ ←
↓
END

Typically, an abbreviated title-page transcription is displayed, with three uniform titles from which one is to be selected. After a choice is made, a "Correct" or "Incorrect" response appears on the lower half of the screen, with a brief explanation. (See Example 4: Sample Question 2.) Alternatively, a uniform title may be shown, with three short descriptions of an edition or collection, from which one is to be selected. After completing the questions about one composer, the student may choose to continue with another, to quit, or to go on to Part Three.

Part Three consists entirely of quiz questions, structured exactly like the ones we have already seen. But now the examples are drawn from many composers, illustrating all periods and styles of

Example 3
Sample Question 1

Select a Number, then Press Carriage Return Key

Bach, Johann Sebastian.
    Six Cello Suites, Transcribed for Trombone Solo.
        1. [Suites, trombone]
        2. [Violoncello music; arr.]
        3. [Suites, violoncello; arr.]

3: Correct.

Because all of the works in this collection are suites, the name of the form begins the uniform title. This is followed by the original instrumentation, and the "arr." designation, which indicates that the music has been transcribed for a new medium.

Example 4
Sample Question 2

Select a Number, then Press Carriage Return Key

Mozart, Wolfgang Amadeus.
    [Piano music. Selections]

        1. Selected piano sonatas.
        2. Complete piano music.
        3. Selected piano sonatas, variations, etc.

1: Incorrect

"Piano music" indicates that this collection contains a variety of forms of piano music, and not just Sonatas. "Selections" identifies a collection that is not complete.

serious music, and no hints are provided. This section was programmed so that the questions come in a random order, and consequently if the student returns another day to try his hand at quiz questions, chances are that many of them will be new to him. Currently, there are about fifty questions in the quiz section, and the design is such that more, or different questions can be added at any time. When the student chooses to exit the quiz, a tally of correct vs. incorrect responses is displayed, along with a percentage score for that session.

Eight IBM-compatible microcomputers recently were purchased to replace the Apple II+ machines in our Music Library. The programming has been rewritten to run on these machines, but the close timing of the project has made it impossible to plan for an actual demonstration of the program at this meeting.

These microcomputer-assisted instruction programs are works in progress. The text of the segment on basic music reference works has been written, and will be programmed within the next weeks. Kathryn Talalay will now describe this segment to you.

Music Bibliographic Instruction on Microcomputers: Part II

Kathryn Talalay

SUMMARY. The role of this reference module is to educate the students in the basics of music bibliography within simple parameters: to select general but comprehensive sources that would answer common reference queries; to teach the students how to decide which tools they might use to answer specific types of questions; to steer clear of more sophisticated sources; and to avoid foreign language texts. Twelve sources were selected for the module. An example of the module on Mozart is included.

Like module one, module two (our bibliographic instruction program on reference tools) was produced during our Seminar in Music Librarianship. Also like module one, it was aimed primarily at the undergraduate population–in particular, freshmen and sophomores. Three students were involved: David Riles, who is currently music librarian at New York University; Shelly Gotz, who is completing both her Masters in Library Science and Masters in Musicology at Indiana University, and Shuk-Han Yu, who has returned to her native Hong Kong. Since Michael Fling was on sabbatical at the time, David Fenske and I directed the project. We are in the final throes of programming and the modules should be available for use within the month.

Kathryn Talalay is affiliated with the Music Library at Indiana University.

[Haworth co-indexing entry note]: "Music Bibliographic Instruction on Microcomupters: Part II." Talalay, Kathryn. Co-published simultaneously in *Music Reference Services Quarterly*, (The Haworth Press, Inc.) Vol. 2, No. 1/2, 1993, pp. 165-181; and: *Foundations in Music Bibliography* (ed: Richard D. Green) The Haworth Press, Inc., 1993, pp. 165-181. Multiple copies of this article/chapter may be purchased from The Haworth Document Delivery Center [1-800-3-HAWORTH; 9:00 a.m. - 5:00 p.m. (EST)].

As Michael Fling has explained, the Indiana University Music Library services a large number of undergraduates with no course-related bibliographic instruction for music students currently available. The role of this reference module then was to educate the students in the basics, and we consequently set up some very simple parameters: to select general but comprehensive sources that would answer common reference queries; to teach the students how to decide which tools they might use to answer specific types of questions; to steer clear of the more sophisticated sources like RISM; and to avoid foreign language texts. Titles such as *The New Grove Dictionary of Music and Musicians,* and *Harvard Dictionary of Music* came readily to mind for all of us.

Before we had the class choose the actual sources, we had them look at the existing module. They praised the program–in particular the general design and approach–but they also found it flawed: it was too dry; it was too long; the difficulty in moving from one section to another was a significant drawback; far too much information was given *before* the user was actually able to interact with the computer; and there were too many review questions. As an aside, many of these suggestions have now been incorporated into the updated version of module one.

A general description of module two began to emerge: the program should be "pithier"–it should engage the user more readily–perhaps some of the questions could be humorous; our module should eschew lengthy definitions in favor of more immediate interactions; and finally, one should be able to begin comfortably with or within *any* section of the module. Since each of the students were providing ten hours of reference desk service each week as part of this course, we hoped this would help them in making a less than random selection.

We let them loose, and they returned with their respective lists. As suspected, there was some overlap. All chose Grove's, (both *The New Grove Dictionary of Music and Musicians,* and *The New Grove Dictionary of Musical Instruments*), *Harvard Dictionary of Music, Baker's Biographical Dictionary of Musicians,* Heyer (*Historical Sets, Collected Editions, and Monuments of Music*), *Music Index, Who's Who in American Music–Classical,* and the two Arthur Wenk indexes: *Analyses of 19th Century Music* and *Analyses of 20th*

Century Music. At that point, the lists diverged, revealing quite a wide range of titles.

There is not enough time today to go through our seemingly endless discussions on why we picked each source or why we decided on only twelve. In the final analysis, some of our decisions were simply arbitrary, based in part on our students' perceptions of the needs of Indiana University undergraduate music students and, of course, of their teachers' infinite wisdom. We also kept in mind that we did not want to simply teach the undergraduates which tools to use in order to answer specific questions. We were equally interested in teaching them HOW to approach a reference question while using a short list of general tools as exemplars.

With all these parameters in mind, we decided to delete the two Wenk books on the grounds that freshmen and sophomores would have little use for them. We also decided to keep only *one* of the Groves (the Music and Musicians one). We discussed other less general reference tools: guides to opera plots; women's music or Afro-American directories; guides to songs in collections; word-by-word translations; general directories like *Musical America,* and guides to recordings, like Schwann. We decided *not* to include them; their subject matter, although undeniably very important, was simply too topical for what we were trying to accomplish. One tool, however, *Musical America,* did engender some debate, and we decided in the end to include it under a more or less miscellaneous category. It seemed to be an appropriate tool, since not only did it cover a wide variety of areas but it was, in a sense, one-of-a-kind. Most compelling, however, was the experience of reference librarians (and now the students doing their practicum) that it was a frequently used source to answer undergraduate questions. Finally, we included the *International Who's Who* along with our *Who's Who in American Music–Classical* feeling that it was important to have our scope be international rather than just national.

There is not enough time under the present limitations to discuss our heated arguments over our next step: whether or not to include on-line computer databases. We finally decided that excluding them was not only intellectually myopic but also untimely. Knowledge is knowledge, after all, whether it rests quietly between the covers of a book or inside a microchip.

There are not a plethora of on-line databases to choose from in music, and therefore our selection was not a difficult one. For coverage of sound recordings, for teaching students that it is possible to obtain books and scores from other libraries, and for examples of different types of subject access, we chose both RLIN and OCLC. RILM, being the only on-line source devoted exclusively to music, was an obvious third choice. And finally, for access to both music and the other arts we selected AHCI (*Arts and Humanities Citation Index*).

At last, we had completed our list: twelve in all–*Harvard, Music Index*, RILM, *The New Grove, Baker's, Who's Who in American Music–Classical, International Who's Who, Heyer,* OCLC, RLIN, AHCI and *Musical America*. Now what? It was time for the actual design phase, and since there is no better way to show a design than to actually look at it, I will now run through a part of one of the modules. The one I have picked is on Mozart, but the students have five composers from which to choose–one from each historical period except Medieval which we excluded on the grounds of its inherent complexities.

MOZART - TOPIC 1

1. Welcome

2. This program is designed to acquaint you with music reference tools. You will be asked to choose a composer, a topic relating to the composer, key words relating to the topic and what types of sources you would like to search. [Name of program] will discuss six types of reference tools, including the twelve listed below. You may elect to complete as many modules as you like during one session.
The reference tools discussed will be:

Arts and Humanities Citation Index (AHCI)
Baker's Biographical Dictionary of Music and Musicians (Baker's)
The New Grove Dictionary of Music and Musicians (Grove's)
Harvard Dictionary of Music (Harvard)

Heyer, Anna Harriet. *Historical Sets, Collected Editions and Monuments of Music: A Guide to their Contents* (Heyer)
International Who's Who in Music
Music Index
Musical America
OCLC Online Computer Library Center, Inc. (OCLC)
Répertoire International de Littérature Musicale (RILM)
Research Libraries Information Network (RLIN)
Who's Who in American Music-Classical

3. A. Press space bar to continue unless otherwise directed.
   B. Type screen number if you wish to return to a previous screen or advance to any subsequent screen.
   C. You may exit system at any time by typing "Q."

4. Screen 5 to choose a composer.
   Screen 6 to choose a topic.
   Screen 9 to choose types of sources.

5. What composer would you like to search?

   A. Monteverdi
   B. Handel
   C. Mozart
   D. Brahms
   E. Stravinsky

6. You have chosen to search Mozart. Now you need to pick a topic relevant to Mozart.

   A. Mozart and the rise of German opera.
   B. Mozart and the development of Italian opera.
   C. Form and structure in Mozart's concerti.

7. You have chosen topic A. Select the pertinent keywords from the list below.

   A. cadenza
   B. Calzabigi
   C. coloratura
   D. da capo aria
   E. Don Giovanni
   F. ensemble finale
   G. Die Entführung aus dem Serail
   H. fugue

I. Idomeneo
J. Lorenzo da Ponte
K. Masonic symbolism
L. La Nozze di Figaro
M. opera buffo
N. opera seria
O. rondo
P. sinfonia concertante
Q. Singspiel
R. sonata-allegro
S. tromba marina
T. Die Zauberflöte

8. Correct keywords for topic A are C,D,G,K,Q and T.

9. What types of sources would you like to search? (We suggest that you start with a biographical search if you are just beginning this program.)

   A. Biographical
   B. Terminological
   C. Bibliographic–Books
   D. Bibliographic–Articles
   E. Bibliographic–Scores and Sound Recordings
   F. Miscellaneous

A. BIOGRAPHICAL SOURCES

10. There are two important biographical sources, the New Grove and Baker's. The New Grove has extensive composer listings, which include both biographical information (sometimes illustrations) and discussions of the composer's music. Grove is arranged alphabetically. Entries in Grove contain a works list which arranges by genre everything the composer is known to have written. There is also a selective bibliography at the end of each article.

11. Baker's is a dictionary comprising solely biographical entries arranged alphabetically. Compared to the New Grove, Baker's is much shorter and more concise. Entries in Baker's contain biographical notes, a short works list and a short bibliography. In general, while Grove is the more comprehensive work, Baker's contains many more performers, conductors and other non-composing musicians than does Grove.

12. Using the information that you have been given, answer the following questions.

13. Where would I find information on Mozart's family?

    A. Grove's
    B. Baker's
    C. Both
    D. Neither

14. The correct answer is A. Baker's may have some information on Leopold Mozart, but even that would be somewhat sketchy. Grove's would have the most substantial information.

15. In which source would I find a list of Mozart's operas?

    A. Grove's
    B. Baker's
    C. Both
    D. Neither

16. The correct answer is A. Remember that Baker's lists only the most important and/or better known works; lesser German operas would be omitted from the list. Grove's would have a complete listing of Mozart's operas.

17. Where is Mozart's birthplace?

    A. Grove's
    B. Baker's
    C. Both
    D. Neither

18. The correct answer is C. Grove's would give not only the town of Mozart's birth but the address as well. Baker's would give only the town, but would be the best source if this is all of the information that you needed (and quickly!).

19. Which of Mozart's operas deals with Masonic symbolism?

    A. Grove's
    B. Baker's
    C. Both
    D. Neither

20. The correct answer is A. Grove would discuss this aspect of Mozart's music in other genres as well should you want further information. Remember, Baker's contains only biographical information.

21. You need information on Schickaneder and Stephanie, two of Mozart's librettists. What source would you consult for the information?

   A. Grove's
   B. Baker's
   C. Both
   D. Neither

22. The correct answer is A. Stephanie is rather obscure and is probably not listed in Baker's. Grove's would have separate articles on Stephanie and Schickaneder in addition to mentioning them in the Mozart article.

B. TERMINOLOGICAL SOURCES

23. Two sources are helpful for finding information on terms. They are the New Grove and the Harvard Dictionary. Terms in the New Grove have full-length articles, often subdivided into national or chronological applications of the term. For instance, the term "opera" is discussed in relation to different countries and different historical periods. Articles discussing terms also contain bibliographies.

24. The Harvard Dictionary is another useful source. It is different from Grove in that it contains only definitions, not biographical information. Articles in Harvard are also frequently subdivided into national or chronological applications. Additional information in the articles includes the names of prominent composers associated with the term and perhaps a short bibliography. Type #12 for questions.

25. Which of the following would you find in the Harvard dictionary of music (answer all that apply)?

A. Singspiel
B. Mozart
C. Stadler
D. basset horn
E. da capo aria

26. A-D-E: Yes! If the term is not exactly as listed, a reference may be given to see a related term. If not, think of some related terms yourself! Let your imagination run wild!

B-C: No! Again, Harvard contains no biographical information.

27. You heard your instructor remark the other day that "Marten aller Arten" from "Die Entführung" is a masterpiece of coloratura writing. But what is coloratura? Where do you find out?

A. Harvard
B. Grove's
C. Both
D. Neither

28. The correct answer is C. Harvard would give you a definition of coloratura, a musical example and a short bibliography for more information. If you needed a detailed account, Grove's would give you the above plus musical examples (including famous coloratura arias), composers who wrote for the coloratura voice and references to famous coloraturas of the past. There would also be a select bibliography and numerous "see also" references. You've hit the jackpot!

29. Oh, these musicologists! Now your instructor babbled something about Katherina Cavalieri, a famous coloratura. Who was she?

A. Harvard
B. Grove's
C. Both
D. Neither

30. The correct answer is B. She would have a separate article in Grove's; from there you could consult the "see also" references to

other articles. Again, Harvard contains no biographical information. She may be mentioned in passing in the coloratura article but the odds are against it!

31. Egad! Not Die Entführung again! The orchestration calls for two basset horns. What are they?

    A. Harvard
    B. Grove's
    C. Both
    D. Neither

32. The correct answer is C. Both sources would have information on the basset horn; although there may be a cross-reference to clarinet since this is a member of the clarinet family. Grove's would give the most substantial information if you needed to do research in depth. You might also consult an encyclopedia of musical instruments.

33. How is Masonic symbolism depicted in Mozart's music?

    A. Harvard
    B. Grove's
    C. Both
    D. Neither

34. The correct answer is D. It is not likely that there will be an entry in Harvard since this is more of a concept than an actual term. Grove's would also be a gamble under this or a related term; although you could check the Mozart article for what information is given there.

C. BIBLIOGRAPHIC–BOOKS

35. Many sources exist to help the researcher find books on a subject. Some of the most important are the New Grove, RILM, AHCI, RLIN and OCLC.

36. The New Grove is very simple to use as a bibliographic device.

Every article has a bibliography. All the researcher needs to do is find which sources he thinks would be most helpful. An important fact to keep in mind is that all of the information contained in Grove is current only up to 1980, the date when Grove was published. To find more current information, you will need to look elsewhere.

37. RILM is an attempt to index all of the significant literature published on music since January 1, 1967. It is available in both computer and print formats. The index includes articles, books, commentaries, dissertations and reviews. The real usefulness of RILM is that it contains an abstract in English for virtually every item indexed. It is important to remember that items usually do not appear in the RILM index until about five years after they are published.

38. AHCI may also be used in print (1976-) or computer (1980-) formats. The index covers many subjects in addition to music. For this reason, it may be used to find books which may have been published in a different subject area applicable to your topic. For example, a book on the house of Hapsburg may have relevant information useful for your topic. AHCI is updated quarterly in paper but weekly on computer.

39. OCLC is a computer tool. It is useful for determining whether a specific book has been published. You can get an idea of what has been published by using a variety of author and title search keys. Subject access on OCLC contains the catalogues of several thousand libraries.

40. RLIN is similar to OCLC and is also a computer tool. The main difference between RLIN and OCLC is that RLIN has a good subject access. This makes subject searching on RLIN much easier than OCLC. RLIN has only a handful of member libraries, making it less useful for finding locations than OCLC. Type #12 for questions.

41. Where would you find a copy of Emily Anderson's translation of Mozart's letters?

    A. OCLC and RLIN
    B. Grove
    C. AHCI

42. The correct answer is A. OCLC and RLIN will list libraries (subscribing to their systems, of course!) that have a copy of the book. OCLC has more locations than RLIN, but at any rate check your own library first.

43. At last! Barely off the press! An earth shattering example of Mozart scholarship has been available for years–in Macedonian!–but has now been released in an English translation. You need to find out any information you can about it. Where would you look?

   A. RLIN and OCLC
   B. Grove's
   C. AHCI

44. The correct answer is A. If available, OCLC and RLIN would contain information about the book; you may even be able to get it through OCLC and RLIN. It is too recent to appear in Grove's, and it is unlikely to be in AHCI unless someone has quoted it or reviewed it.

45. You accept an invitation to a cocktail party–unfortunately, only musicians have been invited. Even worse, most of them are musicologists! You hear someone (after a few drinks) mention the pros and cons of Einstein's biography of Mozart. Alas! You don't know the work at all. Should you? What would be the best source to check in order to find out if this is an important work?

   A. RILM
   B. Grove's
   C. AHCI

46. The correct answer is B–you're old friend, Grove's. This would be listed at the end of the article on Mozart. AHCI will tell you how many people have recently quoted it in papers, but then a lot of people are quoted in such things! The other sources aren't nearly as selective.

47. You've been given a term paper to write on the somewhat ambiguous topic of "Mozart's Tragic Muse." You've read the older works on Mozart but want something a little more recent. You've

found several titles mentioned in articles but you're not sure that they would be helpful. Where would be the best place to look?

　A. RLIN
　B. Grove's
　C. RILM

48. The correct answer is C. RILM contains abstracts as well as citations. By doing a search in RILM, you would be able to deduct whether or not the book may be helpful.

49. Suddenly, you remember hearing of just such a book called Mozart's Tragic Muse, or some such thing. Your library doesn't have it. You remember that it was published sometime recently, but time is of the essence and you need a copy quickly. Where is the best place to find this information?

　A. Grove's
　B. OCLC and RLIN
　C. OCLC and RILM

50. The correct answer is B. OCLC and RLIN are more current than Grove's and RILM.

QUIZ

1. What is the main difference between OCLC and RLIN?

　A. There is no difference.
　B. OCLC indexes articles.
　C. OCLC has good subject access
*　D. RLIN has good subject access

2. You have just tuned in to the Ether Game on WFIU and find that tonight's topic is composers whose names begin with "q." Not recalling any of hand, where would be the best place to look for quick reference?

*　A. Baker's
　B. Harvard

C. RLIN
D. Grove

3. Where would you find a brief definition of sonata da camera?

    A. RILM
* B. Harvard
    C. Musical America

4. Did Brahms write any operas? How would you find out?

    A. RILM
* B. Grove
    C. OCLC
    D. Heyer

5. Richard Taruskin has recently written an article concerning Stravinsky's use of folk themes in the *Rite of Spring*. Where would you find it?

* A. RILM and AHCI
    B. OCLC
    C. RLIN
    D. AHCI

6. Karol Szymanowski's opera *King Roger* was given its American premiere some time ago. Where could you find reviews of this performance?

* A. Music Index
    B. Music Index and OCLC
    C. Music Index and Heyer
    D. Music Index and RILM

7. You want to conduct Strauss' *Don Juan*, but your conducting instructor doesn't like the edition you're using. Where can you locate another one?

    A. Musical America
    B. Grove
    C. Grainger's
* D. OCLC and RLIN

8. You need to find a score for Mozart's aria "Da questa bella mano." Of course, every copy you located was checked out or at the bindery. The reference librarian said it might be in a collected edition or set. What source would you consult to find out?

    A. International Who's Who in Music
    B. International What's What
* C. Heyer
    D. Grove

9. You have checked OCLC for a particular edition of a score that you need to study, but the only place that has it is the University of Southern North Dakota at Hoople. Where can you find the address of the publisher so that you can write them directly?

    A. Heyer
* B. Musical America
    C. AMC Newsletter
    D. Grove

10. Your roommate had to read an article for history class that talked about King George I of England and his court. He said it had a lot about Handel in it. Unfortunately, he has forgotten the author and the title. Where can you find the correct citation of this article?

    A. OCLC
    B. SPCA
* C. AHC
    D. RILM

11. You know that Winton Dean is a Handel expert and must have written a number of books and articles about Handel. Where could you find out some of the more important works that he has written.

* A. International Who's Who in Music
    B. Who Was Who
    C. Baker's
    D. Musical America

12. Your friend wants to start a Lucine Amara fan club. Where could you find her address or the name of her agent?

A. Opera News
B. RILM
C. Heyer
* D. Who's Who in American Music-Classical

13. Your professor told you of an important book on Monteverdi published in 1983. You don't recall seeing it in the bibliography in Grove. Shouldn't such an important work be there?

A. No, Grove doesn't contain bibliographies.
B. Yes, the professor made a mistake as to the importance of the work.
* C. No, Grove is current only to 1980.
D. No, Grove is current only to 1975.

14. You need some information on Brahms for your voice class–in a hurry! You pull Harvard off the reference shelve and Brahms is not listed. Why not?

A. Harvard does not list German composers.
B. Harvard lists only American composers who did not graduate from Yale.
* C. Harvard contains no biographical information.
D. Harvard lists only terms.

15. Your oboe teacher has assigned an obscure piece by Handel. You've never heard of it and have no idea of its interpretation. Is there a recording of it to help you out?

* A. Yes, in OCLC or RLIN.
B. No, you're out of luck.
C. Yes, in Grove.
D. No, you need to know when it was written before you can find out.

16. Brahms revived the principle of cantus firmus technique in some of his works. Would you find a discussion of this technique in Baker's?

A. Sure, why wouldn't you?
* B. No, Baker's contains only biographical information.

C. Yes, Baker's contains both biographical and terminological information.
D. Yes, Baker's contains only terminological information.

17. Your music theory professor's book was just published and he typically assigns it as class reading. You have no intention of reading it, and figure there must be an abstract of it in RILM. Will it be there?

    A. No, but there will be one on OCLC.
    B. Rest assured, it will be there.
*   C. No, it is too recent a publication to be in RILM.
    D. Yes, but the abstract is in French.

18. Your music history professor wants you to find the most current information on the Mozart *Requiem* controversy. In what source would you find the most recent information?

    A. Harvard
*   B. AHCI
    C. RILM
    D. None of the above

19. You are watching *Amadeus* with a friend. Suddenly he shouts, "Hey! There's a tromba marina!" After a subtle reprimand (a quick elbow to the ribs) to your friend for talking during the film, you wonder where you could find out what a tromba marina is (after the film)?

    A. Grove
    B. Harvard
*   C. Grove and Harvard
    D. Baker's and Harvard

20. You've had a paper to write and known about it for six weeks. It's due tomorrow and you haven't begun! Not only that, the best book, which exactly parallels your topic, is checked out! Where can you find another library that may have the book?

    A. RILM
*   B. OCLC
    C. AHCI
    D. Nowhere, and it serves you right!

Integrating Library User Education with the Undergraduate Music History Sequence

Linda M. Fidler
Richard S. James

SUMMARY. An important goal of the undergraduate music history sequence is to provide students with both knowledge and tools for life-long learning. Fundamental to this goal is the ability to use the library effectively. The authors established a library user education program for music majors, integrating it into the music history sequence. This graduated series of library assignments, with accompanying worksheets, can be reinforced from term to term, while the library program enhances the quality of student projects. Larger projects, e.g., a research paper, integrate and solidify the students' research techniques. The authors outline their program and its development as well as indications of its success.

Those who teach music history face the inevitable realization that they can neither convey all a student will ever need to know of music history in a few short semesters nor expect even the brightest of students to retain all that is taught. Thus, it behooves the conscientious instructor to pass along not only the facts, principles and processes of history itself, but also the means by which students

---

Linda M. Fidler and Richard S. James are affiliated with the Music Library, Bowling Green State University.

[Haworth co-indexing entry note]: "Integrating Library User Education with the Undergraduate Music History Sequence." Fidler, Linda M., and Richard S. James. Co-published simultaneously in *Music Reference Services Quarterly*, (The Haworth Press, Inc.) Vol. 2, No. 1/2, 1993, pp. 183-194; and: *Foundations in Music Bibliography* (ed: Richard D. Green) The Haworth Press, Inc., 1993, pp. 183-194. Multiple copies of this article/chapter may be purchased from The Haworth Document Delivery Center [1-800-3-HAWORTH; 9:00 a.m. - 5:00 p.m. (EST)].

can, throughout their careers, seek out the information they need, scholarly information concerning something they are performing, programming, hearing, or simply considering. With access to a library, the college graduate should be able to find what they need. But can they? In reality, they seldom get beyond *The New Grove,* a few synoptic sources like the books of David Ewen, and perhaps a relevant biography. During their college years, the closest most of them will have gotten to independent inquiry into scholarly sources is the ubiquitous music history term paper. As a part of this exercise, they no doubt scrambled about the library in a disorganized search for the elusive Ur-source and, in the end, consulted a number of general sources that frequently repeated the same information. They then eked out a halting summation, without much substantiation or independent thought, of the eloquent generalizations typical of most of their sources, and combined this with enough vague padding to achieve the much-feared minimum page requirement.

The problem is not a new one, nor is it limited to music students. The academic community as a whole, however, has been steadily making some headway against this situation during the past twenty years. Increasingly, college students receive some basic training in information retrieval through library user education programs, usually administered through the library itself or the English department. The students are introduced to the card catalog, general encyclopedias and dictionaries, periodical indexes, and perhaps government documents. As part of the instruction, they may receive a short tour of the library, either by the librarian or the graduate assistant for the class, or perhaps by means of a self-guided tour on cassette or in brochure. While a major step in the right direction, such programs are, of necessity, quite rudimentary. The refinement of these library skills with attention to sources and techniques peculiar to individual disciplines is advisable and, in the case of music, almost essential. The general university program will not, for instance, acquaint them with the use of uniform titles for music, RILM, discographies, or thematic catalogs.

While library user education programs are well established in many universities today, few music curricula have, to date, been modified to reinforce and expand upon the skills taught in the university-wide programs. In 1978, the Midwest Chapter of the Music Library Association established a committee on library instruction. The charge of this committee was first to identify those institutions where students were taught how to use the music library and musical resources, and then to develop workshops which would aid music librarians in establishing programs at their institutions. One outgrowth of this work was a 1984 article, published by the committee in *Notes*, citing the competencies that all undergraduates should have at the conclusion of the undergraduate music degree.[1]

In 1981, the national Music Library Association established a subcommittee of its Reference and Public Services Committee whose charge paralleled that of the Midwest chapter's committee, but at a national level. This subcommittee surveyed 1,400 schools which offer instruction in music. The results of the survey, to appear in a forthcoming article in *Notes,* were discouraging. Of the 565 schools that responded, fewer than 50 made the conscious effort to teach research skills to their undergraduate students, either through a formal course, computer-assisted instruction, or lectures related to or integrated within a required music course. Even more disheartening was the apparent lack of communication between teaching faculty and librarian, music or general.

At Bowling Green State University, the librarian and music faculty have made a concerted, cooperative effort over the past several years to develop a library user education program in music, and the results are very encouraging. The specific nature of the Bowling Green program depends, in some ways, upon the demographics of the institution and the nature of the music program as a whole. BGSU, located in northwest Ohio, serves a total student body of 15,000 students, with approximately 380 music majors and 90 graduate students in music. More than 80% of the undergraduate majors are in music education. The music history and music theory requirements for all music majors begin with a three course core sequence in which history and theory are integrated. The sequence spans music from 1600 to the present, with class sessions alternating between the historical and theoretical issues raised by the repertoire. Class size varies from thirty to seventy-five. The three courses must be taken in chronological order, preferably in successive semesters, and are generally co-taught by an historian and a composer/theorist. With this core as a basis, students may move on to various combinations of courses in Renaissance music, Japanese or Indonesian music, and jazz as well as literature courses covering symphonic music, opera, and chamber music.

When Ms. Fidler was appointed Head of the University's Music Library in 1982, she already had, in addition to her MLA committee work in library user education, experience with a small scale user education program in music, one she had helped develop at Oberlin College. She promptly recommended the implementation of a comprehensive approach to library instruction at Bowling Green and presented a program outline very similar to that seen in Figure 1. In this proposed program, library instruction would be integrated into the core three-semester music history/theory survey. The core would offer the framework for a graduated series of class-related library assignments that could be reinforced and built upon from term to term. The library instruction, in turn, would improve the quality of and pedagogical return on library-based class assignments, provide the skills for efficient use of the library, and thereby increase the chances for greater life-long self-education.

The initial response to this proposal was cautious. Curricular pressures had already reduced the music history/theory core to the bare minimum of credit hours. No one relished losing further time. Ms. Fidler contended, however, that approximately one hour of library instruction time per semester would generate substantial improvement in the students' research techniques and the quality of information gathered in research assignments. The full three semester program was initiated with those students just beginning the history/theory sequence in the fall semester of 1982. Now, four years later, our music library instruction program has evolved into a two-tier structure. The undergraduate music history/theory sequence remains the site of the first-tier, integrated instruction, while the upper division music history classes now incorporate a more advanced, second tier of course-related training.

Figure 1 summarizes the structure of this plan, specifying the overall objectives of each semester, the skills taught, the term project assigned and the types of sources covered. Most students come to college with a dearth of library skills. Since few students will have used a large library before, let alone a music library, it is

FIGURE 1. BGSU Library User Education Program in Music

	Semester I (Baroque Music)	Semester II (Classical and Romantic Music)	Semester III (Twentieth-Century Music)
Unit objectives	Student will obtain information on a musical term using subject headings, card catalog, subject encyclopedias and subject dictionaries	Student will obtain information on a composer using the card catalog, subject encyclopedias, biographical sources and periodical indexes; present sources in correct bibliographic format; annotate a bibliography	Student will write a paper, with bibliography and footnotes, on a specific composition, therein demonstrating an understanding of appropriate sources and logical search strategy.
Term Project	Compilation of definitions	An annotated bibliograhpy	A research term paper
Skills	1. Determine function, uses and limitations of the music library 2. Use of the card catalog - as basic index of library - information on c.c. card - LCSH as list for subjects - basic filing rules - uniform titles 3. Types of coverage in basic encyclopedias and dictionaries	1. Locate biographical information in biographical sources and subject encyclopedias 2. Use subject headings to locate needed subject biographies, dictionaries, encyclopedias, and periodical indexes as well as background information on topic composer 3. Use serials printous to locate periodicals 4. Develop compositional skills to annotate material	1. Apply problem-solving skills to assigned request for information 2. Plan and implement research strategy 3. Use general histories to obtain background information 4. Use discographic sources to identify relevant recordings 5. Organize materials in coherent fashion
Source Types	Card catalog LC subject headings Subject encyclopedias Subject dictionaries	Card catalog LC subject headings Subject encyclopedias Biographical sources Periodical indexes	Card catalog LC subject headings Subject encyclopedias Biographical sources Periodical indexes Discographies, Thematic catalogs Special subject bibliographies Congress reports, Festschrifts

necessary to start with the basics. The initial course in our history/ theory sequence (Baroque music) also emphasizes basic concepts, among them, music terminology. A primary semester assignment in the music history class is the compilation of definitions for some eighty key terms. This assignment, in turn, becomes the vehicle of the library instruction unit, with the students learning how to use the library to find information on music terminology. They are first acquainted with the music library itself by means of a brief slide show. Next a basic subject dictionary–the *Harvard Dictionary of Music*–and a comparable subject encyclopedia–*The New Grove*–are illustrated. The function of each along with the depth and nature of their coverage is compared and contrasted. The instructor then reviews the card catalog in its primary role as an index to the rest of the library. Basic filing rules, call numbers and the interpretation of the data found on the card are explained. Students next become familiar with the Library of Congress Subject Headings system: its abbreviations, organization, and use. A presentation on uniform titles in cataloging scores and recordings concludes the first semester program. These various skills and tools are explained in a series of five presentations, ten to fifteen minutes in length, each of which is reinforced by a worksheet that requires less than an hour of in-library work to complete. The librarian designs the worksheets so that information gathered for them relates directly to their term project in music history, in this first semester the list of definitions mentioned above. At the end of the semester, worksheet grades are averaged and sent to the history/theory team for inclusion in the final course grade.

The second and third semesters of the program follow the same format, in terms of number and length of presentations and also the applicability of worksheet assignments to the final project. Furthermore, a certain amount of reinforcement of the skills learned during the previous semester or semesters is structured into the program. Thus, the first three items listed opposite Types of Sources in Figure 1 appear in each course. These sources are briefly reviewed at the outset of semesters two and three.

During the second semester of the history/theory sequence, the term project towards which both the history and library segments are oriented is an annotated bibliography for a particular composer.

This bibliography must list no fewer than six sources and include both books and articles. After the initial review of past tools, the second-semester student is introduced to various general bibliographical sources and shown how they compare to the subject encyclopedias discussed during the first semester. *The New Grove* and *Baker's Bibliographical Dictionary* illustrate this comparison. The students then learn to use *Music Index* and to locate journals by means of the library's serial printout. The instructor also outlines the value of book reviews and the means of finding them using *Music Index* and other sources. Finally, they are shown how to apply their knowledge of the Library of Congress Subject Headings to select the subject biographies, dictionaries and encyclopedias, along with the periodical indexes, and the general background sources relevant to their composer topics.

Two additional skills are required by the bibliography term project. First, students must master a standard bibliographic format–in this case, Turabian. Each of the library assignments in this course requires citation of one or two different types of sources. The students are taught the format appropriate to each type: books, book reviews, journals and encyclopedias. They are expected to follow it both in the subsequent worksheet assignment and in the term project. Finally, the compositional skills required for annotation are discussed, illustrated, and, in the final library worksheet of the term, practiced.

The library instruction module in the third semester represents the most comprehensive approach of the three. While some new library skills are developed, the over-riding objective is the writing of an eight to ten page research paper, an assignment which requires the students to combine previously learned library skills with problem-solving techniques and research strategy. Their paper focuses on a specific composition, with connections made to the composer's other works, general style and the various stylistic trends of the era. New tools introduced range from special subject bibliographies, discographies and thematic catalogs, to congress reports and Festschriften. Unlike previous semesters, however, students are not taught just about an individual source, but about a type of source, such as thematic catalogs, after which they are expected to be able to find a useful catalog on their own. Once again, the instructor presents and illustrates each topic in relation to the sort of research the students are involved with for their term paper. In the first library presentation of the term, students review some of the library lessons of previous semesters in relation to locating general histories and bibliographic sources for the term paper topics. In addition, the student is presented with a simple process for selecting and refining a topic, and planning an appropriate research strategy, see Figure 2. This plan is then referred to in the subsequent library presentations of the semester. In addition to introducing the above-mentioned new types of sources, the student is acquainted with the distinction between bibliographic and footnote format. Finally, outside of the formal confines of the library instruction program, the teaching faculty member discusses matters of note-taking and paper organization as well as typical writing problems. An outline and bibliography are critiqued and returned before the student begins to write.

In the second level of instruction, the library lectures assume the more familiar "bring the librarian to the classroom" format. This fall, three classes were targeted for instruction: Indonesian Music, Japanese Music, and Medieval/Renaissance Music. Like the first level of integrated instruction, the librarian meets with the faculty to determine the course requirement. However, the lecture developed by the librarian focuses on specific source materials which the students might overlook, including non-music reference books and indexes. The single lecture begins with a reminder of the search strategy, illustrated in the handout, as well as a refresher of the general music sources which might be useful. There is no assignment from the librarian nor are the students expected to complete worksheets.

With the integration of library user education into Bowling Green's already co-taught music history/theory sequence, the librarian becomes the third member of an existing team. At the beginning of each semester, the librarian confers with each of the teams, either singly or together. They review the term project parameters, such as the number of sources required in the bibliographies and the means of making certain that the topics selected by the students can be supported by the resources in the library. They also decide what proportion of the students' final grade will be

FIGURE 2. Strategy for Researching a Topic

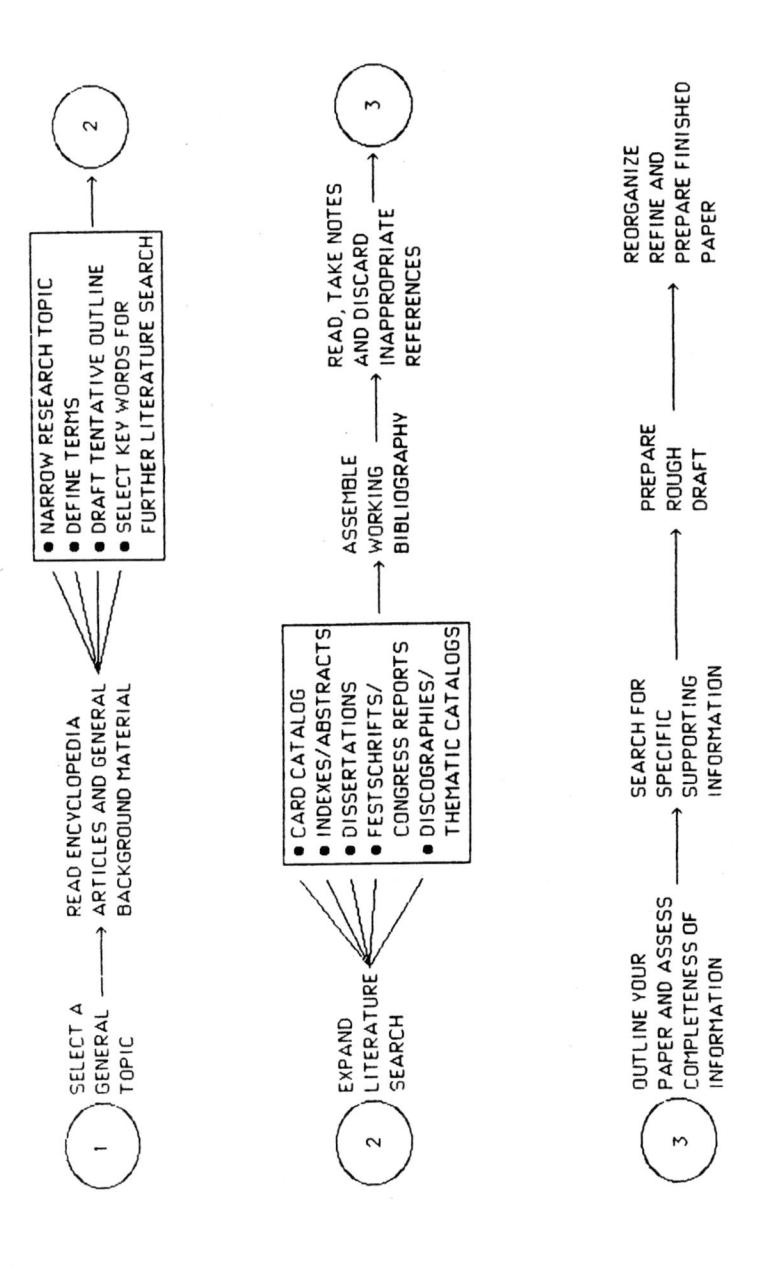

① SELECT A GENERAL TOPIC → READ ENCYCLOPEDIA ARTICLES AND GENERAL BACKGROUND MATERIAL →
- NARROW RESEARCH TOPIC
- DEFINE TERMS
- DRAFT TENTATIVE OUTLINE
- SELECT KEY WORDS FOR FURTHER LITERATURE SEARCH
→ ②

② EXPAND LITERATURE SEARCH →
- CARD CATALOG
- INDEXES/ABSTRACTS
- DISSERTATIONS
- FESTSCHRIFTS/CONGRESS REPORTS
- DISCOGRAPHIES/THEMATIC CATALOGS
→ ASSEMBLE WORKING BIBLIOGRAPHY → READ, TAKE NOTES AND DISCARD INAPPROPRIATE REFERENCES → ③

③ OUTLINE YOUR PAPER AND ASSESS COMPLETENESS OF INFORMATION → SEARCH FOR SPECIFIC SUPPORTING INFORMATION → PREPARE ROUGH DRAFT → REORGANIZE REFINE AND PREPARE FINISHED PAPER derived from the library assignments–usually about 5%–and when to schedule the five library presentations. Frequently she arranges for one of the presentations to be given by either the theorist or the historian. Whether or not the teaching faculty elect to present a unit, he or she is always present for the lecture and almost always participates in some way. The result is a visible support for the library program, and credibility for both librarian and teaching faculty member.

Since the Music Library is not in the Music building, and because the class size is large, transparencies of the sources to be examined in class are used in place of the actual reference books. The instructor also uses transparencies and handouts illustrating bibliographic style and search strategy. At the end of each presentation, the students receive a one-page exercise designed to allow practice with the sources presented in the lecture. Each assignment must be completed by Friday and is returned at the next library lecture. Lectures are generally scheduled on Mondays and Tuesdays to accommodate the necessary time to complete the worksheet.

A presentation from the second semester of this program will serve to illustrate the typical instruction format. In this lecture, the second of five, the students are introduced to periodical indexes, specifically *Music Index*. A transparency of a page taken from *Music Index* is described in detail. One citation is extracted from the excerpt and enlarged in order to analyze it for the various pieces of information. The excerpt is then reformatted into correct bibliographic style. At the conclusion of the discussion, the worksheet is reviewed. The student is asked to locate a journal article on their composer using *Music Index*, and then cite it in correct bibliographic format.

The students' grade depends not only on their being able to locate a journal article but also on their ability to cite according to the bibliographic style as shown on the worksheet. As bibliographic style is quite prescriptive, students are also required to type the assignments; they are penalized for submitting assignments which are messy or not typed.

The impact of the Bowling Green library user education program has been most encouraging. The faculty noticed improvement in term project quality almost immediately, with the magnitude of that improvement increasing steadily. The information presented in the term projects–definitions, annotations and term papers–is much more extensive, substantive and well documented than it was before program implementation. Bibliographic style is largely consistent and the variety of sources consulted has increased considerably. The quality is more consistent as well as higher. Now, when students come in to discuss problems with their assignments, they have already exhausted the basic avenues of inquiry. They ask intelligent questions concerning their problems and can understand far more complex answers and suggestions. They are rarely as lost, upset and intimidated by their research assignments as they used to be. This improvement is also quite apparent to the library staff. Instead of repetitious hand-holding, they are fielding increasingly sophisticated questions. A considerably greater number of students are able to function independently in the library, pursuing logical research strategies of their own.

Student opinions and suggestions concerning the library instruction program have also been sought by means of routine course evaluation forms. Not surprisingly, some of them consider it a waste of time. Many, however, are grudgingly, even openly positive, and see considerable practical value in the training. Most will admit that it made their research projects a good deal less traumatic than they had expected. Most of the students complete the entire sequence of worksheets. While this is partly due to the fact that the assignments account for 5% of their grade, it seems that the way in which the worksheet answers are directly applicable to their term projects is a considerable incentive, too. They know that their project grade will be enhanced as well.

In short, faculty and student evaluation along with the assessment of student assignments, indicate that the Bowling Green library user education program is making a considerable contribution to the undergraduate music curriculum. The structure, goals and objective as originally set forth have proven largely successful. The program has, of course, undergone a number of minor adjustments since its inception. Lecture topics and assignments have been modified and even switched from one course to another, usually to make them more comparable with the research topics or the course syllabus itself. Little else has required attention.

A host of practical lessons have been gleaned from the first several years with this program. The two most important are the critical role of the interplay between librarian and teaching faculty, and the equally important relationship between library instruction and the music history/theory curriculum. A carefully planned and meticulously organized sequence of library presentations is the core of the program, and a major asset to the history/theory sequence. The latter, though, provides a very necessary opportunity for practical application of skills learned to term projects. Likewise, the expertise and continuity provided by the librarian are essential, yet the support and involvement of the teaching faculty are vital to the credibility of the librarian and of the program as a whole.

NOTE

1. "Bibliographic competencies of Music Students at an Undergraduate Level," *Notes*, 40 (1984): 529-532.

Teaching Bibliography to Performers in a University School of Music

Ruth Watanabe

SUMMARY. The paper is a summary of observations gleaned from many years of teaching graduate students in courses on music bibliography. The goal is to point out some differences in perception which have been observed between students in classes designed for music history and theory majors, for majors in music librarianship in schools of library science, and for performance majors in university schools of music. The teaching of bibliography to performers does not need to present insurmountable problems to either students or the instructor.

The following paper is by no means a scholarly document; rather, it is a summary of observations gleaned from many years of teaching graduate students in various courses on music bibliography. My purpose is to point out some differences in perception which have been seen between students in classes designed for music history and theory majors, for majors in music librarianship in schools of library science, and for performance majors in university schools of music. Because other speakers will undoubtedly discuss the materials of music bibliography and the contents of courses which they have designed, I shall confine my remarks to performers and their reactions to classes in research and bibliography.

Ruth Watanabe is affiliated with the Eastman School of Music.

[Haworth co-indexing entry note]: "Teaching Bibliography to Performers in a University School of Music." Watanabe, Ruth. Co-published simultaneously in *Music Reference Services Quarterly*, (The Haworth Press, Inc.) Vol. 2, No. 1/2, 1993, pp. 195-202; and: *Foundations in Music Bibliography* (ed: Richard D. Green) The Haworth Press, Inc., 1993, pp. 195-202. Multiple copies of this article/chapter may be purchased from The Haworth Document Delivery Center [1-800-3-HAWORTH; 9:00 a.m. - 5:00 p.m. (EST)].

© 1993 by The Haworth Press, Inc. All rights reserved.

In university schools of music, the typical student body includes undergraduates and graduates seeking degrees in performance, music history, ethnomusicology, theory, composition, and education. Having experienced music lessons and practice-schedules from a comparatively early age, these students are, for the most part, a dedicated and disciplined group. They have had to achieve a high scholastic rating to meet the requirements for acceptance into an accredited university or a well-established graduate school and–also for the most part–possess a better than average intelligence. They are young people whom it is our privilege to teach, with the aim of guiding them further toward their collegiate and professional goals.

Before the rapid development of music libraries in the late 1950's and the 1960's, the resources of music were more difficult to come by on a university campus than were the resources of, say, English literature. But the post-war publication of a myriad of scores, books, journals, and recordings made possible the founding of new music collections and a dramatic growth of existing libraries. We have at last attained a happy state of affairs in which most of our students have access to a vast variety of musical information. Moreover, with automation and the products of technological development, increasingly rich stores of pertinent data may be tapped more efficiently and more quickly than was thought possible even as late as a decade ago. We know, of course, that libraries are undergoing such rapid and unprecedented changes that it is well-nigh impossible now to describe what in former times could have passed as "a typical music library." And simultaneously, the role of the music librarian is changing and our duties are becoming diversified. Many of us are teaching and assisting in designing curricula.

Most students today are given some sort of library orientation as part of their introduction to the campus or as part of their classroom procedures. Although they tend to be more receptive and are probably better able to derive benefit from this presentation than were their counterparts of yesterday, there are invariably some among them who need further elucidation, while nearly all students may well profit from an increasingly extensive and intensive exposure to library resources, that is, the coverage of a wider field of knowledge leading to a greater depth of understanding. At the moment, more attention is given to graduate students than to undergraduates in most university schools of music in terms of specific course offerings in bibliography.

In the past, music bibliography was typically taught in courses bearing such titles as "Introduction to Graduate Studies" or "Research and Bibliography," similar in nature to parallel class offerings in the humanities (e.g., English literature or European history) and intended for the graduate student embarking upon his master's degree or his doctorate. Their contents traditionally included an overall survey of reference tools and literature of the discipline, a study of principal primary and secondary sources, a review of research methods leading to guidelines for the preparation of seminar papers and the basic principles of thesis writing. Little attention was directed to the distinctively specialized materials of ethnomusicology, music history, theory, or music education. It was presumed that, once having mastered the basic procedures of bibliographical search, the individual student, through his own studies, would become familiar with the sources pertinent to his particular discipline.

More recently as a result of the increasing availability of *musicalia* in university and college libraries (as well as in public collections) and the growing awareness on the part of the faculty of the need for subject-bibliography, new courses have been initiated in many schools of music to satisfy the needs of students in the several branches of music study. In addition, specialized attention to the sources of music history is considered an integral part of many research seminars in musicology. Graduate courses in the history of theory often include first-hand acquaintance with treatises from the earliest times to the present; in the absence of the original work, the splendid reprint editions now available are a worthwhile substitute. Students of non-Western musics have access to field recordings and film clips in special collections on the university campus. Curriculum centers for the music educator provide easy access to pedagogical materials. But in all of these positive developments, the performer and the composer have suffered a degree of bibliographic neglect.

After careful study and due deliberation in the mid-fifties, the Committee on Graduate Studies of the National Association of Schools of Music created the Doctor of Musical Arts degree. Tailored to the needs of performers and composers who aspired to deanships or chairmanships in schools of music or those who hoped for promotion to high academic rank and tenure, the DMA offered a *bona fide* doctorate for those whose interests and backgrounds precluded their pursuit of the traditional Ph.D. The introduction of the DMA created a storm of controversy; there were heated verbal battles and many newspaper accounts of arguments *pro* and *con* between certain educators who favored the new degree for its practicality and certain scholars who feared that doctoral standards would become diluted if not seriously eroded. But the degree has become firmly entrenched in most schools of music, and viable standards have been established for the DMA and for the master's degree program leading to the performance/composition doctorate.

Today the several lecture-recitals and research papers required of DMA candidates place a heavier academic burden upon them than they have previously been accustomed to carry. Courses in bibliography and research methods designed to meet their requirements have been initiated in many institutions.

It is axiomatic that performers spend more time in their practice rooms and rehearsal halls than in the library. Many studio teachers insist that preparation for public performance is much more important than academic study. It comes as no surprise that performers cut academic classes with greater abandon than do theorists and musicologists. But among the greatest concert artists are those whose performances are enhanced by their knowledge of music in all its aspects, history, and other subjects–literature, art, science. Among the most productive and successful creators of music are those whose interests encompass the works of a multitude of other creators–poets, novelists, and essayists as well as composers. To prove the desirability of extensive knowledge is an important phase of courses for performers. In some cases considerable patience and persuasion may be necessary. It helps, of course, if the instructor is or has been a performer himself and thus may qualify as a kindred spirit.

In most schools, no foreign languages are required for the DMA or for the master's degree in performance. In contrast to such students of academic music as ethnomusicologists, music historians, and theorists who know several languages, typical performers (except voice majors who can sing in French, German and Italian) are single-language people to whom polyglot dictionaries of musical terms and lists of foreign phrases, expressions, and abbreviations must be introduced at the outset and appropriate care taken to insure that they are firmly committed to memory. Although a few of the most gifted and conscientious students may, through their own efforts, eventually attain a certain ability to struggle through the shorter entries in *MGG* or *Larousse de la musique,* they cannot be expected to read extensive selections in languages other than their own, a condition which limits the number of sources which may effectively be introduced into class assignments. It stands to reason that in spite of the students' inability to comprehend foreign languages, they must be made familiar with all important bibliographical sources: their purpose, their scope, and their general contents.

Many students, especially the younger ones, place extraordinary faith in what they find in books. "It says right here in this book!" they state as the final *dictum* in settling arguments in case of dissent. They also place more credence in books than in journals as seats of authority. "But that's only a magazine!–Skinny at that." Quite early in the course it may be advisable if not absolutely necessary to admit to them that everything in print may not be the Gospel and to assure them that articles in periodicals may often prove more useful than materials in books (many of which are outdated before they are published) because journals are more nearly up to date. The instructor must see to it, however, that students do not lose faith in the printed word or eschew all books in favor of magazines. A modicum of good judgment on the students' part is much to be desired.

Because most of us have probably started out as performers, we can surely appreciate our students' anxiety about time or the lack of it to spare for pursuits other than preparing for their studio lessons. We can sympathize with the reason why performers tend to consult dictionaries and encyclopedias and favor other similar compilations of knowledge as the most direct path to enlightenment. They experience little difficulty in understanding such succinct articles and will, moreover, even accept the lengthiest encyclopedia entries as being more concise and more readily accessible than are data buried in what they call "regular" books. But an assignment to read a full-length volume (a biography, for example) may be an anathema, no matter how interesting it may be. "But that book is so fat!"

Once convinced of the viability of books, however, students accept fairly happily any volume which appears to contain information closest to their individual interests. They are quite discriminating in their tastes and show considerable judgment in their evaluation of what they read. Instructors obviously need patience and should be willing to plan lessons carefully to gain the students' acceptance of more eclectic resources. Much time may be profitably spent in discovering the primary interests of each pupil and subsequently leading him to a broadening of the parameters of his knowledge. Moreover, conferences with individual members of the class help to dissipate the feeling that bibliography is a desiccated and impersonal study.

Serious performers not only benefit from a comparison of several editions of a given work in their repertoire but often become so interested that they devise projects of their own. At this stage, curiosity about collected editions and historical sets, which they have regarded as "big and awesome," is easy to arouse. Prefaces, introductory remarks, and the critical apparatus in scholarly publications may sometimes lie beyond their interest if not their comprehension, but the music itself is vital to them. They eventually may develop a lively desire to know about articulation, phrasing, dynamics, ornamentation, and even editorial policies. Performance practices, which formerly meant little to them, gradually become meaningful, to the benefit of their playing and/or singing.

Lest students think of all early music as "manuscripts" and every printing of an opus as a separate "edition," they should be taught the distinction between such terms as "autograph," "manuscript," and "typescript"; they must learn the difference between an "issue" and an "edition," and sometimes the definition of "score," "part-book," and "performing parts," or "miniature score," "full score," and "condensed score" needs to be clarified. All such terms are so commonly in use that the distinctions between them seem obvious, but young performers may tend to be surprisingly vague about them.

Performers like to use thematic catalogs and lists of music in print, which in their opinion are closely related to their repertoire and to the development of their concert programs. "You can zero in on a specific composition," they say, "and everything is plain, clear, and relevant." Even in consulting catalogs in German or in French, the students can use identifying keys, opus numbers, titles and sub-titles, and instrumentation and/or texts to locate data on the desired work. They are willing to use dictionaries to help them in their study, at the end of which their feeling of accomplishment is patently clear, while their sense of security with bibliographical sources is strengthened. Their reaction is often expressed: "Why couldn't we have been taught this long ago?"

The materials included in courses for performers should ideally include all of the genres and items studied in classes for academic musicians, with the exclusion (whenever necessary) of highly technical writings in theory and musicology, statistics, and involved articles in foreign languages. Once the interest of the class has been awakened, a wide range of reference tools, catalogs and indexes, histories and biographies, collected editions and historical sets, facsimile and reprint editions, journals and journal literature, recordings and discographies, and microforms can be profitably introduced. But at the same time, the once-over-lightly quick survey to which some instructors are tempted to resort–in an effort to cover the vast literature–produces disappointing and negative results. Students generally feel strongly that if a subject is worthy of being brought up, it should be treated with the proper respect and seriousness to which it is entitled. It is far better, they say, to learn about a few sources thoroughly than to skim over many sources half-way.

A session with illuminated manuscripts, for example, will draw interest and provide a welcome respite from the ordinary class presentation, but unless it can be supplemented by further discussion to bring the manuscripts into some historico-stylistic context, they will remain in the students' memory merely as objects of beauty ("All that gold!") or as curiosities far removed from the present ("How could they read that stuff?"). But given sufficient background, they become meaningful sources to remember with pleasure.

Lastly, music majors often have had less experience in writing papers than have majors in the humanities. There have actually been graduate students who have never written a term paper, for their previous course requirements included few academic subjects. If the bibliography course is also an introduction to graduate studies, the instructor must plan to teach students how to relate library materials to the writing process; time should be set aside during the semester to allow them to practice organizing a seminar report or a research paper under the guidance of the instructor.

Teaching performers does not need to present insurmountable problems to the instructor. Students more often than not show a delighted sense of discovery which is rewarding to one who has devoted much thought, time, and effort to the preparation of the course. If I may be permitted a personal reference, for me a meaningful aspect of music librarianship has been amassing materials for the performing musician as well as for the research scholar, and the opportunity as a teacher to help students find their way through the bibliographic maze.

A Core Literature for Music Bibliography

David Fenske

SUMMARY. Describes the organization and content of a graduate course in music bibliography for musicology and theory students at the masters level and applied students at the doctoral level. The course is designed to be taken early in the student's masters career and it is followed by specialized courses focusing on methodological problems and special literature appropriate to their majors. The course provides instruction in the areas of research methodologies (including an extensive research proposal), computer-based catalogs and databases, documentation techniques, and reference sources. The organization of the course moves from a general core through rings of literature of greater specificity based on the specific research proposal. The article includes a bibliography of approximately 130 citations of core literature.

Music bibliography has been taught at Indiana University to academics, music librarians and performers because: (1) they have common information requirements; (2) all three groups need preparation in information (as opposed to library use) techniques, to documentation techniques, to computer-based systems, and to traditional paper-based reference tools; (3) all groups need an emphasis on methodology and on the information trends.

A RETROSPECTIVE

Prior to 1975, formal bibliographic instruction was limited to an elective graduate course with an enrollment of two to four. During

---

David Fenske is affiliated with the Music Library at Indiana University.

[Haworth co-indexing entry note]: "A Core Literature for Music Bibliography" Fenske, David. Co-published simultaneously in *Music Reference Services Quarterly,* (The Haworth Press, Inc.) Vol. 2, No. 1/2, 1993, pp. 203-226; and: *Foundations in Music Bibliography* (ed: Richard D. Green) The Haworth Press, Inc., 1993, pp. 203-226. Multiple copies of this article/chapter may be purchased from The Haworth Document Delivery Center [1-800-3-HAWORTH; 9:00 a.m. - 5:00 p.m. (EST)].

© 1993 by The Haworth Press, Inc. All rights reserved.

the 1974-75 academic year, the School of Music's Academic Council approved a new course and new regulations requiring this course for musicology and theory students at the masters level and applied students at the doctoral level. The impetus for this change came from two directions: the perceived need to teach what the library called bibliographic instruction and what others generally called library instruction and the need to provide graduate students with some assistance in topic proposal preparation and related writing skills. As a matter of advising, the music bibliography course was to be taken early in the graduate curriculum. As with all academic advising, it is occasionally so given and taken.

The course's current state reflects changes over the last ten years. Documentation techniques have declined in importance. The importance of computer-based systems has increased. In 1975, OCLC was useful for music books but not scores or sound recordings, RLIN and other networks did not exist, local on-line systems weren't a prevalent option, and Dialog or similar systems either did not exist or were of no importance to music. The importance of the literature search has expanded beyond the local collection and its reference shelf. Finally, the reference sources themselves have changed, new sources have replaced some standard ones and new standard sources have emerged. We take it as our mission to create an information literate graduate: to prepare them for the future as best we can see it.

GROUPS SERVED

Nearly five hundred students have completed this course. In the case of the academic areas, the course is designed to be taken early in the student's masters career and it is followed by specialized courses focusing on methodological problems and special literature appropriate to their majors. For example, musicology students take M551, Introduction to Historical Musicology, during the following semester. Theory students take a special seminar for this purpose.

Indiana University also offers a professional education curriculum for music librarianship consisting of music bibliography (three credits), a seminar in music librarianship (three credits), and a six-credit practicum. This curriculum may either be taken as an elective part of the Masters in Library Science or as part of a dual masters between the MLS and the Musicology or Theory masters in the School of Music. In this specialization, the music bibliography course serves as the introductory course. It is taken for three credits as opposed to two credits for music students and involves a bibliographic project in addition to the research proposal required of all students in the course.

Applied doctoral students are required to take the music bibliography course because the degree requires a doctoral document. While the extent of this document varies according to department, many are quite extensive and virtually all are intended to demonstrate research techniques. The importance of research proposal development, literature reviews, and methodological literacy can scarcely be questioned in such an environment. Most departmental curricula have courses which follow logically upon the music bibliography course, e.g., choral literature seminars, piano literature, etc.

TOPICS COVERED

The music bibliography course seeks to educate in four areas: (1) research methodologies including an extensive research proposal; (2) computer-based catalogs and databases; (3) documentation techniques; and (4) reference sources. The course content for each of these areas will be discussed in the following sections.

There are many ways to teach music bibliography. Some focus on a series of individual sources: a type of "great works" approach. Some are taught in a seminar environment with the students reporting upon the sources. Others emphasize the relationships between information systems and de-emphasize the impor- tance of individual reference tools. This course uses the research proposal as a way of applying the information systems and specific sources to a problem currently under examination by the student. The student, it is hoped, learns about the interrelationships, the sources, research methods, and hones writing skills, simultaneously. Since the research proposal is started immediately, the organization of the course moves from a general core through rings of literature of greater specificity.

Introduction to Research Methodologies in Music History, Theory, and Education

The research proposal outlined in the course syllabus (cited at the end of this article) forms the initial sessions of the class. Virtually no students, whether from Indiana University or elsewhere, have developed formal research proposals, and many do not have scholarly writing experience. Within the context of this audience, it is unnecessary to describe all of these sections, but comments are in order on scope and thesis development and on the literature review. They form the principal challenge for all students in this course and the laboratory application of bibliographic research techniques.

Scope and thesis development are problematic for quite different reasons. For most students, they begin the process by describing an idea which is too general. While the literature review causes most to narrow the scope of their ideas, the second problem, thesis development, results from causes much deeper in recent higher education. Most students rarely state the question or the premise they want to test. Throughout the initial consultation session I find myself repeating: "What's the question?" This lack of clarity causes some difficulty in narrowing the scope and allows the students to follow too many relatively unimportant tangents during the literature search.

The literature review is particularly important in this course. During the initial session, the topic search strategy (given below in the course syllabus) is used to start the students on their literature search. In each category, several major tools are briefly introduced. In this initial session, the intent is to give the student a crash mini-bibliography course to get them started on the research proposal. This chart is also the gestalt of the course as a whole. A booklet of approximately 100 pages altered each semester and described later is organized around this chart. As the course proceeds, each of these categories is extended and other important tools are then added. The chart forms the course's core of the information sources.

The research proposal's methodological section is introduced during initial sessions, but this is elaborated upon by guest lecturers from musicology, theory, and music education. By tradition and experience, these faculty usually restrict the range of their comments to historical methodologies, analytical approaches, and statistical studies, respectively.

Computer-Based Information Systems

The student is faced with three problems simultaneously in the research proposal and in the topic search strategy: developing a bibliography of material to examine, bibliographic verification, and location of sources. Since computer-based cataloging systems are the most powerful tool to carry out these simultaneous processes and an area of the least prior information by the student, it forms the next section of the course.

Catalog-Based Systems

Students are introduced to the basic concepts permitting shared computer cataloging–MARC, AACR2, etc.,–and the nature of telecommunicated information. As little time as possible is spent on these discussions for several reasons: (1) they are foreign to any previous experience and nearly unintelligible in the abstract; (2) none of the systems are user friendly and are unlikely to become so until either overlay help screens are designed or new systems, such as OCLC's Oxford, are developed. Nonetheless, it is important for students to understand the national cooperative effort involved and the necessary standardization for the sake of the computer if not the rest of us.

More time is spent on the cataloging networks or bibliographic utilities. OCLC is used as the point of departure simply because it is Indiana University's primary bibliographic utility. The Music Library provides access to OCLC, RLIN, MUMS, etc., all with reference assistance. Public access OCLC terminals are available in the University Library. Under a new proposal, OCLC access may be provided to students in the Music Library through the Bloomington Academic Computing System. Help screens will be designed under this proposal.

Bibliographic access, interlibrary loan, subject access, and bibliographic verification are emphasized in the discussions. Where possible, hands-on experience is given as part of the class. The emerging international applications of these systems is discussed as a likely future trend.

Discussions of MARC, AACR2, OCLC, etc., lend naturally to a rather focused discussion of the card catalog at Indiana University. The computer-assisted instruction module dealing with the card catalog and uniform titles–the subject of an earlier paper by Michael Fling–is used in the place of lecture time on this subject. Class time is devoted to subject heading structures, the public use of the shelf list, and various ancillary tools, such as the Library of Congress Subject Heading List and the Class M schedule, etc.

Databases–External

External databases are introduced again focused upon their applied use in the research proposal. The focus is on *RILM Abstracts, Dissertation Abstracts,* and *Arts & Humanities Citation Index,* but the availability of other databases from Dialog and BRS is also noted.

This fall, there is a new emphasis on downloading information directly from catalog networks and external databases into a database form without typing in the information. We are using PBS software for this purpose. It stores the bibliography on a disk, allows for searching, and exports the data in a variety of bibliographic citation formats.

Documentation Techniques

Alas, despite this electronic future, documentation techniques are still taught in the music bibliography course. What is taught is the most recent version of Turabian's *A Manual for Writers of Term Papers, Theses, and Dissertations àla Fenske.* This manual is not and was not chosen by me. It was chosen by the Graduate Office of the School of Music at a time now shrouded in mystery and for equally clear reasons since it contains but one reference to music. Still, Turabian is one of the widely accepted manuals and the only "national" choice offered by the School of Music. My own variations are achieved by the provision of parallel music examples to those of Turabian's Chapter 8, which I have included in the course syllabus below.

The basic problem remains, there is no standard for music documentation recognized by the music scholarly community and embraced by its professional associations, journals, and major publishers. The teaching of this important subject remains murky. The time devoted must be minimized including that devoted to it in this presentation.

Reference Sources

As a few of you know and many may have guessed, there is a 100 page booklet produced for this course each semester. While it covers all of the topics mentioned in this paper, the emphasis is on documentation, the research proposal, and reference sources. The computer-based systems are taught entirely in the context of lectures. Five years ago the booklet was only 8-10 pages shorter despite many new reference tools. The changes over that period are more dramatic than that indicated by its growth. At the end of this article, at the head of the course syllabus, is the table of contents from the current booklet from which you may at least judge its coverage and its proportions. There are approximately 300 citations in the reference sources parts of the booklet. Of these, one-third consume concentrated class time, one-third are mentioned fairly briefly, and one-third are in the booklet for further student consultation. The order is approximately that of the topic search outline. Non-music tools are included at the end of the course.

The greatest concentration is given to the following sections: encyclopedias, dictionaries, periodical indexes, bibliographies of music literature, catalogs of music libraries, bibliographies of music pre- and post-1800, thematic catalogs, discographies, and non-music reference tools. These categories then constitute the core of the literature taught to this diverse group and would be approximately equal to the 100 citations demanding some in-depth time.

EDUCATION FOR THE FUTURE OF MUSIC INFORMATION

What Is the Core Literature?

What is the core literature taught in this music bibliography course to academics, music librarians, and performers? How can it be conceptualized and understood?

The core literature can be seen as a series of concentric rings with the topic search strategy at the core. The first ring consists of the core's extension adding approximately 100 tools to those previously identified in the core. The next ring consists of approximately

100 reference sources of which the student ought to have some awareness in greater or lesser detail. The third ring consists of another 100 sources for which the booklet serves as a source to look them up and understand their relationship to their topic search strategy. The fourth ring and beyond belongs to specialist literature and is outside the scope of the course.

Considered in this context, it would be difficult to identify any music graduate student who does not need to know in depth the core and the first ring, which include computer-based tools, in order to be music information literate: the goal of this music bibliography course. In order to identify the core plus the first ring a bibliography of ca. 120 reference tools attracting focused attention in the course has been prepared and distributed. Compared to some of the earlier comments in this paper identifying sections emphasized in the course, you will note only a few library catalogs and no thematic catalogs on this list. The Brook and Wettstein bibliographies are included here. Numerous examples from these two categories are discussed in the next "ring" of literature. The emphasis is on dictionaries, encyclopedias, indexes, finding tools, and other similar landmarks or what Hibberd calls pilot works in his 1962 article.[1]

Held notes in his article "Teaching Reference and Bibliography" that: "A rule of thumb is this: The total number of sources studied during the course should equal approximately the number of class meetings ... multiplied by four."[2] Using this formula coincidentally equals 120 sources. But the sources of the core, the first ring, and many of the second ring sources (i.e., music library catalogs and thematic catalogs) exceeds the formula. While different faculty would emphasize different works, the point here is to note that all graduate music students must have an acquaintance with these works to be judged information literate. Understanding how these works are related to one another is more important than what is retained about each source.

Conclusions

The application of this acquired information is immediately made to the semester-long writing of the research proposal. The documentation techniques are applied to the research proposal process, but an emphasis is placed on information sources more than on documentation techniques. Learning about information systems is more important than learning about individual sources. The sources will change fairly quickly, the systems will change more slowly and will remain more relevant to the professional lives of the student for a longer period of time.

Information Prospects

The world of music information has always changed, but changes seem more rapid now; the format of transmission is changing, and access to larger quantities of information is increasing. Educating for the future of music information must include knowledge of traditional reference courses blended with emerging technology. The immediate future contains faster and larger personal computers based on the 386 chip and hard disks commonly in the 60 megabyte range. The CD-ROM technology is already demonstrated in general reference sources. When will Grove's be issued in this format? The read and write optical disk will significantly increase the capacity of future personal computers to perhaps a gigabyte. The ability for an individual to have, store, and manipulate music information will certainly expand in the next five years. The challenge for music libraries will be to change rapidly enough to provide the information bridges, the interface to these information systems, and to place more information in the hands of more people. Bibliographic instruction must prepare the way for today's students to be tomorrow's information literate faculty members and to be able to sort through this mass of information with discernment.

What is retained, actually learned in such a course? In a specific sense, we do not know and we need to know. Roland Person in a 1981 article argues for evaluation and completed a study. He distinguishes between time of course evaluation and long-term evaluation. To measure what has been retained, it is not enough to do pre- and post-test studies, but, "What is needed is an evaluation of the long-term effects of courses in bibliographic instruction and their effects on students' later academic attitudes and achievements."[3] His study of general library bibliographic instruction supports the notion that ". . . the appreciation of the course would increase over time."[4] We need, in music bibliographic instruction, long-term studies to assess that which is learned and retained.

MUSIC BIBLIOGRAPHY CORE LITERATURE

Albrecht, Otto Edwin. *A Census of Autograph Music Manuscripts of European Composers in American Libraries.* Philadelphia: University of Pennsylvania Press, 1953.

Apel, Willi. *Harvard Dictionary of Music.* 2nd ed., rev. and enl. Cambridge, Mass.: Harvard University Press, Belknap Press, 1969.

American Music Center. *Catalog of the American Music Library.* Edited by Karen McNerney Famera and Eero Richmond. 4 vols. New York: The Center, 1975-1983.

_____. *Compositions. Libretti, and Translations Supported by the National Endowment of the Arts Composer-Librettist Program.* New York: American Music Center, 1978.

American Society of Composers, Authors, and Publishers. *ASCAP Concert and Symphonic Band Catalog.* New York: ASCAP, 1970.

_____. *ASCAP Index of Performed Compositions.* New York: ASCAP, 1978. 1423 p.

_____. *ASCAP Symphonic Catalog.* 3rd ed. New York: Bowker, 1977.

Anderson, Ruth, comp. *Contemporary American Composers: A Biographical Dictionary.* Boston: G. K. Hall, 1976.

Arts and Humanities Citation Index. Philadelphia: Institute for Scientific Information, 1976-.

Baker, Theodore. *Baker's Biographical Dictionary of Musicians.* Completely revised by Nicholas Slonimsky. 7th ed. New York: Macmillan Publishing Co., G. Schirmer, 1984.

Bibliographic Guide to Music: 1975-. Boston: G. K. Hall, 1976-.

Bibliographic des Musikschrifttums. Jahrgang 1936-. Leipzig: F. Hofmeister, 1936-.

Le Bibliographie Musical. Reunion d'artiste et d'erudits. 29 vols. in 2. Paris: N.p., 1872-76; reprint ed., Scarsdale, N.Y.: A. Schnase, 1969.

Bibliographie Musicale Française. 47 vols. in 23. Paris: La

Chambre Syndicale des éditeurs de Musique, 1875-1920; reprint ed., Scarsdale, N.Y.: A. Schnase, 1968.
Boston. Public Library. *Dictionary Catalog of the Music Collection.* Boston: G. K. Hall, 1972. 20 vols.
British Library. Dept. of Manuscripts. *Catalogue of Manuscript Music in the British Museum.* By Augustus Hughes. 3 vols. London: Printed by the order of the Trustees, 1906-9.
British Library. Department of Manuscripts. *Handlist of Music Manuscripts Acquired 1908-67.* By Pamela J. Willets. London: British Museum, 1970.
British Library. *The Catalogue of Printed Music in the British Library to 1980.* London: New York: K. G. Saur, 1981(43 vols. to date).
Broadcast Music, Inc. *Symphonic Catalogue.* New York: Broadcast Music, 1971. 375p. *Supplement*, 1978.
Brockhaus-Riemann Musik Lexikon. Herausgegeben von Carl Dahlhaus und Hans Heinrich Eggebrecht. 2 vols. Wiesbaden: Brockhaus, 1978.
Brook, Barry S. *Thematic Catalogues in Music: An Annotated Bibliography Including Printed, Manuscript, and In-Preparation Catalogues; Related Literature and Reviews; an Essay on the Definitions, History, Functions, Historiography, and Future of the Thematic Catalogue.* Hillsdale, N.Y.: Pendragon Press, 1972.
Charles, Sidney. *A Handbook of Music and Music Literature in Sets and Series.* New York: Free Press, 1972.
de Charms, Desiree. *Songs in Collections: An Index.* Detroit: Information Service, 1966.588p.
Choral Music in Print. Philadelphia: Music Data, 1974-. Vol. I: *Sacred Choral Music.* Supplement, 1981. Vol. II: *Secular Choral Music.* Supplement, 1982.
Classical Vocal Music in Print. Edited by Thomas R. Nardone. Philadelphia: Musicdata, 1976.
Coffin, Berton. *Singer's Repertoire.* Part 5: *Program Notes for the Singers Repertoire.* New York: Scarecrow Press, 1978.
_____. *Singer's Repertoire.* 2nd ed. New York: Scarecrow Press, 1960-62. 4 vols.
Comprehensive Dissertation Index: 1861-1972. Vol. 31: *Commu-*

nications and the Arts, pp. 269-589 (Music). Ann Arbor: University Microfilms, 1973.

Comprehensive Dissertation Index Five Year Cumulation 1973-1977. Vol. 16: Language and Literature U-Z, Communications, Arts. Philosophy, Religion, pp. 277-452 (music). Ann Arbor: University Microfilms, 1979.

Cooper, David Edwin. *International Bibliography of Discographies: Classical Music and Jazz and Blues, 1962-1972.* Littleton, Colo.: Libraries Unlimited, 1975.

Coover, James B. *Music Lexicography Including a Study of Lacunae in Music Lexicography and a Bibliography of Music Dictionaries.* 3rd ed. Carlisle, Pa.: Carlisle Books, 1971.

Deutsches Musikgeschichtliches Archiv. *Katalog der Filmsammlung.* Kassel: Bärenreiter, 1955-.

Directory of Music Faculties in Colleges and Universities. U.S. and Canada 1984-1986. Boulder, CO: College Music Society, 1985.

The Directory of the World of Music: The Musician's Guide. New York: Music Information Services, 196-. (Annual)

Dissertation Abstracts International (title varies). Ann Arbor, MI: University Microfilms, 1938 to date.

Dizionario enciclopedico universale della musica e dei musicisti. 8 vols. Torino: Utet, 1984.

Druesedow, John. *Library Research Guide to Music.* Ann Arbor: Pierian, 1982.

Duckles, Vincent, comp. *Music Reference and Research Materials: An Annotated Bibliography.* 3rd ed. New York: Macmillan Publishers, Free Press, 1974.

Eggebrecht, Hans Heinrich. *Handwörterbuch der musikalischen Terminologie.* Wiesbaden: Franz Steiner Verlag, 1972.

Eitner, Robert. *Bibliographie der Musik-Sammelwerke des XVI. und XVII. Jahrhunderts.* Berlin: N.p., 1877; reprint ed., Hildesheim: Olms, 1963. 964p.

_____. *Biographisch-Bibliographisches Quellen-Lexikon der Musiker und Musikgelehrten der christlichen Zeitrechnung bis Mitte des neunzehnten Jahrhunderts.* 2. verbesserte Auflage. 11 vols. in 6. Leipzig: Breitkopf & Härtel, 1898-1904; reprint ed., Graz: Akademische Druck- iu. Verlagsanstalt, 1959-60.

Fellinger, Imogen. *Verzeichnis der Musikzeitschriften des 19. Jahrhunderts*. Regensburg: Gustav Bosse, 1969.

Fétis, Francois. *Biographie Universelle des Musiciens et Bibliographie Générale de la Musique*. Supplement et complément pub. sous la direction de M. Arthur Pougin. 2me ed. 10 vols. Paris: Firmin Didot Freres, 1860-70; 1878-80.

Fink, Robert, and Ricci, Robert. *The Language of Twentieth Century Music: A Dictionary of Terms*. New York: Macmillan Publishing Co., Schirmer Books, 1975.

Gerboth, Walter. *An Index to Musical Festschriften and Similar Publications*. W.W. Norton & Co., 1969.

Gray, Michael, and Gibson, Gerald. *Bibliography of Discographies*. Vol. 1-. New York: Bowker, 1977.

Gribenski, Jean, comp. *French Language Dissertations in Music: An Annotated Bibliography*. New York: Pendragon Press, 1979.

Grigg, Carolyn D., comp. *Music Translation Dictionary: An English, Czech, Danish, Dutch, French, German, Hungarian, Italian, Polish, Portuguese, Russian, Spanish, Swedish Vocabulary of Musical Terms*. Westport, Conn.: Greenwood Press, 1978.

Das Grosse Lexikon der Musik in acht Bänden. Hrsg. von Marc Honegger und Günther Massenkeil. Freiburg: Herder, 1978-.

Harris, Ernest. *Music Education: A Guide to Information Sources*. Detroit: Gale, 1978.

Helm, Eugene, and Luper, Albert T. *Words and Music: Form and Procedure in Theses, Dissertations, Research Papers, Book Reports, Programs, and Theses in Composition*. Rev. ed. Hackensack, N.J.: Joseph Boonin, 1971; Totowa, N.J.: European American Music, 1982.

Heyer, Anna. *Historical Collected Editions and Monuments of Music: A Guide to Their Contents*. 3rd ed. Chicago: American Library Association, 1980.

Hofmeisters Handbuch der Musikliteratur. Bd. 1-. Leipzig: F. Hofmeister, 1844-(Title varies: Vols. 1-3, *C.F. Whistling's Handbuch der musikalischen Literatur*, Vols. 4-6, *Handbuch der musikalischen Literatur*).

Honegger, Marc, ed. *Dictionnaire de la Musique*. Paris: Bordas, 1970.

Hughes, Andrew. *Medieval Music: The Sixth Liberal Art.* Rev. ed. Toronto: University of Toronto Press, 1980.

International Index of Dissertations and Musicological Works in Progress. Edited by Cecil Adkins and Alis Dickinson. Philadelphia: American Musicological Society and the International Musicological Society, 1977. *American-Canadian Supplement.* 1979, 1984.

International Musicological Society and the International Association of Music Libraries. *International Inventory of Musical Sources/Répertoire International des Sources Musicales.* Munich-Duisberg: G. Henle Verlag, 1960-. 3 series.

International *Who's Who in Music and Musicians' Directory.* Edited by Adrian Gaster. 9th ed. Cambridge, England: Melrose Press, 1980.

Jablonski, Edward. *The Encyclopedia of American Music.* Garden City, N.Y.: Doubleday, 1981.

Jahresverzeichnis der deutschen Musikalien und Musikschriften. Jahrgang 1-. Leipzig: F. Hofmeister, 1852-. (Title varies: 1852-53, *Kurzes Verzeichnis sämmtlicher in Deutschland und den angrenzenden Laendern gedruckter Musikalien;* 1929-1942, *Hofmeisters Jahresverzeichnis.*

Kennington, Donald. *The Literature of Jazz: A Critical Guide.* 2nd ed. Chicago: American Library Association, 1980.

Kinkle, Roger D. *The Complete Encyclopedia of Popular Music and Jazz 1900-1950.* New Rochelle, N.Y.: Arlington House, 1974.

Kobbe, Gustav. *The New Kobbe's Complete Opera Book.* Edited and revised by the Earl of Harewood. New York: G. P. Putman's Sons, 1976.

Krummel, Donald. *Guide to Dating Early Music: A Manual of Bibliographic Practices.* Hackensack, N. J.: J. Boonin, 1974.

Leigh, Robert. *Index to Song Books: A Title Index to Over 11,000 Copies of almost 6,800 in 111 Song Books Published between 1933 and 1962.* New York: Da Capo, 1973.

Loewenberg, Alfred. *Annals of Opera 1597-1940.* 3rd ed. Totowa, N.J.: Rowan and Littlefield, 1978

Marco, Guy A., comp. *Information on Music: A Handbook of Reference Sources in European Languages.* Vol. 1: *Basic and Uni-*

versal Sources; Vol. 2: *The Americas;* Vol. 3: *Europe.* Littleton, Colo.: Libraries Unlimited, 1975-84.

_____. *Opera: A Research and Information Guide.* New York: Garland, 1984.

Marcuse, Sibyl. *Musical Instruments: A Comprehensive Dictionary.* Corrected ed. N.Y.: Norton, 1975.

Meadows, Eddie S. *Jazz Reference and Research Materials: A Bibliography.* New York: Garland Publishing, 1981.

Meggett, Joan M. *Music Periodical Literature.* Metuchen, N.J.: Scarecrow Press, 1978.

Miller, Philip L., comp. and trans. *The Ring of Words: An Anthology of Song Texts.* New York: W.W. Norton & Co., 1973.

Modern Language Association. *MLA Handbook for Writers of Research Papers, Theses, and Dissertations.* New York: Modern Language Association of America, 1984.

Music Article Guide: A Comprehensive Quarterly Reference Guide to Significant Signed Feature Articles in American Music Periodicals. Vol. 1-. Philadelphia: Music Article Guide, 1966-.

The Music Index: The Key to Current Music Periodical Literature. Vol. 1, no. 1-. Detroit: Information Service, 1949-.

Music Library Association. *A Checklist of Music Bibliographies and Indexes in Progress and Unpublished.* Compiled by Dee Baily. 4th ed. Philadelphia: Music Library Association, 1982.

Musical America 1986 International Directory of the Performing Arts

Die Musik in Geschichte und Gegenwart. Edited by Friedrich Blume. 14 vols. Kassel: Bärenreiter, 1949-68. 6 supplements in 2 vols.

The New Grove Dictionary of Music and Musicians. Edited by Stanley Sadie. 20 vols. Washington D.C.: Macmillan Publishing Co., 1980.

The New Grove Dictionary of Musical Instruments and Instrument Makers. Edited by Stanley Sadie. 3 vols. London: Macmillan, 1984.

New Serial Titles: A Union List of Serials Commencing Publication After Dec. 31. 1949. Washington: Library of Congress, 1953-.

New York. Public Library. Reference Dept. *Dictionary Catalog of the Music Collection.* 34 vols. Boston: G.K. Hall, 1964. 1964-71, 10 vols.; 1971-74, 1 vol.

New York Times Index. New York: New York Times, 1851-. Semimonthly.

News Bank Review of the Arts. Performing Arts. Stanford, Conn.: Newsband, 1978.

OCLC. On-Line Union Catalog.

Orchestral Music in Print. Edited by Margaret K. Farish. Philadelphia: Musicdata, 1979. Supplement, 1983.

Organ Music in Print. Edited by Walter A. Fraenkel. 2nd ed. Philadelphia: Musicdata, 1984.

Porte, Jacques, ed. *Encyclopedie des Musiques Sacrees.* 3 vols. Paris: Editions Labergerie, n.d.

Répertoire International de Littérature Musicale: RILM Abstracts. Jan. 1967-. Flushing, N.Y.: International RILM Center, Queens College of the City University of New York, 1967-.

Research Libraries Group. Research Libraries Information Network.

Resources of American Music History: a Directory of Source Materials from Colonial Times to World War II. Edited by D.W. Krummel et. al. Urbana: University of Illinois Press, 1981.

Rezits, Joseph. *The Guitarist's Resource Guide: Guitar Music in Print and Books on the Art of the Guitar.* San Diego: Pallma Music, 1983.

Rezits, Joseph and Deatsman, Gerald. *The Pianist's Resource Guide: Piano Music in Print and Literature on the Pianistic Art* Park Ridge, IL: Pallma Music Corp./Neil A. Kjos, 1974. 933p.

Roche, Jerome. *A Dictionary of Early Music from the Troubadours to Monteverdi,* London: Faber, 1981.

Rodgers and Hammerstein Archives of Recorded Sound. *Dictionary Catalog of the Rogers and Hammerstein Archives of Recorded Sound.* 15 vols. Boston:

Sartori, Claudio. *Bibliografia della Musica Strumentale Italiana Stampata in Italia fino al 1700.* 2 vols. Florence: Olschki, 1968.

Schall, Richard. *Abkurzungen in der Musik-Terminologie: Eine Übersicht.* Taschenbücher zur Musikwissenschaft, 1. Wilhelmshaven: Heinrichshofen Verlag, 1969.

Schaal, Richard. *Verzeichnis deutschsprachiger musikwissenschaft-*

licher Dissertationen, 1861-1960. Kassel: Bärenreiter, 1963. *Supplement. 1961-1970.* Kassel: Bärenreiter, 1974.

Schilling, Gustav. *Encyclopaedie der gesammten musikalischen Wissenschaften, oder Universal-Lexikon der Tonkunst.* 6 vols. plus supplement. Stuttgart: Franz Koehler, 1835; reprint ed., Hildesheim: Georg Olms Verlag, 1974.

Schnapper, Edith, ed. *British Union Catalogue of Early Music Printed Before the Year 1801: A Record of the Holdings of Over 100 Libraries Throughout the British Isles.* 2 vols. London: Butterworths Scientific Publications, 1957.

Sears, M.E. *Song Index.* New York: H.W. Wilson, 1926.

Sheehy, Eugene P., comp. *Guide to Reference Books.* 9th ed. with supplements. Chicago: American Library Association, c1976. Supplements, 1980, 1982.

Sibley Music Library. *Catalog of Sound Recordings: The University of Rochester. Eastman School of Music.* Rochester. New York. 14 vols. Boston: G.K. Hall, 1977.

Stieger, Franz. *Opernlexikon.* Tützing: Hans Schneider, 1975. 4 vols.

String Music in Print: 1984 Supplement. Edited by Margart Farish. Philadelphia: Musicdata, 1984.

Terminorum musicae Index septem linguis redactus: Polyglottes Wörterbuch der musikalischen Terminologie: Deutsch. Englisch. Französisch. Italienisch, Spanisch, Ungarisch, Russisch. Edited by Horst Leuchtmann. Budapest: Akademiai Kiado, 1978; Kassel: Bärenreiter, 1978.

Thompson, Kenneth. *A Dictionary of Twentieth-Century Composers (1911-1971).* New York: St. Martin's Press, 1973.

Thompson, Oscar, ed. *The International Cyclopedia of Music and Musicians.* 11th ed. New York: Dodd, Mead, 1985.

Turabian, Kate L. *A Manual for Writers of Term Papers, Theses, and Dissertations.* 4th ed. Chicago: University of Chicago Press, 1973.

Tyrrell, John, and Wise, Rosemary. *A Guide to International Congress Reports in Musicology, 1900-1975.* New York: Garland Publishing, 1979.

Union List of Serials in Libraries of the United States and Canada. Edited by Edna B. Titus. 3rd ed. New York: Wilson, 1965.

Universal-Handbuch der Musikliteratur aller Zeiten und Völker. 9 vols. Vienna: Pazdirek, 1904-1910.

University of Chicago. *A Manual of style.* 13th ed., rev. Chicago: University of Chicago Press, 1982.

U.S. Copyright Office. *Catalog of Copyright Entries.* New Series (1906-1946), Part 3: *Musical Compositions.* Third Series (1947-), Part 5: *Music;* Part 14: *Sound Recordings.* Washington: Library of Congress, 1891-.

U.S. *Library of Congress Catalog: Music and Phonorecords: A Cumulative List of Works Represented by Library of Congress Printed Cards.* Washington: Library of Congress, 1953. Five Year cumulations are published under the title: *National Union Catalog* as follows: 1953-57. Vol. 27, Totowa, N.J.: Rowman and Littlefield, 1966. 1963-67. Vol. 1-3, Ann Arbor, Mich.: Edwards, 1969. 1968-72. Vol. 1-4, Ann Arbor, Mich.: Edwards, 1973. Music books are included in the main volumes of the *National Union Catalog* to which the above are supplements.

U.S. Library of Congress. *Library of Congress Catalogs: Subject Catalog.* Washington, D.C.: Library of Congress, Card Division, 1950 to date.

──────. *The National Union Catalog: A Cumulative Author List.* Washington, D.C.: Library of Congress, Card Division, 1956 to date.

Vogel, Emil; Einstein, A.; Lesure, F.; and Sartori, C., eds. *Bibliografia della musica Italiana Vocale Profana Pubblicata dal 1500 al 1700.* 3 vols. Geneva Minkoff, 1977.

Voigt, John, and Kane, Randall. *Jazz Music in Print.* 2nd ed. Boston: Hornpipe Music Pub. Co., 1978.

Walford, Albert John. *Guide to Reference Materials.* 3rd ed. London: Library Association, 1973-1977. 3 vols.

──────. *Walford's Guide to Reference Material.* 4th ed. London: Library Association, 1980.

Watanabe, Ruth T. *Introduction to Music Research.* Englewood Cliffs, N.J.: Prentice-Hall, 1967.

Wenk, Arthur B. *Analyses of Nineteenth-Century Music. 1940-1975.* Ann Arbor, MI: Music Library Association, 1976.

──────. *Analyses of Twentieth-Century Music, 1940-1970.* Ann Arbor, Mich: Music Library Association, 1975.

_____. *Analyses of Twentieth-Century Music: Supplement. 1970-1975.* Ann Arbor: Music Library Association, 1976. Supplement, Boston, 1984.

Wettstein, Hermann. *Biblioqraphie musikalischer thematischer Verzeichnisse.* Laaber: Laaber Verlag, 1978.

Who's Who in Opera. New York: Arno Press, 1976.

Word by Word Translations of Songs and Arias. Part I: *German and French* by B. Coffin, W. Singer, and P. Delattre. New York: Scarecrow Press, 1966. Part II: *Italian* by A. Schoep and D. Harris. Metuchen, N.J.: Scarecrow Press, 1972.

INTRODUCTION TO MUSIC BIBLIOGRAPHY

Syllabus
Guides to Research/Some Recommended Style Manuals
Glossary
Selection/Acquisition Aids
Research Proposal
Topic Search
Bibliographic Style Worksheet
Bibliographic Examples: Book/Score/Record
Study Examples
I.U. School of Music: General Style Guide
Guidelines for Educational Uses of Music
What teachers & libraries can & can't do under the new law
Catalog Cards
Subject Headings
Music Dictionaries
Encyclopedias
Music Periodical Indexes
Bibliographies of Music Literature
Special Subject Reference Tolls
Catalogs of Music Libraries and Private Collections
Catalogs of Music Instrument Collections/Iconography
Bibliographies of Music Pre-1800
Bibliographies of Music Post-1800
Bibliographies of Music

Thematic Catalogs
Discographies
Non-Music Reference Tools
National Bibliographies

RESEARCH PROPOSAL

All viable studies serve some intellectual purpose other than course and degree requirements. The three primary research methodologies in music (historical, theoretical, and pedagogical) emphasize different parts of a research proposal. The form of proposals differ with their context. Grants frequently are written according to stated detailed outlines, dissertation proposals usually conform to more general outlines or the views of the faculty advisor. The purpose of this proposal is not to present any particular form, but to identify the elements in virtually all research proposals. Additionally, this proposal is intended to apply the bibliographic descriptive and identification techniques taught in this course. The requirement for M539 is the proposal, not completion of the study itself.

TITLE
The title of the project should be descriptive of the scope in the minimum number of words. Amusing titles should not be used. This is not due to a lack of appreciation, but to the imprecision involved. Decide the keywords describing your study before you attempt to form a title, e.g., manuscript, analysis, statistical, survey, random, first edition, etc. The title should accurately characterize the scope and the implied methodology.

SCOPE
The statement of scope fully outlines the parameters of the study indicating the areas it will cover and those it will not. It states the major theses, questions, and hypotheses which distinguish a research study from many pedagogically-oriented, descriptive term papers. In the latter case for example, the assignment may have been an analysis of a work or movement. Except in minute details, it may not have differed significantly from most other analyses of this work. In order for this paper to become a research project, it

must break some new ground. Perhaps you intend to prove the form is not a sonata form as previously believed, but a rondo following a model known to the composer as documented by some contemporaneous evidence. Further, you will show its use by the composer in similarly positioned movements in several other works for the same performing medium as well as for some others.

SOURCES AND EVIDENCE

Cite and summarize the evidence for your theses, review the various editions of work forming the study's focus, or indicate the location and availability of subjects as appropriate to your study. Evaluate the evidence as it is appropriate to your theses or indicate your reasons for choosing an edition. Reference should be made to full citations in the bibliography.

LITERATURE REVIEW

The literature review discusses and summarizes the contents of significant books and journal articles appropriate for the study. The items are cited in the bibliography. This section should demonstrate a familiarity with the literature as a whole and the ability to discern the evolving contributions of many authors.

What evidence was used by these authors? What is their methodological framework? What sampling techniques and statistical tests are used? What is the analytical level? What is ignored? How are the conclusions drawn? What are the conclusions? A lack of discernment is shown when the proposal repetitively describes similar conclusions by many authors. When the literature review groups significant literature with similar findings, methodological frameworks, etc. and traces the intellectual development of the literature, it then informs the reader, permits a discourse, and convinces the reader of your understanding of the field. By default, the literature review establishes the significance of your approach and leads naturally to the next section.

NEED

In the need section, the theses and supporting evidence are compared with the literature review and a statement of need is provided. Except for statistically oriented replication studies, all viable research projects must demonstrate a new approach or significantly different conclusions and convince the reader. The degree of significance is frequently the issue in need statements. The proposal must demonstrate an interesting set of ideas or new supporting evidence not previously discussed in the literature in order for the study to be viable.

METHODOLOGY
The methodology section states the study's methodological framework. While it may refer to established analytical labels (e.g., Schenkerian analyses), to random samples and statistical tests, or a chronological schema, it should elaborate beyond these labels. It should describe how evidence will be handled, viewed, and evaluated.

ORGANIZATION
Outline the proposed study's organization. You may wish to think of this as a tentative table of contents indicating all of the constituent parts.

QUALIFICATIONS
The qualifications section, the only one which may use the first person, simply recounts the required historical, theoretical, language, or statistical training to complete the study possessed by you.

BIBLIOGRAPHY
The organization of the bibliography evolves from its length. Extensive bibliographies frequently require categories, short ones do not. The bibliographic format will be the one used in M539. No abbreviations will be used. Full citations are expected. Citations to standard reference works are not appropriate, but those to the scholarly literature, relevant editions, or primary source material are required. Any item referred to in the proposal must be cited. Other items may be cited if they are published in scholarly sources. The object of this bibliography is not all the literature, but, rather, all the significant literature.

In completing the proposal, you may wish to review style by referring to Strunk & White and research techniques by reading relevant sections of Barzun's book.

TOPIC SEARCH

1. Encyclopedias
   a. International: NGD, MGG
   b. National: see encyclopedia section

2. Periodical indexes: MI, RILM Abstracts, AHCI, MAG, BdM

3. Dissertation indexes: CDI, IIDM, Schaal, Gribenski, DA

4. Festschriften and Congress Reports: Gerboth, Tyrrell, RILM

5. Bibliographic verification sources
   a. OCLC, RLIN, WLN, UTLAS, etc.
   b. Music & Phonorecords, NYPL & Bibliographic Guide

6. Music search
   a. 1-5: a,b above
   b. Thematic catalogs: Brook, Wettstein
   c. Critical editions (Heyer and Charles)
   d. Music in-print sources: see Bibliographies of Music–Music in Print
   e. Bibliographies of Music section

7. Source location search
   a. Thematic catalogs: Brook, Wettstein
   b. RISM-A or B
   c. 5a and multi-library union lists: see Bibliographies of pre-1800 Music section
   d. Large or national Lib. (Music, Books, on Music and Sound Recordings, NYPL, Bibliographic Guide, British Lib.): see Catalogs of Music Libraries section
   e. Lesser Lib. catalogs defined by geography, time and collection emphasis: see Catalogs of Music Libraries section
   f. RISM-C defined by geography, time and collection emphasis

As needed:
Supplemental Literature Search
1. Special topics
2. Performance practice
3. Retrospective bibliographies

NOTES

1. Lloyd Hibberd, "The Teaching of Bibliography," *Notes*, 20 (1962-63):33-40.
2. Ray E. Held, "Teaching Reference and Bibliography," *Journal of Education for Librarianship*, 229.
3. Roland Person, "Long-Term Evaluation of Bibliographic Instruction: Lasting Encouragement," *College & Research Libraries* (January 1981): 20.
4. Ibid., p.23.

The Problem of Definitive Identification in the Indexing of Hymn Tunes

Nicholas Temperley

SUMMARY. The goal of the project is to compile an index of printed sources of hymn tunes with English-language texts from the Reformation to 1820. Each tune is identified in the index by an incipit of ten notes in numerical code. The tune itself is provided, as is the meter of its text, a list of its printed sources, and its composer or compiler. The article describes some of the difficulties encountered in cataloging the many tunes for the index.

The *Hymn Tune Index* project of the University of Illinois started, in its present form, in 1982. It is funded principally by a research grant from the National Endowment for the Humanities, which has been extended, but will run out in the summer of 1987. It is staffed by Charles G. Manns as project associate, several graduate assistants, and myself as project director. What we are doing is to assemble and index all printed sources of hymn tunes intended for use with English-language texts, beginning at the beginning (the Reformation) and ending, for the time being, at the year 1820. Over half of these sources are British in origin and most of the remainder are American. The information is stored in a database and will ultimately be made available on-line as well as in book form.

Nicholas Temperley is affiliated with the School of Music at the University of Illinois.

[Haworth co-indexing entry note]: "The Problem of Definitive Identification in the Indexing of Hymn Tunes." Temperley, Nicholas. Co-published simultaneously in *Music Reference Services Quarterly*, (The Haworth Press, Inc.) Vol. 2, No. 3/4, 1993, pp. 227-239; and: *Foundations in Music Bibliography* (ed: Richard D. Green) The Haworth Press, Inc., 1993, pp. 227-239. Multiple copies of this article/chapter may be purchased from The Haworth Document Delivery Center [1-800-3-HAWORTH; 9:00 a.m. - 5:00 p.m. (EST)].

© 1993 by The Haworth Press, Inc. All rights reserved.

Hymn tunes would seem to be a relatively simple thing to index. That is what I thought when I got into this business. To begin with, the Anglo-Saxon hymn tradition has the unique feature of tune names, which allow hymns to be readily identified independently of the texts that are sung to them. Many enthusiasts in the past have started indexing hymn tunes by means of the names, but it did not take them very long to discover that tunes change their name with disturbing frequency, while names quite often change their tune. Evidently one has to deal with the tunes themselves by some means. Simple codes have been used for hymn tunes in pre-computer days by Katharine Diehl, by Richard Crawford, and by Manns and myself in our pilot study *Fuging Tunes in the Eighteenth Century*. In a computerized index, the need for numerical coding of the music is obvious.

Examples 1 and 2 show our method in action. Example 2 is a facsimile of one of the more complex tunes (only about half the

EXAMPLE 1

```
Incipit: 12231442231
Meter:  888808888
12231442
23345221
00000000
53(2345)432345
[51D7U13221]
3115(43)4545
53(43)23(21)12D7U1
00000000
25(43)23(1)43(4231)D7U1
```

Date	CC	Source	Tune name	Text	Attribution	Key	Setting
1759	e	ArnoJLH 1	Charley	WWOWLT1	Arnold J	g	3/4
1767	e	ArnoJLH 2	Charley	WWOWLT1	Arnold J	g	3/4
1779	a	LawASH b	Cheshire	WWOWLT1	Arnold	a	3/4
1782?	a	LawASH c	Cheshire	WWOWLT1	Arnold	a	3/4
1782?	a	LawASH d	Cheshire	WWOWLT1	Arnold	a	3/4
1784	a	Bay1DSH b	Cheshire	WWOWLT2		a	3/4
1785?	a	LawASH e	Cheshire	WWOWLT1	Arnold	a	3/4
1788	a	Bay1DNHZ a	Cheshire	WWOWLT1		a	3/4
1788	a	Bay1DNHZ b	Cheshire	WWOWLT1		a	3/4
1789	e	DixoWPC a	Zion	WWOWLT1	Arnold J	g	3/4
1791	a	LawARM 3	Cheshire	WWOWLT1	Arnold	a	3/4
1792	a	LawARM 4a	Cheshire	WWOWLT1	Arnold	a	3/4
1794	a	LawACH1 a	Cheshire	WWOWLT2		a	3/4
1796	a	LawAAS 1a	Cheshire	WWOWLT2		a	3/4
1799?	a	LawAAS 1b	Cheshire	WWOWLT2		a	3/4
1801	a	LawAAS 2b	Cheshire	WWOWLT2		a	3/4

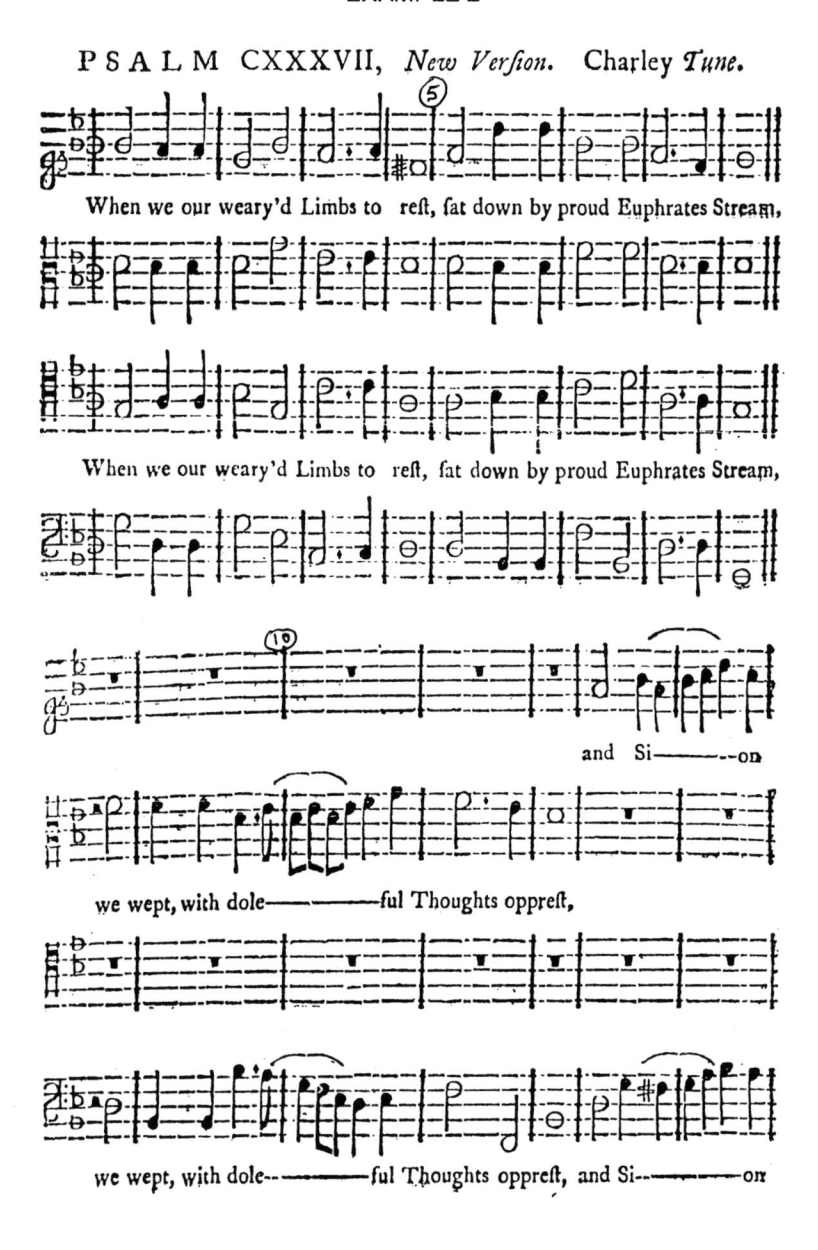

EXAMPLE 2

PSALM CXXXVII, *New Version.* Charley *Tune.*

EXAMPLE 2 (continued)

[Musical notation with lyrics:]

was our mournful Theme, and Si—on was, and Si—on was our

and Si————on wa————s our

and Si————on was our mournful Theme, and Si—on was our

was our mournful Theme, and Si—on was

music is given here), and Example 1 shows how this tune is processed in the index. The entry is in two parts: the tune, and its history. The tune is first identified by an incipit giving its first ten notes as numbers (1 is *do*, 2 is *re* and so on). Next comes the tune itself, divided into phrases or lines of text, and with a few additional coding features: U means move into the next octave upwards, D means move into the next octave downwards; parentheses enclose all the notes of a melisma after the first; brackets enclose notes sung to repeated words of the text; a zero means that the part carrying the tune–here the tenor–is silent for that syllable of text. Finally, we give the text meter, which corresponds to the number of unenclosed digits in each line of the tune above. The meter, besides being a traditional means of classifying hymn tunes, is a basic parameter of our coding system. Our meter code extends the normal one by the use of a zero to indicate a line of tune that repeats a line of text.

Then comes the tune history set out in columns. Each horizontal line represents one printing of the tune. The printed source is identified by source code in the third column. There are ten slots in the source code. The first five are used for an abbreviated entry of the composer or musical compiler–the first four letters of his surname (I should say his or her, although I'm afraid the role of women in this story is not large), then the initial letter of his given name. The sixth and following slots allow an abbreviation of the title of the book. The last slot is reserved for distinguishing different editions of the same book. So, in the first line, ArnoJ LH means John Arnold, *The Leicestershire Harmony,* 1st edition. As you can see from column 1, these sources are arranged in chronological order. The last three sources are ones which we have not yet dated. The other five columns give additional information about the tune as it appears in each source: the tune name, if any; the text (coded by the initial letters of the first six words, plus a number for further identification); the composer to whom the tune is attributed in this source; the final or key of the tune; and the voice setting: 3/4 means that the tune is carried by the third voice from the top in a four-voice setting; that is, probably the tenor. The source codes refer to a bibliography giving full information about each source. The text code leads to an index of texts, and there are also indexes of tune names and composers that refer back to the main tune index.

In Example 3 I have listed the principal questions that our index is designed to answer. The questions in class A can be answered by

EXAMPLE 3

Class	Given	Question	Access
A	a tune	When/where was this tune first printed?	main index
		What was its original form, key, setting?	main index
		With what text was it first associated?	main index
		Who composed it?	main index
		Where else has it appeared?	main index
		In what forms and settings?	main index
		When/where was it most popular?	main index
B	a composer	What tunes did (s)he compose?	composer index
	a tune name	What tune(s) have been given this name?	tune name index
	a text	What tunes have been set to this text?	text index
	a source	What tunes were printed in this source?	source list
C	a text meter	What tunes fit this text meter?	metrical sort
	a book	What were the compilers sources for the tunes?	tune sort
	a period	What tunes originated in this period?	date sort

directly looking up a tune in the main index; those in class B by means of subsidiary indexes; those in class C by further sorts and counts that can be performed by the computer. We hope that this precise information can also help to answer broader, more general questions about hymn singing as a part of musical, religious and cultural history. Here, of course, the index has its limits. It covers only printed sources, whereas tunes were often disseminated by manuscript copies or by oral transmission, or by a fourth method, the barrel organ. Nevertheless, printed sources, at least since about 1700, have probably been the most important means of dissemination for most of the English-speaking churches and for domestic hymn singing; and we believe that this first complete documentation of printed sources of English hymns will be a foundation for new historical understanding.

But the primary function of the index is to answer specific questions, such as those in Example 3. We expect that it will be used in this way by hymnbook editors, church musicians, collectors and librarians as well as musicologists or historians interested in larger matters. For every type of question listed in Example 3, the fundamental unit is a single printing of a tune in a single printed source. This fundamental unit is embodied in a single line in the lower part of Example 1. Unfortunately, the integrity of this unit is not as complete as it appears. It conceals a number of ambiguities in both the basic parameters: the source, and the tune. In neither case have we been able to reach our goal of definitive identification.

As regards sources, we index only what we term prototypes, those in which the compiler made new decisions about what tunes to include or about their settings, keys, or texts. If a source has the same tune content as another already indexed, for example an unrevised second edition of a hymnbook, we call it a "subordinate" source and mention it only in the bibliography, even if, for example, the music has been re-engraved. But it is still possible to get a statistical count of the total number of books in which a tune has been printed by adding these subordinate sources to the prototypes. One might question the meaning of such statistics, in the absence of evidence of the number of copies of each source that were printed or sold, which could be anything from one to a million or more; this is a question seldom asked by bibliographers, though it has been addressed by Richard Crawford and Don Krummel among others. But anyway, a printed book, no matter how many or how few copies were distributed, has a certain status and integrity of its own. By treating it as a counting unit, one can place one's study in the long tradition of bibliographical methodology and draw on the vast experience of that tradition. Unfortunately, compilers and publishers of hymnbooks and tunebooks have not always correctly predicted the guidelines of bibliographical societies.

In the early eighteenth century, some perverse country booksellers in England found it profitable to keep their stock in the form of unbound sheets. Example 4 shows part of the tune history of an old psalm tune called *High Dutch,* and it lists identical appearances of the tune in twelve sources, all compiled by Francis Timbrell and entitled *The Divine Musick Scholar's Guide.* We distinguished the "editions" of this work by the letters A through P, but E, F, J and M do not happen to contain this particular tune. Each "edition" of the work, if that is what we should call it, survives in but a single copy. The title pages are all printed from the same plates, and so are the tunes, on one side of the paper only. The only thing that differs is the selection and order of sheets. Most of the copies are in their original eighteenth-century bindings. It looks very much as if customers came to Timbrell's shop in Northamptonshire, made their

EXAMPLE 4

Date	Incipit	Source	Name	Text	Composer	Final	Setting
1715	55436543131	TimbFDM a	HIGH DUTCH	SAIGTL3		F	3/4
1720	55436543131	TimbFDM b	HIGH DUTCH	SAIGTL3		F	3/4
1723	55436543131	TimbFDM c	HIGH DUTCH	SAIGTL3		F	3/4
1723	55436543131	TimbFDM d	HIGH DUTCH	SAIGTL3		F	3/4
1724	55436543131	TimbFDM e	HIGH DUTCH	SAIGTL3		F	3/4
1725	55436543131	TimbFDM f	HIGH DUTCH	SAIGTL3		F	3/4
1726	55436543131	TimbFDM g	HIGH DUTCH	SAIGTL3		F	3/4
1727	55436543131	TimbFDM h	HIGH DUTCH	SAIGTL3		F	3/4
1728	55436543131	TimbFDM i	HIGH DUTCH	SAIGTL3		F	3/4
1731	55436543131	TimbFDM j	HIGH DUTCH	SAIGTL3		F	3/4
1731	55436543131	TimbFDM k	HIGH DUTCH	SAIGTL3		F	3/4
1733	55436543131	TimbFDM l	HIGH DUTCH	SAIGTL3		F	3/4
1733	55436543131	TimbFDM m	HIGH DUTCH	SAIGTL3		F	3/4
1735	55436543131	TimbFDM n	HIGH DUTCH	SAIGTL3		F	3/4
1737	55436543131	TimbFDM o	HIGH DUTCH	SAIGTL3		F	3/4
1742	55436543131	TimbFDM p	HIGH DUTCH	SAIGTL3		F	3/4
1745	55436543131	TimbFDM q	HIGH DUTCH	SAIGTL3		F	3/4
1748	55436543131	TimbFDM r	HIGH DUTCH	SAIGTL3		F	3/4

personal selection of tunes from the sheets available, and had him bind them up with a title page. Of course, we can index each known copy separately, as shown here; but we know that if another copy turns up, it will probably have a different selection of tunes. Are we really justified in treating each of these sources as a different book? If we do, we will distort the count for the tunes concerned, by making them appear to have been more popular than they probably were. But if we do not treat each one separately, how should we treat them? No satisfactory answer has suggested itself. There are a few other books in this category; and there are less extreme cases like the American publisher Daniel Bayley, who took parts of books and merged them into a new book by gradual stages. A related problem concerns the tune supplement, designed to be bound up at the end of a book of hymn texts. When the identical supplement appears bound with two or more different books of texts, are we to treat them as different sources or not?

Strangely similar problems are found in defining tunes, though they have more ramifications. Suppose, as inputter, you were confronted with the tune shown in Example 5. You might at once recognize it as Old Hundredth; but when you typed in the incipit, the computer would produce the standard form of the tune, shown to the left on the handout. The version of Example 5 has two minor differences in the last phrase, both melismatic passing notes. Is this the same tune? Any musician would say it is, I think, and so did the

EXAMPLE 5

INCIPIT: 11765 12333

1. 11D765U123
2. 33321432
3. 12321D67U1
4. 53124321.

METER: 8888

inputter in this case. It would have been nice to record the variants, but we made an early policy decision not to do so, in the interests of getting the job done in time. We conceive our main task as the bringing together of similar tunes, not differentiation between them. So, in this case, the difference is not recorded at all.

But there must come a point at which two similar tunes are judged different. We have drawn the line at a rather low level of variation. For instance, the version shown in Example 6, while having the same incipit and meter, has been entered as a different tune. Here the difference goes beyond passing notes–the last phrase has two main notes different from the standard version. As a rule of thumb, we tell our inputters that if there is more than one difference per line, on the average, it should be entered as a new tune. This example is just beyond the borderline, as it has five differences in four lines. We still have the option of merging tunes at the editing stage, and we may well do so in this case. Even if we do not, we will insert a footnote pointing out the close resemblance.

Example 7 shows several tunes that have the same incipit with different meters. They all derive from the Old 125th which, in turn, came from Psalm 21 in the Genevan Psalter, the version at left. I have no doubt that the others are all simple adaptations of the tune to texts of different meter. Yet we are almost bound to consider these tunes as *different* for indexing purposes, because meter is a fundamental determinant of a hymn tune. For example, anyone who

EXAMPLE 6

INCIPIT: 1176512333

1. 11D765U123
2. 33321432
3. 12321(D7)67U1
4. 5(4)31234(3)21.

METER: 8888

uses the *Hymn Tune Index* as a way of finding a tune to fit a given text will want to sort tunes by meter. Nevertheless, even the apparently clear-cut question of text meter can produce its own ambiguities. Example 8 shows, in schematic form, four "versions" of a hypothetical tune (and there are many examples of this). Versions 1 and 2 are identical except that in Version 2 the second half of the tune is marked to be repeated. Version 3 is identical to Version 2 in performance, but the repeat is written out in musical notation instead of being indicated by signs, so that the score actually contains six lines of music. Version 4 is musically identical to Version 3 but now the fifth and sixth phrases of music have new lines of text, so the text meter has now changed. We have to conclude that Version 4 is not the same tune as Version 1, but where do we draw the line? If we draw it between 3 and 4 on the basis of text meter, we have two identical pieces of music being treated as different tunes; and moreover, if a source contains the tune alone without a text, there will be no way of deciding whether it is Version 3 or 4. If we divide between 2 and 3, we are separating two tunes entirely on the basis of the way they are notated. And if we put the split between 1 and 2, we are separating on the basis of what was probably an optional repeating practice that could well have been carried out in performance even when not marked in print.

These are intractable problems. But they all concern tunes that have the same ten-digit incipit. Whether we decide to merge these

EXAMPLE 7

1. 55436543	1. 55436543	1. 55436543	1. 55436543
2. 1345565	2. 13455665	2. 134565	2. 13455665
3. 5331321	3. 53313221	3. 531321	3. 53124321
4. 5667567U1	4. 5667567U1	4. 5667567U1	4. 56675U1D7U1
5. D566543	5. D566543	5. D566543	5. D5665543
6. 124321.	6. 124321.	6. 124321.	6. 123(4)532D7U1.
METER: 877866	METER: 888866	METER: 866866	METER: 888888

EXAMPLE 8

Version	1	2	3	4
Tune phrases	A B C D	A B ‖: C D :‖	A B C D C D	A B C D C D
Text lines	a b c d	a b c d	a b c d c d	a b c d e f

tunes or treat them as different, there is no danger of losing track of them. The computer will always produce them all in response to their common incipit. What about similar tunes that have different incipits? Example 9 is a good case in point. Two tunes have been written out with their notes in vertical alignment. The upper stave is the famous Tallis's Canon in the form in which it is most generally known today, from Ravenscroft's *Psalms* of 1621. The lower stave shows a version found in many eighteenth-century books, here taken from Thomas Call's Magdalen Chapel book of 1760. It has been recognized by many scholars as a version of the same melody, altered during several generations of oral transmission. But there are great differences between them, going far beyond passing or inessential notes. Several main notes of the tune are altered: notes 1, 3, 20, 24, 29 and 30; and these changes alter the implied harmonies. The later version no longer works as a canon. Rhythm, too, has been changed, but this does not affect the *Index*; we decided at an early stage to ignore duration as an element in our indexing, precisely because it tends to discriminate between tunes that are fundamentally the same. But the vital point here is that some of the differences occur near the beginning, so that the two versions have quite different incipits. The upper version begins with 1, the lower with 5. So, unless we do something about it, the inputter of one tune will not have the opportunity to compare it with the other, and the user of the index will not be alerted to the connection between the two.

EXAMPLE 9

Can the computer be taught to recognize tune resemblances that are evident to scholars and musicians? In some ways that is the most interesting question of all, and it is now being addressed by several scholars. Ann Dhu Shapiro, for instance, has worked out a new method of classifying Anglo-American folk tunes that seems to lend itself to computer sorting; another method has been adopted by Kate Van Winkle Keller and Carolyn Rabson in the *National Tune Index*. These methods rest mainly on the identification of principal notes in a melody; the principal notes are determined by several factors such as relative duration, stress, and harmonic implication. It is assumed that these parameters are the stable features of a tune which will tend to remain unaltered when melodic details change. This assumption seems well justified for many bodies of folksong, especially those related to dancing, working or other rhythmical movement. It does not apply so well to Anglo-Saxon hymn tunes. You can see in Example 9, for instance, that the rhythmic values are weak. The Ravenscroft version has no barlines to indicate downbeats. Although the stresses are clear in Tallis's original because of harmonic factors such as suspensions, which always occur on strong beats, they are lost in Ravenscroft's version, and are not helped by the text (from Sternhold and Hopkins's metrical psalms). The Call version of 1762 has barlines which do not, in fact, correspond to the stresses implied in the earlier version. The harmonies have also changed. Ravenscroft's harmony has a tonic chord on note 1, a dominant on 2 and 3, a VI on 4 and a I on 5; Call has a dominant on note 1 and tonic harmonies on notes 2-5. The resemblance between the two tunes is founded on two features: the text meter, and the melodic contour, with identity of a large percentage of notes. Such similarity is found between hundreds of pairs and sets of tunes in this repertory, because, for nearly 200 years, the main mode of transmission was by slow, unrhythmical, unaccompanied singing, with the text and melodic contour as the only constant features.

I do not think we will be able to devise programs that will trace all such related tunes. We do, however, have a number of devices which we hope will uncover a large percentage of them. First there is the treatment of melismas. As I have said, all notes of a melisma after the first are placed between parentheses (as in Example 6). If one of these occurs in the ten-note incipit, there is an automatic cross-reference between tunes with and without the extra digits. (You can see from Example 9, however, that the first note of a melisma is not always the main note.) Next there are the subsidiary indexes: the tune name index, the text index, and the composer index. At the editing stage we will compare any two or more tunes that have the same name, the same text, or the same composer attribution. We expect to find many related pairs in this way. Beyond this, there is the memory of each person on the staff. It often happens that a tune will "ring a bell" in the inputter's or editor's mind and that he or she will be able to track down the association to another tune already inputted with a different incipit. We have already caught more than 400 resemblances in this way. Furthermore many such links have been noted by earlier scholars like Walter Frere, Maurice Frost, Henry Wilder Foote, Leonard Ellinwood, Erik Routley, and Richard Crawford. We will, of course, take advantage of their discoveries. Lastly, we may decide to run some programs testing statistical similarity–asking the computer to report any pair of tunes that has more than, say, eighty percent of pitches the same. In a pilot study I found that this method yielded disappointing results. The pairs of tunes it found were either known to me already, or else it turned out on inspection that the resemblance was due to chance rather than to true musical relationship.

I am sure that these piecemeal methods will not lead to the discovery of all related pairs of tunes. Fortunately, we may never know how many we missed. But perhaps someone cleverer than I will be able to devise software that actually duplicates human judgments of tune resemblance in a way that is appropriate for this repertory. Certainly this will not be done in time to be used in the *Hymn Tune Index,* first edition, for we are now in a stage where our overriding concern must be to finish the job. But I will be very interested to hear suggestions for tackling these problems, whether or not they will serve our immediate purposes.

The Cataloging of Chant Manuscripts as an Aid to Critical Editions and Chant History[1]

Theodore Karp

SUMMARY. Gregorian chants having international diffusion are preserved in hundreds of sources ranging from the tenth century onward. It is necessary to collate large numbers of these in order to demonstrate the degrees of faithfulness and change in the transmission of the repertoire and thus construct a history of chant. MS inventories are of inestimable aid in facilitating such editorial comparisons. As demonstrated by means of selected examples, comparative editions help us to interpret illusory notations and to comprehend theoretical writings dealing with chant.

Chant scholars face a curious paradox. Theirs is the oldest branch of musicology. It is likely that over the centuries more work has gone into this field than into any other within our discipline. Yet here more than anywhere else the proportion of the work accomplished is dwarfed by the magnitude of that which remains. Despite the Herculean efforts of generations of scholars, our knowledge remains in many respects primitive. Those involved in chant research refer to the field with a mixture of affection and desperation as a "bottomless pit." A lifetime of work will make only a small impact on its vast terrain.

Theodore Karp is affiliated with the School of Music at Northwestern University.

[Haworth co-indexing entry note]: "The Cataloging of Chant Manuscripts as an Aid to Critical Editions and Chant History." Karp, Theodore. Co-published simultaneously in *Music Reference Services Quarterly,* (The Haworth Press, Inc.) Vol. 2, No. 3/4, 1993, pp. 241-269; and: *Foundations in Music Bibliography* (ed: Richard D. Green) The Haworth Press, Inc., 1993, pp. 241-269. Multiple copies of this article/chapter may be purchased from The Haworth Document Delivery Center [1-800-3-HAWORTH; 9:00 a.m. - 5:00 p.m. (EST)].

© 1993 by The Haworth Press, Inc. All rights reserved.

Two of the major stumbling blocks to a firmer knowledge of chant and chant history are the inordinately large number of sources involved and the lack of sufficient bibliographic control over these. We have relatively few detailed catalogs of individual manuscripts and even lack comprehensive lists of the relevant sources.[2] Thus it is scarcely surprising that, apart from occasional *unica,* we do not possess a critical edition of even a single chant. By critical edition I mean one that for an early chant of international diffusion would make available to the reader the results of a study based on 150 or more sources.[3] In the instance of a later regional or local chant, such an edition should include all known readings. We do, of course, have available photographic reproductions for the *Justus ut palma* melody assembled in Volumes II and III of *Paléographie Musicale.*[4] And a few scholars have published multiple readings for individual melodies.[5] Nevertheless, I regard these as sadly insufficient to our needs. As a preparatory step towards remedying this condition, I have recently embarked on a project to catalog manuscripts created before 1350 that are devoted primarily to chants for the Mass Proper. I am beginning with the indexing of sources in Aquitanian notation and will proceed to other notational families when this group has been completed. Each citation will include the first words of the chant and those of any verses, the folio, the genre, the identity of the Feast, and the mode of the melody where deducible. The project is being undertaken by means of a database program so that when any group is complete it will be possible to merge the information and to sort it according to any desired category. I doubt that there is anything new or unusual about the procedures being followed, and therefore feel no need to comment further on these. Since, however, there is so little impetus among chant scholars to pursue such an endeavor, it may be useful to outline why I feel this project to be urgent and to invite the participation of others with like interests.

Like all historical disciplines, chant history is multidimensional. Individual melodies submit to changes during the course of their transmission, some minor and some of astonishing extent. In part, the history of chant consists of the histories of the individual melodies. We have barely begun this study. The nature of transformations that are possible in the transmission of unstable melodies is largely unknown. For the most part, we gloss over these. Yet if, for example, one studies the Introit, *Eduxit Dominus populum suum,* for the Saturday of Easter Week, we find among readings ending on G, the opening ascent may be either a second, third, or fourth. (See Example 1.) We note further that the descent immediately following may be a minor third, fourth, or fifth. And the first tone may be a fifth, fourth, minor third, or major second above the final, or even a major second or minor third below the final.

> EXAMPLE 1. Eight selected readings of *Eduxit Dominus*: (a) Pistoia, Bibl. cap., MS 120; (b) Paris, Bibl. nat., MS lat. 776;(c) Wolfenbuttel, Herzog August Bibl., MS 40; (d) Rome, Bibl. Vallicelliana, MS C52, (e) Modena, Bibl. cap., MS 0.1.7; (f) Piacenza, Bibl. cap., MS 65; (g) Rome, Bibl. Casanatense, MS 1695; (h) Mo- dena, Bibl. cap., MS 0.1.13.

When concern for modal centricity came to the fore, medieval editors found it possible to change either the first tone of the melody–as in the reading of Modena, Bibl. cap., MS 0.1.7–or the opening of the first phrase–as in the reading of Paris, Bibl. nat., MS lat. 903. In an extreme instance, the Cistercians replaced the opening of the first phase, the cadence to the first half, and the first note of the second half, as shown in Example 2.

> EXAMPLE 2. A comparison of Aquitanian and Cistercian readings of *Eduxit Dominus*; (a) Paris, Bibl. nat., MS lat. 776; (b) Paris, Bibl. nat., MS lat. 17328 and Munich, Bay. Staatsbibl., MS clm 2541.

The same concern resulted also in the alternative replacement of the final cadence with one ending on E. Thus no single version of this melody will provide a chant with any inkling of the complex history of this chant. The small handful of readings for the opening phrase provided by Ruth Steiner in her article, "Introit," for *The New Grove Dictionary*,[6] do not pretend to furnish a full account. It is perfectly true that most chants have far less complex histories than *Eduxit Dominus*. But this chant is by no means unique. Experience would indicate that it is risky to judge the stability of a given chant on the basis of a small handful of readings.

EXAMPLE 1

EXAMPLE 2

[Musical notation: Two-voice comparison (a and b) of the chant "Eduxit Dominus populum suum in exsultatione, alleluia; et electos suos in laetitia, alleluia, alleluia."]

    Even among chants for the Mass, I have found the locating of individual melodies to be a time-consuming process. With regard to the chant being used as an example, we are aided by the fact that it is part of the *Temporale*. Furthermore, it occurs soon after Easter Sunday, whose Introit is often provided with an important decorative initial. Yet even here, one spends needless time looking through manuscripts that do not contain the chant, either because of a chance lacuna or because they do not give the chants for the final days of Easter Week. Were the chant part of the *Sanctorale*, the process would be more complex inasmuch as many of these melodies have multiple assignments or are optional for a particular Feast. And chants for the Office can be even more time-consuming to locate. If we recognize the need for critical editions in the sense previously defined, it is wasteful for the various members of the community of chant scholars to go through the process anew on each occasion. A cumulative index of all major sources would be an inestimable boon.

There are further reasons underlying the need for critical editions of chant melodies. We may uncover these by asking how the various versions of *Eduxit Dominus* sounded. This is not an idle question. For the most part, we have little difficulty in reading the pitch names recorded in the diastematic sources. We know, of course, that these do not refer to any absolute pitch standard. But we tend to forget that there are numerous instances in which sources fail to maintain any uniform reference to a single standard of relative pitch. No medieval scribe was willing to represent a pitch name that did not exist in the gamut prescribed by a theorist whose authority he accepted. Thus most scribes had to find alternative means for the notation of patterns that would have involved the B flat a ninth below middle C. As Marchettus of Padua pointed out, their solutions often conceal the fact that when the chant is notated a fifth higher, other portions of the melody may demand a whole step above E.[7] This too is foreign to the Guidonian gamut. Caught in this dilemma, each scribe had to decide upon the form of misrepresentation that was least distasteful to him. Certain chants elicited multiple alternatives in notation, few of which were accurate representations of the actual pitch relationships observed in performance.[8]

At the present time, I am not prepared to speculate on the intended pitch relationships for each of the many versions of *Eduxit Dominus*, but I propose to illustrate the preceding cautionary remarks by examining a simple instance involving the sixth-mode Introit, *Dicit Dominus: Ego cognito*. This chant posed little problem for the scribe of Graz, Universitatsbibliothek, MS 807.[9] This musician was among the small minority who admitted the existence of a low B flat. Hence he had no difficulty in notating either the low B flats at the opening or the later oscillation between B flat and B natural an octave higher. But this avenue was open to few. Most opted to notate the chant a fifth higher, even though there was no possibility of indicating any alternation between F and F sharp. A few tried to gloss over the opening by notating C instead of B flat.[10] The scribe of Paris Bibliotheque nationale MS n. a. lat. 1669 found the chant to be a particular embarrassment. The melody is subdivided into two halves by a strong medial cadence, and the second half begins with the tone that concludes the first. The scribe in question began by notating the first half of the melody a fifth higher than would have been required had there been no low B flat. Realizing that this tone did not appear in the second half of the chant, he notated the conclusion at normal pitch level for the most part. This resulted in the misleading appearance of a downward leap of a fifth at the juncture of the two parts, a leap that would hardly have occurred in performances that preceded the notation. There was still a further awkward moment to be faced. The scribe was apparently among those who preferred to avoid the notation of any B flat, even if the tone appeared in the middle octave and was part of the Guidonian gamut. When he came to the gesture involving this tone, he therefore notated it a second higher, and then having circumvented this difficulty, returned to the normal level. Any literal performance of this reading will present a false impression to the listener. While instances such as the one discussed probably represent only a tiny proportion of the sum total, they are frequent enough to demonstrate that we cannot securely evaluate the aural import of notation on the basis of isolated readings. Here, too, we require a broad spectrum of sources in order to arrive at dependable conclusions.

Melodic transformations are by no means confined to matters of detail. There are many instances in which readings remain reasonably constant in detail but vary significantly in their form. Variants of such nature spring to light readily in the process of cataloging. Although Tracts were normally performed *in directum* during the Middle Ages, I have previously called to attention the fact that responsorial performance is documented for four second-mode Tracts in one Burgundian and three Aquitanian graduals.[11] Not only do their prescriptions vary in principle from those of other sources, but they vary in detail from each other. Different repetition patterns are also to be observed for the *Benedictiones* of Ember Days. Marion Gushee[12] and later Nancy van Deusen[13] have indicated that antiphons and responsories used in processions may be treated flexibly, being occasionally stripped of their versus and that such versus may appear independently. One of the more interesting of these chants is *Collegerunt pontifices,* used in the procession for Palm

Sunday. Classified variously as a responsory and an antiphon, this chant normally consists of a respond, a verse–*Unus autem*–and a return to the latter half of the respond, beginning with the words, *Ne forte veniant*. However, other schemas also exist. Milan, Biblioteca Ambrosiana MS M. 70 sup., one of a group of eleven sources preserving the tradition of the order of Chartreux, treats the chant as an antiphon and presents only the first half of the respond, the portion terminating immediately before *Ne forte*. This truncated version is one that had originally been entered into Marseilles, Bibl. mun. MS 150, another of the Chartrain sources. When, however, the latter manuscript was nearing completion, the fuller version was recalled. A cross-reference was provided and the omitted material was supplied by a different hand on one of the last folios. At that point, the manuscript presents *Ne forte* as if it were an independent piece and goes on to the verse, *Unus antem*, which is properly rubricated. However, the verse is not presented as a single unit, as is customary. A cue is entered referring the singers to *Si dimittimus*, the concluding phrase for the first half of the respond, entered earlier in the manuscript. Although normative responsorial practice would suggest otherwise, as far as one can tell from the manuscript layout this return would have involved only the one phrase. Following this, we find the music for the final text phase of the verse and a cue for the return to *Ne forte*.

The cataloging process will focus our attention on this unusual repetition pattern. Once we are on the alert, we shall find another unusual change. In many manuscripts, the final phrase of the verse begins with an extensive melisma. In the Marseilles reading, however, this melisma is placed so that it terminates the first section of the verse. The resultant cadence is unusual, but still within the outer boundaries of Gregorian style. Since the transferred melisma occurs earlier in the chant, shortly after the opening of the second half of the respond, its altered placement has a stronger than normal effect on our perception of form. The position of this melisma is of still greater import in Beneventan sources. These amplify the structure of *Collegerunt* by prosulae that are provided for each of the main melismas, and the placement of the melismas is a prime factor in determining the length of the prosulae. In these sources, the melisma that we have been discussing is subdivided, one segment being assigned to each of the major formal divisions and a small linking segment is omitted.

Returning to the Chartrain sources, we find in Avignon, Bibliotheque municipale MS 181 the subdivision into two verses and the melisma placement present in the Marseilles reading. However, the Avignon source does not provide any cue for a return to the respond between the two sections of verse. Was there a return, and, if so, to what point in the respond? I cannot address this question at this time because I have not yet gained access to the remaining Chartrain sources. In Cistercian sources, the normal pattern of respond, verse, and latter portion of the respond is followed. However, the return begins at an earlier part of the respond, with the words, *Quid facimus*.

Once we become involved with *Collegerunt*, we discover still further puzzles to its history. While most of the southern sources that I have consulted begin with the chant on D, the northern ones prefer to notate the melody at a higher level. In the Worcester Cathedral MS F160, the chant is notated so as to begin and end on G, with a consistent use of B-flat, which serves for purposes of a clef.[14] Sarum and other insular sources, on the other hand, begin and end the chant on A,[15] as do others from Paris. The chant may even be written beginning on D, an octave higher. More important, the different classes of readings do not remain in constant pitch relationship to one another. For example, the Sarum readings are variously a fifth or a fourth higher than those of the southern group, which are not in full agreement among themselves. We receive a further surprise when we discover that the reading of *Collegerunt* present in Wolfenbuttel MS Helmstedt 40 presents the respond a fourth higher than usual, and the verse an octave higher. Were this notation to be taken literally, the melisma common to the respond and verse would be performed a fifth higher on its second occurrence, and the return to the middle of the respond would be dislocated by the same interval. It is obvious that in this instance the notation is illusory.

The performance and notation of *Collegerunt* was also of interest to medieval theorists. John informs us that many singers began the chant with the descent of a fifth rather than a fourth, and that they displaced certain tones associated with the word *concilium*.[16] Pursuing this topic further, we learn that Theinred of Dover cites *Col-

legerunt as an instance of a chant employing tones not classified within the Guidonian gamut.[17] Whether there is some interrelationship between these two citations cannot be decided on the basis of evidence presently available. But we can begin to understand that the notations of individual sources may well be glossing over a number of problematic areas. Without a critical edition, any attempt to understand the history of this chant is badly hampered.

> EXAMPLE 3. Selected readings of *Collegerunt pontifices*; (a) Paris, Bibl. nat., MS lat. 903; (b) London, Brit. Lib., MS Harley 4951; (c) Marseilles, Bibl. mun., MS 150; (d) Benevento, Bibl. cap. MS VI.34; (e) Benevento, Bibl. cap., MS VI.35; (f) Rome, Bibl. Vat., MS Rossi 231; (g) Vercelli, Bibl. cap., MS 56; (h) Graz, Universitatsbibl., MS 807; (i) Wolfenbuttel, Herzog August Bibl., MS 40; (j) Worcester, Cathedral Lib., MS F160; (k) London, Brit. Lib., MS Add. 12194; (l) Oxford, Bodleian Lib., MS Rawlinson C892; (m) Rome, Bibl. Casanatense, MS 1695; (n) Paris, Bibl. nat., MS lat. 904; (o) Rome, Bibl. Vat., MS Rossi 76; (p) Northwestern University, 14th-century sequentary without siglum.

Another part of chant history is concerned with the growth and shrinkage of the repertoires comprising the individual genres. This too is a neglected subject. A rich mine of material exists in Karlheinz Schlager's thematic catalog of early Alleluias[18] and in his edition of these melodies.[19] But it remains to put this enormous repertoire into some form of chronological order. Apart from the devoted cataloging efforts of the monks of Solesmes, very little exists with regard to the growth of other genres. The Solesmes scholars generously share their results with their visitors, and I, in particular, am indebted to them. However, their work is still in progress and thus neither complete nor easy to access.

Suppose, for example, you become fascinated by musical problems encountered in dealing with Graduals and wish to extend your horizons beyond the limited materials provided in modern chant books. Suppose too, that you do not have the luxury of a trip to Solesmes. If you consult Bruno Stablein's magisterial article, *Graduale (Gesang)*, in *Die Musik in Geschichte und Gegenwart*,[20] you will find a list of some 115 Graduals that are found in the eleven earliest sources for the Mass Proper. As an addendum, Sta-

EXAMPLE 3

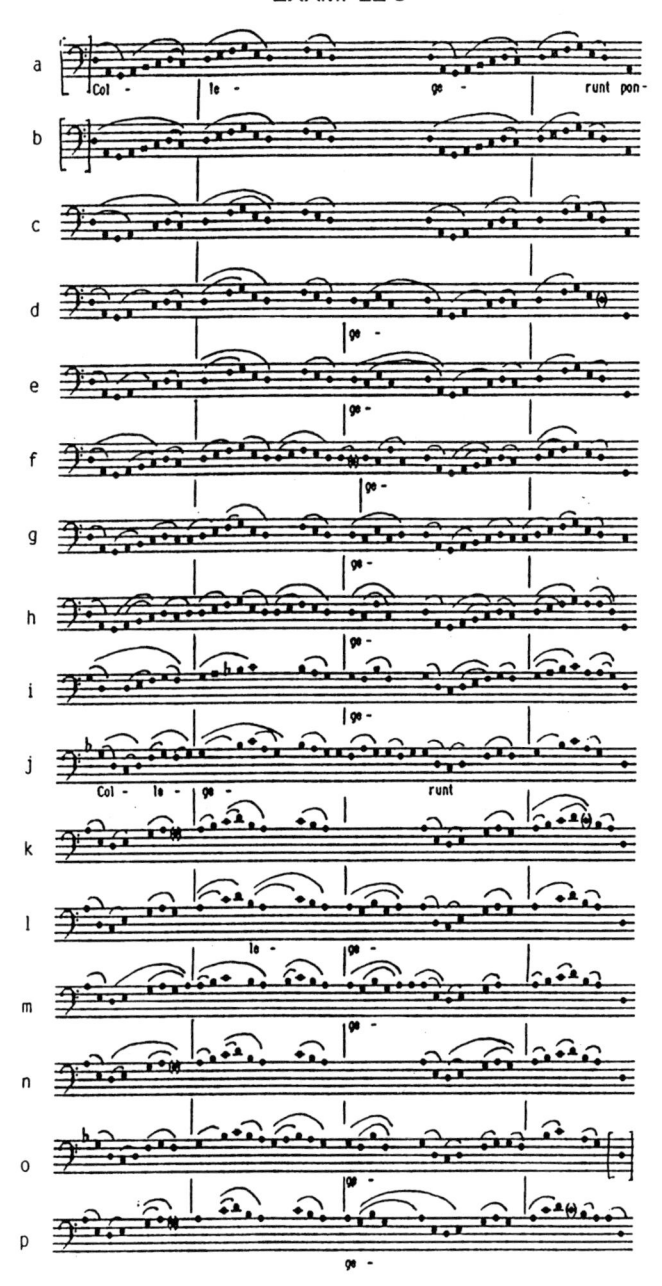

252 FOUNDATIONS IN MUSIC BIBLIOGRAPHY

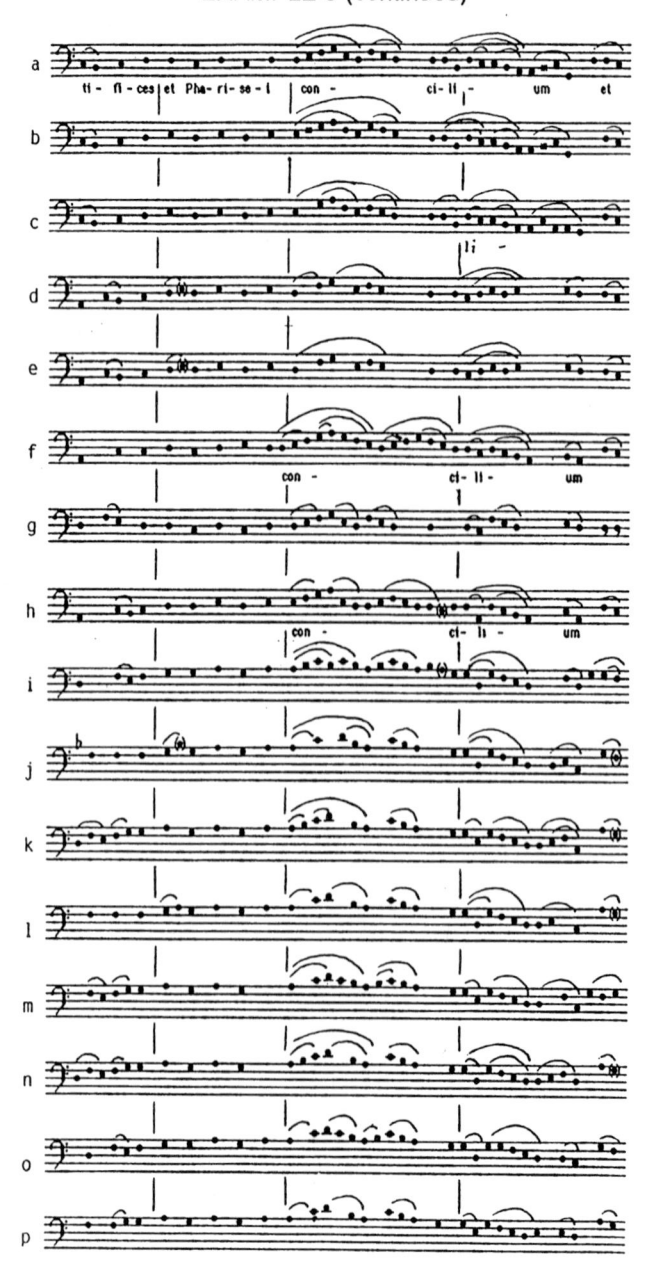

EXAMPLE 3 (continued)

Theodore Karp

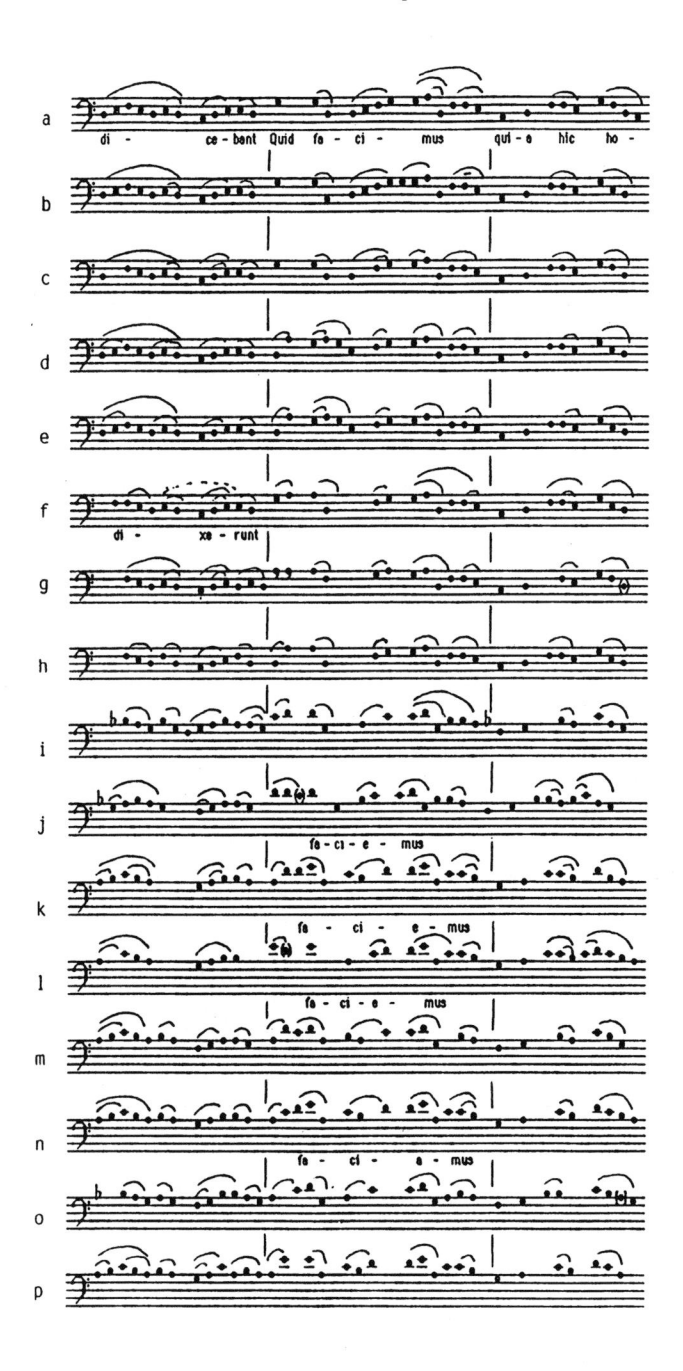

EXAMPLE 3 (continued)

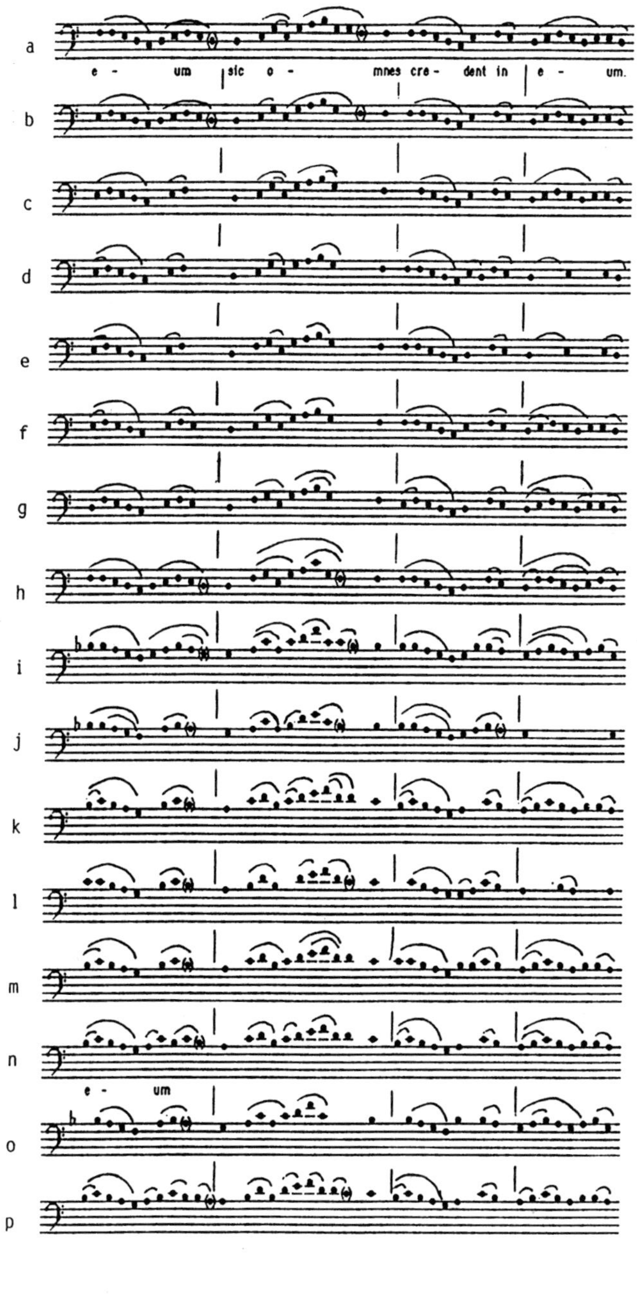
a
e - um sic o - mnes cre- dent in e - um.
b
c
d
e
f
g
h
i
j
k
l
m
n
e - um
o
p

EXAMPLE 3 (continued)

a
et tol - lent no - strum lo - cum et gen -
b
c
d
e
et tol - la no - strum
f
g
h
i
j
k
tol - lent no - strum
l
m
n
et tol - lent no - strum
o
p

EXAMPLE 3 (continued)

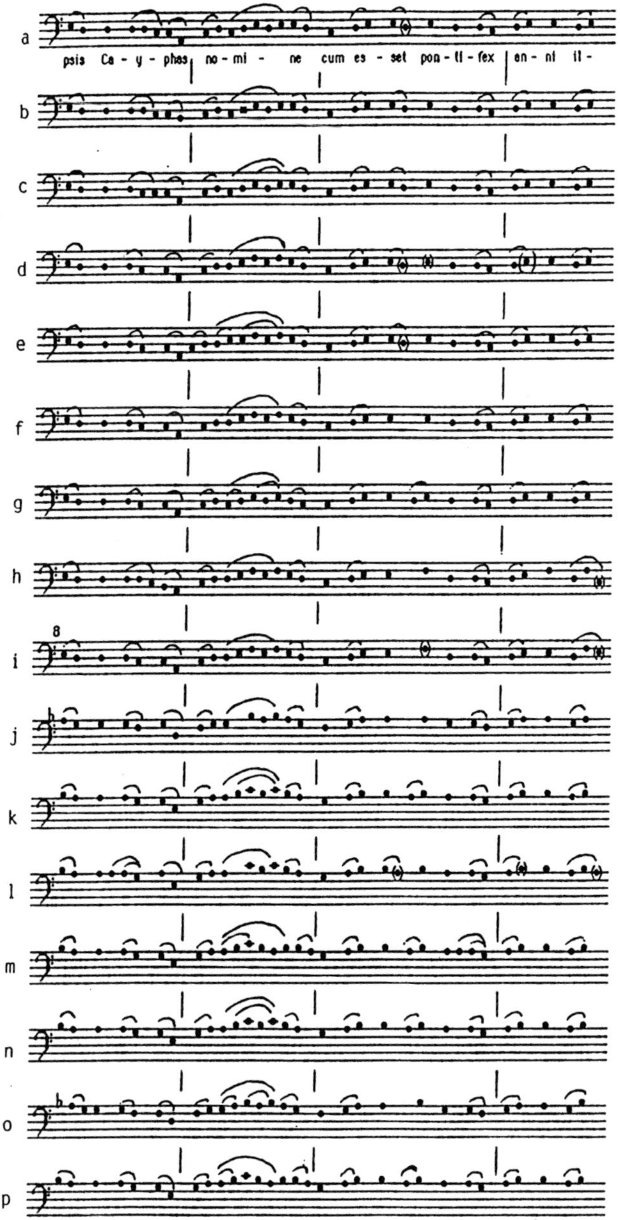
a
psis Ca - y - phas no - mi - ne cum es - set pon - ti - fex an - ni il -
b
c
d
e
f
g
h
i
j
k
l
m
n
o
p

EXAMPLE 3 (continued)

a
vo - bis ut u-nus mo- ri-a-tur ho-mo pro po - pu - lo et
b
c
d
e
f
g
h
i
j
k
po - pu - lo et
l
m
n
o
po - pu - lo et
p

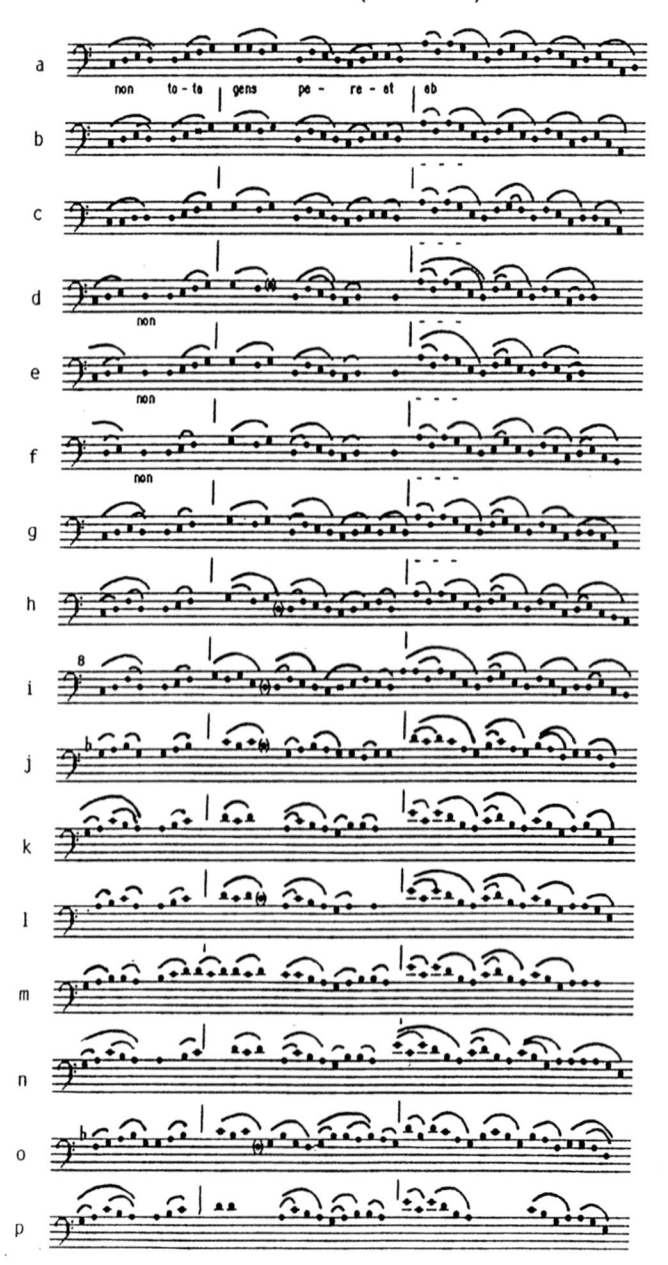

EXAMPLE 3 (continued)

il -lo er-go di - e co - gi - ta - ve - runt in-
ab il - lo
Si dimit- Ab il - lo
timus
Ab il - lo
Ab il - lo
Ab il - lo
Ab il - lo

264   FOUNDATIONS IN MUSIC BIBLIOGRAPHY

EXAMPLE 3 (continued)

blein mentions an additional eight Graduals that fleshed out the repertoire at an early date. The total contrasts with the approximately 170 graduals found in the modern Vatican edition. Stablein further remarks that the medieval repertoire grew but little and that the sharp contrast between the previously cited totals is due mainly to modern compositions created within the past century in conjunction with the movement towards the historical restoration of chant. A similar impression is left by Michel Muglo in his article on the Gradual book in *The New Grove Dictionary*.[21] In certain senses both of these eminent experts are correct in their assessment of the medieval repertoire. Apparently few sources have more than 125 gradual chants, and the growth of the repertoire was certainly modest in comparison with the growth of the Alleluia or Responsory repertoires. But it is probably that the number of medieval Graduals equalled or exceeded the approximately 170 that are found in modern books. The later, unpublished chants are mainly local or regional contributions of the High Middle Ages. Are the compositional techniques underlying these melodies the same as those underlying the main nucleus? At present, we have no means of providing a full answer to this question. But preliminary sketchy exploration would indicate that we will find one or more surprises. If we are determined to obtain a definitive answer and thus provide a basis for a history of this chant genre during the Middle Ages, we shall have to undertake a systematic exploration of our entire manuscript corpus. Having begun such an undertaking with regard to the repertoire of second-mode Tracts, I am fully aware of how laborious and time-consuming a process this is. It would be extremely wasteful to repeat this process for each genre and for each chant.

This apologia ought not be terminated without at least passing reference to the importance of bibliographic control of source material for an understanding of medieval music theory as it pertains to chant. If I do not devote much space to this topic, it is chiefly because the basic points have been raised often enough by others, most forcefully by Calvin Bower in his review of *Hucbald, Guido, and John on Music: Three Medieval Treatises*.[22] As Bower points out, " . . . works that cite chant could be immeasurably improved if the musical examples were taken from sources somewhat contemporary and of related provenance to the texts or examples in question."[23] He shows how the use of readings drawn from the Solesmes editions obscure the meaning of several of Hucbald's remarks.[24] Examples drawn from the treatise of John provide similar cases in point. I shall mention only one of these and that because the discrepancies involved occur on a particularly large scale. In Chapters 15 and 16 of the treatise, John refers twice to the Communion, *Principes persecuti sunt me*.[25] He indicates first that certain ignorant singers begin the word *concupivit*, a whole tone too low, thus introducing the interval of a diminished fifth and displacing the chant from its lawful range. Unfortunately, the Solesmes books present a truncated version of the chant which ends immediately previous to the place mentioned by John. As a consequence, the final cadence appearing in the sources that I have consulted is given its place of the normal medial cadence. This involves a shift in tonal reference. Any reader without access to reproductions of source material will find the first of John's references entirely incomprehensible, while the second–which deals with cadence structures–will lose greatly in force. It is possible that a late insert in the Montpellier Faculte de Medecine MS H.159 may provide an illustration of John's first remark, but this may be only wishful thinking. Its diastemy is not reliable enough to be read with security and the alphabet notation provided in the main body of the manuscript is lacking.[26] Other sources provide a variety of alternatives, but those that I have consulted do not present the pitch relationships recommended by John.

The absence of bibliographic control for our source materials and hence the critical editions has a crippling effect on our knowledge of chant history from the High Middle Ages onward. It creates obstacles to the understanding of an important segment of music theory and to the appreciation of composer's use of chant in polyphony. Even a partial assault on this problem promises significant rewards.

NOTES

1. This author was pleased to dedicate this essay to Janet Knapp and to join it with others in a Festgabe that commemorates her retirement from Vassar College in 1986.

2. An extensive list of sources for chants of the Mass is provided in *Le Graduel Romain, II: Les Sources* (Solesmes, n.d.). A comparable list of sources for

chants of the Office is provided in Vol. 5 of René Jean Hesbert, *Corpus Antiphonalium Officii* (Herder, Rome, 1975), 1-18, but this list does not distinguish between those MSS with music and those without. Additional citations of chant sources are furnished by John Emerson, "Sources, MS, II: Western plainchant," *The New Grove Dictionary of Music and Musicians*, ed. by Stanley Sadie, XVII, 609-633, and by Michel Huglo, "Gradual (ii)," and "Antiphoner (iii)," *ibid.*, vii, 601-9, and I, 483-89. These lists cover most of the important sources, but many others are known to exist. The inventorying of chant MSS has received much more attention since 1985. I cite merely the superb *Cantus* project under the general editorship of Ruth Steiner (to be issued on computer disks) and the *Corpus Antiphonalium Officii Ecclesiarum Centralis Europae (Pars Temporalis)*, (Budapest, 1990), by László Dobszay. Other individual and group projects have been produced on database by a variety of scholars.

3. The Solesmes chant editions are, of course, respected critical editions. But because they are intended for practical use in the liturgy, the critical studies that underlie the editor's choices remain hidden from the editions' users. It is likely that editions prepared for purely historical purposes would vary from those with which we are familiar in a number of instances.

4. Solesmes, 1891-93.

5. See especially Hendrik van der Werf, *The Emergence of Gregorian Chant*, 1,2 (the author, Rochester, 1983), and Dominique Delalande, *Le Graduel des prêcheurs* (*Bibliothèque d'histoire Dominicaine*, 2: Les Éditions du Cerf, Paris, 1949).

6. Ed. by Stanley Sadie, VIII, 282.

7. See Jan Herlinger, *The Lucidarium of Marchetto of Padua* (The University of Chicago Press, Chicago, 1985), 424ff.

8. The gradual, *Salvum fac servum*, which provides the point of departure for Marchettus of Padua's discussion cited in the previous note, provides a case in point. A few dozen readings for this chant are provided in Jeffrey Wasson, *Gregorian Graduals of the First Mode: An Analytical Study and Critical Edition* (doctoral dissertation, Northwestern University, 1987), II, pt. 3, 964-1003. Notational shifts between successive sections of chants such as graduals and responsories occur with modest frequency. The notational shifts occurring within Offertories and their verses need to be considered within this general context.

9. Facsimile edition: *Paléographie musicale, XIX: Le Graduel de Klosterneuburg* (Herbert Lang, Bern, 1974).

10. The 12-century Rouennaise gradual preserved at Leningrad (MS O v 16) is one of the earlier sources to adopt this solution. Facsimile edition: Jean-Baptiste Thibaut, *Monuments de la notation ekphonétique et neumatique de l'Église latine* (St. Petersburg, 1912; rep. 1976).

11. "Interrelationships among Gregorian Chants: An Alternative View of Creativity in Early Chant," *Studies in Musical Sources and Style: Essays in Honor of Jan LaRue*, ed. by Eugene K. Wolf and Edward H. Roesner (A-R Editions, Madison, 1990), 1-40.

12. *Romanesque Polyphony: A Study of the Fragmentary Sources* (doctoral dissertation, Yale University, 1964), 39.

13. *Music at Nevers Cathedral: Principal Sources of Mediaeval Chant* (Musicological Studies, XXX, Institute of Mediaeval Music, Henryville, 1980), I, 70.

14. Facsimile edition of the antiphonary section in *Paléographie Musicale, XII: Codex F. 160 de la Bibliotheque de la Cathédrale de Worcester XIIIe siècle): Antiphonaire Monastique* (Solesmes, 1922-25), 210.

15. A transcription of *Collegerunt* after Oxford, Bodleian Library, MS Rawlinson lit. d. 4, is presented in Terence Bailey, *The Professions of Sarum and the Western Church (Pontifical Institute of Mediaeval Studies: Studies and Texts,* 21; Toronto, 1971), 39. A facsimile of the reading of London, British Library, MS Add. 12194, is provided in Walter Frere, *Graduale Sarisburiense* (Bernard Quaritch, London, 1894; repr. 1966) 84. Additional source citations outside of the Sarum tradition are provided by Bailey, *op. cit.*, 167.

16. *Johannes Affligemensis: De Musica cum Tonario,* ed. by Joseph Smits van Waesberghe (*Corpus Scriptorum de Musica,* I, American Institute of Musicology, Rome, 1950), 134ff. See also *Hucbald, Guido, and John on Music: Three Medieval Treatises;* translated by Warren Babb; edited, with Introduction by Claude V. Palisca (*Music Theory Translation Series,* III; Yale University Press, New Haven, 1978), 147f. One will note that three different opening pitches–D, G, and A– are employed among the readings presented in Example 3 and that those beginning on D all come from southerly sources of the Italo-German orbit. While I have consulted sources beyond those given here, I have not been comprehensive in my coverage and am therefore unable to state whether the latter condition is universal. If needed it is typical of a preponderant majority, the fact that John considers *Collegerunt* to begin and end on D would cast doubt on an association with Afflighem and greatly strengthen Palisca's conclusion that John was located in the south German area between St. Gall and Bamberg.

17. I am indebted to Professor John Snyder for bringing this citation to my attention. (See his doctoral dissertation, *The 'De legitimis ordinibus pentachordorum etetrachordorum' of Theinrea of Dover,* Indiana University, 1982). Dr. Snyder has delivered various papers on Theinred's contributions and is planning a major essay on this subject.

18. *Thematischer Katalog der ältesten Alleluia-Melodien aus Handschriften des 10. und 11. Jahrhunderts* (*Erlanger Arbeiten zur Musikwissenschaft,* ii: Walter Ricke, Munich, 1965).

19. *Monumenta Monodica Medii Aevi,* VII: *Alleluia-Molodien I* (Barenreiter, Kassel, 1968).

20. Ed. by Friedrich Blume, V, cols. 632-59.

21. VII, 598-609.

22. *Journal of American Musicological Society,* 35 (1982), 157-167.

23. *Ibid.,* 158.

24. *Ibid.*, 161f.

25. *De Musica cum Tonario*, 105 and 112. See also, *Hucbald, Guido and John*, 130, 135.

26. Facsimile edition in *Paléographie musicale*, VIII: *Le Codex H. 159 de la Bibliothèque de Médecine de Montpellier (XIe siecle): Antiphonarium Tonale Missarum* (Solesmes, 1901-05), 38.

The Rossini Thematic Catalog: When Does Bibliographical Access Become Bibliographical Excess?

Philip Gossett

SUMMARY. This paper outlines many of the issues involved in the analytical description of sources gathered in the preparation of the Rossini thematic catalog. The compilers are committed to examining every publication of Rossini's operas, either in full score or in reductions for voice and piano. However, except in very special cases, no attempt will be made to provide information about arrangements or adaptations. The central focus of the catalog is the establishment of information pertaining to the authentic versions and authentic sources for each composition.

Barry Brook has provided a useful overview about the past, present, and future of thematic catalogs. I would like to offer, in a rather informal fashion, some personal reflections arising from work in progress at The University of Chicago and the Fondazione Rossini of Pesaro towards a thematic catalog of the works of Gioacchino Rossini.

From the appearance of his *Bibliography of the Musical and Literary Works of Hector Berlioz* in 1951, through the posthumous publication of the second volume of his *Bibliography of the Works*

Philip Gossett is affiliated with the Department of Music at the University of Chicago.

[Haworth co-indexing entry note]: "The Rossini Thematic Catalog: When Does Bibliographical Access Become Bibliographical Excess?" Gossett, Philip. Co-published simultaneously in *Music Reference Services Quarterly*, (The Haworth Press, Inc.) Vol. 2, No. 3/4, 1993, pp. 271-280; and: *Foundations in Music Bibliography* (ed: Richard D. Green) The Haworth Press, Inc., 1993, pp. 271-280. Multiple copies of this article/chapter may be purchased from The Haworth Document Delivery Center [1-800-3-HAWORTH; 9:00 a.m. - 5:00 p.m. (EST)].

© 1993 by The Haworth Press, Inc. All rights reserved.

of Giuseppe Verdi in 1978, Cecil Hopkinson remained a controversial figure to musical scholars. Reviews of his bibliographies often complained that he offered generous (though hardly exhaustive) treatments of intricate bibliographical problems pertaining to secondary sources of scarce musicological interest, while ignoring crucial information about the central sources for a composer's work. Manuscripts were ignored, autographs grudgingly conceded a place in a few of his appendices. Furthermore, his failure to investigate these manuscript sources, and therefore to penetrate fully the textual history of a composition, led inevitably to erroneous judgments about his beloved printed editions. His approach seemed a classic case of putting the cart before the horse: according to Hopkinson's critics, we needed serious thematic catalogs, which could explicate the textual history of works by major composers such as Berlioz, Field, Gluck, Verdi, and Puccini, not accounts of printed sources, many of which were altogether lacking in textual weight.

These criticisms of Hopkinson's work have always struck me as fundamentally unfair. They presume a communality of shared interests on the part of those who employ the resources of our reference collections that has never and will never exist. They presume that the central "facts" in the history of music are a collection of musical works in authentic versions: until those "facts" are established, everything else would appear to be superfluous. Yet the growing importance of studies concerning the history of the reception of musical works belies this prejudice. Though we may not be prepared to follow reception history to its logical conclusion, dethroning the work of art as conceived by its composer (however problematic that concept may be) in favor of the equal historical weight of all its stages, we cannot easily deny that works have a historical life of their own, a life documented in performances, reviews, literature, art, manuscripts, and printed editions, even those published after the death of a composer.

Indeed, a failure to take into account textually unauthentic and unauthorized printed editions can so skew our understanding of reception history as to render incomprehensible the judgments of contemporaries and of later critics. Many assertions about Rossini's *Il Turco in Italia*, from the time of Stendhal's *Vie de Rossini* of 1824 through critical writings well into the twentieth century, make no sense whatsoever when they are referred to an authentic version of that opera. These writings reflect instead a performance given at the Théâtre-Italien of Paris in 1820, later immortalized in a printed score published by the Parisian editor, Raphael Carli.

It would appear that Ferdinand Paer, director of the Théâtre-Italien in this period, produced a pastiche drawing in part from Rossini's *Il Turco in Italia*, in part from other operas by Rossini (including *Ciro in Babilonia, L'Italiana in Algeri, Torvaldo e Dorliska,* and *La Cenerentola*), to which he added a comic aria by Valentino Fioravanti, "Amor perché me pizziche?" Later critics, misled through having studied *Il Turco in Italia* from the Carli edition, often noted wryly that Rossini had borrowed a considerable amount of music from this opera, written in 1814, when he prepared *La Cenerentola* in 1817. And the confusion has persisted into our own day, when Belwin-Mills made the incredible decision to reprint the Carli edition of *Turco*, blissfully unaware that there was any problem at all with this source.[1] Clearly any account of the printed sources for Rossini's music cannot ignore the reception history of his operas, even as manifested in completely non-authentic printed editions.

On a more prosaic level, perhaps, but no less real, a thematic catalog must not scorn the interests and needs of those who love and collect musical editions. Fully aware of its limitations, I have carted Hopkinson's *Puccini* bibliography from store to store all over Italy, comparing title pages, squinting at blind stamps, controlling collations, searching for elusive printed versions of an opera. It was Hopkinson who provided me with the tools to purchase the first edition, first issue of *La Boheme* for $3.50 and that of *Tosca* for $2. There is no reason for me to apologize for this descent into the anecdotal: those of us who work with printed music come to love these objects, to search for them, and to seek as precise information about them as we can obtain, and it behooves us to recognize and empathize with the passion bibliophiles feel in amassing their collections, and their desire for precise knowledge concerning their holdings. Similar information, needless to say, is crucially important to book dealers and music catalogers.

In an ideal world, it would be possible to control the history of all printed music. When we discovered a previously unknown copy of a piece printed by a given publisher, from the proper bibliographies we could place it chronologically, establishing to what edition, issue, state, and impression it belonged. Sufficient data would exist so that previously unknown variants could be inserted readily into our bibliographical narratives for each work. This ideal is not always unrealizable: for very early printed books, as well as music, after all, such information, however incomplete it may be due to the lack of adequate surviving copies, is readily available.

Living in the real world of bibliographical description of nineteenth-century printed music, however, is quite another matter, and its dilemmas come to the foreground in a particularly pressing fashion when one considers the works of Gioacchino Rossini. Under the auspices of the Fondazione Rossini of Pesaro, I have been working fitfully for many years on a Thematic Catalog of Rossini's music. Having just defended the work of Cecil Hopkinson, expressed interest for the studies of reception historians, and affirmed my sympathies for the bibliographical needs of collectors, dealers, and catalogers, let me add that I remain nonetheless hopelessly attached to an old-fashioned belief in the primacy of individual works of art in their authentic garbs. I have no doubt whatsoever that the establishment of information pertaining to the authentic versions and authentic sources for each composition must be the central focus of a thematic catalog.

The problem of printed editions, however, will not just go away, and there is no rug sufficiently large under which to sweep the Rossinian printed sources. Rossini lived at a moment in which the world of music publishing was about to undergo massive changes, in particular owing to the establishment of more coherent procedures for the international copyright protection of music. During the 1810's and 1820's, however, the situation was generally chaotic, and nowhere more so than in the geographical fiction that was Italy. Publishers in Rome were unaffected by agreements made in Naples; those in Florence or Milan blithely plied their trade without restraint.

Recently, for example, spurred on by some bibliographical peculiarities that emerged in Margaret Bent's study of early Italian printed sources for *Il Turco in Italia*, Agostina Zecca-Laterza, director of the library at the Milan Conservatory, began to undertake a fascinating study of the interrelationship between editions of the Florentine music publisher Lorenzi and Ricordi in Milan during the 1810's. She has shown that in many cases, including those identified by Professor Bent, Ricordi obtained copies of Lorenzi's publications and reissued them as *Titelauflagen*. Our earlier failure to recognize this practice has created serious obstacles to the interpretation of Ricordi's plate numbers as found in the 1857 Ricordi *Numerical Catalog* by plate-number.

The profusion of publications in Italy was nothing compared to the situation throughout Europe. In this period, music publishers were springing up like weeds, responding to social and cultural changes that brought music-making ever more frequently into the homes of a rising bourgeois population with its dilettante pretensions to musical culture. Rossini's music became the mainstay of that culture for almost twenty years, whether in the form of reductions for piano and voice of individual arias or entire operas, or in adaptations for any and all combinations of instruments, or as pieces for children in series with such fanciful names as "La gioja delle madri." As the undisputedly favorite composer of the era, the "Napoleon of Music," as Stendhal referred to him, who had conquered European sensibilities as surely as the French Emperor had conquered its territory, Rossini and his music were both the beneficiary and the victim of this historical moment, this confluence of a particular situation in the history of music publishing, largely unrestrained by the niceties of author's rights, and the development of a larger audience interested in printed music.

That Rossini himself was aware of the particularity of his situation is clear from his behavior during the 1820's. One of the major causes of his break in 1822 with Domenico Barbaja, the impresario of the Teatro San Carlo of Naples, was a disagreement over the rights to his last Neapolitan opera, *Zelmira*. Arriving in Vienna with the Neapolitan troupe in 1822, Rossini promptly entered into a contract with the Viennese firm of Artaria to publish his very latest operas, though there is some doubt as to whether the contract really was valid for compositions whose premieres had already taken place abroad. Likewise in Paris, Rossini chose the firm of Troupenas as his publisher, and Troupenas effectively established a European network of publishers to control the distribution of Rossini's French operas.[2] Yet the publisher's efforts to extend his control backwards to at least some of the Italian operas was doomed to failure. Rossini's first French opera, *Le Siège de Corinthe*, is derived from an earlier Italian original, *Maometto II*, and much of the music is unchanged. When Troupenas sought to suppress editions of *Maometto II* made in Paris by his rivals Carli and Pacini, the French courts rejected his stand, asserting that even though many pieces were shared by the two works, the operas nonetheless were sufficiently different as to assure their essential independence. As a result, the rights Troupenas had acquired for *Le Siège de Corinthe* gave him no rights over *Maometto II*. Other publishers in France were free to bring out whatever editions of Rossini's Italian operas they thought might be profitable, and for some of the operas up to four or five competing Parisian editions in multiple issues (often with significant musical variants) were available to the local public.

In England there were few publishers who issued complete operatic reductions for piano and voice, even after the enormously successful visit of Rossini to London in 1824, but the number of competing sets of favorite airs from favorite operas is imposing. However limited their interest may be as sources for Rossini's "works," these publications offer precious testimony about the reception of history of Rossini's operas in England. It is not without importance that certain works were commonly printed rather than others and that the public easily had available extracts but rarely complete scores. Do publishers follow popular taste or do they help to define that taste? The answer, of course, is "both."

Scholars and bibliographers make limiting decisions all the time, without which few projects could be brought to completion. As we contemplate the vast array of Rossinian printed sources, the need for a sense of proportion is constantly with us; but it is tempered by an equally strong belief that we must not miss the opportunity to provide as complete bibliographical control over these sources as we are capable of achieving. This remains true even though, with infrequent and easily identifiable exceptions, most of theses sources have no textual validity whatsoever. Indeed, in the preparation of critical editions of Rossini's works, they offer at best a contemporary opinion for a problematical passage, at worst confused nonsense.

There was one decision that we made at the outset, reluctantly but resolutely: the thematic catalog will not attempt to provide information about arrangements or adaptations of the operas or reductions of vocal music for piano solo except in very special cases. We are fully aware that publications of this kind were crucial to the reception of Rossini's music, but it is not clear that massive documentation of arrangements of entire operas for string quartet or two flutes, or of favorite arias for glockenspiel and timpani would add anything significantly new to the picture charted already by a consideration of reductions of complete operas for voice and piano and excerpts of individual numbers from the operas. The very same pieces that flourished in instrumental arrangements were also issued as extracts for piano and voice by publishers such as Birchall & C. in London, Cappi und Diabelli in Vienna, or Girard in Naples. From the perspective of reception history, the information about arrangements duplicates the information from reductions.

The Rossini catalog, on the other hand, is committed to examining every publication of his operas either in full score or in reductions for voice and piano. Already in Donald Krummel's *I.A.M.L. Guide*, the many problems facing those who seek bibliographical control over printed editions are analyzed in exemplary fashion. Those associated with French editions are complex enough. Parisian editors had an enormously difficult time with many of Rossini's works, partly because they published many of their editions before the composer brought his scores to the French capital in the mid-1820's. In the case of operas such as *Ricciardo e Zoriade* or *Matilde di Shibran*, they presumably based their original editions on faulty manuscript evidence. When more accurate manuscripts or foreign printed sources became available in Paris, they often perceived their mistakes, and hurriedly backtracked, re-engraving large sections, shifting music around, renumbering pages, etc. It was apparent to us from the beginning that only by means of a narrative history of these editions, charting their various stages, can we hope to make sense of these sources.

What we were never quite willing to believe until we began to compare multiple copies of ostensibly identical Ricordi prints of

Rossini's music from the first half of the nineteenth century, was the extent to which practically every copy we examined of these Italian complete piano-vocal scores was bibliographically distinct. Many of their differences do not emerge from standard bibliographical descriptions: title pages, collations, paginations may all be unchanged, even if a larger number of plates were replaced. Similar detailed problems exist among the French editions, though not to the same extent, since most of these editions had a shorter effective life and were not reissued as extensively as were the Ricordi scores. Given the length of these sources and their number, it would be impossible to justify obtaining reproductions of every copy of every score in order to pursue a detailed comparison and history; yet your libraries are loathe (and, I guess, rightly so) to loan early nineteenth-century scores.

As a result, we have begun to provide much more complete bibliographical descriptions of each edition that we examine in the hope of catching more information in our net. We are noting variants in internal pagination, complete caption titles for pieces which were also issued as separate numbers, complete lists of plate numbers, including the engraver's initials typically added to Ricordi plate numbers on every plate (which help identify changes in individual plates even when plate numbers are unaltered), etc. The problem of detailed alteration of plates for which no external bibliographically describable difference can be noted may prove in general beyond the scope of any reasonable amount of labor, although when such information does emerge we accept it readily. (In one case, at least, the Troupenas edition of *Guillaume Tell*, despite the absence of external bibliographical evidence, a significant variant exists in the score: two systems on a single page are completely re-engraved, a change that both represents an important musical alteration by Rossini and one that helps establish the history of the work.[3]) Our aim, ultimately, however idealistic and unrealizable, is to chart the publication history of each edition: for the documentation it provides about each individual opera; for the assistance it gives future bibliophiles and catalogers in evaluating the materials in their possession; for what it reveals about the reception history of Rossini's music.

What can we ultimately do with all this data? It seems clear that any attempt to print a thematic catalog incorporating complete histories of each Rossini printed source brought out even during the composer's lifetime would be absurd, a bloated monster out of proportion to the subject and incapable of even the modest degree of definitiveness that alone justifies hard covers. Instead, we are tending towards a model that would combine regular book publication and computer-stored information, which could be deposited in selected library collections. In describing an edition in the printed thematic catalog, we are imagining a narrative that briefly traces the history of the edition, pausing at a certain point (that point may need to be different for each different edition) to provide an appropriate bibliographical description of what we take to be the most important state of each edition. Thus, one would specify that certain numbers were first published as excerpts, providing plate numbers and years; that these were at a certain point brought together into a complete edition; that this edition in turn underwent several different states, with or without serious changes in the musical text itself. Detailed bibliographical description would normally accompany only one of these states, and not necessarily the earliest, should that earliest state, for example, turn out to have been significantly faulty in a way that was later corrected. As for excerpts that were never gathered into complete editions, short citations without bibliographical paraphernalia, following the order of numbers in the opera, will have to suffice.

In our records, on the other hand, each and every identified stage in the development of complete editions would be sufficiently described to permit a user of this detailed information to identify a new copy with a known stage in the historical process or to fit it within that process. Similarly, each ungathered excerpt would be described completely. Our experience thus far suggests strongly that it will normally be possible to write descriptions that will stand up reasonably well even as additional copies are examined. It is our hope that the fixity of the printed thematic catalog and the flexibility of the computer-stored descriptions will provide the kind of information necessary for a variety of users.

Ultimately we will need to ask the help of music librarians throughout the country in bringing this project to completion. Once we have complete descriptions of at least one copy of every known "printed edition," and of multiple copies wherever possible, and once we have exhausted the holdings of major collections of nineteenth-century printed editions, we shall be sending our descriptions of specific scores to libraries which have reported either to us or to the National Union Catalog that they own certain Rossini editions. Your willingness to check these descriptions against the copies in your libraries will greatly assist us in gathering as accurate and complete data as possible. And I know that were Rossini here to sign our requests for assistance, he would have used the same little recitative phrase he addressed in a letter to the singer Giuditta Pasta when he asked her for a favor during the 1830's, a phrase which derives from his *La gazza ladra:* "E' pure un gran piacer il far del bene!"

NOTES

1. The entire history is recounted by Margaret Bent, in her introduction to her edition of *Il Turco in Italia* in *Edizione critica delle opere de Gioacchino Rossini,* Serie I, vol. 13 (Pesaro, 1988), pp. xxx-xxxiii.

2. This has been studied by Jeffrey Kallberg: see his article "Marketing Rossini: Sei lettere di Troupenas ad Artaria," in *Bollettino del centro rossiniano di studi* (1980), pp. 41-63.

3. Elizabeth Bartlet has examined this problem in more detail in her work on the critical edition of *Guillaume Tell* for the Fondazione Rossini.

Italian Music and Lyric Poetry of the Renaissance

Michael A. Keller

SUMMARY. From approximately 1450-1650, several hundred anthologies of lyric poetry were written and published in Italy. We estimate that there may be as many as 500,000 poems in this literature with a multiple of this number of variants, and as many as 50,000 musical settings. The goal of the project is the development of databases incorporating both full-text transcriptions of Italian lyric poetry from the beginnings of printing to 1650, and bibliographic records of the sources. The texts will be derived initially from contemporary printed anthologies, both literary and musical, and eventually from manuscripts as well. A second goal is the development of another large database of whole texts of abstract Italian instrumental music of the Renaissance.

This paper concerns a project which has had a lengthy gestation period and, we hope will have an even longer life. I intend to discuss the general situation from which the project arose, the goals of the project, and an encapsulation of the methods of the project, interpolating as I go some comments on the applicability of the various components of the project to other literature and music.

This paper will not cover any but a few of the technological factors inherent in the project. While this presentation is not about

---

Michael A. Keller is affiliated with the Sterling Memorial Library at Yale University.

[Haworth co-indexing entry note]: "Italian Music and Lyric Poetry of the Renaissance." Keller, Michael A. Co-published simultaneously in *Music Reference Services Quarterly*, (The Haworth Press, Inc.) Vol. 2, No. 3/4, 1993, pp. 281- 318; and: *Foundations in Music Bibliography* (ed: Richard D. Green) The Haworth Press, Inc., 1993, pp. 281-318. Multiple copies of this article/chapter may be purchased from The Haworth Document Delivery Center [1-800-3-HAWORTH; 9:00 a.m. - 5:00 p.m. (EST)].

© 1993 by The Haworth Press, Inc. All rights reserved.

bits and bytes, the following appendices of this paper do present some of that sort of information. I am obliged at the outset of this presentation to acknowledge with gratitude the generous support from the National Endowment for the Humanities, the IBM corporation, the University of California at Berkeley, Yale University and the Council on Library Resources without which this project would not have been undertaken, even in its present, formative stages. The title of the project is Italian Music and Lyric Poetry of the Renaissance.

Despite the spectacular work of Emil Vogel, Alfred Einstein, François Lesure and Claudio Sartori in the bibliography of the field, many fundamental questions remain unanswered concerning the Italian Renaissance madrigal and particularly the body of poetry and poets which supplied the texts for the music. Here is the situation. From approximately 1450-1650, several hundred anthologies of lyric poetry, principally sonnets, madrigals, canzoni, and terze rime, were written and published in Italy. When the project began, we believed that there might be as many as 100,000 poems in this literature with a multiple of this number of variants. After some research conducted by our Italian co-directors preparing a collated first-line index for about a dozen incipitari, we have revised that estimate upward to perhaps 500,000 poems. We believe that there may be as many as 50,000 musical settings of this literature, well documented by Einstein et al., as musical entities, but not so well connected to the body of literature from which the texts for the music arose. Literary scholars have been aware for a long time that the Renaissance literary style depended heavily upon imitation and parody, especially in lyric poetry, as a creative technique, and as a charming or even ingratiating ingredient directed to readers, especially readers who were or might become patrons. So, imitation and parody of one poem or more usually, of a line or phrase of one poem in another, is a norm in this literature.

All of us in music understand very well another meaning of imitation, that is, successive statements of the same motive or melody among the several voices in a single musical work. Musicologists have been less aware of imitation of the literary sort just mentioned, but there are some examples of this as well in music, and especially in the abstract instrumental musical genres of ricercars and canzonas which appeared in late Renaissance Italy. To date, no one has brought under bibliographic control the enormous body of literature which is Italian lyric poetry of the Renaissance. And though bibliographic control of the musical madrigal and abstract instrumental music of the same provenance is good, no one has found a way to examine the characteristics of this entire body of music. There is simply too much material, with too many variants, and too many subtle distinctions for any scholar working with the classical tools; brains and three-by-five cards; to control and synthesize the characteristics of this literature and music.

The long-term goals of the project are as follows:

> Development of very large databases incorporating both full-text transcriptions of Italian Lyric Poetry from the beginnings of printing to 1650, and bibliographic records of the sources. The texts will be derived initially from contemporary printed anthologies, both literary and musical, and eventually from manuscripts as well. Ninety-five percent of the poems involved in this long-term project are at the present without bibliographical control of any sort.
>
> A second goal is the development of another very large database of whole texts of abstract Italian instrumental music of the Renaissance.

The particular purposes of the long-term goals are seven:

1. To establish bibliographic control over the sources, a task scarcely possible with previous tools, and scarcely begun; sources gathered in Berkeley and will be cataloged on Research Libraries Information Network (RLIN);
2. To enable better chronological control of dates of publication of individual poems;
3. To establish more certain attributions; (The precise origin of the poem set is often a crucial question in studying the musical setting as well as the poem itself.)
4. To enable classification of texts by topoi (by word or phrase searches), or by thematic families (in the case of textless music), and for both by selected formal or stylistic traits, a major

line of investigation that will be opened up by this research tool, we hope;
5. To make possible the identification of imitation of musical passages by previous composers–as important a technique for Renaissance composers as for Renaissance poets and painters. We think many of the instances that have so far been discovered, though recognized as important, have been discovered only by chance;
6. To make possible identification of fragments of texts and texted music cited in literature or visible in paintings of the period, an enterprise important for both musicology and history of art;
7. To understand more systematically and scientifically the development of instrumental genres of the late Renaissance through the study of imitative techniques in ricercars and canzonas, and through other analytical techniques, for instance, examination of cadential structures made possible by the existence of the database.

It has been the opinion of all scholars with whom we have talked that this long-term project promises to expand radically the avenues for linguistic, semiotic, and literary research in poetic texts of the Renaissance, in their musical settings, and in the nascent school of textless music that was detaching itself from texted music during this same period. We have also become aware that the database will assist art historians in identifying text and music fragments in paintings of the period.

We have been structuring the long-term project for about three years now with specialists in Italy who have worked under the sponsorship of two separate scholarly institutes (cited in the Appendix). Our five institutions and eight specialists will continue to work together throughout the long-term project.

We are pursuing several separate sub-projects begun eighteen months ago. Work on one is already completed, that of the computerized incipitari by our Italian co-directors under the sponsorship of the Istituto di studi rinascimentali of the University of Ferrara and the study unit, Europa delle corti, sponsored by the Council of Europe in Strasbourg. Two others have been begun at Berkeley and

Yale and have expanded to incorporate the work of colleagues in other institutions. As we have refined our methods and accumulated experience and data in these pilot projects, we have begun applying to various sources of funding on both sides of the Atlantic to enable us to continue the long-term project and to bring it to the major proportions that will eventually prove necessary.

The Italian project has combined in one database all the first-line indexes that have been made heretofore for the repertory of poetry under study; the indexing of the database has been completed and the final-form distribution is pending. This compendium of previous scholarship obviously forms a broad starting base for the long-term project. Among the many benefits of this Italian project is the package of computer programs which concatenate all spelling versions of words so that first lines with similar texts appear together regardless of spelling variants. Our Italian co-directors and other Italian scholars associated with them have begun to contribute to the growth of the American databases. During our several meetings with them, we have refined the record structure of the databases, discussed the desired and possible attributes of the various search strategies available to us in the SPIRES environment and selected together the next targets of Italian poetry for inputting (SPIRES is the mainframe database manager we have chosen for building, servicing and interrogating the database).

The projects undertaken at Berkeley and Yale might be classified as literary and musical ones, although they have been complementary almost from the beginning. BITNET links to our Italian colleagues have been opened and are being expanded to allow transcontinental transmission of data and interrogation of the database in Berkeley. It is also now possible to query the database from BITNET modes using REMOTE SPIRES.

THE LITERARY PROJECT

The literary project now underway with the first (and most famous) series of poetic anthologies of the 16th century, that of the Roccolte di rime diversi, is entering texts into a database in searchable form, and is entering the bibliographic information about the source volumes into another database linked to the first. Please see the Appendix for the database record structures and field definitions. Sorting, sequencing and displays of and by any of the fields is possible. There is one factor of our techniques which should be pointed out here. In the Poems File Cord Structure of the Appendix, there is a virtual element midway down the page, element 01/09 labeled BIBREC. This element allows us to relate all poems from a single source in the poems database to the source's record in the bibliographic file. There are sample records from the two databases in the Appendix illustrating this capacity. Eighteen volumes (including reprints) are involved in the prototype phase of the project in 1986/87; approximately 4,200 of a total of perhaps 6,000 poems have been entered in the database to date. By including numerous reprints of source volumes, we are confronting immediately and directly the important and difficult matter of variant readings and attributions, which will doubtless be far greater than the number of individual poems.

Among the several poetic anthologies which we intend to input next year are a number of madrigal anthologies, the many editions of the Rime piacevoli di Cesare Caporali, del mauro et d'altri autori, the most popular anthology of madrigal poetry in the late sixteenth century, and the immense and important II Garggiamento poetico del confuso academico ordito (Venice: Barrezzi, 1611). We have undertaken the diffusion of the project among colleague scholars.

Many of the sources for the project have already been obtained from libraries in Europe and America. It should be of interest that this project will have the side-effect of making the content of such resources previously, laboriously, and perhaps redundantly gathered by individuals available to many others with relatively little delay and cost.

Some lyric poetry of concern to us in the project appeared first in musical part-books. The settings of these poetic texts, and thus the texts themselves, are printed in 3 to 6 separate partbooks, one for each of the musical voices in the piece. This means in practice that in any individual partbook some lines of the poem may be omitted or out of order, and that some collections survive only in incomplete form–that is, lacking some partbooks–and hence give incomplete forms of the texts. Despite these difficulties, literary scholars have recently come to realize the authority and importance of the versions of poetic texts contained in musical prints. Because of the close connections between many poets and musicians of the time, a musical print may often turn out to be the earliest known source.

One of the particular purposes of the project from the outset has been the classification of texts by topoi. Until we had sufficient poems in the database, the development and testing of the method by which to identify, classify, and retrieve texts by formal or thematic traits in large enough numbers had to wait. Professor William Graham Clubb will direct the development of a poem analysis methodology based on the poetic database in 1987/88.

POEM ANALYSIS PROJECT DESCRIPTION

Our project is at present limited, in respect of materials stored, almost entirely to bibliographical and biographical facts and to the bare texts with minimal commentary, largely, in short, to external data. Obviously, the value of the eventually complete database would be greatly increased by concomitantly enabling use to retrieve texts or parts of texts on the basis of chosen formal or thematic traits internal to the poems and to make various statistical studies thereof. In this aim, the project plans to adopt and adapt record structures, protocols, and methods developed and used for the analysis of Renaissance poetry by Professor Will Clubb.

The first poem analysis record structure will provide, in addition to identification fields, the general description of poems by listing selected traits in eight fields: praxis, ludus, mode, address, personification, means, realm, and topos. Praxis, for example, indicates the nature of the poetic act, whether it is narration, description, persuasion, etc. Mode indicates praise, dispraise, irony, satire, or simple plain speaking. Realm denotes setting or milieu, explicit or implied, such as courtly, rural, or natural. The data supplied in such fields is coded N for narration, EU for eulogy, and so forth.

A majority of scholars or critics believe, and rightly, that such data is as often as not far from "hard." What is eulogy to one may be irony to another and satire to our neighbor. On the other hand, it is also more often true than not that a consensus on the more obvious and characteristic features of poetic utterances will obtain among informed readers, and indeed our method is intended only for traits of relatively certain identification. Further more, genuinely doubtful cases are to be so identified, demonstrable errors are to be corrected, and plausible alternative identifications by other authorities can be listed in the note field. These remarks will apply also to what follows.

The first poem record structure will store only general information about the central idea or thrust of a poem. Therefore a second record structure is necessary to record all the topoi individually. These will be "translated" or rendered in terms of a formula or protocol language which is somewhat similar to the Basic English developed by Richards and Ogden in being limited to a relatively small number of words (in the case of our protocol less than a thousand, excluding proper nouns) but in which each word can have only one meaning. The protocol, or metagloss, as it will be known to this project, is based on English rather than on Italian, because English has more short words than any of the other possible languages. Future French, Italian, German or Portuguese editors can easily be supplied with a dual language metagloss.

Topoi means here any of the shortest possible phrases in which narrative, expressive, descriptive, metaphorical, etc., elements can be cast. Each is formulated in three parts, like a sentence: subject, or agent; copula or action (if not a true copula, usually a transitive verb); and predicate, or object. In many cases all three parts of the phrase are entered in metagloss language, for example, "pity drives out anger" will be recorded as "pity repel anger," each word appearing in the proper field of the record structure. Certain common subjects and predicates, common copulas, as well as some grammatical features, like modal auxiliaries, comparisons, negation, etc., are coded as two letter abbreviations.

More complex phrases can be built, in two ways. An apostrophe after the subject or predicate will indicate the genitive case, so that "the beloved woman's cheek is like a rose" is rendered "fe' cheek mr rose." An attribute to the rose, or a second subject or predicate word might be added, for both subject and predicate are repeatable fields. Note however that nouns have no number, verbs have no tenses or modes (other than indicated by modal auxiliaries), and prepositions are suppressed. Other kinds of complication, such as the extended simile or antithesis, require the use of two or more templates. In such a case, the CONNECT field will indicate associations with the appropriate templates.

We expect the topoi data-base to facilitate two categories of investigation:

> First, it will function as or generate a concordance of topics, as well as generate indexes of the same, whether of individual words, such as "rose," or of topics complete, like the examples mentioned. The value of these for searches of individual topics is obvious. In addition, various kinds of statistical studies will be possible, such as percentage or absolute numbers of occurrence of words or topics in a given set of poems, of poets, of poets within a given time span, etc.
>
> Second, on the basis of such statistical counts, it will be possible to make comparative studies of imagistic or rhetorical patterns, in short to describe and compare more accurately the characteristic styles or manners of individual poets, of groups or of traditions.

The record structure for the literary analysis phase of the project is not given as it is still under development. It will, however, reside in the poems record structure and thus in the Poems Database.

THE MUSICAL PROJECT

The musical project is developing a database of "abstract" imitative instrumental music (i.e., ricercars and canzonas, but not toccatas, not dances, not variations, not intabulations) for the period 1540-1640 (i.e., from the earliest examples of the forms until the death of Frescobaldi). Entire pieces will be entered using an inexpensive electronic keyboard, MIDI equipment, and microcomputers. We have employed a programmer who is also an advanced graduate student in musicology at Berkeley to develop a program to take the MIDI input and convert it to an ASCII file of defined symbols for use in the SPIRES database of musical and poetic texts (see Appendix). The musical inputting method has been accomplished for other computers using another language by Walter Hewlett of the Center for Computer Assisted Research in the Humanities in Menlo Park, California. Mr. Hewlett has most generously shared his programs, written in HP Basic, to us; our programmer is converting them to the program language "C" so as to make the program more generalizable (to MIDI equipment and various of the IBM PC microcomputers), though this has proven to be a major stumbling block to date. Musical incipits, musical subjects, and simultaneously occurring musical events (i.e., melodic events and harmonic events) can be searched, isolated, and analyzed using the data we will input and SPIRES protocols. Our method has the attractive feature of permitting the matching of text to music, using a sequencing system, or the inclusion of text in the musical fields, or a combination of the two (sequencing and inclusion).

The scholarly importance of this undertaking has several facets. The first and most obvious is the attribution of anonymi and the identification of conflicting attributions. (Since the repertoire is relatively small, some of this has already been done manually.) A more important scholarly task that has hardly been begun is the identification of thematic families in these pieces–the first absolute music, that is music independent of text and verbal logic. These pieces are, as one scholar has observed, "music about music." It would be a small wonder if they did not quote each other's ideas and re-work each other's themes. Beyond this, the Renaissance was a period whose aesthetic prized imitation-emulation as a means of creation.[1] We know of a few famous thematic families in Renaissance music, since they are (sometimes) specified in titles: la sol fa re mi, the hexachord, Ave maris tella, La spagna. There are surely many more in such a self-reflexive tradition. A string search on a powerful database management system such as SPIRES, will allow us to pick up thematic allusions even when ornamental notes had been added to the basic structural tones.

By entering the musical thematic material of particularly famous texted pieces, we could also get an idea of the extent of the imitation and interaction between the worlds of instrumental and vocal music at the time. This question has scarcely been investigated.[2] We know of one Agostino fantasia based on a Striggio madrigal, and of a Bourdeney-codex ricercar and a Ruffo Capriccio both based on Rore madrigals, for instance.

The applicants' initial "quick and simple input method" for

music of this period, using an ordinary computer keyboard has been rejected after testing. As mentioned above, we are in the act of transferring a program developed elsewhere to our hardware configuration. The advantage of our new method is that it uses musical skills, and can be checked by the inputter as he/she is working since the electronic keyboards produce an audible signal as well as an electronic one. Also, we will be able to "play back" the input music on demand; the sound of the music can be checked against the part from which it was entered. Finally, and somewhat more in the future is the possibility that the electronic-keyboard entry method will permit us to print primitive versions of the music for comparison to the source part-books. The method we are now developing will not be useful for the creation of publishable editions of music. Once the method is developed, we will then enter a sizable body of data and practice interrogating it using SPIRES. Indeed we have lately decided to insert a musical record structure in the Poems file record structure given in the appendix. But this must be described in another communication.

An additional challenge that we are experimenting with is this: can one write an algorithm that teaches the computer the Renaissance solmisation system, such that it can look for inganni–those configurations of notes that were considered closely related because, although their melodic contours were different, their solmisation syllables were, or could be, the same. Such hidden relationships were often exploited within individual pieces of abstract instrumental music of the later sixteenth century. Were they also used to link piece to piece in this esoteric art? This question and others like it will be investigated once the musical portion of the database is large and varied enough.

For the foreseeable future we have decided to exclude the lute repertory and the repertory of two voiced ricercars, working only with pieces in score, partbooks or keyboard tablature, and to focus on ricercars, fantasias, and canzonas. Our project will focus for now on the non-Venetian repertory–which means principally the limited body of music from the Po Valley west of Venice, the local tradition in which Frescobaldi grew up–and on that from the school around Macque, which has been alleged to have exercised a strong influence on Frescobaldi. In addition, we will consider at least three important collections at present preserved only in manuscript: those by "Giaches" (Brumel?) preserved in the Bourdeney Codex (F:Pn Res ms VmA 851), those by Macque preserved in a manuscript now at the Biblioteca nazionale of Florence (Magl. XIX 106bis), and those in the recently uncovered manuscript copy of Luzzaschi's Second Book of Ricercars. These three collections, to which little attention has been paid in the secondary literature, seem to constitute the most important surviving monuments of the tradition out of which Frescobaldi came. The immediate goal of this phase is to use the new information and techniques to illuminate Frescobaldi's Fantasie of 1608, his first instrumental publication. We will focus also on the canzonas published by musicians active in Brescia since the first published canzonas and some important subsequent examples emanated from that city famous for builders of fine stringed instruments and organs. Another goal of this phase is to investigate the hypothesis that the instrumental canzona as a separate genre grew out of the ricercar.

We have been following the investigation of the possibility of obtaining copies of the initial tapes of the Josquin complete works entered into a database at Princeton University in the early 1970's. There is a strong possibility that we would be able to translate these tapes to our codes and then enter the Josquin database into our own. The value to musical scholars of this conversion is significant. Josquin's music, the most respected and imitated of its day and of succeeding generations, would be available for comparison to other composers' music. We should expect many examples of shared musical themes, certainly those based on the Gregorian melodies, but also we expect to find examples of composers borrowing Josquin's themes for their own compositions, as emblems of homage, challenges to their inventiveness, and citations of their own merits.

THE COMBINED PROJECTS

Once the poems and the music have been entered into the appropriate files, the SPIRES programs will allow us to search for exact or near matches of words, phrases, and even complete lines and the musical equivalents of words and phrases. Using this facility, we can trace the use of distinctive words, phrases and lines, and also examine their varying uses. Usage is dependent upon poetic and musical context, dialect, linguistic development, and other parameters, but with the systematic examination of a large body of poetic and musical texts, we and other scholars will be able to propose and perhaps even prove new hypotheses. These examinations may be assisted by applying some artificial intelligence programs to the database as well. SPIRES allows us to search for roots of words, for sequences of words by first letter, and for rhyming words. We believe that the combination of those tools will enable us to address our purposes described earlier. The computer will perform, tirelessly and with precision we can define, the comparisons, word searches, and string searches over a very large body of literature and music, and can do so better than any person or persons. Having gathered information to our specifications, the project directors and others are left to make interpretations, judgements, and criticisms which may lead to new understandings of Italian music and poetry of the Renaissance.

By-products of the research will be various lists, indexes and catalogs. We will be able to produce author/composer and first-line indexes (including perhaps musical notation) to individual volumes, various repertories and the whole database. Additionally, we will be able to produce indexes to publishers' products, to volumes published in a given period of time or from a given city, or from combinations of any of the fields. We can produce indexes by dedicatee, persons who were frequently patrons or employers of the creators of the music and poetry; our database thus begins to serve as an aid to the study of the sociology of music and poetry in Renaissance Italy. Very little of this indexing is presently available. For music, there is a patchwork quilt of bibliographic tools. Principal among this of course is *RISM*. If we closely examine a page from the *RISM* volume concerned with anthologies of music published in the sixteenth and seventeenth centuries, however, we see that the entries are in chronological order and list only the names of the composers whose works are contained in each anthology. The indexes in *RISM* provide access only by composer, and generally not by the first line or title of the music (and certainly not by a thematic incipit). Our project will begin to address this lack. For the poetic sources, the indexing and cataloging is in a primitive state.

By the end of our project, we should be able to provide much improved access to the pieces in each anthology than is possible at the present time. Some of these "by-products" may result in new or altered attributions for the poetic and musical texts in our database.

Let us revisit the current situation.

LITERARY PROJECT

At the present time there is no single catalog, bibliography, or index which controls all the sources of Italian lyric poetry either at the volume/codex level, or at the individual poem level. There are several first-line or incipit indices treating poets and schools; these cover only about five percent of the literature in question. Similarly, there is no single compendium of the texts themselves. The prototype project has allowed us to develop a detailed methodology, work out some technical problems (inputting, manipulating, and outputting poetry, poetry set to music, and music alone; how to handle variant lines; linking musical texts to literary texts to bibliographic entries ...), and demonstrate the viability of our approach. The prototype project eventually will enable us to demonstrate the new line of research made possible by computers, that of searching enormous files of texts for topoi. To our knowledge no other group is working on this kind of project on this literature. Also, to our knowledge, this methodology, that of linking bibliographic entries to full texts of music and poetry, is very unusual. The first production phase will use the methodologies proven and tested in the prototype phase to begin the first massive additions to the database and thus permit the poem analysis project to proceed.

MUSICAL PROJECT

There exists no comprehensive catalogue of the contents of the prints and manuscripts of abstract Italian instrumental music prior to 1640 which provides access by thematic content. Thus, no systematic investigation of the quotations, imitations, or thematic families of this repertory has been possible. I hope that it is evident from this description of our work on this music and literature that the methods and tools we develop may well be applicable to other literatures, other musical repertories, and other periods. This investigation should be seen as an experiment leading to some predictable goals, but I hope it will also be of benefit in unforeseen ways to projects in other disciplines.

NOTES

1. See G.W. Pigman, III, "Versions of Imitation in the Renaissance," *Journal of the American Musicological Society,* 35 (Spring 1982), 1-48; David Quint, *Origin and Originality in Renaissance Literature,* New Haven: Yale University Press, 1984.

2. For an idea of potential results, see James Haar, "The Fantasie et recerchari of Giuliano Tiburtino," *Musical Quarterly,* 59 (1973), 223-38.

APPENDIX

ITALIAN MUSIC AND LYRIC POETRY OF THE RENAISSANCE
Report of 9 April 1987
Columbia, South Carolina

I. Abstract

This project is developing a very large data base incorporating both full-text transcriptions of Italian lyric poetry and associated music from ca. 1450 to 1650 and a bibliographic record of the sources. A simultaneous and parallel aspect of the project will pursue similar goals using similar (in many cases the same) hardware and software, but with abstract, untexted instrumental music; entire musical texts will be entered. In both aspects of the project the local goal is to establish bibliographic control over the poems or pieces in their various appearances. In both also, the longer-term goal is to explore, by analogous methods of data base searching, the wide range and the various techniques of imitation in the Renaissance. Thus the search for types of internal connections and various topoi in the poems is paralleled by the exploration of thematic families in the textless instrumental music.

The American branch of this Italian-American endeavor will broaden its focus from the poetry in the *Raccolte di rime diversi* of the proto-type phase, develop a poem analysis method based on topoi, and continue work on the repertory of late Renaissance Italian imitative instrumental music, adding canzonas to the ricercars already entering the data base. These activities are closely linked to and supportive of other research projects. Materials acquired for use in the project will be cataloged in the Research Libraries Information Network (RLIN) and ultimately available on inter-library loan.

The Italian branch of the project has finished preparing a collated first-line index of lyric poetry made from about a dozen smaller such incipitari dating from the Renaissance. The Italian branch has also started contributing poems and bibliographic records to the data base.

BITNET is used as the international telecommunications link and

SPIRES has been chosen as the data base manager, although it is anticipated that the data itself may be inserted into other data base managers (including micro-computer based systems) and interrogated using artificial intelligence programs.

II. Target Literatures

  a. Lyric poetry (madrigals, canzonas, etc.)–initial target has been the Giolito imprints of the late 16th century and will be the Caporali *Le Rime Piacevoli* of 1582 to 1625;
  b. Musical madrigals, and abstract instrumental music (canzonas and ricercars) of the Renaissance (ca 1420-ca 1640). Apx 500,000 poems, apx 30,000 to 50,000 pieces of music (in toto).

III. Directors and Other Personnel

  a. The following specialists are directors of the project:

  Louise George Clubb, Professor of Italian and Comparative Literature, UCB, and Director, Villa I Tatti, the Harvard Center for Renaissance Studies in Florence

  William G. Clubb, Professor of French and Comparative Literature, retired, University of San Francisco, resident and independent scholar at Villa I Tatti

  Anthony Newcomb, Professor of Music, University of California/Berkeley (UCB)

  Michael Keller, Associate University Librarian for Collection Development, Yale University

  Roberto Fedi, Professor, Universita degli Studi, Firenze

  Marco Santagata, Professor, Universita degli Studi, Pisa

  Amedeo Quondam, Professor, Universita degli Stud Roma; Director, Europa degli Corti

  Thomas Walker, Professor of Musicology and Dean of the Facolta diMagistero, Universita degli Studi, Ferrara; Director, Istituto di Stud Rinascimentali

  b. The following specialists are contributing scholar-editors:

  Edmund N. Strainchamps, Associate Professor of Music, State University of New York at Buffalo

Angelo Pompilio, Assistente, Dipartimento di Musica e Spettacolo, Universta' degli Studi di Bologna
Antonio Vasali, Maestro, Istituto di Studi Rinascimentali, Ferrara

c. Computer specialists: Shulamit Roth, Peter Rausch, Allen Konrad, Thom Blum, Austin Shelton, Christopher Newcomb (all University of California/Berkeley)
d. Graduate student research assistants: Jonathan Schiff, Josh Kosman, Andrew dell'Antonio, Naomi Yavneh, Richard Hill, Ellen MacDonald, Brad Rubenstein (all University of California/Berkeley)

IV. Resources

a. IBM ASIS grants of hardware and main-frame computer time;
b. Librarians Association of the University of California grants;
c. Humanities Research Council of the Academic Senate of the University of California grants;
d. Council on Library Resources Faculty/Librarian Research Grant;
e. National Endowment for the Humanities Research Resources Grant (FY1 986/1987 awarded, FY1 987/1988 applied for);
f. various support in funds and otherwise from the home institutions of the members of the directorate.

V. Methods of Adding to the Data Base

a. Pilot phase
  –keyboarding on-site by research assistants (of texts);
  –computer keyboarding by research assistants (of music);
b. Prototype phase
  –OCR test (failed);
  –remote keyboarding by a vendor (of text);
  –electronic keyboarding by research assistants (of music)
c. Production phase
  –remote keyboarding by a vendor (of text);
  –remote keyboarding by specialist editors (of text and music)
  –electronic keyboarding by research assistants (of music).

d. All phases
  –pre- and post-editing of texts and music by project personnel (on-site editors) with sampling by members of the directorate.

VI. Access to the Data Base

a. eventually through BITNET using REMOTE SPIRES as a file server;
b. possibly by downloading portions to micro-computer diskettes (on demand);
c. possibly through purchase of a copy of the data base for loading elsewhere;
d. possibly through various paper products (indexes, catalogs, editions)

VII. Prospective

The data base record structures can accommodate other languages and even versions of one poem in several languages. They can also accommodate various kinds of music, although clearly more complex music from the 18th century and forward will tax, severely, the limits of our coding language; certainly the coding and record structures ought to accommodate medieval and renaissance music of any region. The analytical techniques for text are valid for virtually any lyric poetry. Our hypothesis is that SPIRES provides certain interrogative functions which will be useful for most early music; we are not certain exactly how much we can do in SPIRES with harmonic events, but we are fairly sure that melodic events can be listed, examined, classified, compared and analyzed. The techniques and data we evolve will be available to scholars for their own purposes, although we intend to maintain at least one version of the data base and related programs more or less inviolate for our own research.

(Keller, Columbia, SC 4/87)

SPIRES BIBLIOGRAPHIC RECORD STRUCTURE 2/87

Sec	Occ	Len	Type	St/El	Element
Fix	Sing	4	Int	00/00 slot	BIBID
Opt	Sing		String	00/01	TITLE, T
Opt	Mult		String	00/03	RLIN.ID, RI
Opt	Mult		Struc	00/04	COMPOSERS, C
Opt	Mult		String	01/00	.COMPOSER, C
Opt	Mult		String	01/01	.COMP.PROFESSION, COP
Opt	Mult		String	01/02	COMP.CITY, COC
Opt	Mult		String	01/03	.COMP.INSTITUTION, COI
Opt	Mult		Struc	00/05	AUTHORS, A
Opt	Sing		String	02/00	.AUTHOR, A
Opt	Sing		String	02/01	.AUTH.PROFESSION, AUP
Opt	Sing		String	02/02	.AUTH.CITY, AUC
Opt	Sing		String	02/03	.AUTH.INSTITUTION, AUI
Opt	Mult		Struc	00/06	EDITORS
Opt	Sing		String	03/00	.EDITOR, ED
Opt	Sing		String	03/01	.EDITOR.LOC, EDL
Opt	Sing		String	03/02	.EDITOR.INSTIT, EDIN
Opt	Mult		Struc	00/07	PRINTERS
Opt	Sing		String	04/00	.PRINTER, PRN
Opt	Sing		String	04/01	.PRINTER.LOC, PRNL
Opt	Sing		String	04/02	.PUBLISHER, PUB
Opt	Sing		String	04/03	.PUBLISHER.LOC, PUBL
Opt	Sing		String	04/04	.BOOKSELLER, BKSL
Opt	Sing		String	04/05	.BOOKSELLER.LOC, BKSLLOC
Opt	Sing		String	04/06	.PRINTERS.NOTE, PRNNO
Opt	Sing	4	Hex	00/08	PRN.DATE, PD
Opt	Sing		String	00/09	PRN.PLACE, PP
Opt	Sing		String	00/0A	FORMAT, F
Opt	Sing		String	00/0B	PAGE.FORMAT, PF
Opt	Sing		String	00/0C	PAGINATION, PG
Opt	Mult		Struc	00/0D	DEDICATEE
Opt	Sing		String	05/00	.DEDICATEE.NAME, DNA
Opt	Sing		String	05/01	.DEDICATEE.TITLE, DTI
Opt	Mult		Struc	00/0E	DEDICATION

Opt Sing 1	String	06/00	.DEDICATION.EXIST, DE
Opt Sing	String	06/01	.DEDICATION.TEXT, DT
Opt Sing	String	06/02	.DEDI.SIGNATURE, DS
Opt Mult	String	06/03	.DEDICATION.NAMES, DN
Opt Sing 4	Hex	06/04	.DEDICATION.DATE, DEDA
Opt Mult	Struc	00/0F	AUTHORIZED
Opt Sing	String	07/00	.AUTHORIZED.NAME, AUN
Opt Sing 4	Hex	07/01	.AUTHORIZED.DATE, AUD
Opt Sing 4	Hex	07/02	.AUTH.COMMENT, AUC
Opt Sing	String	00/10	PREFACE
Opt Sing	String	00/11	PREFACE.DATE, PRD
Opt Sing	String	00/12	PREFACE.SIGNAT, PRS
Opt Mult	Struc	00/13	IMPRINT
Opt Sing	String	08/00	.REF.TITLE, RT
Opt Sing	String	08/01	.REF.PLACE, RPL
Opt Sing	String	08/02	.REF.PUB, RPUB
Opt Sing 4	Hex	08/03	.REF.DATE, RDAT
Opt Mult	String	00/14	INDEX.TYPE, IT
Opt Sing	String	00/15	COLLOPHON, COLL
Opt Mult	String	00/16	RISM.NUMBER, RISM
Opt Mult	String	00/17	VOGEL.NUMBER, VOGEL
Opt Sing 1	String	00/18	ERRATA, ERR
Opt Mult	String	00/19	OPERATIONS, OP
Opt Mult	Struc	00/1C	LOCATION
Opt Sing	String	0A/00	.HOLDING.LIB, LIB
Opt Sing	String	0A/01	.PLACE
Opt Sing	String	0A/02	.CALL. NUMBER, CALL
Opt Sing	String	0A/03	.EDITION, EDN
Opt Sing	String	0A/04	.EDITION.DATE, EDD
Opt Mult	Struc	00/1D	NOTES
Opt Sing 4	Hex	0B/00	.NOTE.DATE, ND
Opt Sing	String	0B/01	.NOTE
Opt Sing	String	0B/02	.NOTE.AUTHOR, NA
Opt Sing	Struc	00/1E	ENTRY
Opt Sing	String	0C/00	.INPUTTER, INP
Opt Sing 4	Hex	0C/01	.DATE.ADDED, DA
Opt Mult	Struc	00/1F	MAINTENANCE, MAINT

```
Opt Sing    String  0D/00       .DATA. ENTRY, DE
Opt Sing 4  Hex     0D/01       .DATE.UPDATED, DU
```

(Keller, Columbia, SC 4/87)

SPIRES POEM RECORD STRUCTURE 2/87

```
Sec Occ     Len Type    St/El       Element
--- ----    --- ------  -----       -------

Fix Sing  4 Int         00/00   slot POEMID
Opt Mult    String      00/01        METRICAL.DSC, MD
Opt Mult    Struc       00/02        BIBINFO
Req Sing  4 Int         01/00        .BIBKEY, BI
Opt Sing    String      01/01        .PARTBOOK
Opt Sing    String      01/02        .PAGE
Opt Mult    Struc       01/03        .POETS, P
Opt Sing    String      02/00        .. POET, P
Opt Sing    String      02/01        .. POET.PROFESSION, POP
Opt Sing    String      02/02        .. POET.CITY, POC
Opt Sing    String      02/03        .. POET.INSTITUTION, POI
Opt Mult    Struc       01/04        .COMPOSERS, C
Opt Sing    String      03/00        ..COMPOSER, C
Opt Sing    String      03/01        ..COMP.PROFESSION, COP
Opt Sing    String      03/02        ..COMP.CITY, COC
Opt Sing    String      03/03        ..COMP.INSTITUTION, COI
Opt Mult    String      01/05        .CAPTION, CAP
Opt Mult    String      01/06        .PROPER.NAMES, PN
Opt Mult    Struc       01/07        .CONNECT
Opt Sing  4 Int         04/00        ..CONNECTED.POEM, CP
Opt Sing    String      04/01        ..CONNECTION.TYPE, CT
Opt Mult    Struc       01/08        .STANZA.STR
Opt Mult    Struc       05/00        ..LINE
Req Sing  4 Int         06/00        ... LINE.NUMBER, LN
Opt Mult    String      06/01        ... ITALIAN, IT
Opt Sing  4 Int         05/01        .. STANZA
Vir Sing  4 Struc       01/09        phan . BIBREC
Vir -       -  -/-       . .         (Subfile BIBX)
```

Opt Mult		Struc	00/03	RELATION
Opt Sing 4		Int	0A/00	. RELATED.POEM, RP
Opt Sing		String	0A/01	. RELATION.TYPE, RT
Opt Sing		String	0A/02	. RELATION.COMMENT, RC
Opt Mult		Struc	00/04	AUTHORIZED
Opt Sing		String	0B/00	. AUTHORIZED.NAME, AUN
Opt Sing 4		Hex	0B/01	. AUTHORIZED.DATE, AUD
Opt Sing 4		Hex	0B/02	. AUTH.COMMENT, AUC
Opt Mult		String	00/05	OPERATIONS, OP
Opt Mult		Struc	00/08	NOTES
Opt Sing		String	0D/00	. NOTE
Opt Sing		String	0D/01	. NOTE. AUTHOR, NA
Opt Sing 4		Hex	0D/02	. NOTE.DATE, ND
Opt Sing		Struc	00/09	ENTRY
Opt Sing		String	0E/00	. INPUTTER, INP
Opt Sing 4		Hex	0E/01	. DATE.ADDED, DA
Opt Mult		Struc	00/0A	MAINTENANCE, MAINT
Opt Sing		String	0F/00	. DATA.ENTRY, DE
Opt Sing 4		Hex	0F/01	. DATE.UPDATED, DU

ANTHOLOGIES OF ITALIAN MUSIC AND LYRIC POETRY OF THE RENAISSANCE
PILOT PHASE DIRECTIONS TO INPUTTERS
UPDATED APRIL 1987

NB: Any fields for which information is not specified in the source should be left blank and closed with a semi-colon.

SPIRES BIB File // Field Definitions

In TITLE field, enter locations as they appear in the source; in all other LOCATION fields, enter modern spellings of place names according to [an agreed upon standard Italian source].

BIBID = an unique, system-supplied integer used to identify a particular bibliographic record in the BIB file and to relate particular poem records in the POEMS file and music records in the MUSIC file. Inputters NEVER assign a BIBID number.

TITLE, T = transcription of the entire title page exactly as it appears, using "/" to denote new lines, including imprint information (exactly as it appears). Notes presence of decorative and printer's marks on the title page. Disregard capitalization.

TITLE.ALTERNATE, TA = supply conventional or uniform title as formulated according to AACR2 Cataloging Rules and LC practice.

RLIN.ID, RI = the alphanumeric identification of the catalog record for the source entered by UC/Berkeley into the bibliographic data base of the Research Libraries Group, the Research Libraries Information Network (RLIN). A MARC record with information on the source can be retrieved by searching on this number in the RLIN system.

COMPOSERS, C = a repeatable structure.
    COMPOSER, C = the name of the composer or composers whose name(s) appear on the title page of the source, as it appears on the title page; a repeatable field.
    COMPOSER.PROFESSION, COP = Profession of the composer, if specified on the title page or elsewhere in the volume.
    COMPOSER.CITY, COC = City where composer exercises this profession, as indicated on the title page or elsewhere in the volume.
    COMPOSER.INSTITUTION, COI = Institution (court, church, chapel, etc.) in which composer exercises his profession, as indicated on the title page or elsewhere in the volume.

AUTHORS, A = a repeatable structure.
    AUTHOR, A = the name of the author or authors whose name(s) appear on the title page; the name of the person responsible for the edition may appear as well; a repeatable field.
    AUTHOR.PROFESSION, AUP = Profession of the author, if specified on the title page or elsewhere in the volume.
    AUTHOR.CITY, COC = City where author exercises this profession, as indicated on the title page or elsewhere in the volume.
    AUTHOR.INSTITUTION, COI = Institution (court, church, chapel, etc.) in which author exercises his profession, as indicated on the title page or elsewhere in the volume.

EDITORS, E = a repeatable structure.
EDITOR, ED = Editor of volume, as cited on the title page or elsewhere in the volume.
EDITOR.LOC, EDLOC = Location where editor edits, as cited on title page or elsewhere in the volume.

[NB: Ordinarily we expect that the printer will be cited on the title page, but occasionally publisher will be cited (e.g., ad istanza di . . .) on the title page with printer appearing with designation (e.g., stampatore) on the title page or the colophon. Occasionally also, the bookseller(s) marketing the volume may be cited on the title page or on the colophon with designation (e.g., libraio or si vende da . . .).

PRINTERS, P = a repeatable structure.
PRINTER, PRN = the name of the printer as it appears on the title page or the colophon; if the title page and the colophon display two different names, repeat the structure and show both.
PRINTER.LOC = Location(s) of printer, as cited on the title page or colophon.
PUBLISHER, PUB = Name of publisher as cited on title page or elsewhere in the volume.
PUBLISHER.LOC, PUBLOC = Location where publisher exercises profession as specified on the title page or elsewhere in the volume.
BOOKSELLER, BKSL = Name of Bookseller as cited on title page or else where in the volume.
BOOKSELLER.LOC, BKSLLOC = Location(s) of bookseller as cited on the title page or elsewhere in the volume.

PUB.DATE, PD = the year of publication as it appears on the title page.

FORMAT, F = if musical partbooks, the names of the partbooks.

PAGE.FORMAT, PF = for portrait enter P (portrait format means upright); for landscape enter L (landscape means oblong).

PAGINATION, PG = the number of pages, numbered and unnumbered in the source, giving the number on the last numbered page (i.e., pp. xiv,238 means that the last number on the pages numbered with roman numerals is xiv and the last number on the pages numbered with arabic numerals is 238). Enter unnumbered pages at beginning or end in square brackets preceding or following the numbered pages. Volumes numbered by folios should be indicated by ff. at the appropriate place.

DEDICATEE = a repeatable structure.

DEDICATEE.NAME, DNA = the name of the dedicatee as given in the volume.

DEDICATEE.TITLE, DTI = the title of the dedicatee as given in the volume.

DEDICATION = a repeatable structure.

DEDICATION.EXIST, DE = "yes" if present, "no" if not.

DEDICATION.TEXT, DT = the interesting portions of the text in full.

DEDICATION.SIGNATURE, DS = the name of the person who signed dedication as given in the volume.

DEDICATION.NAMES, DN = names mentioned in the text of the dedication as given in the volume.

DEDICATION.DATE, DEDA = date of dedication as given in volume.

DEDICATION.PLACE, DPL = place dedication signed as given in volume.

AUTHORIZED = a repeatable structure.

AUTHORIZED.NAME, AUN = name of author, composer, dedicatee, or person signing preface as cited in the Library of Congress Name Authority File (LCNAF). Not provided by inputter.

AUTHORIZED.DAT, AUD = dates of birth and death as cited in the LCNAF. Not provided by inputter.

AUTHORIZED.COMMENT, AUC = this field intended to allow project directors and other scholars to note variations from standard forms of names, pseudonyms, aliases, etc., cited in this or other name structures of the record.

PREFACE = a repeatable structure.

PREFACE. DATE, PRD = date at the end of the preface, if present.

PREFACE.SIGNAT, PRS = name of the person, as given in the volume, who signed the preface or is otherwise identified in the source as the author of the preface.

IMPRINT = a repeatable structure referring to modern editions.
REF.TITLE, RT = title of modern edition of the source.
REF.PLACE, RP = place of publication of modern edition.
REF.PUB, RPUB = name of publisher.
REF.DATE, RDAT = year of publication.

INDEX.TYPE, IT = Enter one or more of the following sigla according to whichever types or combination of types of indexes are present in the volume: FN (index by first names of poets); LN (index by last name of poet); MD (index by metrical type of poem, e.g., sonnets, ottave, madrigals); T (index by themes of poems); I (index by incipits of poems).

COLOPHON, COL = the presence of the colophon, where it occurs in the source volume, and the information contained in it.

RISM.NUMBER, RISM = the siglum of the musical edition from the various parts of the Repertoire Internationale des Sources Musicales, an international inventory of early sources of music and works about music.

VOGEL.NUMBER, VOGEL = the siglum of the musical edition from the Nuovo Vogel.

ERRATA, ERR = the full text of any errata list should be entered here. Errata corrections should also be entered in the poems as they are input, with specification in the NOTE field of the altered erratum.

OPERATIONS, OP = an indication of what has been done to the BIB record (index building, editing, modifications, etc.)

LOCATION = a repeatable field.
HOLDING.LIB, LIB = the name of the library owning the source used.

PLACE = the city of the holding library.
CALL.NUMBER, CALL = the shelfmark of the source in the holding library.
EDITION, ED = the number or distinctive name of edition, if any.

NOTES = a repeatable structure.
NOTES. DATE, ND = the date the note was written.
NOTE = the text of the note (may refer to any field in the record or anything at all relating to this bib record).
NOTE.AUTHOR, NA = the name of the person writing the note.

ENTRY = a non-repeatable structure.
INPUTTER, INP = the name of the inputter.
DATE.ADDED, DA = the date the record was first added to the file.

MAINTENANCE, MAINT = a repeatable structure.
DATA.ENTRY, DE = the nature of the alteration to any field, with the field specified, refers to record structure not to data in fields.
DATE.UPDATED, DU = the date the alteration was made.

Note: repeatable structures are meant to be used to control relevant data appearing in multiple sources, etc., so that in most cases only one set of data will appear in one field. This allows indexing and searching by individual names, titles, locations, dates, etc. Inputting multiple sets of data in one element of a structure makes indexing and searching difficult.

SPIRES POEMS File//Field Definitions 4/87

POEMID = a unique, system-supplied integer used to identify a particular poem record in the POEM file and to relate particular poems to records in the BIB file and in the MUSIC file. Inputters NEVER assign a poemid number.

METRICAL.DSC, MD = A one word or phrase descriptor of the poem's type (e.g., sonetto, madrigale, canzona, etc.) NB: WGC and

LGC to provide approved terms in a list. Inputters should fill in only if unambiguous.

BIBINFO = a repeatable structure, allowing variant lines or even identical poems in different bibkeys (i.e., sources) to be associated under the same poemid.
BIBKEY, BI = BIBID (from BIB file record) number of the source containing the poem. Supplied by inputter only when the source is represented in the BIB file and the inputter knows the bibid.
Otherwise, inputter leaves blank, but in some way informs BIRP-central from whence came the poem following. NB-AAN and MAK to work out this latter method in June 1987.
PAGE = page in the source on which the poem begins, as specified in the source. However, when pagination on the source is locally incorrect (e.g., misnumbering of a single page), enter "[recte, p. (or f.) xxx]." If the pagination is more radically wrong, then enter the page as it appears in the volume, supplemented with gathering information [e.g., p. 139, (Biii)]. Note that usually only the first four leaves in the gathering are specifically marked (on the bottom of the recto side); one counts from the last mark (i.e., iiii or iv) forward to the next gathering, supplying the missing Bv, Gvii, or whatever is indicated or appropriate.

POETS, P = a repeatable structure
POET, P = name of poet as found in the source, first name, initials or middle name, last name as given.
POET.PROFESSION, POP = Profession of the poet, if specified.
POET.CITY, POC = City where poet exercises this profession, as indicated on the title page or elsewhere in the volume.
POET.INSTITUTION, POI = Institution (court, church, chapel, etc.) in which author exercises his profession, as indicated on the title page or elsewhere in the volume.

COMPOSER, C = a repeatable structure.
COMPOSER, C = name of the composer setting the poem to music as given in the CANTUS partbook of the source; note varying attribution in repeated field.

COMPOSER. PROFESSION, COP = Profession of the composer, if specified.

COMPOSER.CITY, COC = City where composer exercises this profession, as indicated on the title page or elsewhere in the volume.

COMPOSER.INSTITUTION, COI = Institution (court, church, chapel, etc.) in which composer exercises his profession, as indicated on the title page or elsewhere in the volume.

CAPTION, CAP = Heading of the poem(s) as given in the source. NB AAN, MAK, LGC, and WGC need to work out a method to describe how many poems are affected by the CAPTION (February 12, 1987).

NAMES CITED, NCP = Contemporary historical personnages cited in poem.

CONNECT = a repeatable sub-structure.

CONNECTED.POEM, CP = POEMIDs of poems connected in the source by external connectors (e.g., captions or titles applying to several poems, proposta/risposta headings) and poems joined as an explicit structure (e.g., canzonas, madrigal strings).

CONNECTION.TYPE, CT = A code denoting the type of connection [to be supplied by project directors WGC and LGC February 12, 1987].

STANZA.STR = stanza structure, a repeatable structure.

LINE = a repeatable structure.

LINE.NUMBER, LN = the number of the line of the poem following.

ITALIAN, IT = the text of the line of poetry, exactly as it appears with obvious typographical errors corrected (e.g., upside down letters)

STANZA = the number of the preceding stanza (e.g., 1,2, etc).

BIBREC = a field allowing this structure to be related to other records in this and other files. Inputter NEVER inserts this field or data for it.

RELATION = a repeatable structure.
   RELATED.POEM, RP = a POEMID of a poem related to the one contained in this record by internal reference of various sorts: citation in another poem; copy or servile imitation of another poem or parts of another poem (in theme, development, vocabulary, sentence structure); imitation or emulation of another poem with freedom and personal inventiveness; paraphrase or free translation in another language.
   RELATION.TYPE, RT = specification of one of the sorts suggested above.
   RELATION.COMMENT, RC = free text description of the nature of the relationship.

AUTHORIZED = a repeatable structure, not to be filled out by inputter.
   AUTHORIZED.NAME, AUN = standard form of the poet's name as it appears, if it appears, in the Library of Congress Name Authority File.
   AUTHORIZED.DATE, AUD = established birth and death years of name in AUN as cited in LCNAF.
   AUTH.COMMENT, AUC = free text area to comment upon AUN or AUD.

OPERATIONS, OP = A repeatable structure. Intellectual operations performed on the poem subsequent to input.

EDITORIAL REVIEW, EDR = Authorization of original input–to be filled in with name and date by an authorized project director.

NOTES = a repeatable structure.
   NOTE.DATE, ND = the date a note was entered.
   NOTE. = the text of the note [this field allows us to comment upon peculiarities in any of the fields of the record or in the source, or upon anything else].
   NOTE.AUTHOR, NA = name of the person entering the note.

ENTRY = a repeatable structure.
   INPUTTER, INP = name of the person entering the poem into the file.
   DATE.ADDED, DA = date the record was entered.

MAINTENANCE, MAINT = a repeatable structure. Mechanical operations performed on the record.
DATA.ENTRY, DE = denoting which fields were modified and why.
DATA.UPDATED, DU = dates of modification.

(Keller, Columbia, SC 4/87)

Sample Record from the Bibliographic Data Base

BIBID = 1;
TITLE = Rime/ diverse di/ molti eccellentiss./ auttori nuova-/ mente raccolte. Con gratia & privilegio/ [Printer's mark]/ In Vinetia appresso Gabriel/ Giolito di Ferrarii/ MDXLV.;
RLIN.ID = CUBG85-B23628;
PUBLISHERS;
   PUBLISHER = Gabriel Giolito;
PUB.DATE = 1545;
PUB.PLACE = Venezia;
PAGE.FORMAT = portrait;
PAGINATION = 370, [24];
DEDICATEE;
   DEDICATEE.NAME = Mendozza, Don Diego Hurtado di;
DEDICATION;
   DEDICATION.EXIST = Yes;
INDEX.TYPE = yes, alphabetical by first name of author and by first line of each author's poems, 24 pages.;
COLLOPHON = In Vinegia appresso/ Gabriel Giolito/ de Ferrari.;
LOCATION;
   HOLDING.LIB = Bancroft Library, UC Berkeley;
   PLACE = Berkeley, CA;
NOTES;
   NOTE.DATE = 09/11/85;
   NOTE = Pages 7-8 (last page of dedication) missing in this copy.;
   NOTE.AUTHOR = Jonathan Shiff;
NOTES;
   NOTE.DATE = 08/07/86;

NOTE = "Notes on inputting procedures; While the grave accent is used in the database entries to indicate a grave accent in the text, an apostrophe is used to indicate the straight accent. The metrical description is all in lower-case letters. Names in block capitals in the poems are input normally, with the first letter capital and the rest in lower-case. The inputter calls terze rime terzine. The use of spaces after apostrophes is not consistent, but appears to be correct according to the CLUBB rules.";
NOTE.AUTHOR = A. Dell'Antonio;
ENTRY;
INPUTTER = Jonathan Shiff;
DATE.ADDED = 09/11/85;

(Keller, Columbia, SC 4/87)

Sample Poem from the Data Base Incorporating Elements of the Associated Bibliographic Record

POEMID = 651;
METRICAL.DSC = sonetto;
BIBINFO;
BIBKEY = 1;
PAGE = 332;
POETS;
POET = Baffa, Francesca;
BIBREC;
BIBID = 1;
TITLE = Rime/ diverse di/ molti eccellentiss./ auttori nuova-/mente raccolte. Con gratia & privilegio/ [Printer's mark]/ In Vinetia appresso Gabriel/ Giolito di Ferrarii/ MDXLV.;
RLIN.ID = CUBG85-B23628;
PUBLISHERS;
PUBLISHER = Gabriel Giolito;
PUB.DATE = 1545;
PUB.PLACE = Venezia;
PAGE.FORMAT = portrait;
PAGINATION = 370, [24];
DEDICATEE;
DEDICATEE.NAME = Mendozza, Don Diego Hurtado di;

DEDICATION;
  DEDICATION.EXIST = Yes;
INDEX.TYPE = yes, alphabetical by first name of author and by first line of each author's poems, 24 pages.;
  COLLOPHON = In Vinegia appresso/ Gabriel Giolito/ de Ferrari.;
  LOCATION;
    HOLDING.LIB = Bancroft Library, UC Berkeley;
    PLACE = Berkeley, CA;
  NOTES;
    NOTE.DATE = 09/11/85;
    NOTE = Pages 7-8 (last page of dedication) missing in this copy.;
    NOTE.AUTHOR = Jonathan Shiff;
  NOTES;
    NOTE. DATE = 08/07/86;
    NOTE = "Notes on inputting procedures; While the grave accent issued in the database entries to indicate a grave accent in the text, an apostrophe is used to indicate the straight accent. The metrical description is all in lower-case letters. Names in block capitals in the poems are input normally, with the first letter capital and the rest in lower-case. The inputter calls terze rime terzine. The use of spaces after apostrophes is not consistent, but appears to be correct according to the CLUBB rules.";
    NOTE.AUTHOR = A. Dell'Antonio;
ENTRY;
  INPUTTER = Jonathan Shiff;
  DATE.ADDED = 09/11/85;
STANZA.STR;
  LINE;
    LINE.NUMBER = 1;
    ITALIAN = Cosi tosto vi veggia in alto, e degno;
  LINE;
    LINE.NUMBER = 2;
    ITALIAN = "Seggio posto Rangon dal Re Christiano;";
  LINE;
    LINE.NUMBER = 3;
    ITALIAN = Come farete poi debile, et vano;

```
  LINE;
    LINE.NUMBER = 4;
    ITALIAN = L'ardir' de' suoi nemici, e'l fero sdegno.;
  LINE;
    LINE.NUMBER = 5;
    ITALIAN = Et se il gran Guido con l'ardito ingegno;
  LINE;
    LINE.NUMBER = 6;
    ITALIAN = "Fu insolito splendor de l'armi; e invano";
  LINE;
    LINE.NUMBER = 7;
    ITALIAN = "Squadra non mosse mai; con veder sano";
  LINE;
    LINE.NUMBER = 8;
    ITALIAN = Voi sarete de i gigli alto sostegno.;
  LINE;
    LINE.NUMBER = 9;
    ITALIAN = Ne men di lui col cor grave, et ardito;
  LINE;
    LINE.NUMBER = 10;
    ITALIAN = Maraviglia darete al secol nostro;
  LINE;
    LINE.NUMBER = 11;
    ITALIAN = Del gran vostro valor, chiaro, et gradito.;
  LINE;
    LINE.NUMBER = 12;
    ITALIAN = "Tal che dirassi; ecco di gloria un mostro;";
  LINE;
    LINE.NUMBER = 13;
    ITALIAN = Ecco un d'eterno honor vie piu arricchito,;
  LINE;
    LINE.NUMBER = 14;
    ITALIAN = Ch'altri non fu giamai di gemme, et ostro.;
ENTRY;
  INPUTTER = Jonathan Shiff;
  DATE.ADDED = 04/11/86;
```

(Keller, Columbia, SC 4/87) PG

Coding of Music (Version 2.1, 9/86)

For Storage in SPIRES files the following "words" will be entered in line fields identified as voice fields (Cantus, Altus, Tenor, Bassus, Quintus, etc.). Clef, key signature will be entered as separate "words" before notes are entered.

$A (pitch) $B (duration) $C (horizontal position) $D (poetic text) $E (other)

Content of sub-fields:

$A

1. There will be a maximum of four characters in the $A subfield.
2. Notes will be identified by the letters a through g.
3. Chromatic alterations to letter-named notes will be accomplished by using the short hyphen (-) to denote a flat, @ to denote a natural, and # to denote a sharp. Two short hyphens (--) will denote double flats and # # will denote double sharps.
4. Octave position will be denoted by numerals. The octave beginning with middle c is denoted by the numeral 5. The octave beginning with the c two octaves below middle c is denoted by the numeral 3. The octave beginning two octaves above middle c is denoted by the numeral 7.
5. A rest (the absence of a pitch) will be denoted by a letter r.

The first position in the sub-field will be occupied by the pitch letter (a through g) or the letter r to denote a rest.
The second and possibly the third positions will be occupied by symbols chromatically altering the pitch.
The fourth position will be occupied by a numeral (in our repertory 3 through 7) denoting the octave position of the pitch.

Examples: $A a#4
$A b--6

$B

1. There will be a maximum of 5 characters in the $B sub-field.

2. The character in the first position will denote the duration of the note according to the following scheme –

   l = double breve
   b = breve
   s = semi-breve
   m = minim
   c = crotchet (semi-minim)
   q = quaver (1 flag)
   f = semi-quaver (2 flags).

3. The character t in the second position will denote that the duration in the first position is one-third of the next higher duration value. The character & in the second position will denote that the duration in the first position is two-thirds of the next higher duration value. PG
4. Characters in the third and fourth position indicate ties of the duration indicated to the previous and/or following durations. "+" indicates a tie to the following value and "_" indicates a tie to the preceding value.
5. The character in the fifth position indicates the addition of value to the duration indicated in the first position. "." indicates the addition of one-half the duration value indicated. ":" indicates the addition of three-quarters of the duration value indicated.

$C

There will be a maximum of four characters in the sub-field.

This is the horizontal position indicator. A virtual element is needed as a pointer to a formula to compute the position. The inputter would determine the proportion value(s) and enter them perhaps in the first occurrence of this sub-field. A formula to compute position is needed.

$D

There will be a maximum of 10 characters in the sub-field.

This sub-field is reserved for text.

1. In the ideal circumstance, the sub-field would refer to poems in the data base and not repeat text. One solution: the first occurrence of the sub-field would include a poemid number, a stanza number (if appropriate), and a line number. We have adapted rules of syllabification to develop a formula to allow this. The following symbols would cover some basic text-underlay situations:

   - (the preceding syllable is continued for this note);
   . (move to the next syllable in the line);
   = (a repeating syllable);
   ! (the concluding syllable).

2. In less than ideal circumstances, the sub-field would include actual text.

$E

There will be a maximum of 12 characters in this sub-field.

1. The sub-field will be used to indicate change of key signature, change of meter, change of clef, basso sequente numerals, ornamentation. A scheme for these possibilities has yet to be worked out.

(Keller, Columbia, SC 4/87)

Discography:
Discipline and Musical Ally

Michael Gray

SUMMARY. Discography was "invented" in the 1930's by jazz collectors who wanted to learn more about the records they owned. Honed by a strong informal peer review system, standards for discographies have been well-accepted for decades. Discographies chronicle the formal and informal activities of the world-wide sound recording industry. Yet with the ubiquity of time-altering recording media, typified by editable magnetic tape, discographers face ever more vexing questions and challenges about what their work actually documents.

Discography celebrated its fiftieth anniversary in 1986. I am happy to report that this now middle-aged discipline shows every sign of having achieved the intellectual sophistication many have always hoped it would have. Major discographic publications are now more common than ever, thanks to a large variety of discographic magazines and a few major commercial publishers that cater to the small markets these kinds of books command.

In all discographies three types of information are provided: numerical (treating the producer of the records), artistic (treating the source of the sound on the records) and subject (which considers the material recorded). The first discographers, as we understand the term today, were European jazz fans in the 1930's who wanted

---

Michael Gray is affiliated with Voice of America.

[Haworth co-indexing entry note]: "Discography: Discipline and Musical Ally." Gray, Michael. Co-published simultaneously in *Music Reference Services Quarterly*, (The Haworth Press, Inc.) Vol. 2, No. 3/4, 1993, pp. 319-325; and: *Foundations in Music Bibliography* (ed: Richard D. Green) The Haworth Press, Inc., 1993, pp. 319-325. Multiple copies of this article/chapter may be purchased from The Haworth Document Delivery Center [1-800-3-HAWORTH; 9:00 a.m. - 5:00 p.m. (EST)].

© 1993 by The Haworth Press, Inc. All rights reserved.

to know who the players were on the records, whose catalogs, release sheets and even labels themselves had been omitted or falsified. One of these pioneering fans was a Frenchman named Charles Delaunay. In 1936 Delaunay published a book in Paris called *Hot Discography*[1] in which he tried for the first time to answer some of the questions jazz fans had been asking. His first hurdle was to find the names of those actually performing on the records. Another problem was to discover when the performances had been recorded, and thereby chronicle the work of the artists and ensembles who were shaping evolution of this music. By digging behind the scenes of the record industry, jazz fans were able to answer these questions: who was at the session, what did they play, and when and where did they play it?

By the end of the Second World War, Old World fan-researchers had created a cottage industry of small-circulation magazines in which discographies often drew new information from a research community more interested in expanding knowledge than in claiming credit. By the final edition of *Hot Discography*,[2] published in New York in 1948, a distinctive discographic format had become well-established. The data about the performance was one of the key elements to have been cited, and included lists of the names of performers, the titles of the tunes being played (although not necessarily the names of the composers), and a note about where and when the recording had taken place. Another feature of the discographies documented the recording process itself. In most discographies of pre-LP material, this consisted of the matrix, or internal control number, that identified the disc (and later the master tape) onto which the performances were "cut." Also included were the catalog numbers of the records (and other media) that were issued for sale.

For Delaunay–or for anyone following his format–a complete discographic entry requires information from not only the record itself, but from what are often called "discographic resources." These sources can be anything from reviews in magazines to library catalogs, indexes and even the performers' own datebooks and calendars. Assessing the completeness and accuracy of such sources is one of the pleasure/pains of discographic research.

One of the best–though often most frustrating–sources of discographic information is the files of record companies themselves. Unlike precious master tapes, discographic materials suffer most from cost-cutting executives, the looting of preceding researchers or dispersal among various offices and files sometimes located miles from each other. And while most discographers can work in sympathetic companies with quiet encouragement, there are some companies that consider discographers to be little more than industrial espionage agents bent more on revealing business and financial secrets than discographic ones.

Getting discographic data is regrettably just one of many difficulties facing an intrepid researcher. Take, for instance, problems caused by the sound recording medium itself, and more particularly magnetic tape recording. Tape has been of great benefit to recording artists and their producers, but it has also been hell for discographers. Before tape, a record was a true image of the original sound, unedited and unimproved, as it had been made before the microphones. Not so today. Rare indeed is a taped performance that has not been assembled from fragments whose only relationship to reality frequently lies on the editing room floor. To be sure, composers who had to depend on performers can now create whole works on tape without reference to live sounds. Yet this very flexibility also permits "improvements" to any sequence of magnetically recorded sounds. Over-dubbing, the *sine qua non* of today's pop record industry, can graft further musical elements to existing ones. Even the pitch, tempo, frequency response, and ambience of a performance can be altered, thus changing Studio 8-H by electronic magic into Carnegie Hall.

A discographer's problems, in fact, just begin with the sound itself, for like any other mechanically reproduced medium, records can also suffer from what I like to call "title page boo-boos." Some are as simple as RCA's issue of Erich Leinsdorf's Boston Symphony performance of Beethoven's *Eroica Symphony* on Victrola VICS-1626, in which the label and jacket credited his predecessor, Charles Munch. Other deceptions are a little more deliberate. My favorite victim in this game is EMI, which in the late 1960's bought and issued a tape of a performance of Chopin's *Piano Concerto in E Minor*, played, they thought, by Dinu Lipatti and mysteriously accompanied by an uncredited orchestra and conductor. After years in the catalog (and sales totalling over 40,000 copies)[3] the company discovered that this mysterious tape was not by Lipatti at all, but was in fact a perfectly respectable recording by Helena Czerny-Stefanska that had been aged electronically into a "Lipatti." Fortunately, this story has two happy endings. EMl found, and issued, an authentic performance of this concerto by Lipatti, and Czerny-Stefanska's recording (originally made for the Czech Supraphon label) appeared on Quintessence[4] and became as popular as it had under its Lipatti attribution.

It is one thing for a record company to be fooled, but quite another for it to do the fooling. This happened frequently in the days of 78 rpm recording, when metal parts used to press especially popular records wore out and rendered a master disc unfit for further production. To keep these best-sellers in the catalog, alternate performances, or takes, were quietly issued using the original label, thereby allowing sales to continue without anyone (save the record company) becoming the wiser. As alternate takes wore out, a newly recorded performance, often made years after the original sessions, would be made and issued, still bearing the same old catalog number.

Some of the best deceptions have occurred when the perpetrator has had something to hide. For example, German Columbia, stuck at the outbreak of World War II with three not-yet-issued performances by Sir Thomas Beecham and the London Philharmonic Orchestra, issued them with the politically correct (but fallacious) credit "Dirigent Felix v. Weingartner." Much more recently, producers of the German Acanta and BASF labels were caught by critic David Hamilton trying to palm off pre-War shellac performances of Wagnerian opera excerpts as previously undiscovered German radio tapes.[5]

It is fairly clear that discographers should try to finger this kind of monkey business when and where they know about it. Certainly it creates problems, not only in the examples I have cited, but even more so in popular music, where different versions of one ostensibly original recording make for discographic nightmares. When we consider composed music, however, we run into graver problems. For one thing, there is a lot more to fool around with, in light of the fact that while pop and jazz pieces can last from one to perhaps ten minutes, composed works may extend to six hours. Does it always follow that knowing when the component parts of a performance were recorded is enough to establish its historical provenance? If so, then the rest of a discographic entry will consist of enumerating editions. Still, it will always be necessary to report that some editions of Toscanini's NBC Symphony recordings of Beethoven's *Sixth* and *Seventh Symphonies*[6] contain unacknowledged chunks of broadcast performances of the same pieces; and that Toscanini's version of Mendelssohn's *Italian Symphony*, labeled as "the broadcast of February 28, 1954," was instead taken mostly from a dress rehearsal two days before. And how are we to credit the tone generator that helped the Vienna Philharmonic's double basses get through the opening minutes of Sir Georg Solti's famous 1958 recording of Wagner's *Das Rheingold?*

Historical accuracy, which requires the reporting of such details, also demands reporting all editions that vary in detail from one another. This happens in pop music all the time. But do three different versions of parts of Leonard Bernstein's old New York Philharmonic recording of Beethoven's *Fifth Symphony* (first released on Columbia MS 6468 from sessions on September 25, 1961) each constitute a new edition? Should the remixing, or the reequalizing, of its multi-track tape be considered a new edition? With these and related questions, we need more information before we can even begin to decide whether we have to report where all the splices are.

Another basic question that still does not have a satisfactory discographic answer concerns the scope of our discipline. The easiest answer to this question is simply that discography ought to include everything. Jazz discographers routinely include not just records made at formal recording sessions, but ones made from radio or television broadcasts, film soundtracks, and unofficial transcriptions recorded by collectors from a seat in the concert hall. There is not a good theoretical reason to exclude such material from a discography (the question of format, for instance, has essentially been solved). One reason why such material almost never appears outside of jazz and superstar pop music is a practical one: jazz and pop collectors run small but well-organized networks in which information (and recordings) are constantly exchanged. No one else is so well-organized. More importantly, jazz and pop recordings are often the only way to capture creative inspirations that change each time a chart or "score" is performed.

Yet does it make equal sense to include citations of live, or unofficial recordings in, for example, a discography of Mahler's *Fourth Symphony*? Yes, if they are conducted by Mahler, or by a performer with equal interpretative standing, or because one wants to be complete. Probably not, if one is dealing with Beethoven's *Fifth*, whose multitudinous versions make portraying the characteristics of individual performances impossible in any more than a purely statistical way.

Getting at the music, of course, was what turned jazz collectors into discographers in the first place. Recordings obviously permit the appraisal of performances from a variety of points of view, and are especially useful if one believes that performances *per se* are worth studying as the reflections of a performer's "opinion" of a piece. Certainly jazz and other kinds of vernacular music demand to be studied from recorded performances.

How about art music? Records from the first four decades of this century alone provide evidence of a change from "old-fashioned" to "modern" performance styles, a change in part stimulated by the ability of musicians for the first time to hear, study, and emulate the vocal and instrumental achievements on discs recorded sixty and seventy years ago by Heifetz, Casals and Galli-Curci. Records also allow us to study distinctive national flavors in musical performances, such as the French and Czech "schools" of orchestral playing. Such "trends," of course, are the collective face of thousands upon thousands of individual performers and ensembles whose study is possible only through the evidence they have left on records. Thus far, that appraisal (if that is what we want to call it) has been left to record critics and collectors, whose access to evidence often exceeds that of would-be scholars who lack a recorded inter-library loan network to help assemble the necessary research materials.

Even beyond the records themselves is the history of the industry that made them, an enterprise whose scale (over 100,000 78 rpm records are said to have been issued between 1900 and 1925 alone) has so far eluded systematic consideration. To be sure, those handling the artists have offered their versions of life behind the scenes, motivated, as are all autobiographies, by a desire to settle old scores by concealing or over-dramatizing (or even falsifying) the natural turmoil found in an industry that mixes art and commerce.

If I were asked, "What do you want from discography," I would answer "more discographers"–good ones–who know their sources and who share information. Discography–especially on the scale of a monograph–is, like any bibliographic discipline, a collective enterprise that requires many hands to achieve a successful result. I would also ask for more help from librarians, indexers, catalogers and bibliographers so that discographic materials might receive the same treatment as printed ones. There may never be a recorded *RISM*, or a day in which a Shenkerian analysis of a piece will be accompanied by similar graphs for its performances. There is nonetheless plenty of work to do as discographers slowly build an edifice that needs no apologies as art or discipline.

NOTES

1. Delaunay, Charles. *Hot Discography.* (Paris: Jazz Hot), 1936.
2. *New Hot Discography* (New York: Criterion), 1948.
3. Issued in the U.S. on Seraphim 60007, and in Britain on HMV RLS 749.
4. Issued in the U.S. on Quintessence 7206.
5. David Hamilton, "Gobs and Gobbets of Wagner," *ARSC Journal*, 15/2-3, pp. 98-109.
6. These performances appear at least on RCA CD's RCD-1005 (the *Sixth*) and RCA RCD 1-7197 (the *Seventh*).

Varieties of Analysis:
Through the Analytical Sieve and Beyond

Arthur Wenk

SUMMARY. The author briefly reviews 13 analytical methods and several popular definitions of musical style. The theories of Lerdahl and Jackendoff, and those of Baroni and Jacoboni provide the foundation of a project to define closely the style of Debussy based on the identification of 92 melodic phrases. Each melody is parsed according to a paradigm derived from Baroni and Jacoboni. The project seeks an explanation for the subtleties that we recognize as features of Debussy's style, but which we cannot satisfactorily rationalize.

Several years ago the Music Library Association published a small pamphlet entitled *Analyses of Twentieth-Century Music 1940-1970* [Wenk, 1975]. It contained 1225 entries by some 600 authors drawn from 46 periodicals and 7 Festschriften, covering 225 composers. This project, comprising a single shoe box of index cards, emerged from Harold Samuel's bibliography seminar at Cornell University. The inevitable burgeoning of the index might have been predicted by anyone more foresighted than its compiler. Early in 1987, the MLA will publish a complete cumulation, *Analyses of Nineteenth and Twentieth Century Music,* updated through 1985, containing 5664 entries by some 2400 authors, drawn from 132

Arthur Wenk is affiliated with St. Andrew's College, Aurora, Ontario.

[Haworth co-indexing entry note]: "Varieties of Analysis: Through the Analytical Sieve and Beyond." Wenk, Arthur. Co-published simultaneously in *Music Reference Services Quarterly,* (The Haworth Press, Inc.) Vol. 2, No. 3/4, 1993, pp. 327-348; and: *Foundations in Music Bibliography* (ed: Richard D. Green) The Haworth Press, Inc., 1993, pp. 327-348. Multiple copies of this article/chapter may be purchased from The Haworth Document Delivery Center [1-800-3-HAWORTH; 9:00 a.m. - 5:00 p.m. (EST)].

© 1993 by The Haworth Press, Inc. All rights reserved.

periodicals and 93 Festschriften covering 779 composers, an approximate quadrupling of every dimension.[1] In a review of the 1980 update, François Lesure criticized the quality of certain analyses, lamented the absence of others, and challenged me to define the criteria for inclusion in the index [Lesure, 1985]. (He also suggested that perhaps it was time for the index to be taken over by a committee, a thought that crossed my mind more than once recently as I typed 5600 entries into my word processor.)

My rule-of-thumb definition of analysis, purely for the purposes of the index, has been "technical talk about particular pieces of music." This pragmatic formula attests to my perhaps overly optimistic notion of an ongoing conversation of specialists about questions of the inner workings of musical compositions. It also serves to separate analysis from questions of biography, Zeitgeist, performance practice, paper studies, organology, pedagogy, iconography, sociology, aesthetics, libretto studies, archival research, acoustics, or other subjects within the domain of scholarly musical colloquy. I further distinguish analysis from pure music theory. The analysis index restricts itself to technical talk about particular pieces. One notices right away, however, that this is a rather peculiar kind of conversation. To begin with, most of the participants utter a single remark and then depart. I do not mean to imply that they have nothing more to say, for many of them publish other articles on a variety of non-analytical topics. But it remains the case that 70% of the authors in the analysis index are represented by unique entries.

If we concentrate on those who carry the burden of the conversation, let us say, those with sixteen or more entries, we are struck by their diversity, as a mere listing of their names will indicate: Gerald Abraham, Edward T. Cone, Carl Dahlhaus, Allen Forte, Wilfried Gruhn, Hans Hollander, René Leibowitz, Colin Mason, George Perle, Rudolph Stephan, and Arnold Whittall. Though these interlocutors are nominally engaged in analytical discussion, closer attention gives the impression that they are speaking different languages, quite apart from the several European tongues represented by their prose. This implies that analysis, though conveniently given a single label in order to distinguish it from other musicological activities, might better be regarded as a class of activities, each characterized by its own aims and methods.

Ian Bent adopts this pluralistic perspective in the third section of his magisterial article on analysis in the *New Grove Dictionary* [Bent, 1980]. Under the rubric "Analytical Method," Bent presents seven different approaches, arranged according to their methods of operation, which I shall gloss with well-known examples:

1. *Fundamental structure,* exemplified by Schenker's analyses of late Beethoven piano sonatas, in which, through recursive application of principles of reduction separating the fundamental from the ornamental, the analyst arrives at a final underlying structure [Schenker, 1971a, 1971b, 1972].
2. *Thematic process,* associated with the works of Rudolph Réti, and *functional analysis,* devised by Hans Keller. Here, the analyst attempts to show the underlying unity of a work or group of works by relating all the melodic material to a single, germinal motif. Deryck Cooke's article "The Unity of Beethoven's Late Quartets" illustrates this approach [Cooke, 1963; see also Keller, 1957, 1958].
3. *Formal analysis,* the recognition and classification of recurring formal patterns, ranging in complexity from binary form to sonata form. Bent cites the essays of Donald Tovey and the work of Alfred Lorenz, for example, *Das Geheimnis der Form bei Richard Wagner,* as examples of this method [Lorenz, 1966].
4. *Phrase-structure analysis,* associated with Alfred Riemann, the identification of modules constituting sub-phrase, phrase, period, and subsequent higher levels. Dénes Bartha's work on quatrain patterns in Classic thematic organization, as reported in "Thematic profile and character in the quartet finales of J. Haydn," may be cited as an example [Bartha, 1969].
5. *Category and feature analysis.* Jan LaRue's handy acronym SHMRG, as well as his subdivisions of these basic elements of sound, harmony, melody, rhythm and growth in *Guidelines for Style Analysis,* serve as a useful checklist for those interested in cataloguing the musical features of an individual work or corpus of works [LaRue, 1970; for an extended application of these principles, see Brown, 1980].
6. *Distribution analysis,* as practiced by Nicholas Ruwet, involves breaking down a composition into its component parts

by comparing each unit with every other unit, then grouping similar units in a schema which facilitates the recognition of their resemblances. Ruwet's article, "Notes sur les duplications dans l'oeuvre de Claude Debussy," illustrates this method [Ruwet, 1962; see also Ruwet, 1966, 1972].

7. *Information theory,* associated with the work of Leonard Meyer, among others, deals with the arousal, frustration and fulfillment of a listener's musical expectations. Norbert Böker-Heil's article, "Der Zustand polyphoner Strukturen: Ein Beispiel automatischer Stilbeschreibung," describes a computer-assisted analysis of three Renaissance madrigals resulting in graphic representations of perceptible variations in texture, dissonance and contour [Böker-Heil, 1974]. Gino Stefani, in "Situation de la sémiotique musicale," notes that the distance between information theory and semiotics is rapidly diminishing [Stefani, 1975a: 11].

Several other analytical methods, though they might be accommodated within Bent's categories, seem sufficiently important to merit separate attention.

8. *Pitch-class analysis* draws on the application of mathematical set theory to musical analysis, notably in the formulations of Milton Babbitt and Allen Forte. Notions of subsets and the grouping of sets into larger complexes lie at the heart of this kind of analysis, as illustrated by Forte's study, *The Harmonic Organization of "The Rite of Spring"* [Forte, 1978].

9. *Proportional analysis* shares certain elements with phrase structure analysis, but frequently relies on changes of timbre, texture or dynamics rather than harmonic or melodic articulations to delineate formal divisions. Ernö Lendvai has found Golden Mean relationships based on the Fibonacci series in Bartók's works, while Roy Howat has pointed out the importance of both Golden Mean and symmetrical formations in his recent study, *Debussy in Proportion, a Musical Analysis* [Lendvai, 1983; Howat, 1983].

10. *Formal grammars,* a subject to which I shall return, represent a linguistic approach describing musical events in terms of syntactical rules. *A Generative Theory of Tonal Music,* by

Fred Lerdahl and Ray Jackendoff, offers, among other things, an elegant approach to questions of meter and grouping [Lerdahl and Jackendoff, 1983].

11. *Phenomenology* attacks the issue of musical analysis from the angle of a listener's perception of the work, thus putting into question the traditional assumption of the existence of a composition as an abstract entity. Michel Imberty's essay, *Significance and Meaning in Music: On Debussy's "Préludes pour le Piano,"* for example, tabulates the choice of adjectives used by listeners upon hearing these piano pieces [Imberty, 1976].

12. *Text-music relations,* though fundamental to music in its broadest historical and social contexts, find no place in Bent's pantheon of analytical methods. Yet so varied have been the applications in this area, from melodic-poetic correspondences in Schubert songs to dramatic implications of tonal relations in Verdi and Wagner operas, that some may wish to further subdivide this category. Edward T. Cone addresses the issue of text-music relations, both in terms of general musical aesthetics and in the analysis of particular works, in *The Composer's Voice* [Cone, 1974].

If I may be permitted to round this list off into a baker's dozen, I should like to mention briefly *computer analysis*. Clearly, computer analysis *per se* should not be classified as a methodology, the computer being, as one says, only a dumb tool. But, as Mario Baroni points out in "The Concept of Musical Grammar":

> Paradoxically, it is just because of the computer's inherent lack of intelligence that it proves to be a heuristic device of the utmost importance. In its capacity for repeating a process, the computer increases boundlessly the investigative capabilities of man, but at the same time, it reveals errors of the human cognitive faculty.

For a human analyst, certain obvious musical relationships "go without saying," whereas for a computer, nothing goes without saying. The obligation to provide the computer with a detailed explanation of every element of analysis, Baroni continues, "enriches the range of knowledge, casts doubt on some assumptions, and refines theory" [Baroni, 1983a: 177].

The areas of analysis that I have just outlined vary considerably in accessibility. Discussions of thematic process, form, phrase structure, feature analysis, and text-music relations, at one end of the scale, tend to be conducted in terms comprehensible to the general reader. Most articles in these areas consist of analyses of particular works, in the terms of our index. Proponents of Schenkerian analysis, pitch-class analysis, and distribution analysis, or semiotics, at the other end of the scale, in the interest of rigor, have elaborated specialized vocabularies that the uninitiated reader may find daunting. In addition to studies of particular pieces, these areas of analysis have spawned a formidable meta-literature defining and refining their own theoretical underpinnings. Forte's *The Structure of Atonal Music,* Schenker's *Free Composition,* and Nattiez's *Les fondements d'une sémiologie musicale,* currently in the process of being translated into English, constitute three landmarks of analytical meta-literature [Forte, 1973; Schenker, 1979; Nattiez, 1975].

I should like to turn at this point to the question of style analysis before focussing on a current concern in research on Debussy. Style analysis, traditionally the basis for writing music history, has come under attack by theorists. One recalls, for example, Peter Westergaard's pungent comments at the 1972 IMS Congress:

> In my business "stylistic" and "style" are dirty words. Of course we use them, but rarely with serious intent, and if in print, well insulated by quotation-marks. It seems to me that this attitude of ours is a good indication of how divergent the concerns of historians and theorists have become. Historians, I take it, are interested in comparing pieces with one another in terms of "style" and grouping those with common stylistic features so that they can write histories about groups of pieces rather than about individual pieces. Theorists on the other hand–at least the theorists I know–don't seem to care much about comparing or grouping pieces. They are concerned with (1) understanding the structure of individual pieces and (2) examining the syntactic assumptions we use in understanding such structures. [Westergaard, 1974: 71]

Developments in style analysis in the intervening fourteen years may eventually serve to bridge the gap between historians and theorists. (I do not mean to imply that the chasm will ever disappear. I merely suggest that there may be a way to cross it.)

Leonard Meyer, in an extended essay entitled "Toward a Theory of Style," defines style as "a replication of patterning . . . that results from a series of choices made within some set of constraints" [Meyer, 1979: 3. For a history of the term "style," see Wolff, 1974. See also Ackerman, 1962; Meyer, 1974, 1980, 1983]. "Replication of patterning" is another way of describing the "fingerprints" by which we identify the work of a particular composer. The choices to which Meyer refers have often been internalized by a composer to the point that they become more like unconscious habits. The role of style analysis in this case is to provide a rationale for unconscious knowledge. Meyer writes:

> The constraints of style are *learned* by composers and performers, critics and listeners. . . . Usually such learning is the result of experience in performing and listening rather than of explicit instruction of a formal or theoretical kind. In other words, knowledge of style is usually "tacit.". . . It is the goal of music theorists and style analysts to explain what the composer, performer and listener know in this tacit way. [Meyer, 1979: 11]

Meyer's concept of constraints carries style analysis beyond feature classification toward the realm of formal grammar. We begin, to be sure, by cataloguing traits–with Debussy, for example, the use of the whole-tone scale, parallel chords, and pedal points. But traits do not tell us how a style functions: we must go beyond feature classification to discover the rules by which musical elements interact. In the arts, however, in contrast to the rules of a sport, Meyer continues,

> the constraints governing the choices made are seldom explicitly recorded or consciously known even by those most accomplished in their use. . . . As a result, the theorist/style-analyst must infer the nature of the constraints–the rules of the game–from the "play" of the game itself. [Meyer, 1979: 13]

Meyer distinguishes three levels of constraint: (1) laws, "transcultural constraints–universals, if you will," (2) rules–the constraints that operate within a culture; and (3) strategies, "compositional choices made within the possibilities established by the rules of the style" [Meyer, 1979: 14, 27]. Meyer observes:

> Most changes in the history of musical style in the West have involved the devising of new strategies for the realization of existing rules, rather than the invention of new rules. Rule changes . . . occur only on the highest level of the history of Western music–that is, the levels designated by epochs such as the Middle Ages, the Renaissance, the Age of Tonality (ca. 1600-1918), and the Age of Modernity. Within these epochs what changed were strategic constraints. [Meyer, 1979: 28]

Meyer further divides constraints into three subclasses: (1) dialects, or substyles representing similar constraints employed by more than one composer, for example, Bach and Handel, or Haydn and Mozart; (2) idioms, "the strategies that a composer repeatedly selects from the larger repertory of the dialect"; and (3) idiolects, the patterns replicated within a single work [Meyer, 1979: 30]. "Thus," Meyer concludes, "while dialects have to do with what is common to works by different composers, and idioms have to do with what is common to different works by the same composer, idiolect is concerned with what is common to–replicated within–a single work" [Meyer, 1979: 31-32].

One may think of style analysis as a series of ever finer sieves: the coarsest sieve may pass only works of Western music, a somewhat finer sieve will pass only those of a particular epoch, a still finer sieve will separate works of a single composer, perhaps works of a particular style period of this composer, and finally, a single work. However, the sieve metaphor does not go far enough. One can imagine a checklist of features, along the lines of LaRue's guidelines for style analysis, that would serve to pass or block prospective members of the subset in question. The presence of a multi-voiced texture, for example, would eliminate a candidate for the plainchant set. But even the most ingeniously devised sieve fails to explain the internal workings of a piece of music, a drawback for which theorists have good reason to reject a style analysis that stops at the classification of features.

A formal grammar meets this objection by enabling the analyst to account for every element within a composition in terms of syntactical rules. Once we have identified the whole-tone scale, parallel chords and pedal points as typical traits of Debussy's music–typical elements of his vocabulary–we still have to explain what makes his music sound Debussyan even when these elements are not present; and when they are in evidence, what makes them fit together, what are the rules by which they function. [For an introduction to formal grammars, see Roads, 1979.]

One type of formal grammar, represented by the work of Lerdahl and Jackendoff, culminating in *A Generative Theory of Tonal Music,* proposes rules by which one can parse–that is, offer a consistent formal description of–every element of pitch, harmony, and rhythm in a given composition [Lerdahl and Jackendoff, 1977, 1980, 1981, 1983]. Their formulation includes rules of two types: well-formedness rules defining permissible analytical structures, and preference rules, enabling one to decide which well-formed analysis applies in cases where more than one is possible. These rules reflect the hierarchical quality of musical perception, the tendency of the mind to discriminate among more important and less important elements at any given level for any given parameter. Lerdahl and Jackendoff consider hierarchical structures in four areas: meter (the hierarchy of accents); grouping (the hierarchy of durations); time-span reduction (the hierarchy of pitches considered group by group); and prolongational reduction (the hierarchy of pitches considered across the piece as a whole). Their work, which has been widely reviewed, has brought to general attention the subject of formal grammars which until recently had been the private domain of a handful of specialists. [See Cady, 1983; Child, 1984; Cohn, 1985; Hantz, 1985; Peel and Slawson, 1984; Retzel, 1985; Swain, 1984.]

A second type of formal grammar remains less well-known in this country, perhaps because its leading proponents, Mario Baroni and Carlo Jacoboni, have published their work in specialized journals and symposia. Their *Proposal for a Grammar of Melody: The Bach Chorales,* however, was published by the Presses de l'Université de Montréal in 1978, and recently a translation of Baroni's

"Sulla Nozione di Grammatica Musicale" appeared in *Music Analysis* under the title "The Concept of Musical Grammar" [Baroni and Jacoboni, 1978; Baroni, 1983]. This second type of formal grammar, not content with parsing the elements of a musical entity, offers rules for generating additional examples in the style. For Baroni, "grammar does not mean only the pure and simple description of a set of immediately observable formal characteristics, but also the formulation of hypotheses capable of designing a schematic model of the thought processes that have produced it" [Baroni, 1983: 182].

This kind of approach underlies the teaching of species counterpoint and the harmonization of chorale melodies. By following a set of syntactical rules, a student can produce an original utterance which, if not of imperishable artistic value, is at least grammatically correct. (Both of the examples cited, of course, depend on a given, pre-existing cantus.) Baroni and Jacoboni, taking as their corpus the Lutheran chorale melodies later harmonized by J.S. Bach, have formulated a grammar capable of generating additional melodies in this style. Sundberg and Lindblom have accomplished a comparable task for Swedish nursery tunes [Sundberg and Lindblom, 1975, 1976].

The test of the proposed rules takes the form of a computer program. Why a computer? Because even the best-intentioned musicians applying a prospective rule introduce biases brought about by their musical training, biases that tend to conceal flaws in the grammar that the computer heartlessly exposes. "In this whole procedure," Baroni writes, "the computer performs a decisive heuristic role in permitting the consistency and comprehensiveness of the system of rules to be evaluated; the presence of incompatible rules would cause the programme to fail. . . . Automated production becomes, as a result, an absolutely faithful mirror of the features described by the system of rules; and like a good mirror, it is quite merciless" [Baroni, 1983: 193].

Recent studies suggest that the Baroni-Jacoboni framework, originally derived from an investigation of Lutheran chorale melodies, may be valid in wider applications. Projects now underway have applied the paradigm to an 18th-century chansonnier and to a corpus of Lieder melodies by Schubert [Baroni *et al.*, 1984; Baroni and Callegari, 1984; Camilleri, 1984]. Eventually it should be possible, by comparing the results of a number of such projects, to produce a hierarchy of constraints corresponding to Meyer's three levels: laws, rules, and strategies.

The application of the Baroni-Jacoboni framework to the melodic practice of Claude Debussy, a project still in its early stages, will serve to illustrate in greater detail the methodology and potential of this kind of style analysis. We begin by choosing a limited repertoire of homogeneous examples, in this case, the initial phrases of the first themes of Debussy's instrumental works without a text. (I take up the problem of identifying and segmenting the first themes in "Parsing Debussy: Proposal for a Grammar of His Melodic Practice" [Wenk: 1987].) As a further limitation, we have restricted the repertoire to themes in duple meter.

Two observations are in order here. First, quite aside from questions of rhythmic complexity, the Debussy corpus differs fundamentally from the Lutheran chorale model with regard to its homogeneity, or the absence thereof, and it may well be that the entire project will founder on this point. How can one expect to find consistent rules capable of encompassing the variety of styles represented by *L'Isle joyeuse, La fille aux cheveux de lin, Ce qu'a vu le vent d'Ouest,* and *Golliwogg's Cakewalk*? (I laid the basis of a feature-analysis response in "One Face, Many Masks," but the current project undertakes a comprehensive formal grammar [Wenk, 1983].)

Second, why begin with melody when so much of Debussy's music seems to be based on lightly embellished chord progressions? The stylistic difference between a Bach chorale, where harmonic and polyphonic elements rest in serene equipoise, and a Debussy prelude, whose texture may be purely melodic, purely chordal, or anywhere in between, would seem to reflect entirely new rules, in Meyer's sense, and not simply different strategies. In attempting to write a formal grammar based on chord progressions, an effort described in "Steps Toward a Descriptive Grammar for the Music of Claude Debussy," I constantly confronted the need to define melodic procedures, even if only for brief motifs [Wenk, 1980]. Consequently, a corpus of 92 melodic phrases serves as the point of departure for the current project. As Baroni writes, "In starting with simple structures—at least, relatively simple ones—the aim is to arrive at a set of rules that not only possesses coherence and concision, but also the necessary comprehensiveness, that is, one able to account for all phrases composed—or which one might want to compose—in the style of a particular repertory" [Baroni, 1983: 186].

Having defined the repertoire, our next step is to parse each melody according to a paradigm derived from Baroni and Jacoboni. The generative process begins with a kernel interval ranging from a unison to a fifth for the chorale repertoire and occasionally larger for the Debussy corpus. I shall restrict most of my examples to melodies based on the kernel of a third, which, according to the paradigm, may be filled in to form a kernel scale. "At this primitive level," Baroni writes, "the phrase does not contain absolute pitches, scale degrees, durations or metrical features; we are dealing only with interval relationships and accentual characteristics" [Baroni, 1984: 208]. For the chorale repertoire, the kernel interval serves as the initial and final strong beats of the phrase. For the Debussy corpus, the question of rhythm remains somewhat tenuous, and I rely on your musical intuition to confirm the choices I have made in Example 1. Subsequent steps assign meter and duration, and finally, the arrangement of the pitches on the staff and the attribution of tonality, a step I have labelled "inflection." In the Baroni-Jacoboni paradigm, "every note must become a degree of a scale and may acquire an accidental" [Baroni, 1984: 208]. Additional optional transformations deal with the possibility of an upbeat or arpeggiation.

The original Baroni-Jacoboni scheme suffices to parse the phrases given in Example 1. Other phrases require the insertion of an additional step, called oscillation, after the formulation of the kernel phrase. Example 2 illustrates this operation, which permits us to give a deep-structural account of the quality of stasis—a resistance against forward movement—often associated with Debussy's melodic practice. In the examples given in Example 1, Debussy impedes the forward impulse by rhythmic means: by lengthening note values and by avoiding downbeat accents. In the examples of Example 2, the oscillation between two pitches produces a similar static effect.

The Baroni-Jacoboni paradigm also provides for the application

EXAMPLE 1

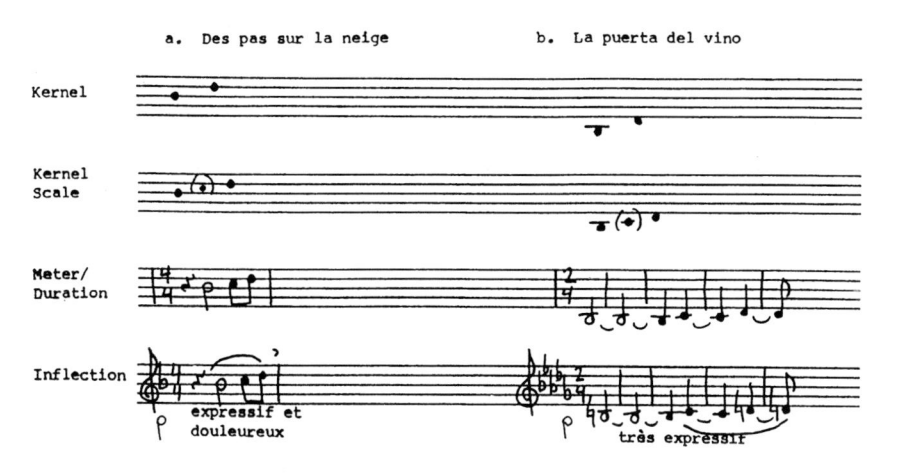

a. Des pas sur la neige   *b. La puerta del vino*

EXAMPLE 2

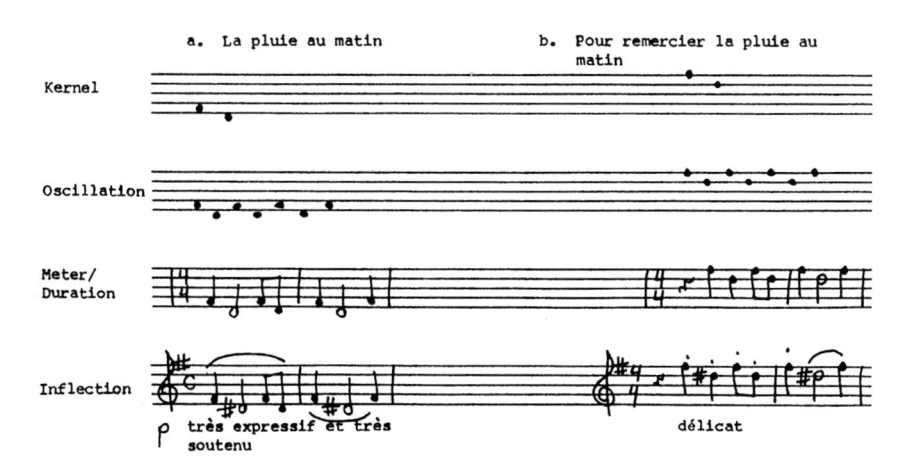

a. La pluie au matin   *b. Pour remercier la pluie au matin*

of insertion rules, or development figures, as a means of elaborating the kernel scale. These figures include repetition, appoggiatura, neighbor tones and skip tones, and may be applied recursively. In our formulation, repetition occupies a separate step, and elaboration figures may be applied only once. Example 3 illustrates these steps.

EXAMPLE 3

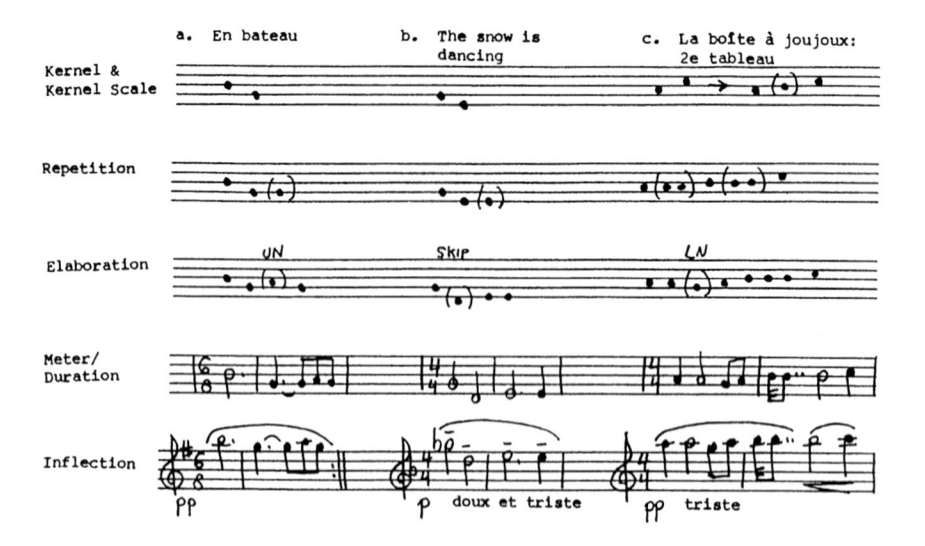

We may observe how repetition also contributes to the quality of stasis: either the immediate repetition of a measure as in 3a–a device that approaches the level of cliché in early Debussy–or repetition as an alternate means of prolonging a single pitch, as in 3c.

Two additional modifications to the Baroni-Jacoboni framework appear in Example 4. Example 4a displays an extension of their fioratura principle to accommodate grace-notes, a step which we include within the category of inflection. Example 4b shows the extension of the neighbor-note principle to include the interval of a third, a feature which leads us to consider the more general question of pentatonic formations in Debussy.

More than twenty-five years ago, Constantin Brăiloiu classified a number of Debussy melodies according to their underlying pentatonic scales and pointed out the prevalence of motives based on perfect fourths and minor thirds [Brăiloiu, 1959]. The formal grammar proposed here allows us to appreciate the importance of pentatonic formations in Debussy's melodic practice even in melodies that are not purely pentatonic. The essential element in Debussy's pentatony seems to have been the conception of the minor-third gap

EXAMPLE 4

a. Minstrels   b. Gigues

Kernel

Kernel Scale

Repetition

Elaboration

Meter/Duration

Inflection

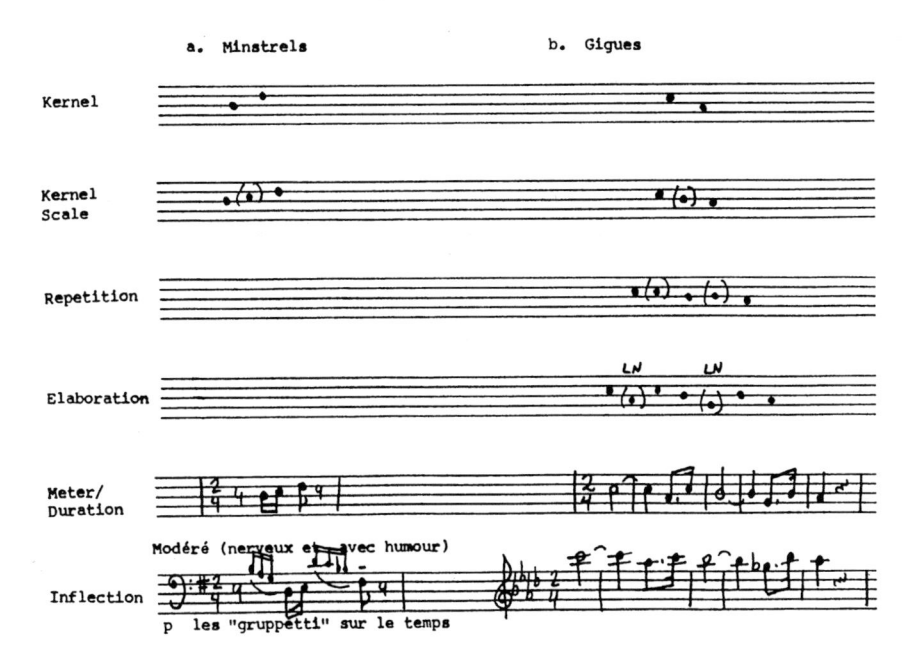

in terms of neighboring scale degrees rather than as an actual skip. We must consequently modify the Baroni-Jacoboni paradigm to admit the possibility of a pentatonic kernel scale. This possibility does not arise in the examples we have considered thus far, since a kernel encompassing the interval of a third only admits one possible kernel scale, namely, that which fills the gap. When we turn to examples based on larger kernel intervals, the possibility of a pentatonic kernel scale becomes evident.

In Example 5a, we see a kernel of a sixth–an interval which exceeds the limits established for the Lutheran chorale repertoire–giving rise to a pentatonic kernel scale. An introductory oscillation completes the pitch outline of this phrase without further elaboration. In Example 5b, a kernel of a fourth gives rise to a pentatonic kernel scale subsequently elaborated by essentially pentatonic figures. The so-called skip figures shown in this example conform entirely to the original paradigm derived from Lutheran chorale

EXAMPLE 5

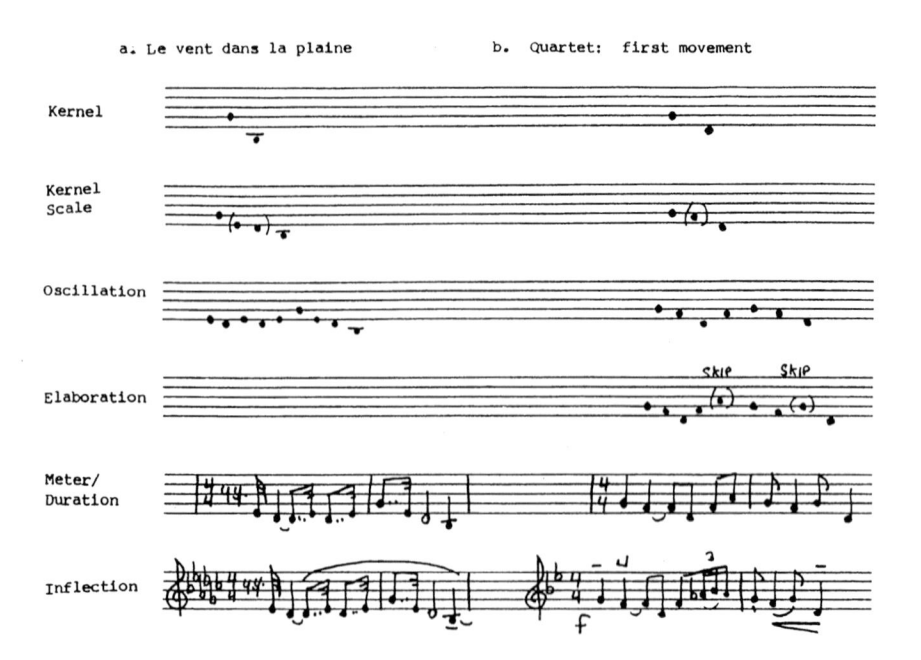

melodies, that is to say, there is nothing peculiarly Debussyan in the elaborative vocabulary. The difference lies in the frequency of these figures, in considerations of rhythm, in the elaboration of a pentatonic rather than a diatonic kernel scale, and in the process of oscillation discussed earlier.

Example 6 illustrates the usefulness of the formal grammar for uncovering unexpected examples of pentatonic thinking in Debussy's melodic practice. A unison kernel receives elaboration by upper and lower neighbor notes including the third, conceived not as a skip but as an adjacent tone in a background pentatonic scale. The next-to-last step of our example, labelled Meter/Duration, in fact resembles a typical Debussyan formation. The final inflection, however, quite apart from the unusual underlying harmonies, produces an exotic, nocturnal transformation. Returning to Examples 3b and 5b, we note similar alterations of underlying pentatonic formations to produce eventual whole-tone or chromatic melodies.

EXAMPLE 6

Kernel

Repetition

Elaboration

Meter/Duration

Inflection

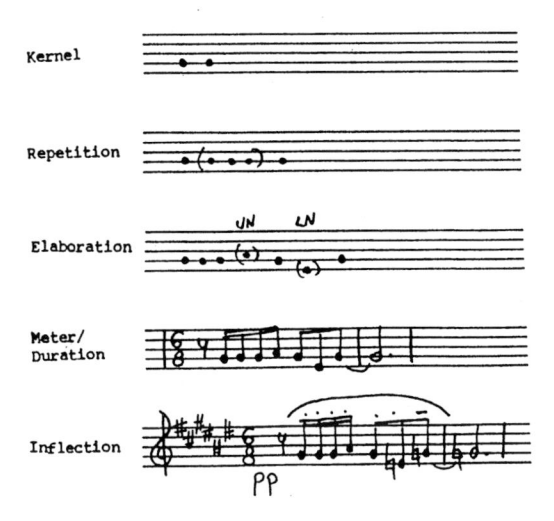

The initial phase of the project, parsing the phrases of the repertoire, has yielded insights into the static quality of Debussy's melodic practice and the inner workings of his pentatonic structures. The next step, a vastly more difficult one, requires the formulation of constraining rules that will define the syntactical limits on repetition, oscillation, and elaboration. The most formidable obstacle remains the question of rhythm. Those who enjoy puzzles may wish to entertain the following problem: given the examples shown in our illustrations, formulate a series of rules for getting to the Meter/Duration level from the level immediately preceding. Examples 1 through 4, for example, display nine melodic phrases based on the interval of a third. Given only the pitches, what are the rules for assigning their durations? A little experimentation will show that not just any rhythms will do. The melodies given in Example 7, for example, also based on the interval of a third, don't sound like Debussy, even though we can parse them without difficulty. There is something too square about the rhythm either of Stravinsky's *Balalaïka* or Brahms's *Intermezzo*, op.118, no. 6.

The current project seeks an explanation for subtleties that we have no difficulty recognizing, but at present cannot satisfactorily

344   FOUNDATIONS IN MUSIC BIBLIOGRAPHY

EXAMPLE 7

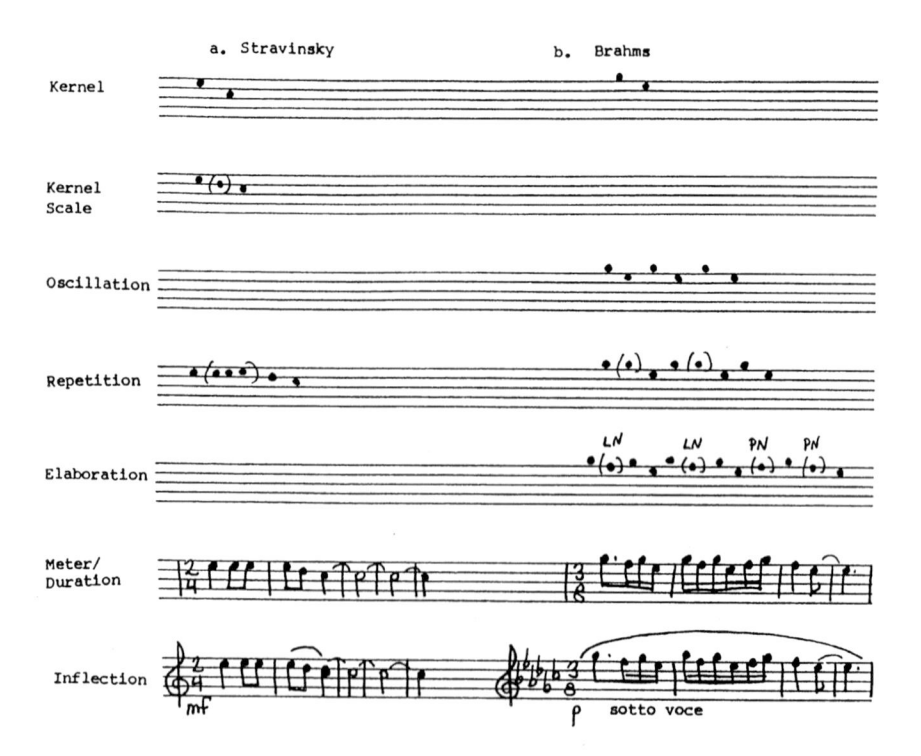

rationalize. Such a grammar, one would hope, might also resolve more difficult questions of what Meyer calls dialect, the constraints shared by several composers in a given epoch. For example, may we regard the melody in Example 8b, the "Forlane" from Ravel's *Tombeau de Couperin,* as a distortion of a pentatonic formation that appears in its pure form in 8a, Debussy's "Pagodes" from *Estampes?* If so, how do the rules of Ravel's distortion differ from Debussy's own as shown in Example 6? In other words, what are the boundaries separating common dialect from personal idiom? We hear these differences, just as we hear the underlying kinship among Debussy's melodies. Our "tacit understanding" of these questions, nonetheless, remains frustratingly mute. The purpose of a formal grammar, finally, is to teach it how to speak.

EXAMPLE 8

a. Debussy b. Ravel

NOTE

1. [The volume has since appeared as *Analyses of Nineteenth and Twentieth-Century Music: 1940-1985*, compiled by Arthur Wenk. MLA Index and Bibliography Series No. 25 (Boston: Music Library Association, Inc.), 1987. Ed.]

REFERENCES

Ackerman, James S. 1962. "A Theory of Style." *Journal of Aesthetics and Art Criticism*, 20 (1961-1962): 227-237.

Baroni, Mario. 1983a. "The Concept of Musical Grammar." *Music Analysis*, 2: 175-208.

_____. 1983b. "A Project for a Grammar of Melody." *Informatique et Musique. Second Symposium International*. Ivry: Elmeratto, p. 55-69.

Baroni, Mario and Carlo Jacoboni. 1975. "Analysis and Generation of Bach's Choral Melodies," in Stefani, 1975: 125-134.

_____. 1978. *Proposal for a Grammar of Melody: The Bach Chorales*. Montréal: Les Presses de l'Université de Montréal.

_____. 1983. "Computer Generation of Melodies: Further Proposals." *Computers and the Humanities*, 17: 1-18.

Baroni, Mario and Laura Callegari. 1984a. "Antiche canzoni francesi. Uno studio di metrica generativa." *Quaderni di informatica musicale*, 5: 3-30.

_____. 1984b. *Musical Grammars and Computer Analysis*. Firenze: Leo S. Olschki Editore.

Baroni, Mario, Rossella Bruenetti, Laura Callegari and Carlo Jacoboni. 1984. "A Grammar of Melody. Relationships between Melody and Harmony," in Baroni and Callegari, 1984b: 201-218.

Bartha, Dénes. 1969. "Thematic Profile and Character in the Quartet Finales of J. Haydn: A Contribution to Micro-analysis of Thematic Structure." *Studia musicologica*, 11: 35-62.

Bent, Ian *et al.* 1974. "Current Methods of Stylistic Analysis of Music." Report of the Eleventh Congress, Copenhagen 1972. Copenhagen: Edition Wilhelm Hansen: Volume 1, p. 43-130.

Bent, Ian. 1980. "Analysis," in Stanley Sadie, ed., *The New Grove Dictionary of Music and Musicians*. London: Macmillan. Vol. 1, p. 341- 388.

Böker-Heil, Norbert. 1974. "Der Zustand polyphoner Strukturen: ein Beispiel automatische Stilbeschreibung," in Bent *et al*, 1974: 108-120.

Braïloiu, Constantin. 1959. "Pentatony in Debussy's Music," in Zoltan Kodaly and Laszlo Lajtha, eds., *Studiae memoriae Belae Bartok*. London: Boosey and Hawkes, p. 377-417.

Brown, A. Peter. 1980. "Approaching Musical Classicism: Understanding Styles and Style Change in Eighteenth-Century Instrumental Music." *College Music Symposium*, 70: 7-28.

Cady, Henry L. 1983. "Review of Lerdahl and Jackendoff, *A Generative Theory of Tonal Music*." *Psychomusicology*, 3: 60-67.

Camilleri, Lelio. 1984. "A Grammar of the Melodies of Schubert's Lieder," in Baroni and Callegari, 1984b: 229-236.

Child, Peter, 1984. "Review of Lerdahl and Jackendoff, *A Generative Theory of Tonal Music*." *Computer Music Journal*, 8: 56-64.

Cohn, Richard. 1985. "Review of Lerdahl and Jackendoff, *A Generative Theory of Tonal Music*." *In Theory Only*, 8/6: 27-52.

Cone, Edward T. 1974. *The Composer's Voice*. Berkeley: University of California Press.

Cooke, Deryck. 1963. "The Unity of Beethoven's Late Quartets." *Music Review*, 24: 30-49.

Forte, Allen, 1973. *The Structure of Atonal Music*. New Haven: Yale University Press.

_____. 1978. *The Harmonic Organization of "The Rite of Spring."* New Haven: Yale University Press.

Hantz, Edwin. 1985. "Review of Lerdahl and Jackendoff, *A Generative Theory of Tonal Music*." *Music Theory Spectrum*, 7: 190-202.

Howat, Roy. 1983. *Debussy in Proportion: A Musical Analysis*. Cambridge: Cambridge University Press.

Imberty, Michel. 1976. *Signification and Meaning in Music (On Debussy's "Preludes pour le piano")*. Monographies de sémiologie et d'analyses musicales III. Montréal: Groupe de recherches en sémiologie musicale.

Keller, Hans. 1957. "Functional Analysis: Its Pure Application." *Music Review*, 18: 202-206.

_____. 1958. "Wordless Functional Analysis: The First Year." *Music Review*, 19: 192-200.

LaRue, Jan. 1970. *Guidelines for Style Analysis*. New York: W.W. Norton.

Lendvai, Erno. 1983. *The Workshop of Bartok and Kodaly*. Budapest: Edition Musica.

Lerdahl, Fred and Ray Jackendoff. 1977. "Toward a Formal Theory of Tonal Music." *Journal of Music Theory*, 21: 111-171.

_____. 1980. "Discovery Procedures vs. Rules of Musical Grammar in a Generative Music Theory." *Perspectives of New Music*, 18: 503-510.

_____. 1981. "Generative Music Theory and its Relation to Psychology." *Journal of Music Theory*, 25: 45-90.

_____. 1983. *A Generative Theory of Tonal Music.* Cambridge, Mass.: MIT Press.

Lesure, François. 1985. "Review of *Arthur Wenk: Analyses of Nineteenth- Century Music. Second edition: 1940-1980. Analyses of Twentieth-Century Music. Supplement. Second edition.*" *Fontis artis musicae,* 32: 181-182.

Lorenz, Alfred. 1966. *Das Geheimnis der Form bei Richard Wagner.* Tutzing: H. Schneider.

Meyer, Leonard. 1974. "Concerning the Sciences, the Arts – and the Humanities." *Critical Inquiry,* 1: 163-217.

_____. 1979. "Toward a Theory of Style," in Berel Lang, ed., *The Concept of Style.* Philadelphia: University of Pennsylvania Press, p. 3-44.

_____. 1980. "Exploring Limits: Creation, Archetypes, and Style Change." *Daedalus,* 111/2: 117-205.

_____. 1983. "Innovation, Choice, and the History of Music." *Critical Inquiry,* 9 (1982-1983): 517-544.

Nattiez, Jean-Jacques. 1973. "Linguistics: A New Approach for Musical Analysis." *International Review of the Aesthetics and Sociology of Music,* 4/1: 51-67.

_____. 1974. "Analyse musicale et sémiologie à propos du Prélude de Pelléas." *Musique en Jeu,* 10: 42-69.

_____. 1975a. *Fondements d'une sémiologie de la musique.* Paris: Union Générale d'Editions.

_____. 1975b. "From Taxonomic Analysis to Stylistic Characterization. Debussy's Syrinx," in Stefani, 1975b: 83-112.

Peel, John and Wayne Slawson. 1984. "Review of Lerdahl and Jackendoff, *A Generative Theory of Tonal Music.*" *Journal of Music Theory,* 28: 271-294. See also the reply by Lerdahl and Jackendoff, 29 (1985): 145-160, and response by Peel and Slawson, 161-167.

Retzel, Frank. 1985. "Review of Lerdahl and Jackendoff, *A Generative Theory of Tonal Music.*" *Music Library Association Notes,* 41: 502-505.

Roads, C. 1979. "Grammars as Representations for Music." *Computer Music Journal,* 3: 48-55.

Ruwet, Nicholas. 1962. "Notes sur les duplications dans l'oeuvre de Claude Debussy." *Revue Belge de Musicologie,* 16: 57-70.

_____. 1966. "Méthodes d'analyse en musicologie." *Revue Belge de Musicologie,* 20: 65-90.

_____. 1972. *Langage, musique, poésie.* Paris: Seuil.

Schenker, Heinrich. 1971a. *Beethoven: Die letzten Sonaten: Sonate C Moll Op. 111.* Vienna: Universal Edition.

_____. 1971b. *Beethoven: Die letzten Sonaten: Sonate E Dur Op. 109.* Vienna: Universal Edition.

_____. 1972. *Beethoven: Die letzten Sonaten: Sonate A Dur Op. 101.* Vienna: Universal Edition.

_____. 1979. *Free Composition.* Translated and edited by Ernest Oster. New York: Longman.

Stefani, Gino. 1975a. "Situation de la sémiotique musicale," in Stefani, 1975b: 9-25.

———. 1975b. *Proceedings of the First International Congress on Semiotics of Music, Belgrade, 1973*. Pesaro: Centro di Iniziative Culturale, 1975.

Sundberg, Johan and Björn Lindblom. 1975. "A Generative Theory of Swedish Nursery Tunes," in Stefani, 1975b: 111-124.

———. 1976. "Generative Theories in Language and Music Descriptions." *Cognition*, 4: 98-122.

Swain, Joseph P. 1984. "Review of Lerdahl and Jackendoff, *A Generative Theory of Tonal Music*." *Journal of the American Musicological Society*, 37: 196-205.

Wenk, Arthur B. 1975. *Analyses of Twentieth-Century Music 1940-1970*. MLA Index and Bibliography Series Number 13. Ann Arbor: Music Library Association.

———. 1980. "Steps Toward a Descriptive Grammar for the Music of Claude Debussy." Masters Thesis, Information Science, Graduate School of Library and Information Science, University of Pittsburgh.

———. 1983. "One Face, Many Masks," in *Claude Debussy and Twentieth-Century Music*. Boston: Twayne Publishers, p. 93-114.

———. 1987. "Parsing Debussy: Proposal for a Grammar of His Melodic Practice," *In Theory Only*, 9/8: 5-19.

Westergaard, Peter. 1974. "On the Notion of Style," in Bent, 1974: 71-74.

Wolff, Christoph. 1974. "Toward a Methodology of Dialectic Style Consideration," in Bent, 1974: 74-80.

Musical Ephemera: Some Thoughts About Types, Controls, Access

James B. Coover

SUMMARY. Ephemera vivify the history of music, illuminate people, events and organizations. This article argues for a general definition of musical ephemera, and the importance of these sources in various types of musicological research. With a consensus on definitions we can proceed to explore what ephemera exists in the U.S., where it is, and what is being done with it. Issues relating to acquisition and bibliographical control are also discussed.

It is curious and surprising that printed musical ephemera has not been discussed in gatherings like this before. There have been neither papers nor panel discussions, and very little has appeared in print, save James Fuld's modest but provocative article from 1981 about two types of musical ephemera, posters and programs.[1] How has it escaped inquiry? It cannot be ignored; it is vast, diverse, and difficult to handle, yet we have had to deal with it, in some fashion, since the invention of printing.[2]

Perhaps its very immensity and variety have kept us from wrestling publicly with the bibliographical problems musical ephemera presents. Donald Krummel rightly sees it as "The Underworld of

---

James B. Coover is affiliated with the Music Department at State University of New York.

[Haworth co-indexing entry note]: "Musical Ephemera: Some Thoughts About Types, Controls, Access." Coover, James B. Co-published simultaneously in *Music Reference Services Quarterly*, (The Haworth Press, Inc.) Vol. 2, No. 3/4, 1993, pp. 349-364; and: *Foundations in Music Bibliography* (ed: Richard D. Green) The Haworth Press, Inc., 1993, pp. 349-364. Multiple copies of this article/chapter may be purchased from The Haworth Document Delivery Center [1-800-3-HAWORTH; 9:00 a.m. - 5:00 p.m. (EST)].

© 1993 by The Haworth Press, Inc. All rights reserved.

Music Bibliography." Michael Ochs says ephemera "gives most of us the gulps." The timeworn, pejorative use of the word does not exactly encourage discussion. With a genteel, but disparaging sniff, libraries attach the label to material difficult to organize and make accessible. Abracadabra, it becomes unimportant. Abracadabra, guilt over its neglect fades away. After all, important things need looking after. But that conceit does not last. The feeling that more can and should be done with "this stuff" just does not go away. We *still* get the gulps.

The word "ephemera" comes from the Greek word for an insect which lives but a day. A lamentable, lexical ancestry! But as early as 1751, Samuel Johnson applied it to printed materials, to what he called "Those papers of the day."[3] The term came into widespread use for such materials only in the 1960's with the publication of John Lewis' book, *Printed Ephemera*.[4] He defined it as "anything printed for a short-term purpose."[5] Even the pronunciation of the word remains a problem–effemmera vs. efeemera–and it is used loosely as either singular or plural. But definitions of it in the current literature hark back to Johnson's. Richard Storey–adopting the plural in 1984–says they are "printed items with an intended lifespan of limited duration, which do not normally lend themselves to standard library processing."[6] Alan Clinton expands that to: "A class of printed or near-print documentation which escapes the normal channels of publication, sale, and bibliographical control . . . [and in libraries] tends to resist conventional treatment in acquisitions, arrangement, and storage, and may not justify full cataloguing."[7]

All of these writers extoll the *value* of ephemera–"The waste of today, the evidence of tomorrow," as Nik Pollard called it.[8] We too sense that ephemera are not just historical curios, but we are naturally often more vexed by the forms than we are excited by the subject content. Much of it is hastily and shabbily printed, in manifold sizes and formats. It appears haphazardly, keyed to irregular events. It is difficult to acquire, retrospectively and currently. It is unfileable, unbindable, unshelveable, and supremely irksome to catalog. Is it any wonder that so much of it remains inaccessible to researchers, known only to its reluctant custodians. Few music librarians today would renounce the purchase of the latest book on

Stravinsky, a recent Stockhausen score, or a new recording of *Parsifal*. At the same time, many ignore collectible ephemera. Some go out of the way to discard it, ostensibly on qualitative grounds, but more probably because it confounds regular procedures.

The custodians of ephemera, however, are not always a predictable lot. In the remorseless *triage* they must practice, they march to various drummers. One, the no-nonsense kind, orders the staff to "get that [blank] stuff in a box and deep-six it."[9] Custodian Number Two, less ruthless, directs the staff to "get that (blank) stuff boxed up and put it in the basement storeroom." (There it sits, no doubt, until a modern manager emulates Custodian One and gets that stuff the [blank] out of there.) A keeper with a still different approach may not seek or purchase ephemera but will accept gifts of it, with reluctance, and will organize some of it, minimally.[10] A Fourth, suffering from "Ephemeraphilia,"[11] seeks, buys, organizes and makes accessible groups of ephemera pertinent to the work of the library's patrons. Few, though, are so afflicted!

And that ought to alarm us. If we view ephemera as wholly transitory, as mere junk, and make few efforts to assess its latent importance, we probably rob future scholarship of useful sources. I do not wish to impute to ephemera greater worth than warranted; many of the other sources of information discussed in this conference are verifiably more important. And none, of course, substitute for the music itself. But if we define primary sources as those created by the actual participants in an event or development, and secondary sources as those created by non-participants retrospectively, then ephemera must be considered primary. If it falls short of the consequence of various autograph materials, ephemera nevertheless vivifies the history of music—the milieu in which artists worked; the dayliness of events; the activities associated with the life of an opera house, a school, a violin maker's atelier; the circumstances attendant upon the genesis of a musical device or procedure and its practice. Ephemera illuminates those people, those events, those organizations.

Not all ephemera are simply factual, however. Some "represent prevailing tastes" in a magical way; others entertain.[12] Aesthetic and iconographic significance often outweigh documentary values.[13] Ephemera can be wondrous, and both nobodies and notables have fallen under its spell. Samuel Pepys' collection of trade cards, street ballads, broadsides and other printed forms is now at Magdalen College. (Pepys, incidentally, called his collection of trade cards, "Vulgariana.") John Bagford's major collection of ephemera formed early in the 18th century is in the British Library. Another collection formed by the American printer Isaiah Thomas in the 19th century serves as the basis of the archive of printed ephemera at the American Antiquarian Society. Bella Landauer's massive collection (including sheet music) is now part of the New York Historical Society. One of the best-known collections of such material is John Johnson's magnificent "Sanctuary of Printing" residing in the Bodleian. Another vast assemblage, the Enthoven Collection of the Theatre in the Victoria & Albert Museum, contains more than 200,000 playbills. This brief recital upholds the old maxim that more often than not, the importance of a collection hinges on its size rather than the essence of single, discrete items within it. (And if it also suggests to you that the British have heretofore placed greater value on ephemera than we, that is correct!)

Are there musical ephemeraphiliacs among us? How many American librarians have systematically gathered and organized musical ephemera? Does *anyone* collect posters? What attention has been paid to such collections? What bibliographies have enumerated those of any one variety? Do we, in fact, even know what those varieties are?

TYPES

Like biologists before Linnaeus, we have not yet agreed on the most basic taxonomy. The meagre literature about ephemera illustrates this dramatically. Various subdivisions have been included under the rubric "Ephemeral Materials" in the index to *Library Literature* beginning with the 1944-45 volume.[14] The year 1944 may, on the one hand, seem like an early start. On the other hand, because printed ephemera began with Gutenberg, who printed single sheet indulgences as broadsides, it is incomprehensibly tardy! And those subdivisions overlap. What are the differences, for example, among literatures variously labeled "minor," "underground," "trivial," "grey," and "fugitive"? And what distinguishes "throwaways" from "giveaways"?

The arrangement is worthless as a classification scheme for printed musical ephemera which, it seems to me, fits into four broad categories: trade literature, "grey" or "fugitive" literature, localia, and graphics. Obviously, these are not mutually exclusive categories.

Trade literature consists of:

1. Trade *journals* issued by businesses such as BMI, ASCAP, Schirmer's and Novello;
2. Trade *catalogs* from publishers and booksellers, auction and antiquarian firms,[15] record manufacturers, instrument makers–and perhaps even dealers in electronics;
3. flyers, brochures, and announcements from those businesses;
4. trade *cards* (not much in vogue in our time but, from earlier decades, rare and important).

"Grey literature" comprises printed materials which are not issued through normal, commercial publishing channels and which do not appear in trade bibliographies like the *Cumulative Book Index* or *Books in Print*. They are sometimes issued in report form without name of author, without imprint, occasionally even without title page.[16] Many are not formally copyrighted.

In this category belong:

1. occasional publications such as newsletters, acquisitions lists, exhibition catalogs, schedules of events, and histories emanating from libraries, schools, museums, and associations. The list is very long. Similar to these are:
2. registration lists, handouts distributed by speakers, programs and summaries of the meetings of musical associations like the CMS, MLA, AMS and Sonneck Society. Anyone who has tried to reconstruct who did what, when, in such organizations–even a short time ago–knows that such items as these are indispensable;
3. some almanacs, membership directories and calendars, especially the beautiful and informative annual productions of publishers such as Moeck and Bärenreiter; and

4. "fake" books, those seemingly indispensable maps for jazz and rock musicians, which until recent years were rarely available through commercial sources.

Local histories are critical resources for music historians. The accuracy of those to be written in the future manifestly depends on present-day efforts to collect and preserve localia, such as:

1. concert programs issued by symphonies, choruses, opera societies, and other musical groups. (I know of two symphony orchestras–both old, one major–which do not have complete files of their own presentations.);
2. catalogs, brochures, concert announcements, posters, and programs documenting the history of local academic music departments;
3. pictorial records of local musical landmarks, such as concert halls, theaters, church organs, and the like;
4. clipping files and scrapbooks, whose future value justifies any efforts required to preserve them.

Posters, playbills, and handbills are the most usual form of "graphics." Historically, musical events have generated more of these than has any other activity. Fuld, in the article mentioned before, describes several early examples. Today there are a number of types, and these sometimes overlap:

1. works of art produced by painters, from Toulouse-Lautrec to Peter Max, for specific musical events, some of them local;[17]
2. others, not necessarily works of art, usually for local events;
3. those for national or international occasions, such as a jazz festival in Copenhagen or Sedona, Arizona, the London premier of Glass' *Akhnaten*, a world-wide piano competition, or concerts and other events abroad in which local musicians are involved; and finally,
4. those which are not tied to specific events. They may include a cutaway view of the Met or Covent Garden, a series parading various opera singers in different roles, another comprising enlarged covers of early Ricordi opera scores;

There is yet another kind of ephemera which belongs under the category "Graphics," and that is:

5. postcards, which may picture singers in various roles, instrumentalists, early stage settings at Bayreuth, or present-day designs for Glyndebourne.[18]

The list falls short of completeness, but it is a start. It emphasizes the strong connection between localia and ephemera. Most concert schedules, programs, posters, clipping files, and the like, relate to a place. We go on to assume–not without reason–that such local history materials can be easily obtained, if needed, from the various archives, libraries, museums or private collectors in that locality. The student, therefore, who in the year 2001 wants to examine all the documents relating to Golschmann's performances with the St. Louis Symphony in the 1940's will find them, suitably organized, in St. Louis institutions. But are they? And if not, how will the research proceed?

The example is broadly drawn, and that study would require vast resources. Some others would not. In collections, whether large or small, ephemera can help us to discover new topics and can furnish new information about old ones. It may confirm facts, cement ideas, supply unexpected interconnections, and document trends, and in so doing, even alter the course or dimensions of a research project. It embellishes the context of human endeavors, and it holds a conspicuous place in scholarship.

Practically every pictorial biography, for example, from Bory's *Mozart* to Jerrold Moore's recent *Elgar* reproduces programs, playbills, invitations, clippings, and other ephemeral documents. What would Kinsky's *Geschichte* be without the same? Music publishers' catalogs have been profitably studied by Johansson, Hopkinson, Lesure, Weinmann, Gossett, Neighbour, and others. Krystyna Kobylanska has combed past auction catalogs by the hundreds to establish the provenance of Chopin autographs. Through a study of the little-known catalogs of a London bookseller, our keynoter, Donald Krummel, has shown that the firm's imports were highly influential in acquainting English musicians with the works of Italian composers in the 17th century.[19]

Masses of such ephemera await study. Just one recent catalog, for example–that for Sotheby's sale of 10 May 1984–contains two lots, each of which should help date some early editions. Lot 127 comprised two music publishers' catalogs, neither of which was known to Humphries and Smith when they compiled their seminal *Music Publishing in the British Isles.*[20] Lot 131 includes a list of, and a bill for, over 150 pieces sold by the music publisher John Bland to another, Robert Birchall, in 1789.[21]

Much ephemera bears heavily on the sociological ambience of music, but some focuses on the music itself, rather than its surroundings. A recent exhibition at Cambridge University, entitled "The Analytial Programme Note," included a program for the prepublication premiere of the Brahms First Symphony. The musical examples in the notes prepared by G.A. Macfarren reveal a slow movement which was significantly different from the one we know and love. Brahms' original version was never published and is available to us only in fragments.[22] Programs of performances conducted by Mahler memorialize his indecision about how to order the movements of his Sixth Symphony. In that same vein, Fuld notes that such programs also disclose to us which of a composer's works he chose to perform or conduct–and which pieces he chose to precede and follow his own compositions.[23]

ACQUISITION

Such discoveries occur haphazardly, for there is no easy access to ephemera, and there are few effective bibliographical controls. But before we fret about those problems, the materials themselves must be acquired. And that is not easy. First it supposes a recognition of ephemera's worth, an ability to look beyond its scruffy, disorderly nature to its future utility. Because our judgments about that may not always be prescient–for it is hard to divine which patterns of collecting will best suit the future needs of scholars–over-acquiring may be the safest path to follow. The acts of acquisition and preservation do not always signal aesthetic or intellectual approval but rather the wisdom to gather evidence at the opportune time.[24]

Collecting current ephemera, though it is mostly free or inexpensive, requires tedious, daily attention. For older materials, the problems are different but no less troublesome. Meaningful, coherent quantities are seldom offered through normal trade channels, and they are becoming expensive. In the market place, also, libraries must compete with growing numbers of collectors and the firms which cater to their needs.

Chiefly out of these interests have grown the Ephemera Society, founded in Britain in 1975, whose journal is *The Ephemerist*, and the Ephemera Society of America, begun in 1980, which publishes *Ephemera News*. Also in that year–called "The Year of Ephemera"–was held the First World Ephemera Congress. Acknowledging that activity, *Bookman's Weekly* now publishes a special, annual issue devoted to the subject.

For ephemerists, the trade bible is *The Price Guide to Paper Collectibles*.[25] Its 1983 edition, in 592 densely-packed pages, provides guidelines to the market value of over 300 types of printed ephemera. Recent music antiquarians' catalogs, mostly from Britain, mirror that surge of interest, as well as gradually escalating prices. Since 1983 offers of ephemera have included a program for a Royal Music Hall command performance in 1912 priced at £30; the same, with souvenir booklet, for £60.[26] Forty-six photographic postcards of composers were offered at from £3 to £5 each.[27] A huge bloc of 1,400 programs for English concerts from 1817 to 1961, important in part because they cover the development of the English Proms, was valued at £850.[28] Another dealer asked £300 for the printed Order of Service for Mendelssohn's funeral in 1847.[29] A 115-page scrapbook descriptive of concert life in London and Brighton between 1916 and 1936 was priced at £180.[30] And a splendid assortment of 160 engraved 18th- and 19th-century music trade cards from the Hill collection was expected to bring an astonishing £4,500.[31]

More items like these appear all the time, but as supplies decrease prices rise.[32] Yet such a condition directs merited attention to ephemera and holds out hope for its preservation.[33] And it cautions us, too, that the time to collect ephemera is when it is current, plentiful, and can be had at little cost.[34] None of us would think of discarding an 18th-century anything. The same could probably be said for most 19th-century materials. Soon we will be looking back on the 20th, and the free and inexpensive "stuff" of today will be just as precious as those 18th-century anythings.

BIBLIOGRAPHICAL CONTROLS

But acquisition and preservation alone are not enough. Bibliographical controls must keep pace. Preserved collections, unused, resemble time capsules unopened. As John Pemberton pointed out in a 1972 survey of "Ephemera in British Libraries," a lack of standards for bibliographical control and handling not only forestalls the use of ephemera–the final step in the process–but also inhibits the first step, its acquisition.[35]

Most of the available literature about ephemeral materials has appeared since 1960. It deals principally with definitions of the word and its types, justifications for its collection, and notions about how to acquire it. Little is said about how it has been, or may be, cataloged and made available. Manuals are lacking, and while a number of superb catalogs of broadsides and sheet music have been produced, there are, otherwise, few worthy models to follow.[36]

Nor has there been much incentive for bibliographers to take on such jobs. In addition to the general uneasiness about ephemera, the scholarly community has not voiced strong desire for bibliographical controls and better access. The lack of such tools has unduly limited the use of ephemera in historical research. These three aspects–acquisitions, controls, and use–might be seen as nodes on a "vicious circle," where all lie gripped by inertia. Significant advance in one would bring improvement in the others.

NEEDS AND RECOMMENDATIONS

Several sessions convened during this conference have been given over to the identification of needs and suggestions about how to satisfy them. When it comes to ephemera, we face an almost clean slate. If we agree that it is useful, we should then start on a national scale, with formal discussions of what we mean by the word itself and how to describe its subdivisions. Such discussions need not be lengthy or laborious; our British colleagues have laid the groundwork for them.

With a consensus on definitions we can proceed to explore what ephemera exists in the U.S., where it is, and what is being done with it. For this, step two, we ought to emulate our British friends and conduct a thorough survey, modeled after theirs, of ephemera in American collections.[37] The results should be incorporated into a computerized and continually-updated central register. For those lacking on-line access to that information, and for libraries' reference shelves, a printed or microfiche directory could be produced occasionally. The register would be generative. It would call attention to collections whose importance and scarcity argue for cataloging or inventories. It would identify areas for collective acquisitions. After all, it is not necessary for everyone to collect auction or antiquarian catalogs. And it ought to lead to more intensive study of certain classes of material, and from that to the design of cataloging manuals,[38] and the compilation of prototypes.

Concurrently, records for groups or blocks of ephemeral materials could be added to the RLIN and OCLC databases. The "US-MARC Format for Archival and Manuscript Control" already provides "form terms" for many ephemera–posters, trade catalogs in general, boadsides, and localia. While those may suffice for RLIN and OCLC, they will need much more precise qualification for the central register, if it is to achieve its maximum value.[39]

As useful as it would be to have many groups of ephemera recorded in RLIN and OCLC, even that accomplishment could be surpassed. Higher goals beckon, and present-day capabilities place additional sophisticated tools within reach. We shall need more than simple access to *groups* of ephemera in certain classes, and so we will hope that bibliographers can provide, in addition, detailed analyses of the discrete items within those groups. These must be computerized, of course, so that we can search databases by dates, places, media of performance, titles of works, and names of conductors, performers, choreographers, set designers, graphic artists, writers, translators, printers, publishers, and sponsors. Such a Boolean Elysium is not unreasonable.[40] The new U.S. *RISM* Libretto Project, with the multiple modes of access to information its planners expect it to provide, serves as an admirable prototype.[41]

* * *

Discovering, understanding, and exploiting that rebarbative but enlightening "stuff" of Professor Krummel's "Underworld" will not be easy. It will take time. I hope you will agree with the goals I have laid out and will find the steps in the proposed agenda both promising and possible. Those are: a collective recognition of the potential usefulness of ephemera; an assumption of responsibility for its collection and preservation (and, as scholars, to make use of it); a determination of what we mean by ephemera, along with a mapping of its boundaries and the salient topography; the construction, through surveys, of a central register of what is available, where, its scope and size, and what is done with it; the development or adaptation of systems for its bibliographical control and access; and the production of both printed and electronic models for those controls. All of this might bring that "Underworld" into what is called the "real world"–*our* real world.

My remaining hope is that you will be as eager as I to get on with it!

NOTES

1. James J. Fuld, "Music Programs and Posters: The Need for an Inventory," *Music Library Association Notes*, 2nd ser., 37 (1980/81): 520-32.

2. Maurice Rickards, one of the more readable writers on the subject, begins one of his articles with: "If you take mankind's five centuries or so of printed record and divide it roughly down the middle, you find half of it on library shelves and the other half in the wastebasket." ("History's other Half," *Private Library* 3rd ser., Spring 1980, p. 8). While it may have been the invention of printing which commenced the production of ephemera–fostering a need for the wastebasket–as Pamela Lurito notes in her "Factories, Trains and Hope: Ephemera in 19th-Century America," *American Book Collector*, 3 (Mar./April 1982): 2, it was the Industrial Revolution which both created the demands for a massive volume of ephemera and, simultaneously, production techniques to meet the need.

3. *The Rambler*, 6 August 1751. It reads in full: "Those papers of the Day, the *Ephemerae* of Learning, have Uses often more adequate to the purposes of common Life than those of more pompous and more durable Volumes." Quoted in Alan Clinton, *Printed Ephemera: Collection, Organization, Access*. London: Bingley, 1981, p. 13.

4. John N.C. Lewis, *Printed Ephemera* ... , London: Cowell, 1962.

5. *Ibid*, p. 278.

6. Richard Storey, "Printed Ephemera–A Chronology and Bibliography," *Archives*, 16(1984): 278-84.

7. Alan Clinton, *Printed Ephemera*, p. 15.

8. Nik Pollard, "Arty Choke: Acquisitions and Ephemera," *Art Libraries Journal*, 2 (Winter, 1977): 15.

9. Some go further and jettison not only ephemera but the ephemer*al* as well– the short-lived, limited circulation, specialized newsletters and bulletins; out-of-date directories of small organizations (like the Amateur Chamber Music Players); polemical pamphlets; almanacs; and even scores of relative unknowns (where are the scores of Cole Porter musicals before *Anything Goes?*).

10. John Cook Wylie notes three ways of dealing with ephemera: "(1) Most libraries don't let it inside the lobby. (2) Some libraries keep some ephemera and say it isn't ephemeral. (3) A few libraries keep everything they can get." In "Pamphlets, Broadsides, Clippings, and Posters," *Library Trends,* 4 (1955): 195.

11. A word coined by Jacquelyn Balish in "Collecting Ephemera: A Personal View," *Antiquarian Bookman,* (1981): 4307.

12. Richard C. Berner, "On Ephemera: Their Collection and Use," *Library Resources and Technical Services,* 7 (1963): 355.

13. Dale Roylance, "Graphic Ephemera: The E. Lawrence Sampler Collection of Printed Ephemera," *Yale University Gazette,* 52 (1976), 101-14.

14. *Library Literature,* 1921/22-(New York: Wilson. 1934-. Other headings used from time to time include "leaflets," "special materials," "clippings," "broadsides," "VF materials," and "social documents."

15. Both A. Hyatt King, in his *Some British Collectors of Music* (Cambridge: University Press, 1963) and Lenore Coral in her dissertation "Music In English Auction Sales, 1675-1750" (Ph.D. diss., University of London, 1971) note the disappearance of important auction sale catalogs and the significance of those losses. It is appropriate to point out that some music antiquarians in business today lack complete files of their own catalogs, already!

16. Some writers and libraries separate "grey" or "minor" literature from ephemera, because "minor" publications receive full cataloging (or ought to), while ephemera does not. Chris E. Makepeace adopts that division in his *Ephemera,* the largest and most serious book on the subject to date (Aldershot, Hants: Gower, c1985).

17. "Art posters," those designed by artists for advertising purposes in the U.S., began with a Grasset poster for *Harper's Magazine* in 1889, according to Elena G Millie, "Posters: A Collectible Art Form," *Quarterly Journal of the Library of Congress,* 39 (1982): 146-64. An uncommon number of them document musical presentations.

18. Evert Volkersz's draft *Guide to Arranging and Handling Printed Ephemera* (without imprint, c1974) also mentions sheet music, maps, and photographs, in addition to the types mentioned here. (His seven-leaf, xeroxed *Guide,* itself, may classify as a bit of "grey" literature–and it is a valuable one!) John Fletcher adds yet another category and a new spectre by foreseeing profound losses of ephemera which now exists in machine-readable form–the electronic journal, superseded statistical data, network mail and correspondence. See "The Importance of Ephemera in Library Collections," in *Acquisition of Foreign Materials for U.S. Libraries,* ed. by Theodore Samore. Metuchen, N. J.: Scarecrow, 1982, p. 190.

19. Donald W. Krummel, "Venetian Baroque Music in a London Bookshop," in *Music and Bibliography: Essays in Honor of Alec Hyatt King*, ed. by Oliver Neighbour. (New York: Clive Bingley, ca. 1980), pp. 1-27.

20. Charles Humphries and William C. Smith, *Music Publishing in the British Isles*, 2nd ed. (New York: Barnes and Noble, 1970; originally published, 1954.)

21. "A great deal of the published history of a book [or score] has to be recovered from sources external to the book itself," especially catalogs, prospectuses, and publishers' announcements, according to John Feather in "The Sanctuary of Printing: John Johnson and his Collection," *Art Library Journal*, 1(1976): 26.

22. Nigel Simeone, *The Analytical Programme Note: An Exhibition in the Faculty of Music, West Road, Cambridge, 26-29 September 1986. Handlist.* [Cambridge?, 1986.] See also an earlier mention of this changed movement in Robert Pascall's "Brahms's First Symphony Slow Movement: The Initial Performing Version," *Musical Times*, 122 (1981): 664-74.

23. Fuld, "Music Programs," p. 528.

24. Pollard, "Arty-choke," p. 13.

25. Thomas E. Hudgeons, ed., *Price Guide to Paper Collectibles* (Orlando: House of Collectibles, 1983).

26. Peter Wood, *Catalogue 34: Theatre* (Cambridge, 1983). In the same year, the firm also issued three catalogs entitled *Entertainment Ephemera*.

27. Burnett & Simeone, *Catalogue 10: Music since Wagner* (London, 1984).

28. Motley Books, Ltd., *Coll. 24/83: Music for the Masses* (Romsey, Hanst, 1983).

29. Lisa Cox, *Music Catalogue*, 7 (Exeter, 1986), lot 178.

30. *Ibid.*, lot 116.

31. Sotheby's auction of 10 May 1984, lot 123. It is interesting to compare these items and their prices with the unpublished Ravel letter knocked down in London last year for an astonishing £38,000, or the free pass to a concert scribbled hastily by Beethoven which was pegged at £11,500 in a recent antiquarian's catalog.

32. Music antiquarians' catalogs of the past decade show clearly this progression; confirmation comes in reports from the dealers themselves. There is an active market for ephemera, and many dealers acquire it, in collections or in bits and pieces, as it comes to hand. In a letter to the author, one of them adds that libraries cannot leave the vital task of acquiring and organizing ephemera to the "whims of private collectors whose heirs then throw the whole lot away."

33. Richard Storey, "Printed Ephemera: A Chronology and Bibliography," *Archives*, 16 (1984): 283.

34. Pollard, "Arty-choke," p. 14: "The period of least cultural acceptance is also the period of lowest market value, and is the time to compile a collection."

35. *ASLIB Proceedings,* 24(1972): 162-77. Pemberton also found that, with few exceptions, university libraries had no acquisition policies covering ephemera. Where policies were in force, some were, in fact, anti-ephemera.

36. A.J. Pischl's "Catalogue of Souvenir Dance Programs," in *Dance Index* (New York: Arno Press, 1970, pp. 76-127) Is one of the few models available. It is

an extremely valuable work even though the citations do not include as many facets of information as they might. Pischl notes in the introduction that the items were "inordinately rare and devilishly hard to secure" (none were earlier than 1909!), "and even dancers . . . are frequently unable to show a copy; nor are managers, publishers or printers much help" (p. 76).

37. I have in mind the "Preliminary Survey of Collections of Ephemera" carried out in the U.K. in 1979, funded by the British Library, which was reported in Alan Clinton's *Printed Ephemera: Its Collection, Organization and Access,* BLRD Report 5593 (Oxford: Bodleian Library, 1980), and was subsequently the subject of much discussion. An expanded version of Clinton's report was published, London: Bingley, 1981. A modest but useful survey of ephemera in U.S. libraries related to "social protest," "the New Left," "dissenters," "social movements," and other such issues was published by Richard Akeroyd, "A Directory of Ephemera Collections in a National Underground Network," *Wilson Library Bulletin,* 48 (1973): 236-54. Akeroyd offers specific details and histories of the collections surveyed.

38. One of the few discussions of ways to handle ephemera in libraries–besides Vokersz's *Guide, op. cit.*–is Walter S. Dunn, Jr.'s "Cataloging Ephemera: A Procedure for Small Libraries," *History News,* 21 (Jan. 1972) Technical Leaflet No. 58.

39. This was proven dramatically by the answers to a test survey which, while this essay was being prepared, was sent to several large U.S. music collections to determine their policies with respect to seventeen types of musical ephemera and their attitudes towards it, in general. I am very grateful to J. Rigbie Turner of The Pierpont Morgan Library; Jean Bowen, Susan T. Sommer, and B. K. Sutherland of the New York Public Library; to William McClellan at the University of Illinois; and to Michael Ochs of the Eda Kuhn Loeb Music Library at Harvard for their thoughtful answers to my queries, suggestions for improving the questionnaire, and wise comments about ephemera in libraries. Any future survey must offer a much wider range of sub-classes and qualifiers for its results to be meaningful. As one of the respondents noted, "collecting habits in this area are not readily described." The experience of those who helped compile that indispensable tool, RAMH *(Resources in American Music History)* would be helpful.

40. For some ephemera, databases such as this already exist; others are being created. Continually being added to SCIPIO, a special RLG database, are records for art auction catalogs from important libraries and museums. Princeton University has received a Title II-C grant to produce bibliographical records for pamphlets, serials, posters, broadsides, and flyers relating to Latin-American economic and political life. The Hoover Institution was awarded a similar grant of $250,000 to preserve its rare international poster collection. Information about musical life which appears in newspapers and journals is, like ephemera, hard upon the events it documents. In London, a group led by Prof. Rosamond McGuinness is gathering grants in support of a Computer Register of Musical Data in London Newspapers, 1660-1800. The Early Concert Life Committee of the Sonneck Society, chaired by Prof. Maryjane Corry, hopes to begin an analo-

gous project dealing with U.S. newpapers to 1783. SIGLE (the System for Grey Literature in Europe), which is supported by a consortium of agencies, had by 1984 constructed a database containing over 40,000 records of pamphlets, reports, and other items of minor literature. The project is more fully described in "Access to European 'Grey Literature' Offered by the British Library," *Library Journal*, 109 (1984): 1082.

41. These manifold points of access are clearly described and illustrated in a recent article by Marita P. McClymonds and Diane Parr Walker in "The U.S. RISM Libretto Project," *Music Library Association Notes*, 2nd ser., 43(1986): 19-35. See especially the examples, pp. 30-35.

Reference Lacunae:
Results of an Informal Survey
of What Librarians Want

Ann Basart

SUMMARY. Summarizes the results of informal surveys of librarians and publishers taken in the 1980's. The indexing of current periodicals is the first priority of many librarians; concern was also expressed over the absence of an effective index to *The New Grove*. Librarians also felt a need for indexes to collections of music, of essays, and of single items on recordings. Respondents said they wanted more databases online, on CD-ROM or on microforms. The surveys reveal what are perceived to be reference lacunae, a variety of source problems, and concern over bibliographic standards.

In 1982, I surveyed a number of colleagues about what they thought they needed in the way of reference tools. In September 1986, I conducted another informal, non-scientific survey, to ascertain what was still needed, which gaps had been filled in the meanwhile, and why some needs were still unmet. Some interesting suggestions emerged for individual reference tools, suggestions that might snag some publishers' attention, such as the following: a subject index of songs; a guide to music publishers' numbers; a list of operas in print; biographical dictionaries of performers–both current and historical–and of rock 'n roll musicians; and indexes of

---

Ann Basart is affiliated with the University of California, Berkeley.

[Haworth co-indexing entry note]: "Reference Lacunae: Results of an Informal Survey of What Librarians Want." Basart, Ann. Co-published simultaneously in *Music Reference Services Quarterly*, (The Haworth Press, Inc.) Vol. 2, No. 3/4, 1993, pp. 365-384; and: *Foundations in Music Bibliography* (ed: Richard D. Green) The Haworth Press, Inc., 1993, pp. 365-384. Multiple copies of this article/chapter may be purchased from The Haworth Document Delivery Center [1-800-3-HAWORTH; 9:00 a.m. - 5:00 p.m. (EST)].

© 1993 by The Haworth Press, Inc. All rights reserved.

separate items on sound recordings. Librarians also wanted to increase access to music in print, mentioning a "chamber music in print," a "songs in print," and just accurate in-print information for scores. Several people expressed their frustration at not having adequate directories of foreign music schools and of foreign music scholars and librarians. A summary of the survey results is appended to this paper.

The most pressing needs are basically the same today as they were in 1982. It will come as no surprise that the indexing of current periodicals is still the first priority of many librarians. One respondent said about the *Music Index,* "It seems positively shameful to me that one of the most essential sources we use isn't current, let alone available on-line or in microform format, like the *Magazine Index,* for example. The lack of cumulation is also absolutely criminal." Another said, "Using the *Music Index* is like going to the dentist!" Numerous others–even if their replies were not as sharply worded–were as concerned about the delayed coverage of *RILM Abstracts,* and a few mentioned the *Music Article Guide* and the *Music Psychology Index* as having similar problems.

What did surprise me a bit was the idea, mentioned by several respondents, that the *Music Index* and *RILM Abstracts* (and perhaps other music periodical indexes) should join forces. They should catch up in their coverage and be available on-line. Someone suggested that the scholarly items in this joint venture could have abstracts (as in *RILM*) and other entries could be provided with simple bibliographic information (as in the *Music Index*). On-line data should be updated every month, and the hard-copy, printed version would appear shortly thereafter.

Retrospective periodical indexing is still a concern. The *RIPM* (*Répertoire International de la Presse Musicale*) project will certainly help in this area, but there are extant resources that need to be made available. As long ago as 1919, Ernst Krohn wrote in *The Musical Quarterly,* "The Music Division of the Library of Congress has developed an extensive card index of the international periodical literature of music published since 1902. It is sincerely to be hoped that some means will be provided of printing this index of at least 40,000 entries." This index has still not been published, nor has the card index generated by the WPA (now housed at Northwestern University). A joint publication of the Library of Congress, WPA, and perhaps New York Public Library lists would be a wonderful first step, but simply publishing them as they are, although it would help to preserve the information on these fragile cards and paper slips, would be merely a stopgap. They need careful editing and cross-indexing.

Next to periodical indexing, my respondents were most concerned with *The New Grove*. A number of people said that they wanted an effective index to the work. (The *Encyclopedia Britannica* was so sharply criticized by many librarians and by Kenneth Kister in his *Encyclopedia Buying Guide* for not having an index that it finally provided one.) Others suggested that *The New Grove* should be available on CD-ROM, for full-text searching, which would obviate the problem of producing a comprehensive index. Many reference works are now available on laser discs, including *Books in Print, Dissertation Abstracts,* Ulrich's *International Periodical Directory,* Grolier's *Academic American Encyclopedia*, and *ERIC*. A four-part dictionary of laser discs, compiled by Bruce Connolly and published in *Database* and *Online* during June through September, 1986, gives some idea of the variety of reference works in this format.

Returning to a world bounded by more usual horizons, librarians also felt a need for indexes to collections–of music, of essays, of single items on recordings. In fact, this was a higher priority than specialized bibliographies, which some thought had been proliferating at too great a rate. Unlike the two major problems that have not been addressed so far–up-to-date periodical indexing and an index for *The New Grove*–this area provided more hope. The inadequacy of Heyer's index, mentioned by several librarians in our first survey, will evidently be largely ameliorated by the Baruch College project, under the supervision of George Hill. A number of indexes to music in collections–piano music, harpsichord music, choral music, songs–have recently appeared or are scheduled to appear soon. But enough remains to be done to keep publishers busy for a long time.

PUBLISHERS' ACTIVITIES

Although I do not have any satisfactory answers, I did manage to discover a little about what publishers are doing in some of these areas. I spoke to Susan Feder, who had worked on the *American Grove*, and who informed me that the final version of *The New Grove* is not on tape (as I had mistakenly thought), and its text is thus not in a state to be put on CD-ROM, unless it were "read by laser." The *American Grove* did a cost-study to see if an index would be economically feasible, and concluded it would not. I also talked with Lynne Thomas, of the *Grove* office, who said that it was not likely that the 1980 *New Grove* would be indexed or made available on CD-ROM. But she added that perhaps the *Grove* people would consider this for the next edition, scheduled for 1995 or so, if enough music librarians make their wants known now. (A number of librarians who had discussed the idea of an index with Stanley Sadie or Macmillan felt that *The New Grove* is not likely to provide one.)

I spoke with Nadia Stratelak of Information Coordinators, who told me that the *Music Index* has recently been purchased by three new owners. Their first priority is to cumulate the monthly issues: they plan to issue a two-year cumulation every year, catching up in about five years. The first such cumulation is due in November, 1986. The *Music Index* is also managing to keep current in its indexing, even though the printed version lags behind the indexing by many months. The *Music Index* will change its policy of selecting periodicals a bit, becoming "broader-based." They have no plans for going online at present, "because of financial constraints," but this idea is "on a back burner." Ms. Stratelak seemed grateful to hear of music librarians' concerns, was receptive to our ideas, and would like to get more feedback from us.

Gary Eslinger of Musicdata, which publishes the various "Music in Print" series, said that the company's aim is "to ultimately publish a catalog for all types of music." Guitar music will be ready before long. Woodwind music is in the works. Piano music is under discussion. Opera is "a very long way off." He added, however, that "since our entire system is computerized, the possibility of going online does exist. But, after a great deal of discussion on the subject, we have realized that there are as many reasons why we shouldn't as why we should. The future may change the way we look at online service, but for now the topic has been tabled." He also seemed very interested in any comments we might have.

Last May, Leo Balk of Garland Publishing held a meeting with several East Coast music librarians to get their ideas about possible, presumably commercially successful, future publishing ventures in music reference. The topics discussed were wide-ranging, and a number of them directly addressed concerns expressed by respondents to my survey. As someone commented to me, "It seemed a positive outreach gesture on the part of the publisher."

TRENDS

A number of trends in music reference tools seemed to be emerging, to judge by my informal survey. Several people mentioned the research guides and bio-bibliographies being done by Garland and Greenwood as a positive step. And we are all now familiar with, and most of us accept, reference works reproduced from camera-ready copy–books which, if conventionally typeset, would be too expensive to publish. A related trend involves desk-top publishing and home computers, which have made self-publishing and very small presses feasible.

Other new technology is firmly here. A large number of respondents felt that the time had come for formats other than printed books for reference tools: they wanted more databases online, on CD-ROM or on microforms. One librarian said, "We need reference works on CD-ROM: there are no online or connect charges." Music librarians are increasingly using OCLC, DIALOG, RLIN, and other computer utilities and vendors to answer reference questions and verify bibliographic data. One librarian said, "The whole question of getting more, and more up-to-date, musical information available on electronic databases is one whose time has come. As I am asked to do more searches of *RILM*, the *Arts and Humanities Citation Index*, etc., I am made increasingly aware of the current limitations in the ways this technology has been applied to music." Another person commented: "as we evolve into a computer-oriented society, I think we will all realize more and more that the instant anything bibliographical is published, it's already out of date." (Of course, this is also true of CD-ROMs.)

And, finally, there is now a possibility of special music-related databases (on RLIN, for example) with shared inputting. These would not be in special files, but would have the capability of being filtered out by people who didn't want to see the results. Richard Koprowski told me that RLIN is considering the following possibilities: the *RISM* libretto project, which would index the Schatz collection; bibliographic records for all known Beethoven scores–a project proposed by the new Beethoven Center at San Jose State; the Rigler-Deutsch index of 78 rpm recordings; and the American holdings of manuscripts for *RISM* A/II. And the Italian music and poetry project with which Michael Keller is associated will load some of its data on RLIN.

PROBLEMS

The librarians I surveyed saw a number of problems. A major one has to do with what they felt was a proliferation of specialized tools but a disregard of the really big, important questions. I will quote a few responses:

> "Perhaps music reference suffers from over-specialization, a lack of scope, and hence a lack of ambition to undertake–even tentatively–projects of general importance and usefulness," said one librarian, who went on to ask provocatively, "Does this result only from a lack of institutional/commercial incentive?"

Another person wrote, "What's being ignored? Projects that are going to be so expensive that a publisher will never break even on the sale of 500 copies. The best-qualified people to create these needed works probably never have the time or financial backing to do them even if a publisher would gamble on them."

And a college librarian commented, "There is still a lot of lousy work being published. However, the problem is that the priorities I've mentioned require more time, talent, and money than most of us would have in a lifetime. I'd like to see the "biggies" addressed rather than see my budget spent on another bio-bibliography of some obscure German baroque composer. Those of us in non-research collections have to focus on the practical and undergraduate-oriented works, given our limited budgets."

Several noted problems with desk-top publishing: one person said, "The home computer has allowed people to take their shoeboxes of cards left over from graduate student days and turn them into books." (To which a colleague of mine retorted, "It's true that the computer is circulating shoebox projects in great numbers. But some of them are wonderful. The WPA periodical index is a shoebox project, after all.") Or again, "Because of computers, people are making new reference books for all sorts of things. Too many are not used. There are too many irrelevant reference books."

One person wrote, rather cynically, "It appears that some publishers take advantage of the fact that many institutions get their works on standing order. I wonder about the need for works like the bio-bibliographic series on contemporary composers. I don't see that the work and money involved really accomplish an equivalent amount of good. Most of the major articles about a contemporary composer will be found in the *Music Index*. Perhaps the information regarding the location of source material is helpful but I still doubt the need for such works. I know it will be impossible to stop such works as long as there are publishers that have to pay the bills and individuals who need to have a book on their vita." Another respondent felt, however, that "The proliferation of research guides and bio-bibliographies is a positive trend, but contributions are uneven. Some are not selective enough, not annotated as well as others. Editorial standards need to be imposed."

Although I have not answered any questions, I will be happy if I have jogged music librarians into thinking in a more focussed way about what they, and their users, really need, and perhaps even into taking the time to express their concerns to the publishers who provide the reference tools for them. Evidently publishers, although constrained by financial considerations, really do care about what we want and need. At least some of them do. But they may not do what we really need unless we pressure them for better indexing, for higher standards, for better currency, for more relevance, for the use of new technology. It worked for those librarians who refused to buy the *Encyclopedia Britannica* until it provided an index. It may work for us.

APPENDIX

REFERENCE LACUNAE: RESULTS OF AN INFORMAL SURVEY OF MUSIC LIBRARIANS

I. WHAT WE NEED

A. Bibliographic Control
  1. Of Printed Music
     a. A more-or-less thorough general bibliographic record of published music [after 1800?] seems to be the most urgent of all desiderata; is its preparation simply unthinkable? Perhaps a reference product could be derived from RLIN/Scores. // We need an international bibliography of printed music [after 1800?], indicating publishers' numbers and which works are arrangements.
     b. In-print lists
        - An equivalent in music of *Books in Print*. Is this too much to hope for? The equivalent in music of *Publishers' Trade List Annual* is a second choice, but would be welcome. // For me, the most frustrating problem is finding accurate in-print information for scores. // We need more broadening of the *Music-in-Print* series.
        - Need a chamber music in print.
        - Need a real songs in print. // While a "songs in print" and its equivalents would be helpful, I can't see how this would be possible for practical and financial considerations.
        - Need in-print lists for operas. // Need an opera-in-print list for obscure works. // Some "in-print" information on operas would be useful.
     c. An updated guide to music in the public domain.

d. A source to bring together information on music publishers' numbers. Something that would cite work by Deutsch and others done over past 50 years and bring together plate numbers, etc., much of this information is hidden in bibliographies.
e. One great project would be an index by title and genre to the musical entries in *NUC pre-1956*. Likewise for later years, incorporating indexing done in *NUC's MBMSR*. Put it all together, in print and online versions, and we have the ultimate weapon.
f. We need more bibliographies of music by performance medium. And other bibliographies of music should have indexes by medium.

2. Of Facsimiles
   - Jim Coover compiled a bibliography of facsimiles in *Notes;* this should be updated as a separate publication.

3. Of Sound Recordings (see also "Items in Collections," 7)
   a. Need an international recordings in print. // Now that Schwann (which was never a perfect tool, but the only one we had) is greatly reduced in usefulness, what are we going to do? Is there anything in the works (except *Phonolog*) that will be a real recordings-in-print? Or does the volatile national of the recording industry make such a source impossible?
   b. List of 78 rpm records reissued on LP8, so we could weed old ones.
   c. Need discographies of ethnic music, e.g., Irish music.
   d. Put Rigler-Deutsch on CD-ROM. // Extend Rigler-Deutsch to LPs.

4. Of Manuscripts
   - Is *RISM* doing enough? // Need cataloging documentation for manuscripts on microfilm.

5. Of Librettos
   a. Need a librettos-in-print list.
   b. Need access at least by first line of arias. People need to locate particular arias.

6. Of Microforms

- Need union lists of microform holdings (books and music) in the U.S. // Better access to microfilm collections in the U.S.
7. Of Items in Collections
   a. Need more types of indexes to music in collections. // An updated song index would still seem to be a high priority. // An update of DeCharms' song index would be a great blessing. // Too much of a gap between the Sears song index and DeCharms. // I would like to see a song index online.
   b. Harvester series of microfilms needs an index: perhaps could be on CD/ROM.
   c. A big problem recently has been up-to-date indexing of songs, symphonic excerpts, etc., available on disc. [This librarian found the answer to one question on OCLC because of a cataloger's careful analytics, saying "It would have been nice if there had been an easier way to obtain this information."] // Need lists of single songs on recordings.
   d. A lot of work needs to be done with the indexing of essays in general collections, published before 1967. Those in Festschriften and congress reports are adequately indexed, but collections of essays dealing with particular topics or periods should be indexed. *Essay Index* does this to some extent, but its coverage is limited to English-language items.
   e. Index to biographies that include scholars.
8. Of Periodical Articles
   a. Indexing of current titles
      - We need up-to-date periodical indexing. // I hope that getting current literature into indexes speeds up. // All levels of research, freshman student to faculty, are hampered by this lack of coverage and/or the difficulty in accessing necessary information.
      - *RILM* is too far behind; not enough people, all volunteer, variety of problems. // We really need *RILM* up to date. // I hope that money keeps coming in to support and, perhaps, expand the operation of *RILM Abstracts*, so that it might be truly up to date. Perhaps some

mechanism could be used so that online coverage is updated monthly or even weekly, such as is done with the *Arts & Humanities Citation Index*. The printed version could be published shortly thereafter. [Barry Brook responded, "*RILM* is bending every effort to become current, and by golly now that we are self-sufficient at our present rate of production we will do so, although it will take a few years."]
- What is happening with the Music Index? // WE NEED TO GET THE *MUSIC INDEX* CUMULATED! // My number one priority is Music Index. It seems positively shameful to me that one of the most essential sources we use isn't current, let alone available online or in microform format like the *Magazine Index*, for example. The lack of cumulation is also absolutely criminal. This is probably the one source that I find most useful for information on contemporary music and musicians. // The Music Index is the single worst disaster in music reference. // *MI* should be online, on schedule, going again; it is almost unusable. // If *MI* cannot convince the online vendors that there is a market, perhaps a joint effort would work.
- *RILM* and *MI* and perhaps the *Music Article Guide* should be online and integrated. // *RILM* and the *Music Index* merged and frequently cumulated. // The *RILM/Music Index* concerns are still major problems. // An updated combined online version of *RILM* and the *MI* is one of the most important tools needed. // The *MI* is hopeless, maddening, and unrealistic; should join forces with *RILM*.
- The *Music Psychology Index* is not well done and is not kept current.

b. Retrospective indexing
- The systematic indexing of 18th-century and early 19th-century periodicals–such as the *Allgemeine deutsche Bibliothek*, the *Teutsche Merkur* (Wieland's journal), and the *Zeitung für die elegante Welt*–for music items (in-

- cluding articles and reviews) would be extremely useful.
- Periodical indexing before 1950 is still a problem. // Retrospective coverage continues to be a problem, particularly with pre-1950 sources. // Is *RIPM* a partial answer? // I hope that there is work being done on retrospective indexing of music periodical literature.
- Someone should index and combine already existing lists: WPA (at Northwestern University) + NYPL + LC. // The home-made catalog of the Library of Congress, together with the one at DePaul [now at Northwestern] should be made available in print in some fashion. // It is imperative that, if the WPA and other early card indexes of music periodicals are published, they be completely edited and cross-referenced; they are not usable as they are.
- We need a pre-1967 index of music articles in nonmusical periodicals; many very useful source materials are buried in literary or general journals, such as Walter Salmen's article on Schubert and folksong published in *Forschungen und Fortschritte,* a journal that generally deals with mathematics and the physical sciences!

9. Of Materials on Specific Topics
   a. Guy Marco's original plans for *Information on Music* have been abandoned and Libraries Unlimited is no longer going to publish the series. Garland's *Composer Resource Manuals* seems to be taking the place of Marco's vols. 4-5, but at one volume per composer it will take many years to cover even the major composers. There is still need for bibliographies on specific topics–Marco's original vol. 3. We still do not have a guide to editions.
   b. We still need a complete bibliography of analyses of standard works, which will separate program notes from real technical analyses. It should have a separate Schenkerian index. Harold Diamond is working on an augmented version of his *Musical Criticism*, which was aimed principally at undergraduates, and maybe that will

fill part of the need at least. He may again be limiting it to English language items. [Barry Brook replies, "in addition to Larry Laskowski's annotated bibliography of Schenkerian analysis . . . Channan Willner is working on an enormous annotated bibliography . . . of Schenkerian analysis by theorists other than Schenker."]
   c. I hope for a continued vigor in the area of guides to the literature on individual composers and on musical topics. These need to be done by experts whose stature permits them to be authoritatively selective, so that the old baggage is disposed of once and for all.
   d. There is a lack of tools in music education. Why must there be separate lists of dissertations-in-progress for music and music education? Why is the list for educators so inadequate? Why have none of the major music education periodicals not received retrospective indexing? Why doesn't *MI* index regional music education mags? Music educators are often the majority audience in our large schools of music, and they are the least-recognized by the community of authors, scholars, and publishers who serve up what is available.
   e. A bibliography of music theorists in translation. Jim Coover compiled one in *JMT*, but should be a separate publication. // We could use a bibliography of music theorists available in translation, updating the old Coover.
10. Of the Works of Individual Composers
    - Thematic indexes remain high on my want list. The new Handel and Telemann are tantalizing, but everything I need to verify is in a yet-unpublished volume. // Thematic catalogs of the works of Liszt, Schumann, Berlioz, and other 19th-century composers not yet adequately covered.
11. Of Dissertations
    - Doctoral dissertations on music-related topics in arts and humanities. The keyword index to *Dissertation Abstracts* is of some help; but we need assistance with foreign dissertations.

B. Dictionaries and Encyclopedias

1. New Grove
   a. Analytical index to *The New Grove*. // It really needs an effective index. [There was much discussion of this topic.]
   b. Full-text *New Grove* on CD/ROM (rather than online). // A CD-ROM version of *Grove's* is one of the two most important tools needed. That would obviate the need of any index and more fully exploit the potential of this important work. The potential for a CD-ROM version of *Grove's* can easily be measured in the number of reference works that would be unnecessary should such searching of *Grove's* be possible. // I doubt if the availability of *The New Grove* online or on CD/ROM would dispense with the crying need for effective indexing of this source, unless the machine-readable product were completely indexed.
2. Terminology
   a. Dictionary of American music terminology.
   b. Polyglot dictionary of major musical terms with definitions, including less-familiar languages, such as Dutch, Norwegian, and Swedish. The big polyglot dictionary published by Bärenreiter includes only synonyms. The *Harvard Dictionary* limits its coverage to major languages.
3. Dictionary of performance practice.
4. A carefully researched encyclopedia of contemporary Christian music, which has become an important subfield of popular music in recent years. Anderson and North's *Gospel Music Encyclopedia* attempts to fill this need, but caters to the lowest common denominator. // A church music dictionary, with terms that don't appear in other music dictionaries.
5. Biographical dictionaries:
   a. Performers, both contemporary and historical.
   b. Decent rock 'n' roll biographical dictionary with quality writing and layout, updated each year–perhaps modeled on *The Blues Who's Who*.
   c. A biographical dictionary of 20th-century French composers.

C. Directories
   1. Of foreign schools of music, publishers, scholars, other data.

(Outside Canada, US, UK.) // Annual directory for foreign music schools. [Mentioned by a number of people.]
  2. Of orchestral personnel (international). There is an *International Conference of Symphony & Opera Musicians* (ICSOM) tied to the AFM, but it is not for sale.
  3. A directory of dealers in second-hand and/or out-of-print music.
D. Guides
  1. A comprehensive pronunciation guide to proper names and titles in music, useful for radio stations, etc.
  2. List of music credits for film and TV. // We get a lot of questions about music commercials (we have a very large number of communications majors); I'd love to see better and more reference works on film, radio, and TV. // Does anyone really care who writes music for commercials? // We need a thorough-going index to musical compositions featured in moving pictures, with entries for films and compositions. It should do things like identify all the music used in Elvira Madigan, list the use of Mozart's music in films (such as the March from *Idomeneo* in "Take This Job and Shove It"). // An update, with some expansion and correction, of the list in the Limbacher would be most helpful. // We need identification of the music in such popular films as *Agnes of God, Kramer vs. Kramer, All That Jazz*, and *The Four Seasons*.
E. Miscellaneous
  1. LC Subject Headings for music should be printed separately.
  2. A documented compilation of music listings from 19th-century bibliographies of general scope (e.g., *Journal général de la littérature de France*).
  3. Subject indexing of songs. The *Great Song Thesaurus* does this only as a keyword index to titles: "Take Me Out to the Ball Game" is there, but not under "Baseball" or "Sports."
  4. Espina's work on repertory for solo voice needs to be indexed (with a sigla index and composer/title index) and reorganized.
  5. Better access to the material in *RAMH*.

6. A Thatcher-Gooch/Hovland type of book indexing musical settings of European poets.
7. An index to biographies that include music scholars.
8. Cooperation
   a. Need an exchange for unanswered reference questions (through the MLA?), like that in RQ.
   b. Perhaps a cooperative effort in sharing reference data would be possible, a data base that could be maintained by MLA members. As individuals came across some information they could add it to the file. Many of us have access to BITNET. A hosting institution could produce the file from various participants, publishing a yearly update or perhaps fielding questions via BITNET.

II. WORKS COMPLETED, IN PROGRESS, OR BEING CONSIDERED SINCE LAST QUESTIONNAIRE
(See also Barry Brook's comments, A9b above)

A. Music in print: Musicdata's aim is "to ultimately publish a catalog for all types of music." Guitar will be ready before long. Woodwind music is in the works. Piano under discussion. Opera "a very long way off." Musicdata has decided not to go online at present.
B. Michael Hovland has completed an index to musical settings of American poetry.
C. Frank Greene's *Composers on Record* partially fills gap for "an index to biographies of little-known composers."
D. More types of indexes to music in collections have been published (piano, harpsichord, songs).
E. Heyer will be much expanded by George Hill's project. // We can look forward to more detailed and up-to-date indexing of collections through the database project being undertaken at Baruch College.
F. *RILM Abstracts* fills in the gap of indexing Festschriften since Gerboth's book was published, so we don't need an update to the Gerboth. [Barry Brook responds, "I believe that an update to the Gerboth Festschriften would still serve a useful purpose to take care of omissions in Gerboth's work and in the early

years of *RILM*, including Festschriften from other disciplines missed by both."]
G. *Find That Tune* helps fill the song-index gap.
H. I've found the *RLIN* online scores file useful in finding in-print information and, given the unreliability of any "in-print" guide, fairly effective for ordering.
I. RLG is considering putting the Rigler-Deutsch Index in its sound recording file.
J. Arthur Wenk has updated his bibliography of analyses of 19th- and 20th-century music.
K. Thatcher and Gooch are doing an index to musical settings of Shakespeare.

III. TRENDS AND RECENT DEVELOPMENTS

A. Resource guides and Composer guides
   1. *Garland Resource Guides*: very good.
   2. Indexes to works on specific composers (Barber, Copland) and guides to research (Josquin, Schutz) are new trends.
B. CD/ROM
   1. We need reference works on CD/ROM: there are no online or connect charges.
   2. Some reference works are now on CD/ROM (e.g., Grolier). Although it may not be financially feasible for *The New Grove*, it would be wonderful.
C. Computer databases
   1. The whole question of getting more, and more up-to-date, musical information available on electronic databases is one whose time has come. As I am asked to do more and more searches of *RILM, A&HCI*, etc., I am made more aware of the current limitations in the ways this technology has been applied to music.
   2. As we evolve into a computer-oriented society, I think we will all realize more and more that the instant anything bibliographical is published, it's already out of date.
   3. Music librarians are increasingly using OCLC, DIALOG, RLIN, and other computer utilities and vendors to answer reference questions and verify bibliographic data. Possibility

of music-related databases (on RLIN, for example) with shared inputting.
D. Publishers' outreach
- Leo Balk of Garland Publishing held a meeting earlier this year with a bunch of East-Coast music librarians (LC, NYPL, Cornell, SUNY Stony Brook, others) to discuss possible, presumably commercially successful, future publishing ventures. It seemed a positive outreach gesture on the part of the publisher.
E. Desk-top publishing
- Desk-top publishing and home computers have made self-publishing and very small presses feasible.

IV. PROBLEMS AND STANDARDS

A. Desk-top publishing
- The home computer has allowed people to take their shoeboxes of cards left over from graduate student days and turn them into books.
B. Selectivity
- I hope for a continued vigor in the area of guides to the literature on individual composers (e.g., the Greenwood and Garland series) and on musical topics. These need to be done by experts whose stature permits them to be authoritatively selective, so that the old baggage is disposed of once and for all. National bibliographies and periodical indexes ought to be accountable for comprehensive lists of writings; subject bibliographers are made for the purpose of pruning the branches intelligently.
C. Complexity
- Am I the only one who finds *RILM* not terribly useful for undergraduates, and the format needlessly elaborate and off-putting?
D. Relevance
  1. There are too many irrelevant reference books: reference librarians can only keep so many books in their heads. Because of computers, people are making new reference books for all sorts of things. Too many are not used.

2. We need fewer specialized bibliographies and more indexes to collections.
3. I'd like to see the "biggies" addressed rather than see my budget spent on another bio-bibliography of some obscure German Baroque composer. Those of us in non-research collections have to focus on the practical and undergraduate-oriented works, given our limited budgets.
4. It appears that some publishers take advantage of the fact that many institutions get their works on standing order. I wonder about the need for works like the bio-bibliographic series on contemporary composers. I don't see that the work and money involved really accomplish an equivalent amount of good. Most of the major articles about a contemporary composer will be found in the *Music Index*. Perhaps the information regarding the location of source material is helpful but I still doubt the need for such works. I know it will be impossible to stop such works as long as there are publishers that have to pay the bills and individuals who need to have a book on their vita.
5. There are more reference books published than we can afford to buy, but would we buy them if money were not a problem? Probably not, which simply means that there are books that do not relate to our collection or curriculum.
6. Our lack of staff makes it impossible for us effectively to use the reference works we have.

E. Up-to-dateness
- One issue that I face regularly is the matter of cost vs. temporality. Consider the $50 (usually much more) annual directory to whatever. I may refer to it twice during the year it is intended to represent, and may not find the information needed either time. How do I justify that expense? Do I buy the next year's, or try to get by every 5-6 years?

F. Quality
1. I'm buying reference books that sound good in the ad but are disappointing in hand. I never understand why I buy a one-volume music dictionary (St. Apel excepted).
2. The proliferation of research guides and bio-bibliographies is a positive trend, but contributions are uneven. Some are

not selective enough, not annotated as well as others. Editorial standards need to be imposed.
    3. Greenwood, Garland, and Scarecrow all publish from camera-ready copy; editing may be a problem.
    4. One point that is of concern to me is sloppy scholarship. A case in point is a discography that won a prize from the MLA: although it contains a great deal of useful material, it is full of omissions and mistakes, and is not as helpful as it could have been had it been more accurate and complete.
G. Very large problems
    1. Perhaps music reference suffers from over-specialization, a lack of scope, and hence a lack of ambition to undertake–even tentatively–projects of general importance and usefulness. Does this result only from a lack of institutional/commercial incentive?
    2. The most qualified people are probably not interested in doing the works we most need.
    3. There is still a lot of lousy work being published. However, the problem is that the priorities I've mentioned require more time, talent, and money than most of us would have in a lifetime.
    4. What's being ignored? Projects that are going to be so expensive that a publisher will never break even on the sale of 500 copies. The best qualified people to create these needed works probably never have the time or financial backing to do them even if a publisher would gamble on them.
    5. We support short-term projects and get nowhere on problems like the *Music Index*. Publishers are not short-sighted; they have to stay in business. Authors have less and less time to work on the major problem areas.

The Bio-Bibliography Series

Don Hixon

SUMMARY. The inaugural volume of the series "Bio-Bibliographies in Music" was the author's *Thea Musgrave* of 1984. Each volume of the series consists of a brief biography, a complete list of works, discography, an annotated bibliography, appropriate appendices, and an index. The bulk of each volume is the annotated bibliography of writing about and, if appropriate, by the composer. One of the purposes of the series is also to provide excerpts from performance reviews, the annotations to which often include quotations from reviews in the contemporary American and foreign press. The article also describes the criteria for the selection of titles and process of preparation and publication.

I am the series adviser to two on-going series by Greenwood Press. One of these is the "Music Reference Collection." While over ten volumes in this series have appeared or are currently in actual production, I have been involved directly with only two titles. The first of these is John and Anna Gillespie's *A Bibliography of Nineteenth-Century American Piano Music, with Location Sources and Composer Biography-Index,* published in 1984. The other is a bibliography of flute music by women composers. This project is still being discussed, however, and you will have to watch for further details on this title!

The series with which I am most involved is "Bio-Bibliographies

---

Don Hixon is affiliated with the University Library, University of California, Irvine, and is Series Advisor, Greenwood Press Bio-Bibliography Series.

[Haworth co-indexing entry note]: "The Bio-Bibliography Series." Hixon, Don. Co-published simultaneously in *Music Reference Services Quarterly,* (The Haworth Press, Inc.) Vol. 2, No. 3/4, 1993, pp. 385-390; and: *Foundations in Music Bibliography* (ed: Richard D. Green) The Haworth Press, Inc., 1993, pp. 385-390. Multiple copies of this article/chapter may be purchased from The Haworth Document Delivery Center [1-800-3-HAWORTH; 9:00 a.m. - 5:00 p.m. (EST)].

© 1993 by The Haworth Press, Inc. All rights reserved.

in Music." To date, four volumes have appeared. The inaugural volume was my own *Thea Musgrave,* published in 1984. Two volumes appeared in 1985: JoAnn Skowronski's *Aaron Copland* and Don Hennessee's *Samuel Barber.* Ms. Skowronski is from California State University, Northridge, and Mr. Hennessee is Librarian Emeritus from California State University in Long Beach, California. The most recent published volume, on Virgil Thomson, appeared only last month, and was authored by Michael Meckna, Assistant Professor of Music from Ball State University. Just last week, I received the final manuscript for a volume on Ester Ballou from James Heintze, Music Librarian at the American University in Washington, D.C. With over sixty other volumes in various stages of preparation, it is difficult to say which will appear next. I have distributed a list of composers represented thus far in this series and the respective contributors. You will note that, at the moment, this series is limited to nineteenth- and early-twentieth-century composers, although there are no restrictions as to nationality.

In order to give an idea of the nature of the series, I would like to briefly describe the major sections of the volume. In addition to front-matter (preface, acknowledgements, etc.), each volume consists of a brief biography, a complete list of works, discography, an annotated bibliography, appropriate appendices, and an index. Since the series is chiefly bibliographical in nature, the bibliographical section intentionally is quite brief, usually consisting of only 10-20 pages providing an overview of life and works of the composer. The "Works and Performances" section is arranged by genre and provides a complete list of works together with data on the compositions (medium, duration, publication information, dedications, librettists, indication of awards, etc.) and data on premiere and other significant performances, including dates, halls, and performers. The "Discography" includes information on recordings, chiefly but not necessarily exclusively commercially-produced, whether or not currently available. The bulk of each volume is the annotated bibliography of writing about and, if appropriate, by the composer. One of the major purposes of this series is to provide excerpts from performance reviews, and annotations often include pertinent quotations from such reviews in the contemporary American and foreign press. This type of material generally is not readily available and this unique emphasis distinguishes volumes in the Greenwood Press series from those in similar series. Generally, each volume contains at least two appendices, one providing an alphabetical list of compositions and the other a chronological list; you will recall that the basic list of works is arranged by genre (opera, orchestral music, solo literature, etc.). All of these sections are tied together through a system of cross-references which enables one to go directly from, say, a composition in the "Works and Performances" section to the "Discography" to find recordings of the work to the "Bibliography" to locate critical discussion on the work, all quite painlessly and without the necessity of flipping back and forth aimlessly among several sections of the book. The nemesis of nearly all bibliographers, an index of personal and corporate names, including all authors and performers cited in the text, concludes the volume.

As series adviser to *Bio-Bibliographies in Music,* I am responsible for selecting appropriate composers for inclusion in the series. A number of considerations are involved here, including the significance of the composer and the degree to which the composer has received similar recent bibliographical treatment which might be considered competitive. In other words, it is the feeling of Greenwood Press that the specialized market to which this series would appeal generally could not bear two or more bibliographies on the same composer unless the treatment differed radically. Implicit in this is that the press has to be convinced of the marketability of the product before they are willing to allocate their human and financial resources to a volume, and this is as it must be. Without intending to speak disparagingly of any publisher of specialized academic books, I believe it is appropriate to note that profit rather than the philanthropic dissemination of knowledge must be the primary motive for publication for the publishers' basic survival. This is a roundabout way of saying that there are times when the significance of a composer, particularly one of fairly recent activity, must be weighed against the potential market for the book. Fortunately, I can recall only a few instances in which proposals have been rejected, and these involved composers of chiefly local rather than international prominence.

After deciding on appropriate figures to be included in the series, these must be matched with qualified writers. I become aware of prospective authors through a variety of sources, including personal knowledge, referrals from other individuals, and from being aware of names attached to other similar bibliographical works. Generally, I make the initial contact, although there have been many times when I have been approached by potential authors. After the writer and I have decided on an appropriate subject, a written proposal is submitted to the press for their consideration, comments, and, hopefully, a contract. Part of the author's proposal is a *vita* noting educational background, degrees, an employment record, and list of prior publications. While academic background and the evidence of previous bibliographic work are carefully considered, one of the most important qualifications is a love of meticulous detail, an enjoyment, or at least a toleration, of searching through endless bibliographies, indexes, and other reference tools in search of the most elusive information, and an ability to organize this mass of detail into a cohesive whole utilizing standard bibliographic conventions. It has been my experience that the librarian, schooled in such approaches, generally makes a very likely candidate for such work, although there certainly have been notable exceptions.

Once the contract has been signed by both parties, my job is to be available for answering questions, providing advice when called upon, and to guide in the preparation of a consistent camera-ready manuscript. This phase of my work generally lasts from a minimum of eight months to several years, depending upon the amount of time available to the writer. The average time required is one and one-half years and, parenthetically, it almost always takes the writer at least six months longer to finish the volume than he or she originally had planned; the number of persistent nitpicking problems which creep up during the last throes is absolutely astounding!

Finally, the day comes when the author is satisfied that the product is as good as it can be and, at that point, he or she sends me a copy of the completed manuscript. I examine the copy very carefully for organizational detail and consistency making certain that everything has been included that is supposed to be there and that everything is presented in the agreed-to bibliographical format. Assuming that all is well on that front, I read very carefully the front-matter, the biography, and any extended narrative passages, looking for typographical errors, misspellings, syntax, and general presentation and appearance. I also spot-check other sections for accuracy, although I am unable to take the time to examine every jot and tittle. The same is true when the final manuscript reaches Greenwood Press: they will re-examine these same sections with a jaundiced eye, but are unable to provide exhaustive proofreading and galleys. The reason for this is an economic one. Because of the perceived relatively small audience for these volumes, the press anticipates a comparatively small profit margin and so cannot afford the tremendous amounts of time which detailed proofreading requires. This also explains the necessity of providing perfect, camera-ready copy. While both the press and I do the most that we are able to ensure an accurate and consistent volume, it must be noted and emphasized that the final product is the responsibility of the author and that he or she must feel personally compelled to carefully examine the manuscript, and then re-examine it, so that the published volume will reflect well on the scholarship and bibliographic expertise of the author.

Following acceptance of the manuscript by me and the press is a period of about six months where the camera-ready manuscript is photographically reduced and published. Then comes publicity, distribution, hopefully sales, royalties, and, even more hopefully, good reviews!

There is much more that I could say about the whole process and my involvement in it, but I would rather wait to respond to questions, if there is time. Let me just say that the preparation of such bibliographies in this series, or in any similar series by any publisher, perhaps will be good for your resume, but will have little immediate effect on your pocketbook, particularly if you place any value on your time. Such work is extremely time-consuming, to a degree realized only by those who have completed such an undertaking. If you are addicted to bibliographic detective-work, however, you just may find it all very much worth the effort.

GREENWOOD PRESS BIO-BIBLIOGRAPHIES IN MUSIC COMPOSERS REPRESENTED AS OF OCTOBER 6, 1986

ANTES, John
BABBITT, Milton
+BALLOU, Esther
*BARBER, Samuel
BASSETT, Leslie
BEACH, Amy Marcy
BERIO, Luciano
BERKELEY, Lennox
BERNSTEIN, Leonard
BLISS, Arthur (Sir)
BLITZSTEIN, Marc
BOND, Carrie Jacobs
BRANSCOMBE, Gena
BUSONI, Ferruccio
CHAMINADE, Cecile
*COPLAND, Aaron
CRAWFORD SEEGER, Ruth
CRESTON, Paul
DIEMER, Emma Lou
DILLON, Fannne Charles
FAURE, Gabriel
FINE, Vivian
GIDEON, Miriam
HARRIS, Roy
HERRMANN, Bernard
HILL, Edward Burlingame
HUSA, Karel
HUSS, Henry Holden
IVES, Charles
KAY, Ulysses
KODALY, Zoltan
KRENEK, Ernst
LANGLAIS, Jean
LIGETI, Gyorgy

LUENING, Otto
LUTOSLAWSKI, Witold
MARTIN, Frank
MASON, Lowell
MESSAGER, Andre
MILNER, Anthony
*MUSGRAVE, Thea
OLIVEROS, Pauline
PENDERECKI, Krzysztof
PERLE, George
PERSICHETTI, Vincent
PINKHAM, Daniel
POULENC, Francis
REGER, Max
ROREM, Ned
ROUSSEL, Albert
RUGGLES, Carl
SCHOENBERG, Arnold
SCHULLER, Gunther
SCHUMAN, William
SCHUMANN, Clara
SMYTH, Ethel
STILL, William Grant
STOCKHAUSEN, Karlheinz
TCHEREPNIN, Alexander
THOMPSON, Randall
*THOMSON, Virgil
TIPPETT, Sir Michael
VILLA-LOBOS, Heitor
WALTON, William
WARD, Robert
WARREN, Elinor Remick
WUORINEN, Charles
ZWILICIH, Ellen Taaffe

*already published
+due Spring, 1987

Three Bibliographic Lacunae

Susan T. Sommer

SUMMARY. This paper addresses three specific lacunae in music bibliography. The first, which has remained virtually ignored by all, concerns our lack of access to visual sources. The second, which is currently trying to address in many ways, is our failure to control primary source material in the 19th and 20th centuries. The third involves the lack of communication with our counterparts in the other performing arts, especially those in dance, theater, film, and in sound archives.

When I was asked to speak on this panel, I was quite at a loss since I had neither embarked on a plan to fill lacunae nor had I taken a survey of existing lacunae and, in fact, I was a little confused by the title itself, which you may notice is grammatically ambiguous. And I thought I had one option, which would be to come and to listen to everything and just sift it all and compare it against the entire universe of known knowledge to locate the gaps, to organize them somehow, and then to describe them to you in either the twenty minutes or twenty seconds which I was allowed. I rejected this and I decided I would try to look at the broadest possible areas where it seemed to me we were lacking in what we might call generally "bibliographic control" and thinking about this from my point of view in New York City and at the New York Public Library. It seemed to me that there were these three areas

---

Susan T. Sommer is affiliated with the New York Public Library, and former editor of Music Library Association *Notes*.

[Haworth co-indexing entry note]: "Three Bibliographic Lacunae." Sommer, Susan T. Co-published simultaneously in *Music Reference Services Quarterly*, (The Haworth Press, Inc.) Vol. 2, No. 3/4, 1993, pp. 391-395; and: *Foundations in Music Bibliography* (ed: Richard D. Green) The Haworth Press, Inc., 1993, pp. 391-395. Multiple copies of this article/chapter may be purchased from The Haworth Document Delivery Center [1-800-3-HAWORTH; 9:00 a.m. - 5:00 p.m. (EST)].

© 1993 by The Haworth Press, Inc. All rights reserved.

which were quite important and significantly I had felt that this evaluation has stood up through this conference.

The first of them, which has remained virtually unmentioned by everyone, is what I feel to be our lack of access to visual sources. I think in Jim Coover's paper this was hidden perhaps under one of the subsections. The second, which some people have mentioned and which obviously we are trying to address in many ways, is our failure to control primary source material in the 19th and 20th centuries particularly. And the third is a lack of communication that I think many of us suffer from, that is, communication with our counterparts in the other performing arts, especially those people who are working in dance, in theater, in film, and in sound archives. I felt the only people to address this directly were my colleagues from the Library of Congress, a non-academically affiliated organization.

To take the first–visual sources. Why should we bother with visual sources? First, it seems to me that ours is a visually-oriented generation. People have been raised on television and spend a lot of time watching it. And whether or not you approve of it, they do. And whether or not you like the fact that it means they read less, they do read less. But there is an advantage to this, and it is that people who have been raised looking at visual information know how to look at it and know how to interpret it. They know how to interpret it in a way which I think those of us, and I will not put myself in the older generation, do not know. And we can expect that there will be more demand for information in this particular form. Certainly there is a demand for it in New York now by the media that soak it up. When they moved to Lincoln Center in 1965, the New York Public Library developed a picture collection out of all the boxes of pictures, those ephemera which had been stuffed in the basement. In those halcyon days we had time and space to do that. Since then, the picture collection has become something of a monster. It occupies an enormous amount of staff time to service it because it is probably one of the most popular and most used collections at the New York Public Library. Although it is not a very good collection there are no others, and obviously people want this information, need this information, and they are not getting it from other places.

We receive a lot of information in this form, in fact an enormous amount. Since the middle of the 19th century the technology has brought us a tremendous number of visual images: still photography, films, video. How would you like to feel that your life was made up of your print collections your birth certificate, your diplomas, and your pictures? If you are looking at your life, you look at your pictures–not at the newspaper clipping where your name was mentioned. What are we going to get from this? What are we looking for? For example, think about an opera you have attended. Do you think just about the music? No, of course not, it was a work which was on stage. It had a set, it had people, people who were dressed in costumes, and who moved about. All of this was part of your experience. All of this went into the artwork itself. All of this matters. It would be wonderful if we had videotapes of all the performances that Verdi or Rossini saw. We have videotapes of many things that are being done today, however, these sources are not being controlled.

Photography has been around for a long time, now but how many photographs exist of Brahms, of Bartok, of any number of other people? Where do you go about finding photographs of music making itself? Music as an art which is being experienced–open-air concerts, jazz, chamber music, theaters. How about film footage? This is probably one of the very worst to be controlled. Suppose you wanted to get film footage of Bruno Walter conducting, or Stravinsky, or the Modern Jazz Quartet–where would you go? I myself would like to know. You may find a place, but is there a source that gives you all of it? I know there is none. And what about television, for goodness' sake, concerts or operas on television. Do you remember the NBC Opera? It is gone, absolutely gone. It exists in your mind, and is as gone as a Rossini opera performed in the middle of the 19th century. Those kinescopes they decided they did not want to save, because they took up too much space? Off they went.

Consider the things that are going on now. You may be building up your own VCR collections of these things, but are your institutions doing that? How about interviews with important musicians, and television programs about them? How about master classes that appear on television? We are building our personal collections but not, I think, our institutional ones. Nor are we developing the tools to control these sources. What can we use as models? The old one is the *Harvard Catalog of Dramatic Portraits* which indexes prints and which is now old and hopeless. But it is all we have. *Redeem*, the effort to index and control the repertoire of econographie musicale, has made a wonderful start but its emphasis seems to have been on the early material, I think because of the special interest of many of the people who have contributed to it. Controlling 19th- and especially 20th-century material is a daunting challenge. One of the best examples that you may use as a model is the *Catalog of the Dance Collection* of the New York Public Library. This a brilliant cataloging effort which is the only thing I can think of that has come to grips with and solved the problem of describing the contents of both still and moving pictures in such a way that it can be united into a bibliographic format–the kind that we are used to.

Finally, I would suggest that when considering visual sources we might remember a very important thing, which is that these are our own sources, sources about music. Let us not abandon the field to the media archivists. Let us not do what I think we made a mistake in doing with sound–to change our collections over to people who are able to handle the technology with the idea that by so doing they would also take full responsibility for what I think is our subject responsibility.

Second, let us consider the issue of controlling 19th- and 20th-century source material, a mass of material which, as I just said, is daunting. Who did what, when, and where in terms of concerts? There is a wealth of primary material in newspapers, in programs, and in other contemporary sources. No one has yet sat down, dug it out, and listed it. There are people who are trying to discover what was published and distributed when and where. But it is an enormous task and we have to do a great deal more. What was heard by people–not just what was performed somewhere–but how do people hear music? In this century, people hear music in many ways other than going to concerts, and you are all too aware of this. How has this been accomplished? We have not got the primary documents that we need to describe this particular event. The 20th century is terribly important, although some think it is not important because it is here. Well, it is here now, to be sure, but it is almost gone. Don't wait, for goodness' sake.

Finally, we should consider music vis-à-vis other performing arts. I think this has come up more perhaps and perhaps again ties into the idea that music is experienced in many settings. Gillian Anderson has vividly pointed out to us how music is experienced in its relationship to film. Music is obviously paramount to dance and yet, for example, try to find out precisely what music is being used in a standard Ballanchine ballet that is based on works by Haydn and Chopin, I mean precisely down to the cuts. Music that has been written for dance companies (a tremendous amount of 20th century music is written for dance companies) goes away with the dance companies, is never published, and remains hidden. Music in the theater, i.e., that beyond opera, is obviously important, too. Incidental music, which occurs either in the course of ephemeral productions or possibly ephemerally in the production itself, should be considered. A character enters singing such-and-such a tune. We have no control over that; a simple reference book has not yet been compiled. The whole field of musical theater obviously concerns drama, music and dance. Finally, let me make another plea not to separate sound archives, but let us re-embrace the sound archives. Let us go to the discographers; let us not wait to have somebody come and tell us what a discography is. Let us use discography as a part of our entire understanding of the art that we claim to serve.

We are talking about bibliography, and the end of it all, presumably, is reference work. But what reference librarians know is that the problem is not the answer. The problem is the question. If you can define the question, then the answer is generally fairly easy to find. So the problem is to define the question, but before we can define the question, we have to realize there *is* a question. What I have tried to suggest here is that there are areas where we have not looked beyond what we expect to find in an academic conference, where there is a very large gap which, indeed, is a question.

Subject Index

Analytical bibliography xi-xviii
Analytical methods 327-345
Arts and Humanities citation index 168-181

Bach, Johann Sebastian 159-163
Baroni, Mario 331-332,335-339
Bartók, Béla 159-163
Bibliographic access 271-280
Bibliographic control 372-377
Bibliographic description 48-49
Bibliographic instruction xi-xviii, 145-151,153-156,157-163, 174-181
Bio-Bibliographies in music 385-390

Cataloging 241-266
Composer identification 59-103
Committee work 153-156
Communication with other performing arts 395
Composers 385-390
Computers 38-40
Core literature 203-224
Critical editions 52-56,241-266

Databases 296-318,381-382
Debussy, Claude 332-345
Discography 319-325

Enumerative bibliography xi-xviii
Ephemera 349-360

Film music bibliography 59-103, 105-144

Graduate students 195-202,203-225
Gregorian chants 241-266

Hymn lyrics 227-239
Hymn tunes 227-239

Indexing 227-239,365-384
Information explosion xi-xviii
Instrumental music 296-318
Italian music 281-318
Italian poetry 281-295

Librarian surveys 365-384
Library of congress uniform titles 29
Library schools 145-146
Library user education 183-194
Lyric poetry 281-295

MacCann, Richard Dyer 105
Manuscripts 241-266
Melody 336-345
Methods of bibliography xi-xviii, 1-21,203-224
Microcomputers 157-163,165-181
Midwest 153-156
Monteverdi, Claudio 159-163
Monumental editions 49-50
Mozart, Wolfgang Amadeus 159-163,168-181
Music education 183-194,195-202
Music history 183-194
Music librarianship 195-202
Music Library Association 153-156
Music performance 195-202
Musical style 327-345
Musicological research 183-194, 203-224,349-350

© 1993 by The Haworth Press, Inc. All rights reserved.

OCLC 168-181
Operas 271-280

Perry, Edward S. 105
Popular music 59-103
Primary sources 394-395

Reference lacunae 365-384
Reference queries 165-181
Reference sources 158,163,
    165-181,366-368,377-380
Renaissance 281-318
RILM 168-181
RLIN 168-181
Rossini, Gioacchino 271-280

Scholarly editions 47-57
Schools of music 195-202
Series 38,385-390
Sound recordings 319-321

Television music 105-144
Thematic catalogs 271-280
Theory of bibliography xi-xviii,1-21

Undergraduate students 183-194
Uniform titles 159-162

Visual sources 392-394

Wescott, Steven D. 105-144

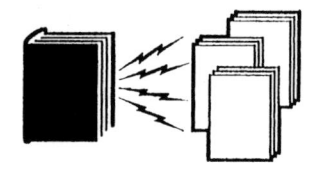

Haworth DOCUMENT DELIVERY SERVICE

and Local Photocopying Royalty Payment Form

This new service provides (a) a single-article order form for any article from a Haworth journal and (b) a convenient royalty payment form for local photocopying (not applicable to photocopies intended for resale).

- *Time Saving:* No running around from library to library to find a specific article.
- *Cost Effective:* All costs are kept down to a minimum.
- *Fast Delivery:* Choose from several options, including same-day FAX.
- *No Copyright Hassles:* You will be supplied by the original publisher.
- *Easy Payment:* Choose from several easy payment methods.

Open Accounts Welcome for...
- Library Interlibrary Loan Departments
- Library Network/Consortia Wishing to Provide Single-Article Services
- Indexing/Abstracting Services with Single Article Provision Services
- Document Provision Brokers and Freelance Information Service Providers

MAIL or *FAX* THIS ENTIRE ORDER FORM TO:

Attn: Marianne Arnold
Haworth Document Delivery Service
The Haworth Press, Inc.
10 Alice Street
Binghamton, NY 13904-1580

or FAX: (607) 722-1424
or CALL: 1-800-3-HAWORTH
(1-800-342-9678; 9am-5pm EST)

PLEASE SEND ME PHOTOCOPIES OF THE FOLLOWING SINGLE ARTICLES:
1) Journal Title: _____
   Vol/Issue/Year: _____ Starting & Ending Pages: _____
   Article Title: _____

2) Journal Title: _____
   Vol/Issue/Year: _____ Starting & Ending Pages: _____
   Article Title: _____

3) Journal Title: _____
   Vol/Issue/Year: _____ Starting & Ending Pages: _____
   Article Title: _____

4) Journal Title: _____
   Vol/Issue/Year: _____ Starting & Ending Pages: _____
   Article Title: _____

(See other side for Costs and Payment Information)

COSTS: Please figure your cost to order quality copies of an article.

1. Set-up charge per article: $8.00
    ($8.00 × number of separate articles) _____
2. Photocopying charge for each article:
    1-10 pages: $1.00 _____
    11-19 pages: $3.00 _____
    20-29 pages: $5.00 _____
    30+ pages: $2.00/10 pages _____
3. Flexicover (optional): $2.00/article _____
4. Postage & Handling: US: $1.00 for the first article/
    $.50 each additional article _____
    Federal Express: $25.00 _____
    Outside US: $2.00 for first article/
    $.50 each additional article _____
5. Same-day FAX service: $.35 per page _____
6. Local Photocopying Royalty Payment: should you wish to copy the article yourself. Not intended for photocopies made for resale. $1.50 per article per copy
(i.e. 10 articles × $1.50 each = $15.00) _____

GRAND TOTAL: _____

METHOD OF PAYMENT: (please check one)

❏ Check enclosed   ❏ Please ship and bill. PO # _____
(sorry we can ship and bill to bookstores only! All others must pre-pay)
❏ Charge to my credit card: ❏ Visa; ❏ MasterCard; ❏ American Express;

Account Number: _____ Expiration date: _____
Signature: X _____ Name: _____
Institution: _____ Address: _____
City: _____ State: _____ Zip: _____
Phone Number: _____ FAX Number: _____

MAIL or *FAX* THIS ENTIRE ORDER FORM TO:

| Attn: **Marianne Arnold**
Haworth Document Delivery Service
The Haworth Press, Inc.
10 Alice Street
Binghamton, NY 13904-1580 | or FAX: (607) 722-1424
or CALL: 1-800-3-HAWORTH
(1-800-342-9678; 9am-5pm EST) |